Democracy for the Few

Fourth Edition

Democracy for the Few

Fourth Edition

Michael Parenti

St. Martin's Press

New York

To Samuel Hendel and Clara Hendel

Library of Congress Catalog Card Number: 82-60475
Copyright © 1983 by St. Martin's Press, Inc.
All Rights Reserved.
Manufactured in the United States of America.
76543
fedcb
For information, write St. Martin's Press, Inc.,
175 Fifth Avenue, New York, N.Y. 10010

cover design: Tom McKeveny
book design: Murray Fleminger

cloth ISBN: 0-312-19359-9
paper ISBN: 0-312-19358-0

ILLUSTRATION ACKNOWLEDGMENTS

Page 9: Tony Auth in *The Philadelphia Inquirer*; page 20: © Ed Valtman in *The Hartford Times*, Conn./Rothco Cartoons; page 27: Fred Wright in *So Long, Partner*, copyright 1975 by the United Electrical, Radio & Machine Workers of America; page 45: drawing by Donald Reilly, © 1974 *The New Yorker* Magazine, Inc.; page 95: copyright 1982 by Herblock in *The Washington Post*; page 103: B.C. by permission of Johnny Hart and Field Enterprises, Inc.; page 109: copyright 1981 by Herblock in *The Washington Post*; page 117: © 1981 Dan Wasserman; page 139: drawing by Mankoff, © 1981 *The New Yorker* Magazine, Inc.; page 152: by permission of Jules Feiffer, copyright 1977, distributed by Universal Press Syndicate; page 167: copyright 1976 by Herblock in *The Washington Post*; page 201: Dunagin's People by Ralph Dunagin © 1980 Field Enterprises, Inc., courtesy of Field Newspaper Syndicate; page 210: © 1982 by the *New York Times* Company, reprinted by permission; page 225: drawing by Dana Fradon, © 1979 *The New Yorker* Magazine, Inc.; page 246: Konopacki in *The Madison Press Connection*/Rothco Cartoons; page 258: Tony Auth in *The Philadelphia Inquirer*; page 262: © 1976 by Don Wright, reprinted by permission of Tribune Company Syndicate, Inc.; page 287: Ed Stein in the *Rocky Mountain News*; page 347: Vadillo in *El Sol de Mexico*/Rothco Cartoons.

Preface to the Fourth Edition

The study of politics is itself a political act, containing little that is neutral. True, we can all agree on certain neutral facts about the structure of government and the like. However, the textbook that does not venture much beyond these minimal descriptions will offend few readers but also will interest few. The truth is that any determined pursuit of how and why things happen draws us into highly controversial subject areas.

Most textbooks pretend to a neutrality they do not really possess. In fact, the standard textbooks are not objective but merely conventional. They depict the status quo and propagate an acceptance of things as they are, fortifying orthodox notions and myths about American politics while avoiding any serious attempt to explain the injustices and inequities that are the realities of socio-political life.

Democracy for the Few offers an alternative interpretation, one that students are not likely to get in elementary school, high school, or most of their college courses, or in the mass media or mainstream political literature. The book directs critical attention to the existing practices and institutional arrangements of the American political system (who governs, what governs, and how?) and critical analysis of the outputs of that system (who gets what?).

I have attempted to blend several approaches. Thus, although the book might be considered an alternative text to the standard works, much attention is given to traditional *political institutions*. The Constitution, Congress, the presidency, the Supreme Court, political parties, elections, and the law-enforcement system are treated in some detail. However, the presentation is organized within a consistent analytic framework so that the nuts and bolts of the various institutions are seen not just as a collection of incidentals to be memorized for the final examination but as components of a larger system, serving certain interests in specific ways. When the institutional, formalistic features of American government are put into an overall framework that relates them to the realities of political power and interest, they are more likely to be remembered by the student because their function and effect are better understood.

In addition, the book devotes considerable attention to the *histori-cal development* of American politics, particularly in regard to the making of the Constitution and the growing role of government. The major eras of reform are investigated with the intent of developing a more critical understanding of the class dimension in American poli-tics and a better appreciation of the struggle waged by democratic forces.

A major emphasis in this book is placed on the *politico-economic aspects of public policy*. The significance of government, after all, lies not in its structure or symmetry as such, but in what it does. And in describing what government does, I have included a good deal of in-formation not ordinarily found in the standard texts. I have done this because it makes little sense to talk about the "policy process" as some-thing abstracted from its content and questions of power and interest, and because students are often poorly informed about politico-eco-nomic issues. Again, this descriptive information on who gets what, when, and how is presented with the intent of drawing the reader to an analysis and an overall synthesis of American political reality.

As I began work on the fourth edition of this book, I was aware that President Reagan had helped to dispel any fears I might have had that *Democracy for the Few* overemphasized the elitist and undemo-cratic aspects of our politico-economic system. For a moment I thought of entitling this new edition *Democracy for the Fewer Still*. But Reaganism also brought out something else about the American political system—how conservative government only increases the people's will to fight and, as a result, how such government must shift some of its attention away from serving the few toward dealing with the many. So I have tried to emphasize this neglected dimension, showing not only the system's denial of democracy but the struggle for democracy by the common people. Every chapter and almost every page of this edition have been revised. I have also included at the end of the book an Information and Resource Guide listing books, periodi-cals, and organizations that students can consult to further their un-derstanding of American capitalism. My hope is that this new edition proves as useful to students and lay readers as were the earlier ones.

I wish to thank Kevin Bailey of North Harris County College (Texas); Farrel Broslawsky of Los Angeles Valley College; Robert To-buren of Louisiana Tech University; Orion White of Virginia Tech University; and also Raphael Marrone, Angela Argento, John Ambro-sio, and Dennis Torigoe for critical comments and other assistance. Most helpful of all was Kathleen Lipscomb, who not only provided a detailed critique of the text but also suggested themes and ideas that have deepened and broadened this book.

I once more benefited from the conscientious assistance of the staff at St. Martin's Press, especially Michael Weber and Ron Aldridge, who remained steadfast in the face of threatening deadlines. My thanks also to the many fine people at the Institute for Policy Studies in Washington, D.C., for making their already crowded facilities and their abundant good will available to me.

The personal inscription remains the same: To Clara and Samuel Hendel, one of the very nicest and best teams in the academic world. Their friendship and support, extending back over many years, have helped me in ways that go beyond the confines of scholarship. In return they have my lasting appreciation. Now into his second or third "retirement," Sam Hendel continues to provide several generations of his former students with the encouragement and guidance we need, and he himself remains an active advocate of the best democratic principles. I hope this book measures up to the standards he has set.

Michael Parenti

Contents

Democracy for the Few

Fourth Edition

1

Politics and "the System"

How does the American political system work and for what purpose? What are the major forces shaping political life and how do they operate? Who governs in the United States? Who gets what, when, how, and why? Who pays and in what ways? These are the central questions investigated in this book. Many of us were taught a somewhat idealized textbook version of American government, which might be summarized as follows:

1. The United States was founded by persons dedicated to building a nation for the good of all its citizens. A Constitution was fashioned to limit political authority and check abuses of power. Over the generations it has proven to be a "living document," which, through reinterpretation and amendment, has served us well.
2. The nation's political leaders, the president and the Congress, are for the most part responsive to the popular will. The people's desires are registered through periodic elections and the operations of political parties and a free press. Decisions are made by small groups of persons within the various circles of government, but these decisionmakers are kept in check by each other's power and by their need to satisfy the electorate in order to remain in office. The people do not rule but they select those who do. Thus government decisions are grounded in majority rule—subject to the restraints imposed by the Constitution for the protection of minority rights.

1

3. The United States is a nation of many different social, economic, ethnic, and regional groups, which make varied and competing demands on public officeholders. The role of government is to act as a mediator of these conflicting demands, formulating policies that benefit the public. Although most decisions are compromises that seldom satisfy all interested parties, they usually allow for a working consensus; hence every group has a say and no one chronically dominates.

4. These institutional arrangements have given us a government of laws and not of men, which, while far from perfect, allows for a fairly high degree of popular participation. Our political system is part of our free and prosperous society, a society that is the envy of peoples throughout the world.

THE POLITICO-ECONOMIC SYSTEM

To be sure, elections have been regular events throughout this country's history; there is a great deal of material abundance, and the United States is the major industrial and military power in the world. Yet there is also a real feeling that something is wrong. In his "Address to the Nation" on July 17, 1979, President Jimmy Carter noted that despite this nation's wealth and power, opinion polls showed that Americans are losing their belief in progress and betterment. More than that, "Our people are losing that faith—not only in government itself, but in their ability as citizens to serve as the ultimate rulers and shapers of our democracy."

Carter offered no explanation for this phenomenon. We are left to suppose that Americans simply have succumbed to a collective gloom that is part of the times. More likely what he describes as a "crisis in confidence" is a reflection of actual social conditions. With the persistence of poverty; unemployment; inflation; overseas interventions; gargantuan military budgets; crises in our transportation, health, educational, and welfare systems; environmental devastation; deficient consumer and worker protection; heavy taxes; a growing national debt; municipal bankruptcies; urban decay; and widespread crime in the streets and in high places, many persons find it difficult to believe that the best interests of the American people are being served by the existing political system.

The central theme of this book is that our government represents the privileged few rather than the needy many, and that participating in elections and the activities of political parties and exercising the right to speak out are seldom effective measures against the influences of corporate wealth. The laws of our polity operate chiefly with undemocratic effect because they are written principally to advance the interests of the haves at the expense of the have-nots and because, even if equitable as written, they usually are enforced in highly discriminatory ways.

Furthermore, it will be argued that this "democracy for the few" is not a product of the venality of particular officeholders but a reflection of the entire politico-economic system, the way the resources of power are distributed within it, and the interests that are served by it.

This investigation might be described as holistic in that it recognizes, rather than denies, the linkages between various components of the whole politico-economic system. When we study any part of that system, be it the media, lobbying, criminal justice, overseas intervention, or environmental policy, we will see how that part reflects the nature of the whole and how in its particular way it serves to maintain the larger system—especially the system's overriding class interests. We will see that issues and problems are not isolated and unrelated, even though they are treated that way by various academics and news commentators. Rather, they are interrelated in direct and indirect ways. This will become more evident as we investigate the actual components of the political system in some detail.

By the "political system" I mean the various branches of government along with the political parties, laws, lobbyists, and private interest groups that affect public policy. One of my conclusions is that the distinction between "public" and "private" is often an artificial one. Government agencies are heavily influenced by private interest groups, and some private interest groups, such as some defense companies, depend completely on the public treasure for their profits and survival.

The decisions made by government are what I mean by "public policy." One characteristic of policy decisions is that they are seldom neutral. They almost always benefit some interests more than others, entailing social costs that are rarely equally distributed. The shaping of a budget, the passage of a piece of legislation, and the development of an administrative program are all policy decisions, all *political* decisions, and there is no way to execute them with neutral effect. If the wants of all persons could be automatically satisfied, there would be no need to set priorities and give some interests precedence over others, indeed, no need for policies or politics as the words have just been used.

Politics extends even beyond the actions of state. Decisions that keep certain matters within "private" systems of power—such as leaving rental costs or health care to the private market—are highly political, having important effects on the distribution of social costs and benefits. Private power is even more inequitable and difficult to evade than public power. However, in this book we will focus on the public realm and how it fosters and responds to private power.

Someone once defined a politician as a person who receives votes from the poor and money from the rich on the promise of protecting each from the other. And with uncharacteristic wit, President Jimmy Carter observed: "Politics is the world's second oldest profession, closely related to the first." Many people share this view. For them, politics is little more than the art of manipulating appearances and evoking desires in order to sell oneself, with the politician as a more subtle and less honest kind of prostitute. While not denying the large measure of truth in such observations, I take a broader view of politics; it is more than just something politicians do. Politics is the process of struggle over conflicting interests carried into the public arena; it may also involve the process of muting and suppressing conflicting interests. Politics involves the activation and mediation of conflict, the setting of public priorities, the choosing of certain values, interests, and goals and the denial of others. For instance, the way prisons and mental institutions are run is not only an administrative matter but also a political one, involving the application of a particular ideology about normality and social control that protects certain interests and suppresses others.[1]

Politics involves not only the competition among groups within the present system but also the struggle to change the entire system, not only the desire to achieve predefined ends but the struggle to redefine ends and to pose alternatives to the existing politico-economic structure.

Along with discussing the political system as such, I frequently refer to "the politico-economic system." Politics today covers every kind of issue, from abortion to school prayers, but *the bulk of public policy is concerned with economic matters*. The most important document the government produces each year is the budget. Probably the most vital functions of government are taxing and spending. Certainly they are necessary conditions for everything else it does, from delivering the mail to making war. The very organization of the federal government reflects the close involvement the state has with the economy: thus one finds the departments of Commerce, Labor, Agriculture, Interior, Transportation, and Treasury, and the Federal Trade Commission, the National Labor Relations Board, the Interstate Commerce Commission, the Federal Communications Commission, and

---

1. See the section in chapter 9 entitled "Mind Control for Law and Order."

the Securities and Exchange Commission all involved in regulating economic activity. Most of the committees in Congress can be identified according to their economic functions, the most important having to do with taxation and appropriations.

If much of this book seems concerned with economic matters, it's because that's what government is mostly about. Nor should this relationship be surprising. Politics and economics are but two sides of the same coin. Economics is concerned with the allocation of scarce resources for competing ends, involving conflicts between social classes and among groups and individuals within classes. Much of politics is a carryover of this same struggle. Both politics and economics deal with questions affecting the material survival, prosperity, and well-being of millions of people; both deal with the first conditions of social life itself.

This close relationship between politics and economics is neither neutral nor coincidental. Large governments evolve through history in order to protect large accumulations of property and wealth. In nomadic and hunting societies, where there is little surplus wealth, government is rudimentary and usually communal. In societies where wealth and property are controlled by a select class of persons, a state develops to protect the interests of the haves from the have-nots. As Adam Smith wrote in 1776: "Civil authority, so far as it is instituted for the security of property, is in reality instituted for the defense of the rich against the poor, or of those who have some property against those who have none at all."[2] Smith, who is above suspicion in his dedication to capitalism, argued that as wealth increased in scope, a government would have to perform more extensive services on behalf of the wealthy. "The necessity of civil government grows up with the acquisition of valuable property."[3]

Many political scientists have managed to ignore the relationship between government and wealth, treating the corporate giants, if at all, as if they were but one of a number of interest groups. Most often this evasion is accomplished by labeling any approach that links class, wealth, and capitalism to politics as "Marxist." To be sure, Marx saw such a relationship, but so did more conservative theorists like Hobbes, Locke, Adam Smith and, in America, Hamilton, Adams, and Madison. Indeed, just about every theorist and practitioner of

2. Adam Smith, *An Inquiry into the Nature and Causes of the Wealth of Nations* (Chicago: Encyclopaedia Britannica, Inc., 1952), p. 311. A century before Smith, John Locke, in his *Second Treatise of Civil Government*, noted that "the great and chief end" served when men put themselves "under government is the preservation of their property."

3. Smith, *Wealth of Nations*, p. 309.

politics in the seventeenth, eighteenth, and early nineteenth centuries saw the linkage between political organization and economic interest, and between state and class, as not only important but *desirable* and essential to the well-being of the polity. "The people who own the country ought to govern it," declared John Jay. A permanent check over the populace should be exercised by "the rich and the well-born," urged Alexander Hamilton.

Unlike most of the theorists before him, Marx was one of the first in the modern era to see the existing relationship between property and power as *un*desirable, and this was his unforgivable sin. Marx wrote during the mid-to-late nineteenth century, when people increasingly criticized the abuses of industrial capitalism and when those who owned the wealth of society preferred to draw attention away from the relationship between private wealth and public power and toward more "respectable" subjects. The tendency to avoid critical analysis of American capitalism persists to this day among business people, journalists, lawyers, and academics.[4]

Many economists pay no heed to politics and many political scientists give but a passing thought to economic forces. Yet there exists in the real world a close interrelationship between political power and economic wealth, between state and class. As the sociologist Robert Lynd once noted, power is no less political because it is economic. By "power" I mean the ability to get what one wants, either by having one's interests prevail in conflicts with others or by preventing others from raising conflicting demands. Power presumes the ability to control the actions and beliefs of others through favor, fear, fraud, or force and to manipulate the social environment to one's advantage. Power belongs to those who possess the resources that enable them to control the behavior of others, such as jobs, organization, technology, publicity, media, social legitimacy, expertise, essential goods and services, and—the ingredient that often determines the availability of these things—money.

UNDERSTANDING "THE SYSTEM"

We hear a great deal of talk about "the system." What is often lacking is any precise investigation of what the system is and what it does or doesn't do. Instead, some people will attack the system and others

---

4. See William Appleman Williams, *The Great Evasion* (Chicago: Quadrangle Books, 1964) for an analysis of the way Marxist thought has been stigmatized or ignored by American intellectuals and those who pay their salaries. See also Sidney Fine,

will defend it. Some say it does not work and should be changed or overthrown; others say it does work or, in any case, we can't fight it and should work within it. Some argue that the existing system is "the only one we have" and imply that it is the only one we ever *could* have. Hence some people fear that a breakdown in this system's social order would mean a breakdown in all social order, an end to society itself or, in any case, a creation of something monstrously worse than the status quo. These fearful notions keep many people not only from entertaining ideas about new social arrangements but also from taking a critical look at existing ones.

Sometimes the complaint is made: "You're good at criticizing the system, but what would you put in its place?" the implication being that unless you have a finished blueprint for a better society, you should refrain from pointing out existing deficiencies and injustices. But this book is predicated on the notion that it is desirable and necessary for human beings to examine the society in which they live, possibly as a step toward making fundamental improvements. The purpose here is to understand what *is* and not to present a detailed, speculative study of what could be. It is unreasonable to demand that we refrain from making a diagnosis of an illness until we have perfected a cure. Such a method of solving problems, medical or social, would be futile.

Like so much else in the existing society, political life is replete with deceit, corruption, and plunder. Small wonder that many people seek to remove themselves from politics. But whether we like it or not, politics and government play a crucial role in determining the conditions of our lives. Readers might go "do their own thing," pretending that they have removed themselves from the world of politics and power. They can leave political life alone, but it will not leave them alone. They can escape its noise and its pretensions but not some of its worst effects. One ignores the doings of the state only at one's own risk.

If the picture that emerges in the pages ahead is not pretty, this should not be taken as an attack on the United States, for this country and the American people are greater than the abuses perpetrated upon them by those who live for power and profit. To expose these abuses is not to denigrate the nation that is a victim of them. The greatness of a country is to be measured by something more than its

---

Laissez-Faire and the General-Welfare State (Ann Arbor: University of Michigan Press, 1964) for a description of capitalist, anti-Marxist orthodoxy in the United States in the late nineteenth century and its control over business, law, economics, university teaching, and religion.

rulers, its military budget, its instruments of dominance and destruction, and its profiteering giant corporations. A nation's greatness can be measured by its ability to create a society free of poverty, racism, and sexism and free of domestic and overseas exploitation and social and environmental devastation. Albert Camus once said, "I would like to love my country and justice too." In fact there is no better way to love one's country, no better way to strive for the fulfillment of its greatness, than to entertain critical ideas and engage in the pursuit of social justice at home and abroad.

2

Wealth and Want in the United States

If politics is concerned with who gets what, then we might begin by considering who's already got what. How is wealth accumulated, distributed, and used in the United States? What we discover will tell us something important about the economy of American capitalism[1] and the political viability of American democracy.

WEALTH AND CLASS

One should distinguish between those who own and control the wealth and institutions of the society, the "owning class," and those who are dependent on that class for their employment, the "working class." The latter includes not only blue-collar workers but also many white-collar professionals. Many of us have been taught that "America belongs to the people," but in fact almost all Americans are tenants, debtors, and hired hands in their own country, with most of the advantages going to the employers, landlords, and banks. The manufacturer hires us to make a profit from our labor by selling the product of our labor back to us at a profit. The landlord rents to us so that he

---

1. By "capitalism" I mean the system of production, ownership, and consumption found in most Western and Third World countries and Japan that manifests two essential conditions: (1) the means of production, specifically the factories, land, mines, banks, offices, etc., are under private ownership; (2) their primary function is to make money for those who own them. Terms like "corporate capitalism" and "corporate system" refer herein to modern-day capitalism, a system in which economic power is embodied in a relatively small number of large banks and other corporations.

9

can make an income on the rental. The bank extends credit so that it can get back substantially more than it lends.

The distinction between classes is blurred somewhat by the range of wealth within the owning and working classes. Thus although "owners" include both the owners of giant corporations and the proprietors of small stores, the latter control a miniscule portion of the wealth and hardly qualify as part of the *corporate* owning class. Usually small-business people devote much of their own labor to their enterprises, are dependent on larger contractors and suppliers for their existence, and are easily snuffed out when markets decline or bigger competitors move in.

Likewise, among the employee class are professionals and middle-level executives who in income, education, and life style tend to be identified as "middle class." Then there are entertainment and sports figures, some lawyers, doctors, and executives who earn such lavish incomes that they become in part, or eventually in whole, members of the owning class by investing their surplus wealth.

You are a member of the owning class when your income is very large and comes mostly from the labor of other people, that is, when others work for you, either in a company you own, or by creating the wealth that allows your money and realty investments to increase in value. Hard work seldom makes anyone rich. *The secret to wealth is to have others work hard for you.* This explains why workers who spend their lives toiling in factories or offices retire with little or no wealth to speak of, while the owners of these businesses, who may not work in them at all, can amass riches from such enterprises.

Wealth is created by the labor power of workers. What transforms an unmarketable tree into a profitable commodity such as paper or furniture is the labor that goes into harvesting the timber, cutting the lumber, and manufacturing, shipping, advertising, and selling the commodity (along with the labor that goes into making the tools, trucks, and whatever else is needed in the production process). For their efforts, workers are paid wages that supposedly represent "a fair day's pay for a fair day's work." In reality, the wages represent only a portion of the wealth created by labor. The unpaid portion is expropriated by the owners for their personal consumption and for further investment.

Workers suffer an exploitation of their labor as certainly as did slaves and serfs. They labor to make giant corporations bigger and richer. The difference is that with wage labor, the portion taken from the worker is not visible. All one sees is five days' pay for five days' work. Under feudalism, when serfs worked three days for themselves and three days for the lord, the expropriation was readily apparent; so with the sharecropper who must give, say, a half of his crop to the landowner (as still happens in many countries and in some rural regions of the United States). If wages did represent the total wealth created, there would be no surplus wealth, no funds for production costs, no profits for the owner, no great fortunes for those who do not labor. But don't managers and executives make a contribution to production for which they should be compensated? Yes, if they are performing useful labor for the enterprise, and usually they are paid very well, indeed. But income from ownership is apart from salary and apart from labor; it is money you are paid *when not working*. The author of a book, for instance, does not make "profits" on his book; he *earns* an income from the labor of writing it, proportionately much less than the sum going to those who own the publishing house and who do none of the writing, editing, printing, and marketing of books. The sum going to the owners is profits; it is *unearned* income.

While the corporations are often called the "producer" interests, the truth is that they produce nothing. They are organizational devices for the expropriation of labor and for the accumulation of capital. The real producers are those who apply their brawn, brains, and talents to the creation of goods and services. The primacy of labor was noted years ago by a Republican president. In his first annual message to Congress, Abraham Lincoln stated: "Labor is prior to and independent of capital. Capital is only the fruit of labor and could not have existed had not labor first existed. Labor is the superior of capital and deserves much the higher consideration."

Lincoln's words went largely unheeded. The dominance of capital over labor remains the essence of the American economic system, bringing ever greater concentrations of wealth and power into the hands of a small moneyed class. And as we shall see in the pages ahead, the interests of this class are antithetical to the interests of a democratic society.

WHO OWNS AMERICA?

Contrary to a widely propagated myth, the wealth of America is not owned by a broad middle class. Approximately 1.6 percent of the population own 80 percent of all capital stock, 100 percent of all state and municipal bonds, and 88.5 percent of all corporate bonds. In just about every major industry a few giant companies do from 60 to 98 percent of the business. Some 200 companies account for 80 percent of

all resources used in manufacturing. Five New York banks hold a controlling share of stock in three-fourths of the top 324 corporations.[2]

The trend is toward ever greater concentrations of economic power as giant corporations are bought up by supergiant corporations. Thus Mobil Oil purchased Montgomery Ward, Philip Morris inhaled Miller Brewing, and Coca-Cola swallowed Paramount Pictures. The top 20 coal producers are now controlled by a handful of oil, utility, and steel companies, such as Exxon, Kerr-McGee, and U.S. Steel. Some of these firms also dominate the nuclear supplying system and uranium reserves. Indeed, America's energy resources are now controlled by a clique of multinational corporations, dominated by the major oil companies.[3]

---

2. For a good collection of readings on corporate America, see Mark Green and Robert Massie, Jr. (eds.) *The Big Business Reader* (New York: Pilgrim Press, 1980); also Ferdinand Lundberg, *The Rich and the Super-Rich* (New York: Lyle Stuart, 1968); Robert Lampman, *The Share of Top Wealth-Holders in National Wealth* (Princeton, N.J.: Princeton University Press, 1962). The five banks alluded to above are Chase Manhattan, Morgan Guaranty Trust, Citibank, Bankers Trust, and the Bank of New York. See the Corporate Data Exchange study of banks summarized in the *Washington Post*, May 2, 1980.

3. Michael Pertschuk and Kenneth Davidson, "What's Wrong with Conglomerate Mergers?" in *The Big Business Reader*, pp. 484–97.

Yet Americans are taught that the economy consists of a wide array of independent producers. We refer to "farmers" as an interest apart from businessmen, at a time when the Bank of America has a multimillion-dollar stake in California farmlands and Cal Pak and Safeway operate at every level from the field to the supermarket. Every month about 1,000 small family farms go out of business. The larger agribusiness firms now operate over half of all the farmland in the United States. Just one percent of all food corporations control 80 percent of all the industry's assets and close to 90 percent of the profits, while totally monopolizing food advertising on television. Just three companies control 60 to 70 percent of all the country's dairy products. Six multinational firms handle 90 percent of all the grain shipped in the world market.[4]

This centralized food industry represents an American success story—for the big companies. Independent farmers are going ever deeper into debt ($160 billion by 1981) as income plummets and fuel, feed, and seed costs rise sharply.[5] Regional self-sufficiency in food has virtually vanished. The Northeast, for instance, imports more than 70 percent of its food from other regions. For every $2 spent to grow food in the U.S., another $1 is spent to move it. Giant agribusiness farms rely on intensive row crop farming and heavy use of chemical spraying and artificial fertilizers, all of which cause massive erosion and place a strain on water supplies. The nation's ability to feed itself is being jeopardized, as each year more and more land is eroded by large-scale, quick-profit commercial farming.[6] Thus the concentration of monopoly capital—as in agribusiness—begets not only bigness but also a pursuit of profits that produces serious economic and environmental costs.

Many corporations are owned by stockholders who, because of their scattered numbers, have little say over the management of their holdings. From this fact it has been incorrectly inferred that control of most firms has passed into the hands of corporate managers who own but a tiny segment of the assets and who therefore run their companies with a regard for the public interest that is not shared by their profit-hungry stockholders. Since Berle and Means first portrayed the

---

4. Jim Hightower, "Food Monopoly," in *The Big Business Reader*, pp. 9–18; see also the excellent documentary film "September Wheat," produced by Peter Krieg (New Time Films, New York, 1980).

5. Fifty percent of farm income goes to servicing this debt.

6. Hundreds of millions of acres of topsoil are blown away each year, a result of "hard pan," a deadening and hardening of soil due to the use of insecticide and artificial fertilizer and to intensive farming. See the two-year study by the Cornucopia Project, reported in the *Washington Post*, November 18, 1981; also Jim Hightower, *Eat Your Heart Out* (New York: Crown, 1975); *Washington Post*, February 7 and 8, 1982.

giant firms as developing "into a purely neutral technocracy," controlled by disinterested managers who allocated resources on the basis of public need "rather than private cupidity,"[7] many observers have come to treat this fantasy as a reality.

In fact, the separation of ownership from management is far from complete. Almost one-third of the top 500 corporations in the United States are controlled by one individual or family. Furthermore, the decline of family capitalism has not led to widespread ownership among the general public. *The diffusion of stock ownership has not cut across class lines but has occurred within the upper class itself.* In an earlier day three families might have owned companies A, B, and C respectively, whereas today all three have holdings in all three companies, thereby giving "the upper class an even greater community of interest than they had in the past."[8]

Some "family enterprises" are of colossal size. Indeed, a small number of the wealthiest families, such as the Mellons, Morgans, DuPonts, and Rockefellers, dominate the American economy. The DuPont family controls eight of the largest defense contractors and grossed over $15 billion in military contracts during the Vietnam war. The DuPonts control ten corporations that each have over $1 billion in assets, including General Motors, Coca-Cola, and United Brands, along with many smaller firms. The DuPonts serve as trustees of scores of colleges. They own about forty manorial estates and private museums in Delaware alone, and, in an attempt to keep the money in the family, have set up thirty-one tax-exempt foundations. The family is frequently the largest contributor to Republican presidential campaigns and has financed right-wing and antilabor organizations such as the proto-fascist American Liberty League and the American Conservative Union.[9] In 1976 Pierre DuPont won the governorship of Delaware.

Another powerful family enterprise, that of the Rockefellers, holds over $300 billion in corporate wealth, extending into just about every industry in every state of the Union and every nation in the nonsocialist world. The Rockefellers control five of the twelve largest oil companies and four of the largest banks in the world. They finance universities, churches, "cultural centers," and youth organizations. At one time or another, they or their close associates have occupied the

---

7. A. A. Berle, Jr., and Gardner C. Means, *The Modern Corporation and Private Property* (New York: Harcourt, Brace, 1932), p. 356.

8. G. William Domhoff, *Who Rules America?* (Englewood Cliffs, N.J.: Prentice-Hall, 1967), p. 40.

9. Gerald C. Zilg, *DuPont: Behind the Nylon Curtain* (Englewood Cliffs, N.J.: Prentice-Hall, 1974).

offices of the president, vice-president, secretaries of State, Commerce, Defense, and other cabinet posts, the Federal Reserve Board, the governorships of several states, key positions in the Central Intelligence Agency (CIA), the U.S. Senate and House, and the Council on Foreign Relations.[10]

In companies not directly under family control, the supposedly public-minded managers are large investors in corporate America. Managers award themselves stupendous salaries and other benefits. Thus, despite recessions and widespread layoffs in various industries, compensation for executives has been rising more than 13 percent annually, with top managers of the largest firms making between $500,000 and $3,000,000 a year in salaries, bonuses, and stock options.[11] The executives of large corporations are almost always wealthy individuals who have a direct interest in corporate profits. Far from being technocrats dedicated to advancing the public welfare, they represent the more active element of a self-interested owning class. Their power does not rest in their individual holdings but in their corporate positions. "Not great fortunes, but great corporations are the important units of wealth, to which individuals of property are variously attached," C. Wright Mills reminds us. "The corporation is the source of, and the basis of, the continued power and privilege of wealth."[12]

THE DYNAMIC OF CAPITALISM

There is something more to capitalism than just the concentration of wealth. Vast fortunes existed in ancient Egypt, feudal Europe, and other pre-capitalist class societies. What is unique about capitalism is its perpetual dynamic of capital accumulation and expansion—and the dominant role this process plays in the economic order.

In a sense, capital is dead labor. Unless it can be invested in production, that is, mixed with living labor to create more capital, it has

---

10. See Peter Collier and David Horowitz, *The Rockefellers: An American Dynasty* (New York: Holt, Rinehart and Winston, 1976).

11. Paul Blumberg, "Another Day, Another $3,000: Executive Salaries in America," in *The Big Business Reader*, pp. 316–32; *Wall Street Journal*, April 18, 1978. As one top executive, J. Richard Munro, president of Time, Inc., noted: "Corporate managers lead just about the most privileged lives in our society." *Washington Post*, February 11, 1982.

12. C. Wright Mills, *The Power Elite* (New York: Oxford University Press, 1956), p. 116. See also Ralph Miliband, *The State in Capitalist Society* (New York: Basic Books, 1969), pp. 28–36, and Paul Baran and Paul Sweezy, *Monopoly Capital* (New York: Monthly Review Press, 1968).

no function and no value. The capitalist likes to say that he is "putting his money to work," but money as such cannot create more wealth. What the capitalist really means is that he is putting more human labor power to work for him, paying workers less in wages than they produce in value, thereby siphoning off more profit for himself. That's how money "grows."[13]

Normally when we think of work, we think of the worker using the means of production (tools, machines, vehicles). But under capitalism, the means of production use the worker. The ultimate purpose of work under capitalism is not to produce goods, such as cars or breakfast cereals, or to perform services, such as insurance or banking, but to make more money for the investor. Money harnesses labor in order to convert itself into goods and services that will produce still more money. Capital annexes living labor in order to create more capital.[14]

Corporate profit is surplus wealth that must be either distributed to stockholders as dividends or reinvested by the corporation for more profits. As a corporation grows, it must find ways of continuing to grow. It faces the problem of constantly having to make more money, of finding new profitable areas of investment for its surplus earnings. Ecologists who worry about the way industry devastates the environment and who dream of a "no-growth capitalism" as the solution seem not to realize that such a goal is unattainable, for a "no-growth capitalism" is a nonexpanding, noninvesting, nonprofit capitalism, a contradiction in terms, no capitalism at all.

The first law of capitalism is: accumulate profits or go out of business. "Profits provide the internal funds for expansion. Profits are the sinew and muscle of strength. . . . As such they become the immediate, unique, unifying, quantitative aim of corporate success."[15] The function of the corporation is not to perform public services or engage in philanthropy but to make as large a profit as possible. The social uses of the product, its effects upon human well-being and the natural environment win consideration in capitalist production, if at all, only to the extent that they do not violate the profit goals of the corporation.

---

13. Investments having no direct link to the employment of labor still indirectly rely on labor for their income. The earnings on real estate, for instance, ultimately depend on the rents that can be extracted from wage earners and on the capital accumulations of investors. Money in the bank or invested in bonds earns interest only because others can invest it, that is, use it to extract a profit from labor greater than the interest they must pay on the original bank loan.

14. For the great statement on the nature and function of capital, see Karl Marx, *Capital*, vol. 1, available in various editions.

15. Baran and Sweezy, *Monopoly Capital*, pp. 39–40.

When pressed on this subject, business leaders will admit as much. They will tell you, quite correctly, that they could not survive if they tried to feed or house the poor, or if they tossed millions into non-profit projects for the environment, or if they based their investment decisions on something so nebulous as a desire to "get the economy moving again." Nor can they invest simply to "create more jobs." In fact, most of their investments in new plants and equipment and in overseas areas are designed to cut labor costs by creating fewer jobs and lower wages.

This relentless pursuit of profit results from something more than just greed—although there is enough of that. It is an unavoidable fact of capitalism that enterprises must expand in order to survive. To stand still amidst growth is to decline, not only relatively but absolutely. A slow-growth firm is less able to move in on new markets, hold onto old ones, command investment capital, adapt to new technologies, and control suppliers. A decline in the rate of production eventually cuts into profits and leads to a company's decline. Even the very biggest corporations, enjoying a relatively secure oligopolistic control over markets, are beset by a ceaseless drive to expand, to find new ways of making money. Ultimately the only certainty, even for the giants, is uncertainty. (Witness the near demise in recent years of General Dynamics, Lockheed, and Chrysler.) Larger size, greater reserves, and better organizational control might bring security were it not that all other companies are pursuing these same goals. So survival can never be taken for granted. The search for security through economic superiority becomes an endless race for dear life.[16]

Recession

By doing everything possible to hold down wages and increase profits, capitalists work against themselves, for such measures also cut into the buying power of the very public that is supposed to buy their services and commodities. Every owner would prefer to pay his employees as little as possible while selling his goods to better-paid workers from other companies. "For the system as a whole, no such solution is possible; the dilemma is basic to capitalism. Wages, a cost of production, must be kept down; wages, a source of consumer spending, must be kept up."[17] This contradiction is a source of great instability, leading to chronic overproduction and underconsumption.

---

16. Robert L. Heilbroner, "Inflationary Capitalism," in *The Big Business Reader*, p. 514.
17. "Economy in Review," *Dollars and Sense*, March 1976, p. 3.

When markets sag, prices are raised to compensate for diminished sales, and layoffs and wage cuts are imposed. As workers lose their jobs, their buying power declines and sales drop further; prices are rigged still higher; inventories accumulate; investment opportunities disappear; more cutbacks and speedups are imposed; and the country moves deeper into a recession, characterized by stagnant production and inflation, or "stagflation."[18] So productive capacities are underused and human resources misused. There is a glut of nonessential goods and services for those with money and a shortage of essential ones for those without money. Stores groan with unsold commodities, while many people are ill-housed and ill-fed.

Recessions are not unmitigated gloom—for the big owners. Economic slumps keep labor from getting too aggressive in its wage demands and help weed out the weaker capitalists—to the benefit of the stronger. In boom times, with nearly full employment, workers are more ready to strike for better contracts. Other jobs are easy to get, and business finds it too costly to remain idle while markets are expanding. Wages are able to cut into profits during good times, but a recession reverses the trend. As the job market tightens, business is better able to resist labor demands. A reserve army of unemployed helps to deflate wages. Unions are weakened and often broken and profits rise faster than wages. A review of the U.S. economy shows big business "coming out ahead of the workers. . . . The general pattern reveals increased profits, decreased buying power, increased unemployment, higher labor productivity and decreased strike activity."[19]

Corporations draw subsidies from the public treasure; enter into monopolistic mergers; rig prices at artificially high levels; impose speedups, layoffs, and wage cuts; and move to cheaper domestic and overseas labor markets. In these ways they are often able to increase profits amidst widespread want and unemployment. Business does fine; only the people suffer. According to *Fortune* magazine, between 1970 and 1980, a decade beset by sluggish growth and a decline in real wages, total after-tax profits for the 500 largest corporations increased about 300 percent, from $41 billion to $163 billion.[20] In 1980–81, a period of recession and hardship for many Americans, giant firms like GE, AT&T, and Exxon reported record earnings. Whether there be boom or bust, giant firms rarely go bankrupt. As

---

18. David M. Gordon, "Recession Is Capitalism as Usual," *New York Times Magazine*, April 27, 1975.

19. Ben Bedell, "Workers Lose Out in 1975," *Guardian*, January 14, 1976, p. 4.

20. Carol Loomis, "Profitability Goes Through a Ceiling," *Fortune*, May 4, 1981, pp. 114–20. See also Robert Lekachman, "Profits Explode," *Nation*, April 7, 1979, p. 357.

the steel companies have shown, firms can be inefficient and still make profits. While operating at 20 percent below capacity, at a time of high unemployment and price squeeze, U.S. Steel showed a handsome profit growth throughout the 1970s.

The idea that all Americans are in the same boat, experiencing good and bad times together, should be put to rest. Millions of working people suffer dearly during economic recession. But the very rich, enjoying vast reserves, endure few privations and may prosper all the more. As of 1979 there were 520,000 American millionaires, up 15 percent from the previous year. In the recession years of 1974–75 and 1981–82, sales of jewelry, antiques, art work, executive apartments, mansions, yachts, and luxury cars were booming among upper-class patrons. One top executive confessed, "The last two recessions have been poor man's recessions. People who have money have not suffered that much."[21]

The economically strongest are able to turn the adversity of others into gain for themselves, gathering control over the broken holdings of smaller competitors, limiting wage increases, and increasing profits. Such has been the good fortune of the Morgans, Rockefellers, and others in every recession since at least 1873.

Inflation

We often hear that the American economy suffers from inflation. More precisely, the suffering is done by small business, wage earners, salaried employees, and persons on low or fixed incomes. For big business, inflation—like recession—has its compensations: higher prices mean bigger profits. Soaring prices are portrayed as the *symptom* of inflation when actually they are the *cause*. And the major impetus behind higher prices is the grab for profits.

Corporation leaders maintain otherwise, claiming that inflation is caused by the wage demands of labor unions. In fact, wages have not kept pace with profits. Prices of manufactured goods increased 25 percent faster than labor costs during the 1970s, causing significantly larger profit margins. In the coal industry, after-tax profits per ton of coal climbed 800 percent over a 5-year period, while miners' wages rose only 160 percent in *twenty* years, and unemployment in the mines increased drastically.[22]

---

21. Gilbert Maurer of Hearst Corp., in *Business Week*, October 5, 1981; also *Dollars and Sense*, April 1976, p. 9, and September 1979, p. 11.

22. For a discussion of inflation, see Dick Cluster, Nancy Rutter, et al., *Shrinking Dollars, Vanishing Jobs* (Boston: Beacon Press, 1980).

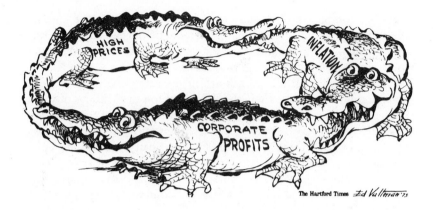

The Hartford Times   Ed Vallman '75

Hardest hit by inflation are the four essentials, which devour 70 percent of the average family income: food, fuel, housing, and health care. But in these necessities, the share of costs going to labor has been dropping. For example, from 1972 to 1979, wages in the oil industry climbed only 50 percent, but gas and fuel prices rose over 100 percent and oil company profits jumped a dazzling 126 percent. Likewise, high interest rates and real-estate speculations rather than wages have caused inflation in the construction industry. Labor costs in home construction have actually declined, as construction unions have failed to win contracts and have been broken.[23]

Those who blame organized labor for inflation should observe that over the last decade the percentage of union members in the U.S. labor force has declined from 25 to 18 percent, or by more than one-fourth. Labor has been relinquishing benefits and sometimes even taking wage cuts, yet inflation has increased dramatically. To be sure, the struggle for better wages always threatens to cut into profits, but wage demands cannot be blamed for inflation. If anything, wages have been limping behind, unable to increase as fast as prices. The real wages of Americans declined more than 20 percent in the last decade.[24] The "wage-price spiral" is really a profit-price spiral, with the worker more the victim than the cause of inflation.[25]

23. See the inflation studies and quarterly releases from the National Center for Economic Alternatives (Washington, D.C.); also "An Energy Special Report," in *Public Employee* (Washington, D.C.), July 1979, pp. 8–9.

24. "Real wages" are the actual purchasing power of wages after discounting for inflation. In 1980 the real wages of the average family plunged a record 5.5 percent; see *Los Angeles Times*, August 21, 1981.

25. As one senior White House advisor in the Carter administration commented: "If we aren't able to get a handle on inflation, it won't be the fault of the working people of this country. . . . There's been substantial deceleration on the wage side. [But] prices have not decelerated . . ." *Washington Star*, April 19, 1979.

The causes of inflation are not to be found in wage demands so much as in the monopolistic structure of the corporate economy itself. Consider the following:

1. In most industries prices are held at artificially high levels through price fixing or other monopolistic practices. Instead of lowering prices when sales drop, the big companies often raise them to compensate for sales losses. The oil, steel, and automotive industries have repeatedly done this. Wheat shortages in 1972 were used as an excuse for a rise in bread prices. In 1977 a bumper wheat crop brought a surplus, which, according to the "free market" principles of supply and demand, should have lowered bread prices; yet the price of bread still rose. According to the U.S. press this was due to the increased costs and increased profits of the middlemen—millers, bakers, and retailers—all of whom are mistakenly treated as different people. In truth, companies like ITT control production from the planting of wheat to the wrapping and selling of bread. The law of supply and demand is thus rewritten according to monopolistic rules: first, the giant companies manipulate the supply, then they demand still higher prices.[26]

2. Prices are rigged at high rates through government subsidies, price supports, and limits on production. Thus acreage-reduction programs award billions of dollars to agribusiness for producing nothing—certainly a situation conducive to inflation. When the big companies sell steel, wheat, tobacco, cotton, and other products at world prices lower than those inside the United States, the U.S. government makes up the difference with subsidies, enabling the oligopolies not only to compete favorably in foreign markets but to maintain high prices on the domestic market.

3. Massive military expenditures, many of which duplicate each other and are of dubious defense value, represent a huge investment of taxpayers' money in nonproductive, inflationary programs. While creating jobs and distributing billions in income, military and security appropriations produce nothing that would absorb the spending power that is artificially generated. The same is true of the billions spent on the national security establishment (FBI, CIA, DIA, etc.). The military helps create inflationary scarcities by consuming vast amounts of labor and material resources (for instance, it is the largest single consumer of fuel in the U.S.),

---

26. Cluster, Rutter, et al., *Shrinking Dollars, Vanishing Jobs*, pp. 84–89; Bill Del Vecchio, "U.S. Bread Prices Up Despite Overflow Harvest," *Workers World*, July 15, 1977.

but it does not produce the goods and services needed by the civilian population. "Outlays for defense," notes the *Wall Street Journal*, "happen to be a particularly inflation-producing type of federal spending." The *Journal* quotes one leading conservative economist as saying: "National defense spending makes an already grim inflation picture even grimmer."[27]

4. Other inflationary expenditures include the billions spent for unemployment payments and welfare expenditures to assist the economic victims of capitalism (the poor, the disabled, the unemployed), or at least to provide palliatives to keep them from becoming too troublesome. These programs provide them with some minimum buying power but little or no opportunity to become productive members of society.

5. More and more of the labor force is absorbed by the nonproductive private bureaucracies of big business engaged in extending managerial control over production, finance, and distribution. These bureaucracies employ increasing numbers of persons in planning, job supervision, banking, billing, data accumulation, advertising, marketing, and so on. In addition, public bureaucracies servicing the activities of giant corporations at home and abroad create inflationary spending.

6. Some $200 billion has been spent in foreign aid over the last 25 years, mostly to protect overseas business investments and the right-wing dictatorships friendly to U.S. corporations. This aid consists of sending weapcnry, capital goods, and commodities abroad, thereby producing more inflationary buying power and scarcity at home.

NEEDS, PRODUCTIVITY, AND BIGNESS

Those who insist that private enterprise can answer our needs seem to overlook the fact that private enterprise has no such interest, its function being to produce private profit. People may *need* food, but they offer no market until their need (or want) is coupled with buying power to become a market *demand*. When asked by the Citizens Board what they were doing about the widespread hunger in the United States, food manufacturers responded that the hungry poor were not their responsibility. As one company noted: "If we saw evidence of profitability, we might look into this."[28]

---

27. *Wall Street Journal*, August 30, 1978.
28. Quoted in *Hunger, U.S.A.*, a report by the Citizens Board of Inquiry into Hunger and Malnutrition in the United States (Boston: Beacon Press, 1968), p. 46.

The difference between *need* and *demand* shows up on the international market also. When buying power rather than human need determines how resources are used, then poor nations feed rich ones. Much of the beef, fish, and other protein products consumed by North Americans (and their livestock and domestic pets) comes from Peru, Mexico, Panama, India, Costa Rica, and other countries where grave protein shortages exist. These foods find their way to profitable U.S. markets rather than being used to feed the children in these countries who suffer from protein deficiencies. In Guatemala alone, 55,000 children die before the age of five each year because of illnesses connected to malnutrition. Yet the dairy farmers of countries like Guatemala and Costa Rica are converting to more profitable beef cattle for the U.S. market. The children *need* milk, but they lack the pesos, hence there is no market. Under capitalism, money is invested only where money is to be made.

Some defenders of the established system contend that the pursuit of profit is ultimately beneficial to all since corporate productivity creates mass prosperity. This argument overlooks several things: high productivity frequently *detracts* from the common prosperity even while making fortunes for the few, and it not only fails to answer to certain social needs but may generate new ones. The coal mining companies in Appalachia, for example, not only failed to mitigate the miseries of the people in that area; they *created* many miseries, swindling the Appalachians out of their land, underpaying them, forcing them to work under inhumane conditions, destroying their countryside, and refusing to pay for any of the resulting social costs.

Furthermore, an increase in productivity, as measured by a gross national product (GNP) of more than $2 trillion a year, may mean *less* efficient use of social resources and more waste. The GNP is the total value of all goods and services produced in a given year. Methods of measurement are often arbitrary and imprecise. Important nonmarket services like housework and child rearing go uncounted, while many goods and services of negative social value *are* tabulated. Thus, highway accidents, which lead to increased auto repairs, wreckage and insurance costs, car sales, and ambulance, hospital, and police costs, add quite a bit to the GNP but take a lot out of life.

The *human* value of productivity rests in its social purpose. Is the purpose to plunder the environment without regard to ecological needs, fabricate endless consumer desires, produce shoddy goods designed to wear out quickly, create wasteful, high-priced forms of production and service, pander to snobbism and acquisitiveness, squeeze as much compulsive toil as possible out of workers while paying them as little as possible, create artificial scarcities in order to jack up prices—all in order to grab as big a profit as one can?[29] Or is productivity geared to satisfying the communal needs of the populace in an equitable and rational manner? Is it organized to serve essential needs first and superfluous wants last, to care for the natural environment and the health and safety of citizens and workers? Is it organized to maximize the capabilities, responsibilities, and participation of its people?

Capitalist productivity-for-profit gives little consideration to the latter set of goals. Indeed, what is called productivity, as measured by *quantitative* indices, may actually represent a decline in the *quality* of life—hence the relationship between the increasing quantity of automobiles and the decreasing quality of the air we breathe. Such measurements of "prosperity" offer, at best, a most haphazard accounting of many qualities of social life.

The apologists for capitalism argue that the accumulation of great fortunes is a necessary condition for economic growth, for only the wealthy can provide the huge sums needed for the capitalization of new enterprises. Yet a closer look at many industries, from railroads to atomic energy, suggests that much of the funding has come from the government—that is, from the taxpayer—and most of the growth has come from increased sales to the public—from the pockets of consumers and from the wealth created by the labor power of workers. It is one thing to say that large-scale production requires capital accumulation but something else to presume that the source of accumulation must be the purses of the rich.

It is also argued that the concentration of corporate wealth is a necessary condition for progress because only big companies are capable of carrying out modern technological innovations. Actually, giant companies leave a good deal of the pioneering research to smaller businesses and individual entrepreneurs. The inventiveness record of the biggest oil companies, Exxon and Shell, is strikingly undistinguished.[30] Referring to electric appliances, one General Electric vice-president noted: "I know of no original product invention, not even electric shavers or heating pads, made by any of the giant laboratories or corporations. . . . The record of the giants is one of moving in, buying out, and absorbing the small creators."[31]

---

29. Regarding the last point, American oil companies have repeatedly (1920, 1929, 1947, 1973, and 1977) announced major "crises" in oil supplies—which mysteriously disappeared immediately after the companies got big price increases; see "The Making of a Gas Shortage," *Dollars and Sense*, September 1979, pp. 3–5.

30. Anthony Sampson, "How the Oil Companies Help the Arabs to Keep Prices High," *New York*, September 22, 1975, p. 55.

31. Quoted in Baran and Sweezy, *Monopoly Capital*, p. 49.

Defenders of the present system claim that big production units are more efficient than smaller ones, a highly questionable contention, for in many instances, huge firms tend to become less efficient and more bureaucratized with size, and after a certain point in growth there is a diminishing return in productivity. Moreover, bigness is less the result of technological advance than of profit growth. When the same corporation has holdings in manufacturing, insurance, utilities, amusement parks, and publishing, it becomes clear that giantism is not the result of a technological necessity that supposedly brings greater efficiency but the outcome of capital concentration. The search is not for more efficient production but for new areas of investment.

Likewise the concern is not to maintain the well-being of the industry as such, but to extract as large a profit as possible. Ultimately, "efficiency" is not measured by the technical condition of the productive unit but by the return on the investment. One need only recall how railroads, shipping lines, mines, factories, and housing complexes have been bought and sold like so many game pieces for the sole purpose of extracting as much profit as possible, often with little regard for maintaining their functional capacity.[32] The long-term survival and capacity of an enterprise are of less concern to the investor than the margin of profit to be had. If firms sometimes totter on the edge of ruin, to be rescued only by generous infusions of government funds, it is after stockholders have collected millions in high profits. Thus during the years 1967 to 1971, the "depressed" aerospace industry, plagued by climbing costs and layoffs and repeatedly rescued from the brink of insolvency by fat government subsidies, netted for its investors $3 billion in after-tax profits.

Whose "Low Productivity"?

For all its self-congratulations, big business wins no special prizes for efficiency and productivity. The costly managerial bunglings of private companies are even more likely to go unreported than those of government. Management is fond of blaming its poor performance on "low worker productivity," which supposedly can be corrected only with speedups and cutbacks in the work force. But studies show that American workers are far more productive than workers in most other capitalist nations.[33] Actually the low productivity is among U.S.

---

32. Matthew Josephson, *The Robber Barons* (New York: Harcourt, Brace, 1934), pp. 19, 203.

33. See Paul Sweezy and Harry Magdoff, "Productivity Slowdown: A False Alarm," *Monthly Review*, June 1979, pp. 1–12.

managers, most of whom are paid too much for too little work. In 1980, business administrative costs exceeded $800 billion, of which $500 billion went to executives and corporate professionals. Factory-worker productivity soared 80 percent in the last decade, while white-collar productivity rose only 4 percent. One study estimates that as little as one-fourth of a manager's time is actually spent working, that is, developing, analyzing, or executing company policies.[34]

Low productivity in U.S. industry results from widespread over-capitalization, which means idle machines and a relatively low output for the existing plant. Technological obsolescence is another factor. Big companies are unwilling to spend their own money to modernize their plants. Corporations cry poverty and call for federal funds to finance technological renovations ("reindustrialization"), supposedly to help them compete against more productive Japanese and German firms. Yet these same companies then produce huge cash reserves, which they use to buy up other companies in multibillion-dollar mergers. One example says a lot: after laying off 20,000 workers, refusing to modernize its aging plants, and milking the government of hundreds of millions of dollars in subsidies and tax write-offs, U.S. Steel came up with $6.2 billion to purchase Marathon Oil in 1981. (U.S. Steel still cries poverty and uses the threat of additional factory closings to force concessions from its remaining work force.)

Giant corporate mergers have little to do with productivity. They seldom create new capital assets but merely rearrange old ones for quick paper profits. In recent years some $100 billion of corporate cash resources have been spent on mergers at a great profit to company executives and big stockholders (who are often one and the same). Such mergers absorb money that could have been spent on new technologies, new factories, and other productive uses. Instead of enlarging the economic pie, corporate and financial elites are busy cutting bigger slices for themselves.[35] This is how profits can grow while American productivity declines.

A source of waste is the continual shift of capital from one location to another, in the search for cheaper labor markets. These plant closings may bring higher profits, but they create inefficient uses of the society's overall resources and have a disastrous effect on communities, generating serious social costs that do not show up on the corporate balance sheet. Sometimes perfectly sound small businesses or

---

34. Josh Martin, "Managers Are the Main Reason for Poor Productivity," *In These Times*, October 14–20, 1981, p. 17, and the study conducted by management consultants referred to therein.

35. Robert Reich, "Pie-Slicers vs. Pie-Enlargers," *Washington Monthly*, September 1980, pp. 13–19.

small units of larger firms are closed as a way of amassing capital for future takeovers and concentrating on corporate divisions that produce the highest profits. These maneuvers also result in a loss of jobs and an overall decline in productive enterprise.[36]

---

36. David Moberg, "Shutdowns Inflict Massive Social Cost," *In These Times*, April 30–May 6, 1980, p. 2.

In sum, the pursuit of profits enriches the few at the expense of the many. Productivity, efficiency, and technological innovation are retarded or advanced, depending on how they best serve capitalism's supreme consideration, which is to accumulate the largest amount of capital at the fastest rate possible.

The power of the business class is not total, "but as near as it may be said of any human power in modern times, the large businessman controls the exigencies of life under which the community lives."[37] The giant corporations control the rate of technological development and the terms of production; they fix prices and determine the availability of livelihoods; they decide which labor markets to explore and which to abandon; they create new standards of consumption and decide the quality of goods and services; they divide earnings among labor, management, and stockholders; they transform the environment, devouring its natural resources and poisoning the land, water, and air; they command an enormous surplus wealth while helping to create and perpetuate conditions of poverty for millions of people; they exercise trustee power over religious, recreational, cultural, medical, and charitable institutions and over much of the media and the educational system; and they enjoy a powerful voice in the highest councils of federal, state, and local governments.

THE DISTRIBUTION OF WANT AND MISERY

The United States has been portrayed as a land of prosperity and well-being, but closer scrutiny brings little cause for celebration. In life expectancy, 20-year-old American males rank 36th among the world's nations, and 20-year-old American females rank 21st.[38] The infant mortality rate in the U.S. is worse than in thirteen other nations. In eleven countries women have a better chance to live through childbirth than in the United States.[39] One out of every four Americans lives in substandard housing.[40] One out of every five American adults is functionally illiterate.[41] Almost 80 million Americans live on in-

37. Thorstein Veblen, *The Theory of the Business Enterprise* (New York: New American Library Edition, n.d., originally published in 1904), p. 8.

38. James S. Turner, *The Chemical Feast* (New York: Grossman, 1970), p. 1.

39. Samuel Shapiro et al., *Infant, Prenatal, Maternal and Childhood Mortality in the United States* (Cambridge, Mass.: Harvard University Press, 1968).

40. "The Nation's Housing Needs: 1975–1985," a report published by the MIT-Harvard Joint Center for Urban Studies, Cambridge, Mass., March 1977.

41. According to U.S. Government surveys; see the *Washington Post*, September 8, 1981.

comes estimated as below a comfortable adequacy by the Department of Labor, and the U.S. Census Bureau reports that almost 32 million Americans live below the poverty level.[42] Of the latter, less than half get either food stamps or free food. Racial minorities suffer disproportionately in every area of life, including housing, health, education, or employment. Thus, a Black child has nearly one chance in two of being born into poverty and is twice as likely as a White baby to die during the first year of life.[43]

The Hungry Americans

Some people contend that those described as "poor" in the United States would be considered fairly well off by Third World standards. However, one study found that more than 12 million Americans suffer from conditions of acute hunger comparable to anything found in poorer nations.[44] Another study found that some 50 percent of children from the very poorest families grow to maturity with impaired learning ability, while 5 percent are born mentally retarded because of prenatal malnourishment.[45] An estimated one million babies and young children in the nation are suffering brain damage from malnutrition caused by extreme poverty.[46]

Children who live in chronic hunger, according to the noted psychologist Robert Coles, "become tired, petulant, suspicious and finally apathetic." Malnourished four- and five-year-olds interpret the

---

42. *Los Angeles Times*, August 21, 1981. The designation of $8,414 annual income for a family of four as the 1980 official poverty line has been criticized for being unrealistically low and for taking insufficient account of the severe inflation of recent years. Critics argue that as many as 46 million people live in conditions of economic want that can only be called poverty. See the *Guardian*, January 14, 1981. In addition, official tabulations usually underestimate the number of poor, being based on a national census that undercounts transients, homeless people, and those living in remote rural areas and crowded inner-city neighborhoods. Numerous cities complained of undercounting in the 1980 census.

43. Statistics based on government surveys reported in the *Washington Post*, January 7, 1981. Blacks compose about 12 percent of the population but poor Blacks represent 30 percent of the officially designated poor, 8.6 million of the 32 million. Another 3.5 million of the poor are Latinos and the other 19 million or more are White; see the Census Bureau findings reported in the *Los Angeles Times*, August 21, 1981. Of the people living in poverty, 11.4 million are children.

44. *Hunger U.S.A.*, Citizens Board of Inquiry.

45. Nick Kotz, *Let Them Eat Promises: The Politics of Hunger in America* (Englewood Cliffs, N.J.: Prentice-Hall, 1969).

46. *New York Times*, November 2, 1975. A Senate select committee reported that "infectious diarrhea, dehydration, malnutrition and anemia" were typical health conditions among children of the rural poor; see "Rural Housing Famine," *Progressive*, April 1971, pp.7–8.

aches of the body as a judgment made by the outside world upon them and their families, causing them to reflect upon their own worth.

> They ask themselves and others what they have done to be kept from the food they want or what they have done to deserve the pain they seem to feel. . . .
> All one has to do is ask some of these children in Appalachia who have gone north to Chicago and Detroit to draw pictures and see the way they will sometimes put food in the pictures. . . . All one has to do is ask them what they want, to confirm the desires for food and for some kind of medical care for the illnesses that plague them.[47]

In the well-known Field Foundation report, a team of doctors investigating rural poverty noted:

> In child after child we saw: evidence of vitamin and mineral deficiencies; serious untreated skin infestation and ulcerations; eye and ear diseases, also unattended bone diseases secondary to poor food intake; the prevalence of bacterial and parasitic disease as well as severe anemia, with resulting loss of energy and ability to live a normally active life; diseases of the heart and lungs—requiring surgery—which have gone undiagnosed and untreated; epileptic and other neurological disorders; [and] severe kidney ailments, that in other children would warrant immediate hospitalization.[48]

During the 1970s progressive groups were able to exert sufficient political pressure to get federal food programs started. These served to reduce *some* of the more extreme cases of hunger among the children of the poor. The Field Foundation hailed the programs as "the most valuable dollar spent by the federal government" and called for larger allocations.[49] However, the cutbacks in food programs made by the Reagan administration in the early 1980s reversed the trend of the previous decade, and the conditions of misery that never left many youngsters were returning to more children throughout the land.[50]

In the United States today, there are people living in abandoned cars and shacks who pick their food out of garbage cans and town

---

47. Robert Coles, quoted in *Hunger U.S.A.*, pp. 31–32.
48. Quoted in *Hunger U.S.A.*, p. 13.
49. *Washington Post*, May 1, 1979.
50. Thomas Morgan, "Hunger and Malnutrition Stalk Poor in a Land of Plenty," *Washington Post*, June 9, 1980; Michael Harrington and Jack Clark, "Reagan: Taking Food From the Poor," *Mother Jones*, September/October 1981, pp. 50–51; also "Food Stamps, Child Nutrition Facing $2.8 Billion in New Cuts," *Washington Post*, December 25, 1981.

dumps. Despite prolonged illness and destitution, many cannot get on welfare, even after repeated tries. Public assistance and private charities reach only a portion of the poor and sometimes not the neediest. In Philadelphia, one investigator found people starving to death, and "tens of thousands" of men, women, and children "desperate for food."[51] In Detroit, according to the mayor's office, 200,000 are starving and hunger has reached epidemic proportions. Fully one-third of that city's residents are eligible for food stamps but only 18 percent are receiving them.[52] And in New York state alone an estimated one million people who need food stamps are not getting them.[53]

The inflation of recent years has meant additional misery for the poor. As grocery prices soar, families with somewhat higher incomes are forced to buy less expensive foods such as beans, rice, and flour. The prices on these commodities are then raised still higher by profiteering producers and retailers. (Thus in 1974, the price of dried beans climbed 256 percent and that of rice over 100 percent.) Poor families, already buying the cheapest foods, are hit the hardest as a result. One last response has been an increased human consumption of dog food: an estimated one-third of all dog food sales in low-income area supermarkets goes for human consumption.[54] According to a 1976 Department of Agriculture survey, substandard diets are increasing among low-income Americans.[55]

Even more prosperous Americans are becoming victims of poor nutrition as the food industry offers increasing amounts of highly processed, chemicalized, low-nutrition foods. Bombarded by junk-food television advertising over the last thirty years, Americans have changed their eating habits dramatically: per-capita consumption of vegetables, fruits, and dairy products is down 20 to 25 percent while consumption of cakes, pastry, soft drinks, and other snacks is up 70 to 80 percent.[56] According to a U.S. Senate report, the plethora of junk foods and the paucity of wholesome ones "may be as damaging to the nation's health as the widespread contagious diseases of the early part of the century."[57]

51. Loretta Schwartz-Nobel, "Starving in the Shadow of Plenty," *Mother Jones*, September/October 1981, p. 50; also Jeri Barr, "What? Hunger in My Town?" *Food Monitor*, January/February 1979.

52. *Workers World*, February 28, 1975.

53. According to six members of the House Subcommittee on Domestic Marketing, reported in *ibid.*, July 1, 1977.

54. John Cook, "Hunger: High Prices Drive Many to Dog Food," *Guardian*, July 3, 1974, p. 3.

55. Survey by the Department of Agriculture, *New York Times*, March 13, 1976.

56. Catherine Larza and Michael Jacobson (eds.) *Food For People Not For Profits* (New York: Ballantine Books, 1975), p. 165.

57. Quoted in the *Guardian*, March 30, 1977.

Economic deprivation is a common condition among the elderly. More than half of the 26 million Americans 65 years or older live below the poverty level. Most of these live on nutritionally deficient diets, and one-third of them have a daily intake of less than 1,000 calories—amounting to a slow starvation diet. "We do see regularly those [elderly] who are found dead in their homes who are almost like walking skeletons," noted one county medical examiner in Florida.[58] Each winter throughout the country, hundreds of people, mostly the very old and very young, freeze to death in unheated apartments or perish in fires caused by the use of gas stoves after heat cutoffs. During the January 1982 cold spell alone, over 280 such deaths were reported, with the actual figure probably much higher. Many elderly cannot afford medical and nursing care or decent housing and transportation that would allow them to maintain normal social relations. They face loneliness and boredom in a market society that treats old people like used cars.[59] One out of ten elderly persons who live with a member of the family is subjected to serious abuse, such as forced confinement and beatings. With inflation and unemployment, some families resent having to feed and care for an old person. The mistreatment of elderly parents is a problem that is growing dramatically as economic conditions worsen.[60]

Unemployment

According to official statistics, as of December 1982 there were 12 million unemployed in the United States, or 10.8 percent of the work force. This figure includes only persons collecting unemployment insurance or registered as looking for employment. It does not count the several million people whose benefits have run out or who never qualified for benefits, nor those who have given up looking for work, nor the 5.5 million part-time or reduced-time workers who need full-time jobs, nor the many youths who fail to find work after leaving school, nor the many women who need jobs but are classified as "house-

---

58. Quoted in the *Buffalo Evening News*, October 13, 1974; also *Hunger, U.S.A.*, pp. 9, 24; also the Health and Nutrition Examination Survey, 1971–1972, sponsored by the U.S. Department of Health, Education, and Welfare; and Sharon Curtin, *Nobody Ever Died of Old Age* (Boston: Little, Brown, 1972).

59. *Workers World*, January 22, 1982. "Every winter in Boston people have frozen to death," observed Methodist minister Rev. Charles Stith, *Boston Globe*, July 29, 1979; also John Clairborne, "Old Age in Capitalism," *Monthly Review*, November 1972, p. 52; Robert Butler, *Why Survive? Being Old in America* (New York: Harper and Row, 1975).

60. Lewis Koch and Joanne Koch, "Parent Abuse—A New Plague," *Washington Post*, January 27, 1980, and the various studies cited therein.

wives," nor the many who join the armed forces because they cannot find employment. A conservative estimate is that 20 million people do not have sufficient full-time employment.[61]

It has been argued that people are unemployed because they are indolent. Certainly there are a few individuals in almost every society who sometimes will evade gainful employment. But when unemployment jumps 2.3 million, as it did from 1981 to 1982, is this because that many people suddenly found work too irksome? Do people really want to lose their homes, cars, medical coverage, and pensions, and be unable to provide for their families because they prefer idleness and impoverishment?[62] Apparently President Reagan thinks so. In a January 1982 press conference he said he counted 24 pages of help-wanted ads in the Sunday newspapers. There are, you see, plenty of jobs available. Yet in 1981 when 75 new job openings, at a pathetic starting salary of $7,000 a year, were advertised in Baltimore, 12,000 people lined up for them. And a survey of employment ads throughout New York state found that 85 percent of the jobs required college training or special skills. For the remaining 1,305 "entry-level" openings 29,316 people applied. People caught up in this desperate search for employment hardly deserve to be labeled as lazy laggards.

The groups hardest hit by unemployment are racial minorities, youths, women, and unskilled workers. Official unemployment figures for inner-city Black youths exceed 40 percent, while actual figures may be much higher. Unemployment among Blacks in general is more than twice that of Whites and the Black-White income gap continues to widen, giving lie to the racist claim that Afro-Americans are "making it" at the expense of others.[63]

Even when regularly employed, many workers do not earn enough to support themselves and their families in any comfort or security. "They work for a living but not for a living wage."[64] A Census Bureau survey of 51 urban areas found that more than 60 percent of

---

61. *Dollars and Sense*, January 1976, p. 10.

62. Opinion surveys indicate that people want jobs, not welfare. See, for instance, the Los Angeles Times poll, "Nation's Basic Work Ethic Found to Endure," *Los Angeles Times*, April 20, 1981.

63. U.S. Bureau of Labor Statistics report, January 1982; *Chicago Tribune*, February 18, 1979. Women are concentrated in the low-paid employment market (especially Black and Latin females). Women who move into the better-paying professional and business jobs are mostly from higher-income families, the well-to-do wives and daughters of fairly affluent males. See "Women at Work," *Wall Street Journal*, September 8, 1978. Women who work full-time average less than 60 cents for every dollar earned by men; *Washington Post*, September 2, 1981.

64. William Spring, Bennett Harrison, and Thomas Vietorisz, "Crisis of the *Under-employed*—In Much of the Inner City 60% Don't Earn Enough for a Decent Standard of Living," *New York Times Magazine*, November 5, 1972.

all *employed* workers in the inner city could not make enough to maintain a decent standard of living and 30 percent were earning wages below the poverty level.[65] Most of the poor in America have jobs. *It is not laziness that keeps them in poverty but the low wages their bosses pay them and the high prices, rents, and taxes they have to pay others.*

One hears many references to the "affluent workers" of America, of plumbers and construction workers who make more than doctors, and sanitation workers who earn more than college professors. Such stories are unfounded. First, it is not clear why sanitation workers should not be paid more than college professors, since they work harder and at more unpleasant, unhealthy tasks. Second, as a matter of fact, they make substantially less. Even the well-paid "labor aristocracy" of construction workers, given seasonal layoffs and assuming that they can find work at all, averages about $15,000 in income in a good year. The average auto worker, operating in one of the better-paying labor markets, takes home less per year after decades on the assembly line than the young college graduate who enters a management trainee program for that same auto industry. In any case, discussions on "how good labor has it" always focus on these better-paying jobs and ignore the 50 million or more people who earn subsistence wages and who face high injury rates, job insecurity, and chronic indebtedness. To make ends meet, millions of workers are obliged to hold down two jobs. Millions more are compelled by their employers to work involuntary overtime for extended periods. Owners prefer to impose overtime hours on the work force they have rather than hire more help, thereby saving on the benefits that must be paid to additional employees.[66] And from New York to Los Angeles, hundreds of thousands of workers, mostly immigrants, toil in unsafe and unhealthy sweatshop conditions, sometimes ten to twelve hours a day for less than the minimum wage and without medical coverage, sick pay, or other benefits.[67]

In greater numbers each year, unemployed workers and their families are wandering around the country in the hope of finding employment, traveling in all directions—"only to find there are no jobs when they arrive."[68] Mortgage foreclosures in many areas are ten

---

65. *Ibid.*

66. Victor Perlo, "Why Bosses Push Overtime," *Daily World*, July 20, 1978; also Dan Georgakas and Marvin Surkin, *Detroit: I Do Mind Dying* (New York: St. Martin's Press, 1975).

67. *New York Times*, February 26, 1981; *Los Angeles Herald Examiner*, March 13–28, 1981.

68. Rod Such, "In Search of Work, Jobless Workers Roam U.S.," *Guardian*, March 26, 1975, p. 3.

times what they used to be. Unable to keep up payments, many jobless persons abandon their homes and take to the road. Unemployed workers have resorted to selling their blood in order to feed their families. The father, mother, and oldest son of one destitute family, homeless because they could not pay their rent, and denied welfare assistance because they had no permanent address, took to selling weekly pints of plasma until they were rejected because of the low iron content of their blood—a condition caused by malnutrition.[69] A jobless worker ran an advertisement in a Pittsburgh newspaper offering to sell one of his kidneys for $5,000. The Kidney Foundation reported one hundred such offers from persons who "needed money."[70]

Social Pathology

Unemployment and economic hardship are not just material conditions; they affect every aspect of life, generating a great deal of misery and social pathology. It is difficult for those who have never known serious economic want to imagine the stress, anxiety, pain, depression, and unhappiness it causes. A major study at Johns Hopkins University found that each extra percentage point of unemployment brought a noticeable rise in illness, alcoholism, homicide, and suicide.[71] The suicide rate among young people has tripled in the last two decades. Suicide is the third major cause of death among U.S. youths and is especially common among unemployed youths. In all, over 27,000 Americans take their own lives each year.[72] The FBI Crime Report noted that 13 million serious crimes were reported in 1980 (including 23,044 murders), a 55 percent increase from the decade before. As crime grows so does the prison population—which more than doubled between 1973 and 1980; over half a million people are incarcerated in local, county, state, and federal prisons, and each week 300 more people go to jail than leave. The United States "is now in the midst of a prison building boom."[73]

Each year some 50,000 people are killed and more than a million are injured in auto accidents, many of which are linked to drunk driv-

69. *Guardian*, April 21, 1976.

70. *New York Daily News*, March 28, 1975.

71. The study by Dr. Harvey Brenner reported in the *Wall Street Journal*, August 25, 1980; also Brenner's earlier work, *Mental Illness and the Economy* (Cambridge, Mass.: Harvard University Press, 1973).

72. U.S. Census Bureau, *Statistical Abstract of the United States*, 95th ed. (Washington, D.C., 1974); *Newsweek*, August 23, 1978; Herbert Hendin, *Black Suicide* (New York: Basic Books, 1969).

73. *New York Times*, July 2, 1978; and the U.S. Bureau of Justice Statistics reported in the *Guardian*, July 16, 1980. A summary of the FBI Crime Report is in the *Washington Post*, September 11, 1981.

ing. Over 10 million adults have serious alcohol problems, and the number has increased most dramatically during recession years. Heroin addiction, which currently plagues 450,000 Americans, similarly increases during hard times.[74] Millions more are addicted to amphetamines, barbiturates, and other drugs. The pushers are doctors; the suppliers are the drug industry; the profits are stupendous.[75] Millions of Americans have spent time in mental hospitals or have received psychiatric care. Emotional illness is highly, though not exclusively, related to poverty and economic insecurity.[76] Another 35 million Americans, a disproportionate number of them poor, suffer cerebral and physical handicaps, many of which could have been corrected with early treatment or prevented with better living conditions.[77]

Some 28 million women are beaten each year by men, with 4.7 million sustaining serious injury.[78] Nearly 2 million children, predominantly but not exclusively from low-income families, are brutalized abused, abandoned, or neglected each year. Child abuse kills more children annually than leukemia, automobile accidents, and infectious diseases combined.[79] With growing unemployment, incidents of child abuse by jobless fathers have increased dramatically. Child labor is still practiced in the United States, with almost one million children, some as young as seven years old, serving as underpaid farm hands, dishwashers, laundry workers, and domestics for as long as ten hours a day in violation of child labor laws.[80]

THE PLIGHT OF THE MIDDLE AMERICAN

It is said that the prosperity of the United States is widely shared and incomes are becoming more equally distributed among a broad-based middle class. But the average annual pay for employees covered by state and federal unemployment insurance was $14,363 in 1980, or almost $9,000 less than the "moderate budget" for a family of four set

---

74. For reports on alcoholism and heroin addiction, see the *Washington Post,* January 13, 1980, and May 13, 1979.

75. *Washington Post,* January 13, 1980; *In These Times,* November 8–14, 1978, p. 23.

76. See the study cited in the *Progressive,* November 1977, p. 13.

77. NBC radio report, May 23, 1977.

78. *Newsweek,* January 30, 1978.

79. *New York Times,* September 30, 1981; *Washington Post,* May 27, 1979. Up to one million children in the United States run away from home each year, mostly because of abusive treatment from adults. Of the many sexually abused children among runaways, 83 percent come from White families, according to the federal Health and Human Services Administration; see *Washington Post,* February 7, 1982.

80. *New York Times,* September 4, 1972; *Los Angeles Times,* August 26, 1981.

by the Department of Labor.[81] And studies show that the gap between upper and lower income levels has been widening over the last 25 years. For example, between 1968 and 1975 there was a marked upward shift in income, with close to $10 billion being redistributed from the bottom three-fifths of American families to the richest one-fifth.[82] And by 1981–82, with the Reagan administration's taxation and spending policies designed to augment the income of the rich, the upward redistribution accelerated.

As noted earlier, there are many high-paid professionals who live quite well in the United States, but millions of middle-income people are feeling the combined squeeze of recession and inflation (albeit not as drastically as lower-income persons). They have little to cushion them against the loss of earning power that comes with layoffs, prolonged illness, or old age. While they may be earning a sufficient income, they have virtually no wealth—in a society where wealth is the only certain measure of economic security.

Middle-income people are finding it increasingly hard to maintain a middle-class standard of living. One journalist notes how the American Dream has been "revised":

> Young people today are less likely ever to own a home. We shall reach old age and be poor, not retired. Fewer of our children will go to college. We'll bleed to buy a new car, to heat our homes. . . . Remember the fine print of the American Dream: Hard work, decency and an enthusiasm for living do not always translate into homes, cars, college educations and dreams realized.
>
> . . .My father built a career . . . and lost it. . . . He and my mother invested their savings in a home they cannot sell. Their vision of retirement has evaporated. They were made promises that have not been kept, and they are not alone.[83]

By the end of 1981 over 80 percent of American families were in debt (up dramatically from 54 percent nine years earlier), most of them so heavily that they were seriously worried about how to meet their bills. A majority indicated they had borrowed money not for

81. These figures were given to me by the Bureau of Labor Statistics in Washington, D.C. The $14,363 represents gross income (actual take-home pay after the many deductions would be closer to $10,000), and it does not average in the various lower-paying occupations not covered by unemployment insurance.

82. See findings reported in the *Progressive*, July 1977, p. 11; also studies cited in the *Washington Post*, August 22, 1979. The top fifth of U.S. families receive almost half of the country's net income, while families in the bottom fifth receive between 5 and 6 percent.

83. Walt Harrington, "The Great American Dream (revised)," *Washington Post Magazine*, February 28, 1982, pp. 16–17.

luxuries but for necessities. The 1974 consumer debt for goods and services was $200 billion; by 1979 it had grown to $500 billion. The home-mortgage debt climbed to $600 billion by 1974, then mushroomed to $956 billion as of 1980.[84] According to one conservative publication, mounting debts "are threatening a financial crackup in more and more families."[85] As consumers, Americans are also victimized by shoddy, unsafe products; deceptive packaging; swindling sales; and numerous other unscrupulous practices.[86]

In sum, the story of the great "affluence" in the post–World War II United States is of people becoming increasingly entrapped in a high-priced, high-profit, high-pressured, highly unequal system. It is not enough to denounce the inequities that exist between the highly affluent and the majority of the population; it is also necessary to understand the connection between them. For it is the way wealth is organized and used that creates most of the existing want. By its very nature, the capitalist system is compelled to exploit the resources and labor of society for the purpose of maximizing profits. This systemic imperative creates the imbalances of investment, neglect of social needs, privation, wastage, and general economic oppression and inequality that bring misery to so many. And, as we shall see in the chapters ahead, it is corporate power that prevents both a reordering of our priorities and a move toward a healthier, more equitable society.

84. On the indebtedness problems of Americans, see *Washington Post*, February 7, 1982; also Susan Trausch, "Inflation and the Working Poor," *Boston Globe*, July 29, 1979; Paul M. Sweezy, "Crisis Within the Crisis," *Monthly Review*, December 1978, p. 8; Douglas Casey, "That Tricky Housing Market," *Washington Post*, April 5, 1981.

85. *U.S. News and World Report*, June 22, 1970; also David Caplovitz, *The Poor Pay More* (New York: Free Press, 1967) for a study of how the poor are victimized as consumers and debtors. The victimization of the poor by insurance companies is treated by Max Apple, "Dreams of Immortality," *Mother Jones*, June 1977, p. 46.

86. See the collection of exposé articles in David Sanford et al., *Hot War on the Consumer* (New York: Pitman, 1969).

3

The Plutocratic Culture: Institutions, Values, and Ideologies

In trying to understand the American political system we would do well to look at the social context in which it operates. What are the predominant values, ideologies, and institutional practices of American society?

AMERICAN PLUTOCRACY

It is said we live in a democratic society, but more accurately it should be described as a plutocracy, or rule by and for the rich, because our nation's industrial and cultural institutions serve the interests of the dominant owning class. American capitalism represents more than just an economic system; it is an entire cultural and social order. Most universities and colleges, publishing houses, mass circulation magazines, newspapers, television and radio stations, professional sports teams, foundations, churches, private museums, charity organizations, and hospitals are organized as corporations, ruled by self-appointed boards of trustees (or directors or regents) composed overwhelmingly of affluent business people. These boards exercise final judgment over all institutional matters.[1]

Consider the university: most institutions of higher education are public or private corporations (e.g., the Harvard Corporation, the Yale Corporation) run by boards of trustees with authority over all

---

1. My book *Power and the Powerless* (New York: St. Martin's Press, 1978) has a more detailed discussion of business power within social and cultural institutions.

matters of capital funding and budget; curriculum, scholarships, and tuition; hiring, firing, and promotion of faculty and staff; degree awards; student fees; etc. Most of the tasks related to these activities have been delegated to administrators, but the power can be easily recalled by the trustees, and in times of controversy it usually is. These trustees are granted legal control of the property of the institution, not because they have claim to any academic experience but because as successful business people they supposedly have proven themselves to be the responsible leaders of the community.[2]

This, then, is a feature of real significance in any understanding of political power in America: *almost all the social institutions existing in this society, along with the immense material and vocational resources they possess, are under plutocratic control, ruled by non-elected, self-selected, self-perpetuating groups of affluent corporate representatives who are answerable to no one but themselves.*

The rest of us make our way through these institutions as employees and clients, performing according to standards set by the ruling oligarchs or their administrative agents. The power exercised over us is hierarchical and nondemocratic. These institutions shape many of our everyday experiences and much of our social consciousness; yet we have no vote, no portion of the ownership, and no legal decision-making power within them.

Many Americans believe as they were taught, that they are a free people, a belief held even by persons who refuse to voice controversial opinions for fear of jeopardizing their career opportunities. By controlling the wealth and economic life of the country, the corporate elites are able to control the major institutions that, in turn, enable them to control the flow of mainstream ideas and information and even the behavior and choices of otherwise recalcitrant persons. The ruling ideas, as Karl Marx once said, are the ideas of the ruling class. Those who control the material production of society are also able to

---

2. *Ibid.*, pp. 156–63; also David N. Smith, *Who Rules the Universities?* (New York: Monthly Review Press, 1974); James Ridgeway, *The Closed Corporation* (New York: Random House, 1969). Even if it were true that trustees' guidance is needed on financial questions, should they have authority over all matters? In fact, on most financial and technical problems, the trustees rely on advisors and accountants. The argument is made that trustees take the financial risks for the university and therefore should have the authority. In fact, they seldom take on personal liabilities. Legal judgments made against their decisions are covered by insurance paid out of the university budget. If anything, trustees are likely to profit personally by awarding university contracts to their own firms or those of business associates. Another argument for trustee power is that students, faculty, and staff compose a transient population and therefore cannot be expected to run the university. But their stay at the university is longer than that of the average trustee, who serves for three years, often resides out of town, and visits the campus for board meetings once a month.

control the mental production. What exactly are the dominant values of our society and how are they propagated?

SOCIALIZATION INTO ORTHODOXY

The power of business does not stand naked before the public; rather it is enshrouded in a mystique of its own making. The agencies of the plutocratic culture, namely the media, the schools, the politicians, and others, associate the capitalist system with the symbols of patriotism, democracy, prosperity, and progress. Criticisms of the system are equated with un-Americanism. Capitalism is treated as a force that breeds democracy, although, in truth, capitalism also flourishes under the most brutally repressive regimes, and capitalist interests have supported the overthrow of democracies in Chile and other Third World countries and the installment of right-wing dictators who make their lands safe for corporate investments. Capitalism is presented as the sole alternative to "communist tyranny." The private enterprise system, it is taught, creates equality of opportunity, rewards those who show ability and initiative, relegates the parasitic and slothful to the bottom of the ladder, provides a national prosperity that is the envy of other lands, safeguards (through unspecified means) personal liberties and political freedom, promises continued progress in the endless proliferation of goods and services, and has made America the great and beautiful nation it is.

Among the institutions of plutocratic culture, our educational system looms as one of the more influential purveyors of dominant values. From the earliest school years, children are taught to compete against each other for grades and for the teacher's approval rather than work together for common goals and mutual benefit. Grade-school students are regularly exposed to the rituals of the nation-state. They are taught to salute the flag, pledge allegiance, and sing the national anthem. They read stories of their nation's exploits that might be more valued for their inspirational nationalism than for their historical accuracy. Students are instructed to believe in America's global virtue and moral superiority and to fear and hate the Great Red Menace. They are taught to hold a rather uncritical view of American politico-economic institutions. One nationwide survey of 12,000 children (grades two to eight) found that most youngsters believe "the government and its representatives are wise, benevolent and infallible, that whatever the government does is for the best." Teachers concentrate on the formal aspects of representative government and accord little attention to the influences that wealthy and powerful groups exercise over political life.[3]

Schools are regularly inundated with millions of dollars worth of printed materials, video tapes, and films, which the Pentagon and the giant corporations provide at no cost, to promote a glorified view of the military and argue for tax subsidies to business and deregulation of industry. Pro-business propaganda on nutrition, nuclear power, environmental issues, and the wonders of free enterprise are also widely distributed in schools and communities. Corporations encourage their employees to serve on local school curriculum committees to help develop pro-business materials.[4]

Teachers in primary and secondary schools who wish to introduce radical critiques of American politico-economic institutions do so at the risk of jeopardizing their careers. High school students who attempt to sponsor unpopular speakers and explore progressive views in student newspapers have frequently been overruled by administrators and threatened with disciplinary action.[5]

Colleges and graduate and professional schools offer a more sophisticated extension of this same orthodox socialization. One gets a Ph.D. in political science at Yale, Harvard, Princeton, Cornell, and most other graduate schools in the nation usually without ever studying Marxist or other socialist literature and without ever having the opportunity to do research with a professor using a Marxist conceptual framework. Faculty, and even students, have been subjected to discriminatory treatment because of their political orientations and dissenting activities, suffering negative evaluations, loss of scholarships, loss of research grants, and nonrenewal of contracts.[6]

So it is that socialization into the orthodox values is achieved not only by indoctrination but also by economic sanctions designed to

---

3. A Carnegie Corporation three-year study reported in the *New York Times*, September 23, 1970.

4. Sheila Harty, *Hucksters in the Classroom: A Review of Industry Propaganda in Schools* (Washington, D.C.: Center for Study of Responsive Law, 1979); Betty Medsger, "The 'Free' Propaganda That Floods the Schools," *Progressive*, December 1976, p. 42; Samuel Bowles and Herbert Gintis, *Schooling in Capitalist America* (New York: Basic Books, 1976).

5. John Birmingham, *Our Time Is Now* (New York: Bantam, 1970); also the report of the Commission of Inquiry into High School Journalism, *Captive Voices: High School Journalism in America* (New York: Schocken Books, 1974). A survey of 500 high school newspapers found censorship to be widespread; see *Washington Post*, December 30, 1981.

6. Michael Miles, "The Triumph of Reaction," *Change, The Magazine of Higher Learning*, 4 (Winter 1972–73), p. 34; J. David Colfax, "Repression and Academic Radicalism," *New Politics*, 10 (Spring 1973), pp. 14–27; Michael Parenti, "Political Bigotry

punish the radical critics and reward the more faithful, conservative conformists. This is true of the training and certification of lawyers, doctors, journalists, engineers, managers, and bureaucrats, as well as teachers. To get along in one's career, one learns to go along with things as they are and avoid the espousal of views that conflict with the dominant economic interests of one's profession, institution, and society.[7]

Another agent of orthodox political socialization is the government itself. The concern of government officials with trying to prevent leaks of potentially embarrassing information does not keep these same officials from flooding the public and the media with press releases and planted information supporting the viewpoints of government, industry, and the military. Hardly a day passes without the president or some White House official feeding us reassuring pronouncements about the economy and alarming assertions about communist threats from abroad. The federal government allocates about $400 million yearly for its "public information" efforts, double the combined expenditures of the major wire services, television networks, and 10 largest newspapers in the United States.[8]

One cannot talk about political socialization without mentioning the mass media. Almost all our views and information about the political world come from newspapers, popular magazines, movies, radio, and, above all, television. Owned by big-business interests, the media allow little room for ideological heterodoxy either in their news or entertainment sectors. Arguments and analyses from leftist sources are either ignored or quickly dismissed from an orthodox perspective, as are most controversial and troublesome issues. Occasionally the media might carry a reformist-type complaint about corporate behavior, but rarely if ever will one be exposed to an overall critique of *capitalism as a system*—of a kind found in this book, for instance. Political leaders may be criticized in limited ways about particular policies,

---

in Academe," *Chronicle of Higher Education*, January 21, 1980, p. 56. As of 1982, in the field of political science alone, radical professors who claim to be victims of politically motivated firings are contesting their cases in New Hampshire, Massachusetts, Maryland, California, New York, and Colorado. See also Martin Nicolaus, "The Professional Organization of Sociology: A View from Below," in Robin Blackburn (ed.), *Ideology in Social Science* (New York: Vintage, 1972), pp. 45–60.

7. On the conservative socialization in law school, see Scott Turow, *One L* (New York: Putnam's, 1977); Ralph Nader, "Law Schools and Law Firms," *New Republic*, October 11, 1969, p. 20.

8. William Rivers and Wilbur Schramm, *Responsibility in Mass Communications* (New York: Harper and Row, 1969), p. 97.

but generally the media accept the same view of the world espoused by America's political, military, and corporate elites.[9]

Although we are often admonished to "think for ourselves," we might wonder if our socialization process allows us to do so. Ideological orthodoxy so permeates the plutocratic culture, masquerading as "pluralism," "democracy," and the "open society," that it is often not felt as indoctrination. The worst forms of tyranny are those so subtle, so deeply ingrained, so thoroughly controlling as not even to be consciously experienced. So there are Americans who conform unswervingly to the capitalist orthodoxy, afraid to entertain contrary notions, but who think they are "free." Perhaps they should be more selfish, demanding for themselves the same good things they desire for the Russians and Chinese, namely the opportunity to hear and advocate iconoclastic views without fear of reprisal. Only then can we move to a genuinely free flow of information and a truly open competition of ideas.

INDIVIDUALISM AND THE STRUGGLE
FOR SURVIVAL

Living in a capitalist society, one is bombarded daily with inducements to maintain values and a life style that promote the plutocratic culture. Each year business spends billions to get people to consume as much as they can—and sometimes more than they can afford. Mass advertising offers not only commodities but a whole way of life, teaching us that the piling up of possessions is a worthwhile life goal, a measure of one's accomplishment and proof of one's worth.

In the plutocratic culture, one is admonished to "get ahead." Ahead of whom and what? Of others and of one's present material status. This kind of "individualism" is not to be mistaken for the freedom to choose deviant political and economic practices. Each person is expected to operate "individually" *but in more or less similar ways and similar directions.* Everyone competes against everyone else but for the same things. "Individualism" in the United States refers to *pri-*

---

9. A fuller treatment of the media can be found in chapter 10. For general studies of ideological orthodoxy and political repression in the United States, see William Preston, Jr., *Aliens and Dissenters* (Cambridge, Mass.: Harvard University Press, 1963); William Appleman Williams, *The Great Evasion* (Chicago: Quadrangle Books, 1964); Michael Parenti, *The Anti-Communist Impulse* (New York: Random House, 1969); Francis X. Sutton et al., *The American Business Creed* (New York: Schocken Books, 1962); Sidney Fine, *Laissez-Faire and the General-Welfare State* (Ann Arbor: University of Michigan Press, 1964); Parenti, *Power and the Powerless*, chapter 11.

"Religious freedom is my immediate goal, but my long-range plan is to go into real estate."

Drawing by Donald Reilly; © 1974 The New Yorker Magazine, Inc.

vatization and the absence of social forms of ownership, consumption, and recreation. You are individualist in that you are expected to get what you can for yourself and not to be too troubled by the needs and problems faced by others. This attitude, considered inhuman in some societies, is labeled approvingly as "ambition" in our own and is treated as a quality of great social value.

Whether or not this "individualism" allows one to have control over one's own life is another story. The decisions about the quality of the food we eat, the goods we buy, the air we breathe, the prices we pay, the way work tasks are divided, the opinions and values fed to us by the media—the controlling decisions concerning the palpable realities of our lives—are made by people other than ourselves.

This competitive individualism spawns a good deal of loneliness and limits the opportunities for meaningful and joyful experiences with other people. The emphasis is on self-absorption: "do your own thing" and "look out for number one." We are taught to seek more possessions and more privacy: a private home, private car, private vacation place; and we "feel more and more alienated and lonely" when we get them.[10] Born of a market economy, the plutocratic culture is essentially a market culture, one that minimizes cooperative efforts and human interdependence and keeps us busily competing as workers and consumers.

Public man gives way to private competitor. One's peers are potentially one's enemies; their successes can cause us envy and anxiety, and their failures bring secret feelings of relief. The ability or desire to work collectively with others is much retarded.

As products of a competitive, acquisitive society, some Americans do not welcome equality; they fear and detest it and have a profound commitment to inequality. People who have invested much psychic energy and years of toil in maintaining or furthering their positions within the social hierarchy become committed to the hierarchy's preservation. Even those perched on modest rungs of the ladder—the millions of small proprietors, low-paid semiprofessionals, and white-collar workers, often described as "middle Americans," who could have much to gain from a more egalitarian social order—fear that they might be overtaken by those below, making all their toil and sacrifice count for naught.[11] The plutocratic culture teaches us that proximity to the poor is to be shunned, while wealth is something to be pursued and admired. Hence the road upward should be kept open, free of artificial impediments imposed by the government on those who can advance, while the road behind should not be provided with special conveyances for those who wish to catch up.

To be sure, Americans have their doubts about the rat race, and those who are able to, seek an alternative life style, consuming less and working in less demanding jobs. But the economy does not always allow such a choice. With wage cutbacks, inflation, and growing tax burdens, most people must keep running on the treadmill just to stay in the same place.

---

10. Philip Slater, *The Pursuit of Loneliness* (Boston: Beacon Press, 1970), p. 7.

11. On the "fear of equality," see Robert E. Lane, *Political Ideology* (New York: Free Press, 1962), pp. 57–81. According to one community study, the higher their income and education, the less people believe that all groups should have equal political power. Low-income people and Blacks were the firmest supporters of equality; see William Form and Joan Rytina, "Ideological Beliefs on the Distribution of Power in the United States," *American Sociological Review*, 34 (February 1969), pp. 19–31.

The insecurities of capitalism propagate a scarcity psychology even among people well above the poverty level. There is always more to get, more to hang on to, and more to lose. The highly paid professional feels the pressure of "moreness," as does the lowly paid blue-collar worker. Economically deprived groups are seen as a nuisance and a threat to the affluent because they want more, and more for the have-nots might mean less for the haves. The scarcity psychology, then, leaves some people with the feeling that the poor and the racial minorities (potential competitors) should be kept in their place, away from what others have and want.

Those possessed by a scarcity psychology will sometimes convince themselves of the inferiority of deprived groups. Unfortunately, the racism, sexism, and class bigotry thus activated militate against working people's understanding of their common interests and leave some of them inclined to exclude groups and categories of people from competing for the desired things in life. So bigots can convince themselves that the hardships endured by victimized groups are due to the groups' deficiencies. "Those people don't *want* to better themselves," say the bigots, who then become quite hostile when deprived groups take actions intended to better their lot.

During recessions, as economic anxieties intensify, so does scarcity psychology and so does the bigotry aimed at potential competitors. Not surprisingly, hate groups like the Ku Klux Klan and the American Nazi Party and organizations like the Moral Majority begin to gather momentum (and win generous publicity from the media). Often well-financed by moneyed persons, these groups take the anger that working Americans might feel toward the profiteering corporate class and try to redirect it in a right-wing direction against irrelevant foes such as Blacks, Jews, women, trade unionists, secular humanists, and radicals. They attempt to channel economic class grievances into noneconomic issues such as school prayers, abortion, and the teaching of evolution.

A special word should be said about *class* bigotry, which, along with racism and sexism, is one of the widely held forms of prejudice in American society and the least challenged. In movies, on television, in school textbooks, and in popular fiction, the world is portrayed as a predominantly White upper-middle-class place. Working-class people are often presented as villainous characters or as uncouth, unintelligent, and generally undesirable persons. A TV series like "All in the Family," while supposedly exposing bigotry, practices a bigotry of its own by stereotyping the working-class lead character, Archie Bunker, as a loud-mouthed ignoramus and bully whose mispronunciations, life style, and physical appearance are held up to ridicule.

If material success is a measure of one's worth, then the poor are not worth much and society's resources should not be squandered on them. If rich and poor get pretty much what they deserve, then it is self-evident that the poor are not very deserving. Such is the attitude that permeates the money-success-power-status-oriented plutocratic culture.[12] As the American humorist Will Rogers once said: "It's no disgrace to be poor, but it might as well be."

ARE AMERICANS CONSERVATIVE?

It would be easy to fault Americans, who manifest these competitive, acquisitive, jingoistic traits, as people who lack some proper measure of humanity. But most such attitudes evolve as products of plutocratic class dominance. The emphasis placed on getting ahead, on making money, on putting others down in order to boost oneself is not the outcome of some genetic flaw in the American character. In a society where money is the overriding determinant of one's life chances, the competitive drive for material success is not merely a symptom of greed but a factor in one's very survival, shaping the texture of one's life. Rather than grasping for fanciful luxuries, most Americans are still struggling to provide for basic necessities. If they need more money than was essential in earlier days, this is largely because essentials cost so much more.

Because human services are based on ability to pay, money becomes a matter of life and death. To have a low or modest income is to run a higher risk of illness, insufficient medical care, and job exploitation, and to have a lesser opportunity for education, leisure, travel, and comfort. The desire to "make it," even at the expense of others, is not merely a wrong-headed attitude but a reflection of the material conditions of capitalist society wherein no one is ever really economically secure except the very affluent.

There is another side to the values of Americans that should not be overlooked. Despite all the ideological and economic pressures to the contrary, millions of Americans manifest a generous and cooperative community spirit. One out of four does some kind of unpaid volunteer

---

12. James T. Patterson, *America's Struggle Against Poverty* (Cambridge, Mass.: Harvard University Press, 1981); Janet M. Fitchen, *Poverty in Rural America* (Boulder, Colo.: Westview, 1981). These books discuss the low esteem in which the poor are held, often by the poor themselves. See also Sidney Lens, "Blaming the Victims, 'Social Darwinism' is Still the Name of the Game," *Progressive*, August 1980, pp. 27–28; an earlier statement on this subject is William Ryan, *Blaming the Victim* (New York: Harper and Row, 1969).

work. (Even today, 85 percent of U.S. firefighters are volunteers.) In 1980, Americans donated $43 billion to charity.[13] A national survey found that Americans ranked "close friends" and "a good family life" as the two most important priorities, while "making a lot of money" and "making a good impression on others" were down toward the bottom of the list. Such responses might indicate that many persons desire to live—whether they actually can or not—by less selfish values. "If one looks under the rhetoric about the 'me decade' and the meanness supposedly poisoning the American psyche," Harry Boyte observes, "evidence of a new spirit of civic idealism and community self-help can be found everywhere."[14]

A Gallup survey of American youth found that young people were less self-centered than supposed; many wished to be of service to others. The survey concluded: "The problem we face in America today is not a lack of willingness to serve or to help others, but to find the appropriate outlet for this."[15] Other studies arrive at similar conclusions: deprived of an opportunity to participate in something of value to their society, young (and not-so-young) people lapse into egoistic pursuits and authoritarian cults.[16] This suggests that the problem of alienation lies less in our "human nature" or "national character" than in the way our resources, institutions, and social relations are organized.

Many Americans, including millions of the more conventionally minded, have serious questions about the institutions and practices of their society. Opinion polls show that among all groups of Americans there has been a growing distrust of economic and political elites. Between 1966 and 1976, public confidence in those who ran the major corporations declined from 55 percent to 16 percent. Confidence in religious, military, and other establishment elites showed comparable drops.[17] Fifty-five percent of the respondents in another poll believe that both the Democratic and Republican parties favor big business over the average worker. Forty-one percent want "sweeping changes" in our economy; only 17 percent are for letting the economy

13. Those who have the most to give, business and rich foundations, account for only 10 percent of all U.S. philanthropy—and much of this is from small business. *Time*, October 19, 1981, p. 47.

14. Quoted in the *New York Times*, October 10, 1980. On the choice of priorities, see the Louis Harris survey, "How the Baby Boom Generation Is Living Now," summarized in the *Daily World*, May 16, 1981. A 1980 survey of college freshmen by the University of Michigan's Institute for Social Research got similar results, reported in the *Washington Post*, December 28, 1981.

15. Gallup poll quoted in the *Washington Post*, December 29, 1981.

16. See the reports on American youth in the *Washington Post*, December 27-31, 1981; also the discussion in Parenti, *Power and the Powerless*, chapter 8.

17. Harris survey, *Ithaca* (N.Y.) *Journal*, March 22, 1976; also Harris survey, *Ithaca* (N.Y.) *Journal*, March 25, 1976.

straighten itself out. Most respondents seem open to new and bold experiments in economic matters. A whopping 66 percent would like to work for a company owned and controlled by its employees.[18]

Other polls found that majorities of more than two to one favor increased government efforts to (a) curb air and water pollution, (b) aid education, and (c) help the poor. At the same time they are against increased spending for highways and the space program. By a margin of 80 to 13 percent, Americans feel the tax system favors the rich at the expense of the average person. By 72 to 20 percent they judge that "too much money is going into wars and defense," and by an overwhelming 4 to 1 margin they would support a freeze on nuclear armaments and a 50 percent cut in arms by the United States and the Soviet Union. Despite the cold-war alarms repeatedly sounded by political elites and media pundits, fear of "the threat of communism or aggression by a communist power" has declined from 29 percent in 1964, to 13 percent in 1974, to 8 percent in 1981.[19]

A CBS News/*New York Times* survey found that by lopsided majorities, both conservatives and liberals favored more public spending on the environment, schooling, medical care, the elderly, employment, and job safety. But differences between them do appear on social and cultural questions, such as abortion, legalization of marijuana, gun control, and gay rights.[20] Surveys have found little evidence of a "shift to the right" among college students; even the ones who labeled themselves conservative were quite liberal on most issues.[21] Studies of the 1980 election of a conservative president, Ronald Reagan, indicate his victory was *not* a mandate for conservative policies. By 1982, opinion polls reported that Americans were complaining that President Reagan favored the rich over the poor and big business over labor. Most respondents opposed Reagan's cuts in human services and his astronomical increases in defense spending. Instead, they thought it important to balance the budget by "cutting down on defense, increasing corporate taxes and not by cutting social services."[22]

Americans have become more tolerant of cultural and political dissenters. Large majorities found atheists, Black militants, student demonstrators, and homosexuals "dangerous or harmful to the coun-

18. Peter Hart poll in *Ithaca* (N.Y.) *Journal*, September 5, 1975.

19. Findings by William Watts, "Americans' Hopes and Fears," *Psychology Today*, September 1981; Gallup poll, *Washington Post*, December 22, 1981.

20. *New York Times*, February 3, 1981, and January 22, 1978. Surveys show that 74 to 79 percent of Americans favor legal abortions; see Associated Press/NBC News poll, January 20, 1982, and *Washington Post*, February 22, 1982.

21. CBS News/*New York Times* survey in *New York Times*, January 22, 1978.

22. Yankelovich, Skelly, and White survey reported in *New York Times*, January

try" in the late sixties. But by 1974, lopsided majorities now labeled as dangerous the following: politicians who engage in secret wiretapping, businessmen who make illegal campaign contributions, and generals who conduct secret bombing raids.[23] A Harris poll concluded that substantial majorities of Americans are no longer willing to be stampeded by the kind of fear appeals that characterized past conservative campaigns—such as the "soft on communism," "soft on Blacks," and "soft on crime" issues.[24] And throughout the sixties and seventies, Americans slowly but steadily changed their attitudes in a progressive direction, especially in regard to race relations.[25]

In short, on almost every major issue, Americans seem to hold opinions contrary to the policies pursued by corporate and political elites.

Political activism, supposedly a passing phenomenon of the 1960s, remained very much a reality through the late 1970s and seemed to be gathering momentum by the early 1980s. There were campus demonstrations, strikes, sit-ins, and arrests to protest university investments in firms doing business in South Africa, the firing of radical professors, tuition increases, and cuts in scholarship aid. In November 1981, rallies and teach-ins protesting nuclear weapons were held on more than 150 college campuses across the nation.[26] And in that same year, the Selective Service System admitted that some 800,000 young men had defied the law and refused to register for the draft (the actual number was probably much higher). Religious groups, including previously conservative ones like Roman Catholics and Southern Baptists who usually could be counted on to bless any military venture the nation embarked upon, denounced as dangerous and immoral the nu-

---

13, 1982; also Arthur Miller, "What Mandate? What Realignment?" *Washington Post*, June 28, 1981, and *Washington Post*, September 23, 1981. Nearly two-thirds of those interviewed in a February 1981 *Washington Post*/ABC News poll agreed that "the Government should work to substantially reduce the income gap between rich and poor."

23. Harris survey, *New York Times*, January 21, 1974.

24. Harris survey, *Chicago Tribune*, January 5, 1975. "For the period through 1978, with few exceptions, liberal or left-wing options were endorsed by majorities as large as ever—or larger," conclude David Paletz and Robert Entman after an analysis of opinion data in their book *Media—Power—Politics* (New York: Free Press, 1981), p. 197.

25. Surveys reported in *Scientific American*, June 1978; Harris poll in *New York Times*, February 19, 1979; Gallup poll reported in *Daily World*, August 29, 1978. In 1968–69, 63 percent of White Americans thought Blacks should have the right to live anywhere they could afford to; by 1978 the percentage had climbed to 93 percent of those interviewed; see *Public Opinion*, January/February 1979. All this does not gainsay that well-financed, virulent forms of racism and reaction emerge during times of economic stress and recession.

26. *Washington Post*, November 12, 1981.

clear arms build-up.[27] SANE, an anti-war organization, nearly tripled its membership during 1980–81, and civil-liberties, environmental, and women's-rights groups also reported increases in membership.[28]

In 1981, in Santa Monica, California, a city of 100,000, the voters elected a militantly progressive slate to the city government, while in Burlington, Vermont, an avowed socialist won the mayorality race and five of his supporters subsequently won city-council seats. In April 1981 in New York, and in May 1981 and May 1982 in Washington, D.C., hundreds of thousands marched against U.S. military intervention in Central America.[29] From Maine to California, tens of thousands demonstrated against nuclear power plants, with several thousand people getting arrested.[30] And in June 1982, upwards of a million people marched in New York to support a freeze on nuclear weapons.

Various regions of the country have witnessed major strikes by coal miners, farm workers, teachers, and newspaper, hospital, and utility workers. In September 1981, detachments from virtually every sector of organized labor, numbering over 400,000, descended upon Washington to protest President Reagan's anti-working-class programs. Additional protests during 1980–82 were staged by farm, labor, minority, and religious groups to combat conservative domestic and foreign policies.[31]

In sum, despite all the propaganda and indoctrination by plutocratic institutions, Americans have not been taken in. The disparities between what elites profess and what they practice remain glaringly apparent to large numbers of people. There is a limit to how effectively the sugar-coated orthodoxies of capitalist culture can keep Americans from tasting the bitter realities of economic life.

Furthermore, political socialization does not operate with perfectly conservative effect, there being unexpected and contradictory spin-offs. Thus when the plutocratic opinion makers indoctrinate us with the notion that we are a free and prosperous people, we, in fact, begin to demand the right to be free and prosperous. The old trick of

---

27. See the stance taken by the National Conference of Catholic Bishops and other Christian groups, *Washington Post*, December 25, 1981; also the editorial comment in the *Daily World*, November 25, 1981.

28. *Washington Post*, November 30, 1981; and "Lashing Back at the Right," *Mother Jones*, September/October 1981, p. 15.

29. *New York Times*, May 24, 1981.

30. *Washington Post*, September 18, 1981.

31. *New York Times*, October 19, 1981. On the development of a farmer-laborer coalition in Illinois called the Public Action Coalition, see *Daily World*, February 25, 1982; on grassroots protest groups, see Harry Boyte, *The Backyard Revolution: Understanding the New Citizen Movement* (Philadelphia: Temple University Press, 1980).

using democratic rhetoric to cloak an undemocratic class order will backfire if people begin to take the rhetoric seriously and translate it into substantive economic demands. Also, there are many people who love justice more than they love money or a narrow professional success, and who long not for more things for themselves but for a better quality of life for all. It is not that they are without self-interests but that they define their interests in a way that conflicts with the interests of the privileged and the powerful. In general, Americans are hardly as conservative as we have been led to believe. If they were given more truthful information and if they could see a way to change things, they would be more likely to move in a progressive direction on most economic policies—and, indeed, despite everything, they show signs of wanting to do just that. A conservative newspaper, the *Brooklyn Tablet*, ran an editorial on a senior-citizens conference that serves as a good description of the mood of many Americans:

> They all are concerned about the economy. They had worked hard all their lives and felt themselves entitled to freedom from money worries at this stage of their lives. They felt betrayed by inflation, government promises and the general lack of fairness in the way they were treated by society. . . .
> Yet once they began to articulate what they wanted from society it was also obvious that they were demanding deep social changes in our economic system.
> They wanted their income protected from inflation. They wanted their decreased income sheltered from taxation, and taxes shifted to those who had greater ability to pay them. They wanted corporate profits limited in order that adequate pensions could be paid workers. Yet it was a federalized program of income maintenance, social security, that they most trusted and respected. They felt that medical services and housing were rights they were entitled to and at government expense.
> They were not trying to write a socialistic charter. They would deny that they were anything but conservative Americans. . . . Yet when they looked carefully at the social problems that they understood and wanted to help solve, they came up with some very radical solutions.[32]

CONSERVATIVES, LIBERALS, SOCIALISTS, AND DEMOCRACY

Political ideologies in the United States might be roughly categorized as conservative, liberal, and socialist. Each of these terms carries certain ambiguities and within each category there are variations and

---

32. The *Tablet* editorial is quoted in Gus Hall, "The New Political Reality: Analysis and Perspective," *Political Affairs*, January 1981, pp. 2–3.

differences. Here we will try to draw the broad outlines of the three tendencies. The *conservative* ideology, held most firmly by corporate and political elites and by many—but not all—persons of high income and substantial property, supports the system of capitalism and defends the interests of business as the primary mainstays of the good society. Conservative leaders believe that most reforms should be resisted. They may recognize that there are some inequities in society, but these will either take care of themselves or, as with poverty, will always be with us. Conservatives believe that people are poor usually because, as Richard Nixon once noted, they are given to a "welfare ethic rather than a work ethic."

Conservatives are for strong or weak government depending on what interests are being served. They denounce as government "meddling" those policies that appear to move toward an equalization of life chances, income, and class, or that attempt to make business more accountable to public authority. But they usually advocate a strong government that will enforce "law and order,"[33] restrict dissent, intervene militarily in other countries, and regulate our private lives and personal morals.[34]

Conservatives say they are for cutting government spending and bureaucracy, but the cuts they propose are selective, focusing on domestic services to the needy, while ever greater sums are given to the largest bureaucracy within the federal government—the Department of Defense. Far from being frugal, a conservative administration produced a budget deficit for 1983 estimated at between $150 billion and $200 billion, the largest in history and more than twice that of any peacetime liberal administration. Conservatives decry all government handouts except defense contracts, corporate subsidies, and tax breaks for business and the well-to-do. They believe taxes reduce the freedom of people to spend their own money, so they prefer to shift the tax burden onto those with less money, presumably thereby taking away less freedom.

"Supply-side" conservative theorists argue that recessions occur because corporations do not have enough money to invest, inflation

---

33. The law-and-order issue focuses on street crimes. Corporate crimes and organized crimes are of less concern to conservatives; see chapter 8.

34. Conservatives talk about "getting big government off the back of the American people" (President Reagan's words), yet in 1981 they pushed through a $30 million bill to create a new federal agency, the Office of Adolescent Pregnancy, which will oversee a network of storefront "chastity centers" to teach adolescents that celibacy is the one foolproof way of avoiding pregnancy and retaining one's virtue. The bill was sponsored by right-wing Senator Jeremiah Denton (R.–Ala.), who once half-seriously advocated the death penalty for adultery. *Working Papers*, November/December 1981, p. 6. So much for keeping government out of our lives.

occurs because people have too much money to spend, and unemployment occurs because people prefer to live off welfare. In other words, the rich must be given more money before they will work, while the poor must have money taken from them before they will work.

For conservatives, the keystone to individual rights is the enjoyment of property rights, especially the right to make a profit off other people's labor. Indeed, conservatives cherish private enterprise quite independently of the value placed on human beings, so when the two values conflict, private profit is often protected in preference to individual life and sometimes at a cost to individual life.[35] In sum, conservative leaders put their stock in individual acquisitiveness and other established values of the plutocratic culture such as institutional authority and hierarchy, support of big business, a strong police force, and a large and powerful military establishment.

Many people who are not members of the corporate elite, but who witnessed the failure of liberal programs to solve major social problems, oppose big government and high taxes and call themselves conservatives—for want of an alternative. As noted earlier, ultraconservative religious groups like Moral Majority, adhering to fundamentalist Christian doctrines—if not to Christian practices—have tried to direct this popular discontent toward moralistic life-style issues that have little to do with economic problems but that work against liberal and progressive candidates. While giving an appearance of offering something new, the "Christian" Right and the New Right in general, in their financing, leadership, and politics, are little more than a warmed-over version of right-wing Republicanism.[36]

There are, however, differences among conservatives (as among liberals and socialists). The true believers of the New Right dream of a mythic "free enterprise" in which business, once totally free of government restraints and taxes, will become so productive as to bring prosperity to all. In contrast, the more conventional corporate elites understand that government's true historic role is not to keep hands off business but to enhance business profits with subsidies, price supports, manipulated money supplies, market protections, and restrictions on labor. Differences also emerge in foreign policy as the corporate and financial elites, for profit's sake, show themselves willing to

---

35. See, for instance, the discussion on health, environment, and occupational safety in chapter 7.

36. Michael Lienesch, "Right-Wing Religion: A Study of Interest-Group Conservatism," (paper given at the annual meeting of the American Political Science Association, New York, September 1981). For an earlier statement of how irrational symbols are used for rational, dominant class interests, see Michael Rogin, *The Intellectuals and McCarthy* (Cambridge, Mass.: M.I.T. Press, 1967).

trade with, and lend money to, existing socialist nations, while the New Rightist ideologues are more likely to call for embargos and holy-war confrontations with socialist countries.

A *liberal*, like a conservative, accepts the basic structure and values of the capitalist system but believes that social problems should be rectified by a redirection of government spending and by better regulatory policies. Liberals do not usually see these problems as being interrelated and endemic to the present system. Since they assume that the ills of the politico-economic system are aberrations in the workings of capitalism, they believe that the fault must be with the particular policies of the personages who have gained power. If the right persons finally win office, and with the right combination of will, public awareness, and political push, the system will be able to take care of its major crises. Liberals generally support government intervention in the economy in the hope of curbing some of the worst abuses of the economic system and changing "our warped priorities" so that more money will be spent on needed public services and less on private privileges. Yet while liberals call for cuts in "excessive" military spending and advocate protection of individual rights against government suppression and surveillance, and assistance for the poor and needy, in the world of action many liberals vote for huge military budgets, support security and intelligence agencies, and make cuts in human services for the needy.

Some liberals are not overly fond of capitalism, but they like socialism even less. Socialism, in their minds, conjures up stereotyped images of "drabness" and "regimentation," of people waiting in line for shoddy goods wrapped in dull gray packages and of Stalinist purges and labor camps. The liberal's concern seems to be that freedom would be lost or diminished under socialism. (Many liberals believe they are free under the present politico-economic system.) They are also worried about the diminution of their own class and professional privileges and the loss of status they might suffer with the democratization of institutions advocated by American socialists. In this respect, they often resemble conservatives.

In matters of foreign policy, liberals generally have shown themselves as willing as conservatives to contain the spread of socialism in other lands and make the world safe for American corporate investments and markets. Since Vietnam, many liberals have come to think that we should not get involved in suppressing social revolutionary movements in other countries. But whatever their feelings about revolution abroad, most liberals have little tolerance for revolutionary struggle in the United States.

Only a small portion of Americans currently identify themselves as socialists—although many more adhere to views that are close to socialist principles, and socialist opinion has shown a modest but steady growth in recent years.[37] A *socialist* is someone who wants to replace the capitalist system with a system of public and communal ownership. Socialists are distinguished from liberal reformers in their belief that our social problems cannot be solved within the very system that is creating them. Socialists do not believe that *every* human problem at *every* level of existence is caused by capitalism but that many of the most important ones are and that capitalism propagates a kind of culture and social organization that destroys human potentials and guarantees the perpetuation of poverty, racism, sexism, and exploitative social relations at home and abroad. Socialists even argue that much of the unhappiness suffered in what are considered purely "interpersonal" experiences relates to the false values and insecurities of an acquisitive, competitive capitalist society.

Socialists believe that American corporate and military expansionism abroad is not the result of "wrong thinking" but the natural outgrowth of profit-oriented capitalism. To the socialist, American foreign policy is not beset by folly and irrationality but has been quite successful in maintaining the status quo and the interests of multinational corporations, crushing social change in many countries and establishing an American financial and military presence throughout much of the world.

Democracy: Form and Substance

Conservatives, liberals, and socialists all profess a dedication to "democracy," but tend to mean different things by the term. In this book, *democracy* refers to a system of governance that represents in both *form* and *content* the needs and desires of the ruled. Decision-makers are not to govern for the benefit of the privileged few but for the interests of the many. In other words, their decisions and policies should be of substantive benefit to the populace. The people exercise a measure of control by electing their representatives and by subjecting them to open criticism, the periodic check of elections, and, if necessary, recall and removal from office. Besides living without fear of political tyranny, a democratic people should be able to live without fear of want, enjoying freedom from economic, as well as political,

---

37. See, for instance, Paul W. Valentine, "The Coming Out of U.S. Socialists," *Washington Post*, March 25, 1979.

oppression. In a real democracy, the material conditions of people's lives should be humane and roughly equal.

Some people have argued that democracy is simply a system of rules for playing the game, which allows some measure of mass participation and government accountability, and that the Constitution is a kind of rule book. One should not try to impose, as a precondition of democracy, particular class relations, economic philosophies, or other substantive arrangements on this open-ended game. This argument certainly does reduce democracy to a game. It presumes that formal rules can exist in a meaningful way independently of substantive realities. Whether procedural rights are violated or actually enjoyed, whether one is treated by the law as pariah or prince, depends largely on material realities that extend beyond a written constitution or other formal guarantees of law. The law in its majestic equality, Anatole France once observed, prohibits rich and poor alike from stealing bread and sleeping under the bridges. And in so doing the law becomes something of a farce, a fiction that allows us to speak of "the rights of all" divorced from the class conditions that place the rich above the law and the poor below it. In the absence of certain substantive conditions, formal rights are of little value to millions who lack the time, money, and opportunity to make a reality of their rights.

Take the "right of every citizen to be heard." In its majestic equality, the law allows both the rich and the poor to raise high their political voices: both are free to hire the best-placed lobbyists and Washington lawyers to pressure public officeholders; both are free to shape public opinion by owning a newspaper or television station; and both rich and poor have the right to engage in multimillion-dollar election campaigns in order to pick the right persons for office or win office themselves. But again, this formal political equality is something of a fiction, as we shall see in the pages ahead. Of what good are the rules for those millions who are excluded from the game?

Some people think that if you are free to say what you like, you are living in a democracy. But freedom of speech is not the sum total of democracy, only one of its necessary conditions. A government is not a democracy when it leaves us free to *say* what we want but leaves others free to *do* what they want with our country, our resources, our taxes, and our lives. Democracy is not a seminar but a system of power, like any other form of governance. Freedom of speech, like freedom of assembly and freedom of political organization, is meaningful only if it keeps those in power responsible to those over whom power is exercised.

Nor are elections and political-party competitions a sure test of democracy. Some two-party or multiparty systems are so thoroughly controlled by like-minded elites that they discourage broad participation and offer policies that serve establishment interests no matter who is elected. In contrast, a one-party system, especially in a newly emerging, social revolutionary country, might actually provide *more* democracy—that is, more popular participation, more meaningful policy debate within the party, and more accountability and responsiveness to the people than occurs between the parties in the other system.

In the chapters ahead, we will take a critical look at our own political system and measure it not by its undoubted ability to hold elections but by its ability to serve democratic ends. It will be argued that whether a political system is democratic or not depends not only on its procedures but on the *substantive* outputs—that is, the actual material benefits and costs of policy and the kind of social justice or injustice that is propagated. By this view, a government that pursues policies that by design or neglect are so inequitable as to deny people the very conditions of life is not democratic no matter how many competitive elections it holds.

4

A Constitution for the Few

To help us understand the American political system, let us investigate its origins and its formal structure, the rules under which it operates, and the interests it represents, beginning with the Constitution and the men who wrote it. Why was a central government and a Constitution created? By whom? And for what purposes?

It is commonly taught that in the eighteenth and nineteenth centuries men of property preferred a laissez-faire government, one that kept its activities to a minimum. In actuality, while they wanted government to leave them free in all matters of trade and commerce, not for a moment did they desire a weak, inactive government. Rather they strove to erect a civil authority that worked *for* rather than against the interests of wealth, and they frequently advocated an extension rather than a diminution of state power. They readily agreed with Adam Smith, who said that government was "instituted for the defense of the rich against the poor" and "grows up with the acquisition of valuable property."[1]

CLASS POWER AND CONFLICT IN EARLY AMERICA

During the period between the Revolution and the Constitutional Convention, the "rich and the wellborn" played a dominant role in public affairs.

---

1. For citation and fuller quotation, see the discussion in chapter one.

Their power was born of place, position, and fortune. They were located at or near the seats of government and they were in direct contact with legislatures and government officers. They influenced and often dominated the local newspapers which voiced the ideas and interests of commerce and identified them with the good of the whole people, the state, and the nation. The published writings of the leaders of the period are almost without exception those of merchants, of their lawyers, or of politicians sympathetic with them.[2]

The United States of 1787 has been described as an "egalitarian" society free from the extremes of want and wealth that characterized the Old World, but there were landed estates and colonial mansions that bespoke an impressive munificence. From the earliest English settlements, men of influence had received vast land grants from the crown. By 1700, three-fourths of the acreage in New York belonged to fewer than a dozen persons. In the interior of Virginia, seven persons owned a total of 1,732,000 acres.[3] By 1760, fewer than 500 men in five colonial cities controlled most of the commerce, banking, mining, and manufacturing on the eastern seaboard and owned much of the land.[4] In contrast, the bulk of the agrarian population were poor freeholders, tenants, and indentured hands. The cities also had their poor—craftsmen, servants, and laborers, who worked long hours for meager sums.[5]

As of 1787, property qualifications left perhaps more than a third of the White male population disfranchised.[6] Property qualifications for holding office were so steep as to prevent most voters from qualifying as candidates. Thus, a member of the New Jersey legislature had to be worth at least 1,000 pounds, while state senators in South Caro-

---

2. Merrill Jensen, *The New Nation* (New York: Random House, 1950), p. 178.

3. Sidney H. Aronson, *Status and Kinship in the Higher Civil Service* (Cambridge, Mass.: Harvard University Press, 1964), p. 35.

4. Ibid., p. 41; see also the estimates in Jackson Turner Main, *The Social Structure of Revolutionary America* (Princeton, N.J.: Princeton University Press, 1965); Allan Kulikoff, "The Progress of Inequality in Revolutionary Boston," *William and Mary Quarterly* (1971), 28, pp. 375–412.

5. Herbert Aptheker, *Early Years of the Republic* (New York: International Publishers, 1976). Historians like Robert Brown who argue that little or no poverty existed in post-Revolutionary America ignore the large debtor class and the rebellions, poorhouses, and debtor jails that held the attention of both rich and poor.

6. This is Beard's estimate regarding New York. Charles A. Beard, *An Economic Interpretation of the Constitution of the United States* (New York: Macmillan, 1936), pp. 67–68. In a few states like Pennsylvania and Georgia, suffrage was more widespread; in others it was even more restricted than in New York; see Arthur Ekrich, Jr., *The American Democratic Tradition* (New York: Macmillan, 1963). For a pioneer work on this subject, see A. E. McKinley, *The Suffrage Franchise in the Thirteen English Colonies in America* (Philadelphia: B. Franklin, 1969, originally published 1905).

lina were required to possess estates worth at least 7,000 pounds, clear of debt.[7] In addition, the practice of oral voting, rather than use of a secret ballot, and an "absence of a real choice among candidates and programs" led to "widespread apathy."[8] As a result, men of substance monopolized the important offices. "Who do they represent?" Josiah Quincy asked of the South Carolina legislature. "The laborer, the mechanic, the tradesman, the farmer, the husbandman or yeoman? No, the representatives are almost if not wholly rich planters."[9]

Not long before the Constitutional Convention, the French *chargé d'affaires* wrote to his Foreign Minister:

> Although there are no nobles in America, there is a class of men denominated "gentlemen." . . . Almost all of them dread the efforts of the people to despoil them of their possessions, and, moreover, they are creditors, and therefore interested in strengthening the government, and watching over the execution of the law. . . . The majority of them being merchants, it is for their interest to establish the credit of the United States in Europe on a solid foundation by the exact payment of debts, and to grant to Congress powers extensive enough to compel the people to contribute for this purpose.[10]

The Constitution was framed by financially successful planters, merchants, and creditors, many linked by kinship and marriage and by years of service in Congress, the military, or diplomatic service.[11] They congregated in Philadelphia in 1787 for the professed purpose of revising the Articles of Confederation and strengthening the powers of the central government. They were aware of the weaknesses of the United States in its commercial and diplomatic dealings with other nations. There were also problems among the thirteen states involving trade, customs duties, and currency differences, but these have been exaggerated and in fact some reforms were being instituted under the Articles.[12]

---

7. Beard, *An Economic Interpretation*, pp. 68, 70. Seven thousand pounds was equivalent to almost a million dollars today.

8. Aronson, *Status and Kinship*, p. 49.

9. *Ibid.*, p. 49.

10. Quoted in Aptheker, *Early Years of the Republic*, p. 41.

11. Even Forrest McDonald, a critic of Charles Beard's "economic interpretation" of the Constitution, documents the opulent background of 53 of the 55 delegates; see his *We, the People: The Economic Origins of the Constitution* (Chicago: University of Chicago Press, 1958), chapter two.

12. Aptheker, *Early Years of the Republic*, pp. 34–35.

Most troublesome to the framers of the Constitution was the increasingly insurgent spirit evidenced among poorer people. Fearing the popular takeover of state governments, the wealthy class looked to a national government as a means of protecting their interests. Even in states where they were inclined to avoid strong federation, the rich, once faced with the threat of popular rule "and realizing that a political alliance with conservatives from other states would be a safeguard if the radicals should capture the state government . . . gave up 'state rights' for 'nationalism' without hesitation."[13]

The nationalist conviction that arose so swiftly among men of wealth during the 1780s was not the product of a strange transcendent inspiration; it was not a "dream of nation-building" that suddenly possessed them as might a collective religious experience. (If so, they kept it a secret in their public and private communications.) Rather, their newly acquired nationalism was a practical response to material conditions affecting them in a most immediate way. Gorham of Massachusetts, Hamilton of New York, Morris of Pennsylvania, Washington of Virginia, and Pinckney of South Carolina had a greater identity of interest with each other than with debt-burdened neighbors in their home counties. Their like-minded commitment to federalism was born of a common class interest stronger than state boundaries.

The rebellious populace of that day has been portrayed as irresponsible and parochial spendthrifts who never paid their debts and who believed in nothing more than timid state governments and inflated paper money. Most scholars say little about the actual plight of the common people, the great bulk of whom lived at a subsistence level. Farm tenants were burdened by heavy rents and hard labor. Small farmers were hurt by the low prices merchants offered for their crops and by the high costs for goods. They often bought land at inflated prices, only to see its value collapse and to find themselves unable to meet their mortgage obligations. Their labor and their crops usually were theirs in name only. To survive, they frequently had to borrow money at high interest rates. To meet their debts, they mortgaged their future crops and went still deeper into debt. Large numbers were caught in that cycle of rural indebtedness, which is the common fate of agrarian peoples in many countries to this day. The artisans, small tradesmen, and workers in the towns were not much

---

13. Merrill Jensen, *The Articles of Confederation* (Madison: University of Wisconsin Press, 1948), p. 30.

better off, for they were "dependent on the wealthy merchants who ruled them economically and socially."[14]

Throughout this period newspapers complained of the "many beggars troubling our doors" and the "increasing numbers of young beggars in the streets."[15] Economic prisoners crowded the jails. In 1785 in one county jail in Massachusetts, for instance, 86 of the 103 prisoners were debtors and six had failed to pay their taxes. In 1786 the same jail held 88 persons, of whom 84 were incarcerated for debts or nonpayment of taxes.[16] Among the people there grew the feeling that the revolution against the English crown had been fought for naught. Angry armed crowds in several states began blocking foreclosures and forcibly freeing debtors from jail. They gathered at county towns to prevent courts from sentencing honest men to jail for being unable to pay mountainous debts and ruinous taxes.[17] Disorders of a violent but organized kind occurred in a number of states. In the winter of 1787, debtor farmers in western Massachusetts led by Daniel Shays took up arms. But their rebellion was forcibly put down by the state militia after several skirmishes that left eleven men dead and scores wounded.[18]

CONTAINING THE SPREAD OF DEMOCRACY

The specter of Shays's Rebellion hovered over the delegates who gathered in Philadelphia three months later, confirming their worst fears about the populace. They were determined that persons of birth and fortune should control the affairs of the nation and check the "leveling impulses" of the propertyless multitude that composed "the majority faction." "To secure the public good and private rights against the danger of such a faction," wrote James Madison in *Federalist* No. 10, "and at the same time preserve the spirit and form of popular govern-

---

14. *Ibid.*, pp. 9–10; also Beard, *An Economic Interpretation*, p. 28. The historian Richard B. Morris writes: "Unable to pay for seed and stock and tools, farmers were thrown into jail or sold out to service. Except for the clothes on the debtor's back, no property was exempt from seizure or execution. . . . But imprisonment for debt is only part of the story. The records disclose case after case of debtors sold off for sizable terms to work off their debts to their creditors—peonage lacking only the Mexican term"; quoted in Aptheker, *Early Years of the Republic*, p. 33. Interest rates on debts ranged from 25 to 40 percent and taxation systems discriminated against those of modest means; Aptheker, p. 36.

15. Aptheker, *Early Years of the Republic*, p. 137.

16. *Ibid.*, pp. 144–45.

17. *Ibid.*, p. 145.

18. David Szatmary, *Shays' Rebellion: The Making of an Agrarian Insurrection* (Amherst: University of Massachusetts Press, 1980).

ment is then the great object to which our inquiries are directed." Here Madison touched the heart of the matter: how to keep the *spirit* and *form* of popular government with only a minimum of the *substance*, how to provide the appearance of republicanism without suffering its leveling, democratic effects, how to construct a government that would win some popular support but would not tamper with the existing class structure, a government strong enough to service the growing needs of an entrepreneurial class while withstanding the egalitarian demands of the poor and propertyless.

The framers of the Constitution could agree with Madison when he wrote in the same *Federalist* No. 10 that "the most common and durable source of factions has been the various and unequal distribution of property. Those who hold and those who are without property have ever formed distinct interests in society," and "the first object of government" is "the protection of different and unequal faculties of acquiring property." The framers were of the opinion that democracy was "the worst of all political evils," as Elbridge Gerry put it. Both he and Madison warned of "the danger of the leveling spirit." "The people," said Roger Sherman, "should have as little to do as may be about the Government." And according to Alexander Hamilton, "All communities divide themselves into the few and the many. The first are the rich and the well-born, the other the mass of the people. . . . The people are turbulent and changing; they seldom judge or determine right."[19]

The delegates spent many weeks debating their interests, but these were the differences of merchants, slave owners, and manufacturers, a debate of haves versus haves in which each group sought safeguards within the new Constitution for its particular concerns. Added to this were disagreements about how best to achieve agreed-upon ends. Questions of structure and authority occupied a good deal of the delegates' time: How much representation should the large and small states have? How might the legislature be organized? How should the executive be selected? What length of tenure should exist for the different officeholders? *Yet questions of enormous significance, relating to the new government's ability to protect the interests of property, were agreed upon with surprisingly little debate.* On these issues, there were no dirt farmers or poor artisans attending the convention

---

19. The comments by Gerry, Madison, Sherman, and Hamilton are from Max Farrand (ed.), *Records of the Federal Convention* (New Haven: Yale University Press, 1927), vol. 1, passim. For further testimony, see John C. Miller, *Origins of the American Revolution* (Boston: Little, Brown, 1943), pp. 491 ff. and Andrew C. McLaughlin, *A Constitutional History of the United States* (New York: Appleton-Century, 1935), pp. 141–44.

to proffer an opposing viewpoint. The debate between haves and have-nots never occurred.

The portion of the Constitution found in Article I, Section 8, giving the federal government the power to support commerce and protect property, was adopted within a few days.[20] This section delegated to Congress the power to:

1. Regulate commerce among the states and with foreign nations and Indian tribes
2. Lay and collect taxes and impose duties and tariffs on imports but not on commercial exports
3. Establish a national currency and regulate its value
4. "Borrow Money on the credit of the United States"—a measure of special interest to creditors
5. Fix the standard of weights and measures necessary for trade
6. Protect the value of securities and currency against counterfeiting
7. Establish "uniform Laws on the subject of Bankruptcies throughout the United States"
8. "Pay the Debts and provide for the common Defence and general Welfare of the United States"

Congress was limited to powers specifically delegated to it by the Constitution or implied as "necessary and proper" for the performance of the delegated powers. Over the years, under this "implied power" clause, federal intervention in the private economy grew to an extraordinary magnitude.

Some of the delegates were land speculators who expressed a concern about western holdings; accordingly, Congress was given the "Power to dispose of and make all needful Rules and Regulations respecting the Territory or other Property belonging to the United States." Some of the delegates speculated in highly inflated and nearly worthless Confederation securities. Under Article VI, all debts incurred by the Confederation were valid against the new government, a provision that allowed speculators to make enormous profits when their securities, bought for a trifling, were honored at face value.[21]

---

20. John Bach McMaster, *The Political Depravity of the Founding Fathers* (New York: Farrar, Straus, 1964), p. 137. Max Farrand refers to the consensus for a strong national government that emerged after the small states were given equal representation in the Senate. Much of the work that followed "was purely formal"; see his *The Framing of the Constitution of the United States* (New Haven: Yale University Press, 1913), pp. 134–35.

21. Beard, *An Economic Interpretation, passim.* The profits accrued to holders of public securities were in the millions. The debt assumed by the newly established fed-

In the interest of merchants and creditors, the states were prohibited from issuing paper money or imposing duties on imports and exports or interfering with the payment of debts by passing any "Law impairing the Obligation of Contracts." The Constitution guaranteed "Full Faith and Credit" in each state "to the Acts, Records, and judicial Proceedings" of other states, thus allowing creditors to pursue their debtors more effectively.

Slavery—another valuable form of property—was afforded special accommodation in the Constitution. Three-fifths of the slave population in each state were to be counted when calculating the representation deserved by states in the lower house. The importation of slaves was allowed to continue for another twenty years. And slaves who escaped from one state to another had to be delivered up to the original owner upon claim, a provision that was unanimously adopted at the Convention.

The framers believed the states acted with insufficient force against popular uprisings, so Congress was given the task of "organizing, arming, and disciplining the Militia" and calling it forth, among other reasons, to "suppress Insurrections." The federal government was empowered to protect the states "against domestic Violence." Provision was made for "the Erection of Forts, Magazines, Arsenals, dock-Yards and other needful Buildings" and for the maintenance of an army and navy for both national defense and to establish an armed federal presence within the potentially insurrectionary states—a provision that was to prove a godsend to the industrial barons a century later when the army was used repeatedly to break strikes by miners, railroad employees, and factory workers.

In keeping with their desire to contain the majority, the founders inserted "auxiliary precautions" *designed to fragment power without democratizing it.* By separating the executive, legislative, and judicial functions and then providing a system of checks and balances among the various branches, including staggered elections, executive veto, Senate confirmation of appointments and ratification of treaties, and a bicameral legislature, they hoped to dilute the impact of popular sentiments. In keeping with this goal, they contrived an elaborate and difficult process for amending the Constitution, requiring proposal by two-thirds of both the Senate and the House, and ratification by

---

eral government consumed nearly 80 percent of the annual national revenue during the 1790s: Aptheker, *Early Years of the Republic*, p. 114. On the question of speculation in western lands, Hugh Williamson, a delegate, wrote to Madison, "My opinions are not biassed by private Interests, but having claims to a considerable Quantity of Land in the Western Country, I am fully persuaded that the Value of those Lands must be increased by an efficient federal Government." Quoted in Beard, p. 50.

three-fourths of the state legislatures.[22] (Such strictures impede progress to this day. Thus, although national polls show a substantial majority of Americans supports the Equal Rights Amendment, the proposal failed to make its way through the constitutional labyrinth.) To the extent that it existed at all, *the majoritarian principle was tightly locked into a system of minority vetoes, making swift and sweeping popular action less likely.*

The propertyless majority, as Madison pointed out in *Federalist* No. 10, must not be allowed to concert in common cause against the established social order.[23] First, it was necessary to prevent a unity of public sentiment by enlarging the polity and then compartmentalizing it into geographically insulated political communities. The larger the nation, the greater the "variety of parties and interests" and the more difficult it would be for a majority to find itself and act in unison. As Madison argued, "A rage for paper money, for an abolition of debts, for an equal division of property, or for any other wicked project will be less apt to pervade the whole body of the Union than a particular member of it." An uprising of impoverished farmers may threaten Massachusetts at one time and Rhode Island at another, but a national government will be large and varied enough to contain each of these and insulate the rest of the nation from the contamination of rebellion.

Second, not only must the majority be prevented from finding horizontal cohesion, but its vertical force—that is, its upward thrust upon government—should be blunted by interjecting indirect forms of representation. Thus the senators from each state were to be elected by their respective state legislatures. The chief executive was to be selected by an electoral college voted by the people but, as anticipated by the framers, composed of political leaders and men of substance who would gather in their various states and choose a president of their own liking. It was believed that they would usually be unable to muster a majority for any one candidate, and that the final selection would be left to the House, with each state delegation therein having only one vote.[24] The Supreme Court was to be elected by no

---

22. Amendments could also be proposed through a constitutional convention called by Congress on application of two-thirds of the state legislatures and ratified by conventions in three-fourths of the states.

23. *Federalist* No. 10 can be found in any of the good editions of the *Federalist Papers*. It is one of the most significant essays on American politics. With clarity and economy of language it explains how government may preserve the existing undemocratic class structure under the legitimating cloak of democratic forms.

24. The delegates did expect George Washington to be overwhelmingly elected the first president, but they anticipated that in subsequent elections the electoral college would seldom be able to decide on one person.

one, its justices being appointed to life tenure by the president and confirmed by the Senate. In time, of course, the electoral college proved to be something of a rubber stamp, and the Seventeenth Amendment, adopted in 1913, provided for popular election of the Senate.

The only portion of government directly elected by the people was the House of Representatives. Many of the delegates would have preferred excluding the public entirely from direct representation: John Mercer observed that he found nothing in the proposed Constitution more objectionable than "the mode of election by the people. The people cannot know and judge of the characters of Candidates. The worst possible choice will be made." Others were concerned that demagogues would ride into office on a populist tide only to pillage the treasury and wreak havoc on all. "The time is not distant," warned Gouverneur Morris, "when this Country will abound with mechanics [artisans] and manufacturers [industrial workers] who will receive their bread from their employers. Will such men be the secure and faithful Guardians of liberty? . . . Children do not vote. Why? Because they want prudence, because they have no will of their own. The ignorant and dependent can be as little trusted with the public interest."[25]

When the delegates agreed to having "the people" elect the lower house, they were referring to a select portion of the population. Property qualifications disfranchised the poorest White males in various states. Half the adult population was denied suffrage because they were women. American Indians had no access to the ballot. About one-fourth, both men and women, had no vote because they were held in bondage, and even of the Blacks who had gained their legal freedom, in both the North and the South, none were allowed to vote until the passage of the Fourteenth Amendment after the Civil War.

PLOTTERS OR PATRIOTS?

The question of whether the framers of the Constitution were motivated by financial or national interest has been debated ever since Charles Beard published *An Economic Interpretation of the Constitution* in 1913. Beard believed that the "founding fathers" were guided by their class interests. Arguing against Beard are those who say that the framers were concerned with higher things than just lining their purses. True, they were moneyed men who profited directly from

---

25. Farrand, *Records of the Federal Convention*, vol. 2, pp. 200 ff.

policies initiated under the new Constitution, but they were motivated by a concern for nation building that went beyond their particular class interests, the argument goes. To paraphrase Justice Holmes,
these men invested their belief to make a nation; they did not make a
nation because they had invested. "High-mindedness is not impossible
to man," Holmes reminds us.

That is exactly the point: high-mindedness is a common attribute
among people even when, or especially when, they are pursuing their
personal and class interests. The fallacy is to presume that there is a
dichotomy between the desire to build a strong nation and the desire
to protect wealth and that the framers could not have been motivated
by both. In fact, like most other people, they believed that what was
good for themselves was ultimately good for the entire society. Their
universal values and their class interests went hand in hand, and to
discover the existence of the "higher" sentiment does not eliminate the
self-interested one.

Most persons believe in their own virtue. The founders never
doubted the nobility of their effort and its importance for the generations to come. Just as many of them could feel dedicated to the principle of "liberty for all" and at the same time own slaves, so could they
serve both their nation and their estates. The point is not that they
were devoid of the grander sentiments of nation building but that
there was nothing in their concept of nation that worked against their
class interest and a great deal that worked for it.

People tend to perceive issues in accordance with the position
they occupy in the social structure; that position is largely—although
not exclusively—determined by their class status. Even if we deny
that the framers were motivated by the desire for personal gain that
moves others, we cannot dismiss the existence of their class interest.
They may not have been solely concerned with getting their own
hands in the till, although enough of them did, but they were admittedly preoccupied with defending the wealthy few from the laboring
many—for the ultimate benefit of all, as they understood it. "The
Constitution," as Staughton Lynd noted, "was the settlement of a revolution. What was at stake for Hamilton, Livingston, and their opponents, was more than speculative windfalls in securities; it was the
question, what kind of society would emerge from the revolution
when the dust had settled, and on which class the political center of
gravity would come to rest."[26]

---

26. Staughton Lynd, *Class Conflict, Slavery and the United States Constitution* (Indianapolis: Bobbs-Merrill, 1967). For discussions of the class interests behind the
American Revolution, see Alfred F. Young (ed.), *The American Revolution: Explora-*

The small farmers and debtors who opposed a central government have been described as motivated by self-serving, parochial interests—unlike the supposedly higher-minded statesmen who journeyed to Philadelphia and others of their class who supported ratification.[27] How or why the wealthy became visionary nation builders is never explained. In truth, it was not their minds that were so much broader but their economic interests. Their motives were neither higher nor lower than those of any other social group struggling for place and power in the United States of 1787. They pursued their material interests as single-mindedly as any small freeholder—if not more so. Possessing more time, money, information, and organization, they enjoyed superior results. How could they have acted otherwise? For them to have ignored the conditions of governance necessary for the maintenance of their enterprises would have amounted to committing class suicide—and they were not about to do that. They were a rising bourgeoisie rallying around a central power in order to protect their class interests. Some of us are quite willing to accept the existence of such a material-based nationalism in the history of other countries, but not in our own.

Finally, those who argue that the founders were motivated primarily by high-minded objectives consistently overlook the fact that the delegates repeatedly stated their intention to erect a government strong enough to protect the haves from the have-nots. They gave voice to the crassest class prejudices and never found it necessary to disguise the fact—as have latter-day apologists—that their uppermost concern was to diminish popular control and resist all tendencies toward class equalization (or "leveling," as it was called). Their opposition to democracy and their dedication to moneyed interests were unabashedly and openly avowed. Their preoccupation with their class interests was so pronounced that one delegate, James Wilson of Pennsylvania, did finally complain of hearing too much about how the sole or primary object of government was property. The cultivation and improvement of the human mind, he maintained, was the most noble object—a fine sentiment that evoked no opposition from his colleagues as they continued about their business.

If the founders sought to "check power with power," they seemed chiefly concerned with restraining mass power, while assuring the

---

tions in the History of American Radicalism (DeKalb, Ill.: Northern Illinois University Press, 1977).

27. See several of the essays in Robert Goldwin and William Schambra (eds.), *How Democratic Is the Constitution?* (Washington, D.C.: American Enterprise Institute, 1980); also David G. Smith, *The Convention and the Constitution* (New York: St. Martin's Press, 1965).

perpetuation of their own class power. They supposedly had a "realistic" opinion of the rapacious nature of human beings—readily evidenced when they talked about the common people—yet they held a remarkably sanguine view of the self-interested impulses of their own class, which they saw as inhabited largely by virtuous men of "principle and property." According to Madison, wealthy men (the "minority faction") would be unable to sacrifice "the rights of other citizens" or mask their "violence under the forms of the Constitution."[28] They would never jeopardize the institution of property and wealth and the untrammeled uses thereof, which in the eyes of the framers constituted the essence of "liberty." Recall Hamilton's facile reassurance that the rich will "check the unsteadiness" of the poor and will themselves "ever maintain good government" by being given a "distinct permanent share" in it. Power corrupts others but somehow has the opposite effect on the rich and the wellborn—so believed many of the rich and wellborn.

An Elitist Document

More important than to conjecture about the framers' motives is to look at the Constitution they fashioned, for it tells us a good deal about their objectives. The Constitution was consciously designed as a conservative document, elaborately equipped with a system of minority checks and vetoes, making it easier for entrenched interests to endure. It provided ample power to build the services and protections of state needed by a growing capitalist class but not the power for a transition of rule to a different class. The Constitution was a historically successful ruling-class undertaking whose effects are still very much with us—as we shall see in the chapters to come.

The Constitution championed the rights of property over the rights and liberties of persons. For the founders, liberty meant something different from and antithetical to democracy. It meant liberty to invest, speculate, trade, and accumulate wealth and to secure its possession without encroachment by sovereign or populace. The civil liberties designed to give all individuals the right to engage in public affairs won little support from the delegates. When Colonel Mason recommended that a committee be formed to draft "a Bill of Rights," a task he said could be accomplished "in a few hours," the other convention members offered little discussion on the motion and voted unanimously against it.

---

28. *Federalist* No. 10.

If the Constitution was so blatantly elitist, how did it manage to win ratification? Actually, it did not have a wide backing, initially being opposed in most of the states. But the same superiority of wealth, organization, and control of political office and the press that allowed the rich to monopolize the Philadelphia Convention enabled them to orchestrate a successful ratification campaign. The Federalists also used bribes, intimidation, and other discouragements against opponents of the Constitution.[29] What's more, *the Constitution never was submitted to a popular vote*. Ratification was by state convention composed of delegates drawn mostly from the same affluent strata as the framers. Those who voted for these delegates were themselves usually subjected to property qualifications.[30]

DEMOCRATIC CONCESSIONS

For all its undemocratic aspects, the Constitution was not without its historically progressive features.[31] Consider the following:

1. The very existence of a written constitution with specifically limited powers represented an advance over more autocratic forms of government.
2. No property qualifications were required for any federal officeholder, unlike in England and most of the states. And salaries were provided for all officials, thus rejecting the common practice of treating public office as a voluntary service, which only the rich could afford.
3. The President and all other officeholders were elected for limited terms. No one could claim a life tenure on any office.
4. Article VI reads: "no religious Test shall ever be required as a Qualification to any Office or public Trust under the United States," a feature that represented a distinct advance over a number of state constitutions, which banned Catholics and Jews from holding office.

---

29. Jackson Turner Main, *The Antifederalists* (Chapel Hill: University of North Carolina Press, 1961).

30. Even if two-thirds or more of the adult White males could vote for delegates, probably not more than 20 percent actually did; see the studies cited in Beard, *An Economic Interpretation*, pp. 242 ff.; McDonald agrees with this estimate in *We, the People*.

31. This section on the progressive features of the Constitution is drawn from Aptheker, *Early Years of the Republic*, pp. 71 ff. and *passim*.

5. Bills of attainder, the practice of declaring by legislative fiat a specific person or group of people guilty of an offense, without benefit of a trial, were made unconstitutional. Also outlawed were ex post facto laws, the practice of declaring an act a crime and punishing those who had committed it *before* it had been unlawful.

6. As noted earlier, the framers showed no interest in a Bill of Rights, but supporters of the new Constitution soon recognized their tactical error and pledged the swift adoption of such a bill as a condition for ratification. So in the first session of Congress, the first ten amendments were proposed and swiftly adopted by the states; these rights included freedom of speech and religion; freedom to assemble peaceably and to petition for redress of grievances; the right to keep arms; freedom from unreasonable searches and seizures, self-incrimination, double jeopardy, cruel and unusual punishment, and excessive bail and fines; the right to a fair and impartial trial; and other forms of due process.

7. The Constitution guarantees a republican form of government and explicitly repudiates monarchy and aristocracy; hence, Article I, section 9 states: "No title of Nobility shall be granted by the United States . . . ." According to James McHenry, a delegate from Maryland, *at least 21 of the 55 delegates favored some form of monarchy.* Yet few dared venture in that direction out of fear of popular opposition. Furthermore, delegates like Madison believed that stability for their class order was best assured by a republican form of government. The time had come for the bourgeoisie to rule directly without the baneful intrusions of kings and nobles.

Time and again during the Philadelphia convention, this assemblage of men who feared and loathed democracy found it necessary to remind each other that they had best show some regard for popular sentiment (as with the direct election of the lower house). If the Constitution was going to be accepted by the states and if the new government was to have any stability, it had to gain some measure of popular acceptance; hence, the founders felt compelled to leave something for the people. While the delegates and their class dominated the events of 1787–89, they were far from omnipotent. The class system they sought to preserve was itself the cause of marked restiveness among the people. Had the common folk been merely compliant and quiescent, there would have been little need for the extraordinary undertaking at Philadelphia and the subsequent ratification campaign, little need to erect a strong central authority to contain democratic struggles.

Land seizures by the poor, food riots, and other violent disturbances occurred throughout the 18th century in just about every state
and erstwhile colony.[32] This popular fomentation spurred the framers
to their effort *but it also set a limit on what they could do.* The delegates "gave" nothing to popular interests, rather—as with the Bill of
Rights—they reluctantly made concessions under the threat of democratic rebellion. Like every elite before and since, they kept what they
could and grudgingly relinquished what they felt they had to, driven
not by a love of the people but by a prudent desire to avoid popular
uprisings. The Constitution, then, was a product not only of class
privilege but also of class struggle—a struggle that continued and intensified as the corporate economy and the government grew.

---

32. Howard Zinn, *A People's History of the United States* (New York: Harper and
Row, 1980), chapter three.

5

The Rise of the Corporate State

Although the decisions of government are made in the name of the entire society, they rarely benefit everyone. Some portion of the populace, frequently a majority, loses out. What is considered *national* policy is usually the policy of dominant groups strategically located within the political system. The standard textbook view is that American government manifests no consistent class bias. The political system is said to involve a give-and-take among many different groups, "a plurality of interests." What government supposedly does is act as a regulator of conflict, trying to limit the advantages of the strong and minimize the disadvantages of the weak.

I will argue for a very different notion—that the existing political system may regulate but it does not equalize and that its overall effect is to deepen rather than redress the inequities of capitalist society. The political system enjoys no special immunity to the way power resources are distributed in society. It responds primarily to the powers and needs of the corporate system. "The business of government is business," President Calvin Coolidge once said. In this chapter we will explore the meaning of that statement, noting how the rise of corporate society also brought the rise of the corporate state.

SERVING BUSINESS: THE EARLY YEARS

The upper-class dominance of public life so characteristic of the founding fathers' generation continued throughout the nineteenth century. In the 1830s, the period of "Jacksonian democracy," supposedly an era of the common man, an informal but financially powerful aristocracy controlled "the economic life of the great northeastern cities" and exercised a "vast influence" over the nation, while "the common man appears to have gotten very little of whatever it was that counted for much."[1] President Andrew Jackson's key appointments were drawn overwhelmingly from the ranks of the rich, and his policies regarding trade, finances, and the use of government lands reflected the interests of that class.[2]

Destitute people inhabited large sections of the cities. "In Philadelphia, working-class families lived fifty-five to a tenement, usually one room per family, with no garbage removal, no toilets, no fresh air or water. There was fresh water newly pumped from the Schuylkill River, but it was going to the homes of the rich."[3] Similar conditions in New York brought the cholera and typhoid epidemics of 1832, 1837, and 1842, during which "the rich fled the cities, the poor stayed and died."[4]

Through the nineteenth century laboring people struggled under horrendous conditions. The press carried articles about adolescent girls laboring from six in the morning until midnight for three dollars a week, of women who fainted beside their looms, of children as young as nine and ten toiling 14-hour shifts, falling asleep beside the machines they tended, suffering from malnutrition, sickness, and stunted growth.[5] In an address before "the Mechanics and Working Classes" in 1827, a worker lamented:

> We find ourselves oppressed on every hand—we labor hard in producing all the comforts of life for the enjoyment of others, while we ourselves obtain but a scanty portion, and even that in the present state of society depends on the will of employers.[6]

Through the next 70 years the industrial oppression intensified.[7] Contrary to the view that the nation was free of class conflict, the

1. Edward Pessen, *Riches, Class and Power Before the Civil War* (Lexington, Mass.: D. C. Heath, 1973), p. 278 and p. 304.
2. See Howard Zinn, *A People's History of the United States* (New York: Harper & Row, 1980), pp. 125–29, *passim*.
3. *Ibid.*, p. 213.
4. *Ibid.*
5. Richard Boyer and Herbert Morais, *Labor's Untold Story* (New York: United Electrical, Radio and Machine Workers, 1972), p. 25 and *passim*; also John Spargo, *The Bitter Cry of the Children* (Chicago: Quadrangle, 1968) originally published in 1906.
6. Zinn, *A People's History*, p. 216.
7. *Ibid.*, pp. 206–99.

class struggles of 19th century America "were as fierce as any known in the industrial world."[8] After the sporadic uprisings and strikes of the early decades of the nineteenth century, there came the railroad strikes of the 1870s, followed by the farmers' rebellions and the industrial strikes of the 1880s and 1890s. Involving hundreds of thousands of people, these struggles were highly developed in organization, while militant and sometimes even revolutionary in political tone.

How did the government respond? When public authority intervened, it was almost invariably on the side of the wealthy element and against the laboring class. The hardships that beset people failed to enlist the efforts of government, but when rebellious workers seized the railroads or tried to prevent factories and mines from operating, as happened repeatedly, civil authorities took energetic measures on behalf of capitalist interests, using first the police and state militia and later federal troops to crush strikes.[9] "The industrial barons made a habit of calling soldiers to their assistance; and armories were erected in the principal cities as measures of convenience."[10] Short of having the regular army permanently garrisoned in industrial areas, as was the desire of some owners, government officials took steps "to establish an effective antiradical National Guard."[11]

The high-ranking officials who applied force against workers often were themselves men of wealth. President Cleveland's attorney general, Richard Olney, a millionaire owner of railroad securities, used antitrust laws, court injunctions, mass arrests, labor spies, deputy marshals, and federal troops against workers and their unions. From the local sheriff and magistrate to the president and Supreme Court, the forces of "law and order" were utilized to suppress the "conspiracy" of labor unions and to serve "the defensive needs of large capitalist enterprises."[12] The very statutes they had declared to be unworkable against the well-known monopolistic and collusive practices of business were now promptly and effectively invoked against "labor combinations."

---

8. The historian David Montgomery quoted in *ibid.*, p. 221. The monumental study on the labor struggle is Philip Foner, *History of the Labor Movement in the United States* (New York: International Publishers, 1947, 1955, 1964, 1965, 1980, 1981).

9. Boyer and Morais, *Labor's Untold Story*; and Jeremy Brecher, *Strike!* (Greenwich, Conn.: Fawcett, 1974). Hundreds of strikers and supporters were wounded, beaten, given long jail terms, or killed.

10. Matthew Josephson, *The Robber Barons* (New York: Harcourt, Brace, 1934), p. 365.

11. William Preston, Jr., *Aliens and Dissenters* (Cambridge, Mass.: Harvard University Press, 1963), p. 24.

12. Matthew Josephson, *The Politicos, 1865–1896* (New York: Harcourt, Brace, 1938), pp. 562, 566.

The same federal government that remained immobilized while violence was perpetrated against abolitionists, and while slaves were imported into the United States in violation of the Constitution right until the Civil War, was able to comb the land with bands of federal marshals and troops to capture fugitive slaves and return them to their masters. The same government that could not find the constitutional means to prevent the distribution of contaminated foods and befouled water supplies could use federal troops to break strikes, shoot hundreds of workers, and slaughter thousands of Indians. The same government that had not a dollar for the indigent (poverty being a matter best left to private charity) gave 21 million acres of land and $51 million in government bonds to the few railroad financiers.[13]

While insisting that the free market worked for all, most businessmen showed little inclination to deliver their own interests to the stern judgments of an untrammeled, competitive economy; instead they resorted to such things as tariffs, public subsidies, land grants, government loans, high-interest bonds, price regulations, contracts, patents, trademarks, and other services and protections provided by civil authority.

Well before the Civil War, the common law was redone to fit the needs of capitalism, as the historian Morton Horowitz notes. Mill owners could flood other people's property in order to carry on their business. Through the law of "eminent domain" the government took land from farmers and gave it as subsidies to canal and railroad companies. The idea of a fair price for goods was replaced in the courts by the free-market notion of *caveat emptor* (let the buyer beware). Contract law was used to deny back pay to workers who wished to quit undesirable jobs, and to deny compensation to injured employees. Workers were killed or maimed because of blatantly unsafe conditions imposed by owners—without the latter being held liable for criminal intent. By the Civil War, "the legal system had been reshaped to the advantage of men of commerce and industry at the expense of farmers, workers, consumers, and other less powerful groups." The law promoted "a legal redistribution of wealth against the weakest groups in the society."[14]

In the late nineteenth century, the millions of dollars collected by the government "from the consuming population, and above all from the . . . poor wage earners and farmers," constituting an enormous budget surplus, was paid out to big investors in high-premium gov-

---

13. Zinn, *A People's History*, p. 253.
14. Morton Horowitz, *The Transformation of American Law*, quoted in Zinn, *A People's History*, pp. 234–35.

ernment bonds.[15] Likewise, a billion acres of land in the public domain, *almost half of the present area of the United States*, was given over to private hands. Josephson describes the government's endeavors to transform the common wealth into private gain:

> This benevolent government handed over to its friends or to astute first comers, . . . all those treasures of coal and oil, of copper and gold and iron, the land grants, the terminal sites, the perpetual rights of way—an act of largesse which is still one of the wonders of history. To the new railroad enterprises in addition, great money subsidies totaling many hundreds of millions were given. The Tariff Act of 1864 was in itself a sheltering wall of subsidies; and to aid further the new heavy industries and manufactures, an Immigration Act allowing contract labor to be imported freely was quickly enacted; a national banking system was perfected. . . . Having conferred these vast rights and controls, the . . . government would preserve them.[16]

For all its activities on behalf of business, the government did exercise a kind of laissez-faire in certain areas, giving little attention to unemployment, work conditions, the spoliation of natural resources, and the living conditions of millions of destitute Americans.

PROGRESSIVE REPRESSION

In the twentieth century, as in the centuries before, the men of wealth looked to the central government to do for them what they could not do for themselves: to repress democratic forces, limit competition, regulate the market to their advantage, and in other ways bolster the process of capital accumulation.

Contrary to the view that the giant trusts controlled everything, price competition with smaller companies in 1900 was vigorous enough to cut into the profits of various industries.[17] Suffering from an inability to regulate prices, expand profits, and free themselves from the "vexatious" reformist laws of state and local governments, big business began demanding action by the national government. As the utilities magnate Samuel Insull said, it was better to "help shape the right kind of regulation than to have the wrong kind forced upon

---

15. Josephson, *The Robber Barons*, p. 395.
16. *Ibid.*, p. 52.
17. See the evidence for this in Gabriel Kolko, *The Triumph of Conservatism* (Chicago: Quadrangle, 1967), chapters 1 and 2.

[us]."[18] During the 1900–1916 period, known as the Progressive Era, federal price and market regulations in meat packing, food and drugs, banking, timber, and mining were initiated at the insistence of the strongest companies within these industries. The overall effect was to raise prices and profits for the larger producers, tighten their control over markets, and weed out smaller competitors.

The several men who occupied the presidency during the Progressive Era were the faithful collaborators of big business. Teddy Roosevelt, for one, was hailed as a "trust-buster" because of his occasional verbal attacks against the "malefactors of great wealth," yet his major legislative proposals reflected the desires of corporate interests. He was hostile toward unionists and reformers, derisively dubbing the latter "muckrakers," and enjoyed close relations with business magnates, inviting them into his administration. Similarly, neither William Howard Taft nor Woodrow Wilson, the other two White House occupants of that period, "had a distinct consciousness of any fundamental conflict between their political goals and those of business."[19] Wilson railed against the corrupt political machines and the big trusts, but his campaign funds came from a few rich contributors, and he worked closely with copper magnate Cleveland Dodge and other associates of Morgan and Rockefeller, showing himself as responsive to business as any Republican.[20] "Progressivism was not the triumph of small business over the trusts, as has often been suggested, but the victory of big businesses in achieving the rationalization of the economy that only the federal government could provide."[21]

The period is called the Progressive Era because of the flurry of muckraking against big-business abuses. In addition, there was the much publicized but largely ineffectual legislation to control monopolies; the Sixteenth Amendment, which allowed for a graduated income tax; the Seventeenth Amendment, which provided for the direct popular election of U.S. Senators; and such dubious municipal and state electoral reforms as the long ballot, the referendum and recall, and the nonpartisan election. Given the persistent oppression of working people by the plutocracy, the era was "progressive" more in tone than substance. Yet some victories were won. By 1915, many states had passed laws limiting the length of the workday and providing workman's compensation for industrial accidents. By 1913, several

---

18. James Weinstein, *The Corporate Ideal in the Liberal State* (Boston: Beacon Press, 1968), p. 87.

19. Kolko, *The Triumph of Conservatism*, p. 281.

20. Frank Harris Blighton, *Woodrow Wilson and Co.* (New York: Fox Printing House, 1916).

21. Kolko, *The Triumph of Conservatism*, pp. 283–84.

states had passed minimum wage laws and 38 states had enacted child labor laws restricting the age children could be employed and the hours they could work. And in a few industries workers won an eight-hour day and time-and-a-half overtime pay.[22]

These enactments represented longstanding demands by American workers, in some cases going back over a century. One might think such gains were "given" to labor by benign legislators and corporate bosses who responded to friendly persuasion and partook of a peaceful, gradualistic progress. In fact, they were wrested from fiercely resistant elites by democratic forces after bitter and sometimes bloody struggle. Even with these victories, the conditions of labor remained far from good. The American workers' "real wages—that is, their ability to buy back the goods and services they produced—were lower in 1914 than during the 1890s."[23] Millions worked 12- and 14-hour days, usually six or seven days a week, and 2 million children, according to government figures, were still forced to work in order to supplement the family income. As is the case today, much of the reform legislation went unenforced.

Making the World Safe for Hypocrisy

In 1915, at the insistence of the House of Morgan, President Wilson revoked the policy of American neutrality in World War I and approved a huge Wall Street loan to Britain and France—without telling the American public about it. (The next year he campaigned for reelection on the slogan "He kept us out of war.") The Morgan people raked in $22 million in commissions on that deal, and more loans followed. Allied purchases of munitions and other war supplies (shipments that were repeatedly attacked by German submarines) now became a major source of industrial production and profit in the United States. The repayment of the Allied debt, grown to over $2.5 billion, depended on an Allied victory, while a German triumph would have brought a disastrous financial loss and would have plunged the country into panic and depression.[24] As one Morgan partner allowed: "Our firm had never for a moment been neutral. We didn't know how"—certainly not when billions of dollars were involved. In the end Wilson's announced neutrality was put aside and the U.S. entered the

---

22. Boyer and Morais, *Labor's Untold Story*, p. 180; Zinn, *A People's History*, p. 341.
23. Boyer and Morais, *Labor's Untold Story*, p. 181.
24. *Ibid.*, p. 194.

war "to defend American interests" and "to make the world safe for democracy."

After the United States entered World War I, relations between industry and government grew still closer. Sectors of the economy were converted to war production along lines proposed by business leaders—many of whom now headed the government agencies in charge of defense mobilization.[25] The war also gave authorities an opportunity to intensify the oppression against labor.

As of 1916 millions worked for wages that could not adequately feed a family. Each year 35,000 were killed on the job, mostly because of unsafe work conditions, while 700,000 suffered injury, illness, blindness, and other work-related disabilities.[26]

The war helped quell class conflict at home by focusing people's attention on the menace of the "barbarian Huns" of Germany, who supposedly threatened Anglo-American civilization. Patriotic feelings ran high as Americans were exhorted to make sacrifices for the war effort. Strikes were now treated as seditious interference with war production. Federal troops raided and ransacked IWW headquarters and imprisoned large numbers of workers suspected of socialist sympathies.

Nor did things improve during the postwar "Red scare," as the government resorted to mass arrests, deportations, political trials, and congressional investigations to suppress labor unrest and anticapitalist ideas.[27]

During the "normalcy" of the 1920s, prosperity was supposedly within everyone's grasp; stock speculations and other get-rich-quick schemes abounded. Not since the Gilded Age of the robber barons had the more vulgar manifestations of capitalist culture enjoyed such an uncritical reception. But the bulk of the population still lived in conditions of want. In 1928, Congressman Fiorello La Guardia reported on his tour of the poorer districts of New York: "I confess I was not prepared for what I actually saw. It seemed almost incredible that such conditions of poverty could really exist."[28]

---

25. Paul A. C. Koistinen, "The 'Industrial-Military Complex' in Historical Perspective: The Inter War Years," *Journal of American History*, 56, March 1970, reprinted in Irwin Unger (ed.), *Beyond Liberalism: The New Left Views American History* (Waltham, Mass.: Xerox College Publishing, 1971), pp. 228–29.

26. Boyer and Morais, *Labor's Untold Story*, p. 184 and *passim*; see also Zinn, *A People's History*.

27. Preston, *Aliens and Dissenters, passim*.

28. Zinn, *A People's History*, p. 376. According to the figures of the Brookings Institution, in the 1920s almost 60 percent of U.S. families did not receive enough income to provide for "the basic necessities" of life. See Boyer and Morais, *Labor's Untold Story*, p. 237.

The stock market crash of 1929 brought years of extreme economic hardship. Millions of people who had remained untouched by the prosperity of the 1920s were soon joined by millions more.

THE NEW DEAL: HARD TIMES AND TOUGH REFORMS

Speaking about the Great Depression of the 1930s, banker Frank Vanderlip admitted: "Capital kept too much and labor did not have enough to buy its share of things."[29] Such candor was not characteristic of most members of the plutocracy, who treated economic misery as if it were a natural disaster, a product of some blameless thing called "hard times." Others blamed the depression on its victims. Millionaire Henry Ford said the crisis came because "the average man won't really do a day's work unless he is caught and cannot get out of it. There is plenty of work to do if people would do it." A few weeks later Ford laid off 75,000 workers.[30]

With a third of the nation ill-fed, ill-clothed, and ill-housed, and at least another third just managing to get by, a torrent of strikes swept the nation. In the San Francisco general strike of 1934, 127,000 people stopped work for four days in support of sailors and longshoremen who were fighting for union recognition. Employers were forced to make concessions in wages and union rights. A few months later 475,000 textile workers in various states struck for implementation of safety and working conditions ignored by the bosses. In 1935 some 400,000 coal miners carried out a successful general strike. This was followed in 1936 by the historic sit-down strike in General Motors's huge automobile plants. Almost 150,000 workers walked picket lines, fought off goon squads, refused to allow strike breakers through, and kept food and other supplies moving into the plants, which were occupied by 40,000 workers for six weeks. With its factories paralyzed, GM was forced to recognize the United Auto Workers union.[31]

Between 1936 and 1940 the newly formed Congress of Industrial Organizations (CIO) organized millions of workers on an industry-

---

29. Boyer and Morais, *Labor's Untold Story*, p. 249. Senator Hugo Black (D-Ala.) observed in 1932: "Labor has been underpaid and capital overpaid. This is one of the chief contributing causes of the present depression. We need a return of purchasing power. You cannot starve men employed in industry and depend upon them to purchase." Quoted in Rhonda F. Levine, "Crisis and Intra-Capitalist Conflict: The Formulation of the National Industrial Recovery Act," paper presented at the American Political Science Association meeting, New York, September 1981.

30. Zinn, *A People's History*, p. 378.

31. Boyer and Morais, *Labor's Untold Story*, *passim*.

wide basis and achieved a significant betterment in wages and work conditions. But these victories were achieved only after protracted struggles in which hundreds of thousands went on strike, demonstrated, or occupied factories in sit-downs; thousands were locked out, fired, blacklisted, beaten, and arrested; and hundreds were wounded or killed by police, soldiers, and company thugs.[32] The gains were real but they came at a high cost in human suffering.

The first two terms of President Franklin D. Roosevelt's administration have been called the New Deal, an era commonly believed to have brought great transformations on behalf of "the forgotten man." Actually the New Deal's central dedication was to business recovery rather than social reform. The first major attempt was the National Recovery Administration (NRA), which set up hundreds of "code authorities," usually composed of the leading corporate representatives in each industry, whose task was to restrict production and set minimum price requirements. The NRA parceled out portions of the "free market" to firms at rigged prices, in effect suspending the antitrust laws—with results that were more beneficial to big corporations than to smaller competitors.[33] In attempting to spur production, the government, in an early version of supply-side economics, funneled large sums from the public treasure into the hands of the moneyed few. In nine years the Reconstruction Finance Corporation alone lent $15 billion to big business.

Faced with mass unrest, the federal government created a relief program that eased some of the hunger and starvation and—more importantly from the perspective of business—limited the instances of violent protest and radicalization. But as the New Deal moved toward measures that threatened to compete with private enterprises and undermine low wage structures, businessmen withdrew their support and became openly hostile. While infuriating Roosevelt, who saw himself as trying to rescue the capitalist system, business opposition probably enhanced his reformist image in the public mind.

The disparity between the New Deal's popular image and its ac-

---

32. Brecher, *Strike!*; Boyer and Morais, *Labor's Untold Story*; and Zinn, *A People's History*, provide numerous and vivid accounts. See also Irving Bernstein, *Turbulent Years, A History of the American Worker 1933–1941* (Boston: Houghton Mifflin, 1970).

33. Barton Bernstein, "The New Deal: The Conservative Achievements of Liberal Reform," in Barton Bernstein (ed.), *Toward a New Past* (New York: Pantheon, 1963), p. 269; Douglas Dowd, *The Twisted Dream* (Cambridge, Mass.: Winthrop, 1974), pp. 102–3. The NRA was established by the National Industrial Recovery Act of 1933, a bill written largely under the guidance of business representatives. It was eventually declared unconstitutional by a Supreme Court still hostile to "government meddling" in the economy.

tual accomplishments remains one of the unappreciated aspects of the Roosevelt era. To cite specifics: the Civilian Conservation Corps provided jobs at subsistence wages for 250,000 out of 15 million unemployed persons. At its peak, the Works Progress Administration (WPA) reached about one in four unemployed, often with work of unstable duration and wages below the already inadequate ones of private industry. Of the 12 million workers in interstate commerce who were earning less than forty cents an hour, only about a half-million were reached by the minimum wage law. The Social Security Act of 1935 made retirement benefits payable only in 1942 and thereafter, covering but half the population and providing no medical insurance and no protection against illness before retirement. Similarly, old-age and unemployment insurance applied solely to those who had enjoyed sustained employment in select occupations. Implementation was left to the states, which were free to set whatever restrictive conditions they chose. And social-welfare programs were regressively funded through payroll deductions and sales taxes.[34]

The federal housing program stimulated private construction, with subsidies to construction firms and middle-class buyers and protection for mortgage bankers through the loan insurance program—all of little benefit to the many millions of ill-housed poor. Like so many other of its programs, the New Deal's efforts in agriculture primarily benefited the large producers through a series of price supports and production cutbacks, while many tenant farmers and sharecroppers were evicted when federal acreage rental programs took land out of cultivation.[35]

Piven and Cloward argue that it was not the misery of millions that brought government aid—since misery had prevailed for years before—but the continued threat of acute political unrest. Government programs were markedly inadequate for the needs of the destitute, but they achieved a high visibility and did much to dilute public discontent. Once the threat of political unrest and violence subsided, federal relief was drastically slashed, as in 1936–1937, reducing many families to a destitution worse than any they had known since the 1929 crash. "Large numbers of people were put off the rolls and thrust into a labor market still glutted with unemployed. But with stability restored, the continued suffering of these millions had little political force."[36]

---

34. Frances Fox Piven and Richard Cloward, *Regulating the Poor* (New York: Pantheon Books, 1971), chapters 2 and 3; Paul Conkin, *The New Deal* (New York: Crowell, 1967).

35. Piven and Cloward, *Regulating the Poor*, p. 76; see also Bernstein, "The New Deal . . . " pp. 269–70.

36. Piven and Cloward, *Regulating the Poor*, p. 46.

Several laws were passed during this period giving labor the right to bargain collectively, most notably the Wagner Act of 1935. Such legislation was both a measure of organized labor's growing legitimacy and a support to that legitimacy. But legal guarantees did not bring automatic compliance by business or vigorous enforcement by government. Labor victories against the "open shop" came only through direct struggle at the workplace—and mostly on terms that soon proved functional to the corporate system. Labor leaders, including most of those who had earned reputations as "militants," were dedicated to maintaining the capitalist system. In 1935 John L. Lewis warned that "the dangerous state of affairs" might lead to "class consciousness" and "revolution as well"; he pledged that officials of his own union were "doing everything in their power to make the system work and thereby avoid [revolution]."[37] Men like Lewis cooperated closely with management in introducing speed-up methods into production, limiting strikes, and maintaining a "disciplined" labor force.[38] Many owners relied on union leaders to keep a "production-minded" control over the workers, utilizing the good will of the union for management's purposes.

The Roosevelt administration's tax policies provide another instance of the disparity between image and performance. New Deal taxation was virtually a continuation of the Hoover administration's program. Business firms avoided many taxes during the depression by taking advantage of various loopholes.[39] The 1935 tax law "did not drain wealth from higher-income groups."[40] When taxes were increased to pay for military spending in World War II, the major burden was taken up by those of more modest means, who had never before been subjected to income taxes. "Thus, the ironic fact is that the extension of the income tax to middle- and low-income classes was the only original aspect of the New Deal tax policy."[41]

In sum, the New Deal introduced some long-overdue social-welfare legislation, extended the opportunities for collective bargaining, and created a number of worthwhile public-works projects. Yet the Roosevelt era was hardly a triumph for the "forgotten man." Of the New Deal's "three Rs"—relief, recovery, and reform—it can be said that *relief* was markedly insufficient for meeting the suffering of the times and, in any case, was rather harshly curtailed after the 1936

---

37. Quoted in Ronald Radosh, "The Corporate Ideology of American Labor Leaders from Gompers to Hillman," in Unger, *Beyond Liberalism*, p. 226.

38. *Ibid.*, p. 224; also Brecher, *Strike!* Union leaders were often pushed into more militant positions than they cared to take by the actions of their rank and file, as was true of the sit-down strikes of 1936–1937.

39. Conkin, *The New Deal*, p. 67.

40. Bernstein, "The New Deal . . . " p. 275.

41. Gabriel Kolko, *Wealth and Power in America* (New York: Praeger, 1962), p. 31.

electoral victory; *recovery* focused on business and achieved little until the advent of war spending; and *reform*, of the kind that might have ended the maldistribution and class abuses of the capitalist political economy, was rarely attempted.

As with class reform, so with race reform. In regard to school desegregation, open housing, fair employment practices, voting rights for Blacks, and antilynch laws, the New Deal did nothing. Blacks were excluded from jobs in the Civilian Conservation Corps, received less than their proportional share of public assistance, and under the NRA were frequently paid wages below the legal minimum.[42]

By 1940, the last year of peace, the number of ill-clothed, ill-fed, and ill-housed Americans showed no substantial decrease. Unemployment was over 20 percent, almost as high as in 1933, and the national income was still lower than in 1929. One historian of the period offers this conclusion:

> The New Deal failed to solve the problem of depression, it failed to raise the impoverished, it failed to redistribute income, it failed to extend equality and generally countenanced racial discrimination and segregation. It failed generally to make business more responsible to the social welfare or to threaten business's pre-eminent political power. In this sense, the New Deal, despite the shifts in tone and spirit from the earlier decade, was profoundly conservative and continuous with the 1920s.[43]

Only by entering the war and remaining thereafter on a permanent war economy was the United States able to maintain a shaky "prosperity" and significantly lower the Depression era unemployment.

To comment on some of the points raised in this chapter:

It is commonly taught that the U.S. government has been a neutral arbiter presiding over an American polity free of the class antagonisms that beset other societies. The truth is, our history has been marked by intense and often violent class struggles, and government has played a partisan, repressive role in these conflicts. Government has responded to the existing social formation and not to an imaginary world; it has responded to the business interests of society, which control the money, resources, labor, cultural institutions, and established ideology. When divisions have arisen *within* the business class, as between large and small competitors, not surprisingly, government usually has resolved matters to the satisfaction of the more powerful.

---

42. Bernstein, "The New Deal . . . " pp. 278–79.
43. *Ibid.*, pp. 264–65.

Government's growing involvement in economic affairs was not at the contrivance of meddling Washington bureaucrats, but was a response to the increasing concentration of production, wealth, and labor. Along with the many small local labor conflicts, handled by small local government, there developed large-scale class struggle—which had to be contained by a large state. The centralization and growth of the powers of the federal government, a process initiated by the framers of the Constitution to secure the class interests of property, continued at an accelerated pace through the nineteenth and twentieth centuries. Government provided the regulations, protections, subsidies, and services that business could not provide for itself. The corporate society needed a corporate state.

This ostensibly democratic government did little for the democratic interests of working people. While the populace won formal rights to participate as voters, the state with its judges, courts, police, army, and officialdom remained firmly at the disposal of the wealthy class. The law was cut loose from its ancient moorings and rewritten and reinterpreted to better serve capital and limit the ability of labor to fight back. However, working people were not without resources of their own, specifically the ability to disrupt and threaten the process of capital accumulation by withholding their labor through strikes, and by engaging in other acts of protest and resistance, thus making claims on the public mind for the rights of labor as against the prerogatives of wealth. The concessions wrested from the owning class and the state brought some real material gains for the better organized segments of the working class but fell far short of any all-out attack on capitalism. By giving a little to keep a lot, the corporate state sought to contain the class struggle. Nonetheless, the minimum-wage reform, the eight-hour workday, the right to organize, and the Social Security and unemployment compensation legislation won by labor-led coalitions of the 1930s were giant stepping stones that put working people on higher ground from which to continue struggling.

6

Politics: Who Gets What?

With the advent of World War II, business and government worked ever more closely in formulating economic policy. The large corporations picked up the lion's share of government war contracts, thereby enjoying a dramatic rise in production and profits. This development accelerated the trend toward greater concentrations of wealth. The war demonstrated to business and political leaders that the way to avoid economic disaster was to use the immense borrowing, taxing, and spending powers of government to sustain capital accumulation. Since the war, successive Democratic and Republican administrations have dedicated themselves to this endeavor, first, through an elaborate system of subsidies and services; second, through a massive military program, which transformed the United States into a permanent war economy.

WELFARE FOR THE RICH

In any given year the U.S. Treasury distributes some $30 billion in direct subsidies or benefit-in-kind subsidies to just about every major industry and enterprise.[1] For example, anywhere from $7 billion to $9

---

1. See *The Economics of Federal Subsidy Programs* prepared by the Joint Economic Committee (Washington, D.C.: U.S. Government Printing Office, 1972); also Morton Mintz and Jerry S. Cohen, *Power Inc.* (New York: Viking Press, 1976); William Proxmire, *Uncle Sam: The Last of the Bigtime Spenders* (New York: Simon and Schuster, 1972); and various issues of *Multinational Monitor* (a Ralph Nader publication, Wash-

billion a year is allocated to limit acreage production and buy up surplus crops, mostly from large commercial farms. The effect is to keep agribusiness prices and profits high while subsidizing an expansion of giant corporate farms at the expense of family farms. (About 2,000 family farms go under each year.) Among the unlikely recipients of agriculture subsidies are rich oil companies and the Queen of England (who got $68,000 for not producing anything on her plantation in Mississippi).[2]

The government gives additional billions to the nuclear industry, the airlines, and the shipping, timber, mining, and manufacturing companies, and hundreds of millions to the wheat, tobacco, peanut, sugar, and dairy industries. Much of the export costs in iron, steel, petroleum, farm crops, chemicals, automobiles, and other products are financed by the federal government (while the profits remain with the exporters). In 1976 Congress allocated over $6 billion to subsidize railroads, thus ensuring high dividends to stockholders and bank creditors while railroads continued to deteriorate.[3]

Even the relatively limited assistance given to *small* business helps fatten the big firms. The Small Business Administration (SBA) stands behind $1 billion easy-term loans and loan guarantees to over 16,000 "independent" businesses, most of which are actually franchises of such large corporations as General Motors, McDonald's, and Texaco. The General Accounting Office (an oversight agency of the U.S. Congress) has criticized the SBA for risking federal money without requiring the parent companies to share some of the burden.[4]

The government provides billions to cushion business losses. The most intriguing case of compensation involves corporations like Du-Pont, General Motors, Ford, Exxon, and ITT, which owned factories in enemy countries during World War II and produced everything from tanks to synthetic fuels for the Nazi war effort. In its German plants, ITT manufactured bombers that wreaked havoc on Allied convoys. After the war, rather than being prosecuted for aiding and abetting the enemy, ITT collected $27 million from the U.S. govern-

ington, D.C.); "The Kindest Cuts of All—Cutting Business Subsidies in Fiscal Year 1982," (a report by Congress Watch, Washington, D.C., 1982).

2. William Robbins, "Farm Policy Helps Make the Rural Rich Richer," *New York Times*, April 5, 1970; Larry Casolino, "This Land Is Their Land," *Ramparts*, July 1972, pp. 31–36; Dan Morgan, "New Study Finds Small Farms Hurt by Many Federal Policies," *Washington Post*, January 14, 1981.

3. Blessed with such bounty from the public treasure, the railroads in question stripped themselves of their own cash assets of over $9 million and distributed the money to their stockholders in what was one of the highest dividend payments in New York Stock Exchange history. See *Workers World*, March 12, 1976.

4. *Sacramento Bee*, November 27, 1980.

ment for war damages inflicted on its German plants by Allied bombings. GM collected more than $33 million in compensation for damages to its enemy war plants.[5]

Along with its subsidies, grants, loans, and loss compensations, the government serves the business class by maintaining prices at monopolistic levels in "regulated" areas of the economy at an estimated annual cost of $80 billion to American consumers.[6] The government engages in preferential enforcement—or nonenforcement—of regulatory standards, as when the FCC sets an "allowed rate of return" for the telephone company and then ignores it, enabling American Telephone and Telegraph to overcharge customers a half-billion dollars each year on interstate long-distance calls.[7]

Private electric utilities offer another illustration of government "regulation." Utilities are nonrisk enterprises whose expenses are virtually guaranteed by the government. They never go bankrupt; they pay high dividends to their shareholders and give their managers handsome salaries and stock options. Their rates are regulated so as to allow them a net income as high as 20 to 30 percent of sales, which explains why private utility rates are sometimes more than four times those of publicly-owned utilities.[8]

Under corporate state capitalism the ordinary citizen pays twice for most things—first as a taxpayer who provides the subsidies and supports, then as the consumer who buys the high-priced commodities and services. Every year the government distributes from $20 billion to $30 billion in research-and-development grants, mostly to corporations, which are permitted to keep the patents and charge working people high prices when the products are sold.[9] Whole new technologies are developed at public expense, as with nuclear energy, electronics, aeronautics, space communication, mineral exploration,

---

5. The information comes from documents declassified in 1974. See Bradford Snell, "GM and the Nazis," *Ramparts*, June 1974, pp. 14–16; "Memo from COPE" (AFL-CIO report), August 30, 1973. Some plants were spared because they were owned by American companies. Thus while Cologne was leveled by saturation bombing, its Ford plant, providing military equipment for the Nazi army, was untouched—and used by German workers as an air-raid shelter. See eyewitness correspondence by E. F. Patterson, *Ramparts*, August 1974, p. 8.

6. *New York Times*, March 2, 1975.

7. Frye Gaillard, "Trouble on the Line," *Progressive*, February 1978, p. 31. The author cites a Federal Communications Commission study.

8. See Lee Metcalf and Vic Reinemer, *Overcharge* (New York: McKay, 1967); also Richard Morgan, Tom Riesenberg, and Michael Troutman, *Taking Charge: A New Look at Public Power* (Washington, D.C.: Environmental Action Foundation, 1978).

9. Three-fifths of the technical research done in this country is funded by the government; three-fourths is controlled by the corporations. See Harry Braverman, *Labor and Monopoly Capital* (New York: Monthly Review Press, 1975), p. 166 *fn*; also "Double Jeopardy," *Progressive*, February 1978, p. 8.

and computer systems, only to be handed over to industry for private gain. Thus AT&T managed to have the entire satellite communications system put under its control in 1962—after U.S. taxpayers had put up the initial $20 billion to develop it.[10]

Sometimes the state forces the public to pay for the capital investments of a private corporation because no one else will. In 1981, the oil and gas companies pushed for the construction of a 4,800-mile natural-gas pipeline from Alaska to California and Illinois, costing an estimated $59 billion. The venture was rejected as too risky and too costly by the banks, so the Reagan administration sponsored, and Congress passed, a bill that pre-charges to hundreds of millions of consumers—through their monthly gas bills—the expense of the pipeline, even if it is never completed or a drop of gas delivered. The charge is as much as $200 per family each year and will continue for some twenty years. Since no person would voluntarily agree to such a deal, business and government use the law to impose a new market relationship upon consumers and workers, forcing them to provide all the risk capital with no possibility of gain for themselves, while the big companies risk nothing and reap the profits.[11]

As in olden days, government continues to give away, lease, or sell at bargain rates the national forests, grasslands, wildlife preserves, and other public lands containing priceless timber, minerals, oil, water, and recreational resources—with little consideration for environmental values or for desires other than those of the favored corporations.[12] For instance, several petroleum companies leased acreage in Alaska for oil exploration, paying a sum of $12 million for leases worth upwards of $2 *billion*. In a subsequent oil-lease auction, the companies paid the government $900 million for lands that are expected to be worth some $50 billion within a decade.[13]

The government pays out many billions in unnecessarily high interest rates, and permits billions of government dollars to remain on deposit in banks without collecting interest. It tolerates overcharging by firms doing business with the government. The government

---

10. Steve Babson and Nancy Brigham, "Why Do We Spend So Much Money?" *Liberation*, September/October 1973, p. 19.

11. Coleman McCarthy in the *Washington Post*, November 28, 1981, also *Daily World*, December 16, 1981.

12. See James Ridgeway, *The Politics of Ecology* (New York: E. P. Dutton, 1970); also The Ralph Nader Study Group Report, *The Water Lords* (New York: Grossman, 1971), James M. Fallows, project director; The Ralph Nader Study Group Report, *The Vanishing Air* (New York: Grossman, 1970), John C. Esposito and Larry J. Silverman, project directors.

13. Barry Weisberg, "Ecology of Oil: Raping Alaska," in Editors of *Ramparts*, *Eco-Catastrophe* (San Francisco: Canfield Press, 1970), p. 107, 109.

awards highly favorable contracts and provides emergency funding to ensure the survival and continued profits of large companies; it furnishes big business with long-term credits and tariff protections and provides lowered tax assessments and write-offs amounting to many billions of dollars yearly; it makes available to defense industries billions of dollars worth of government-owned land, buildings, machinery, and materials, thereby in part "saving them the job of financing their own investments";[14] and it applies the antitrust laws so lackadaisically as to make them inconsequential.

MILITARY SPENDING: BUTTERING THE GUNS

Another way the corporate state keeps the corporate economy afloat is through defense spending. While the military budget is probably the most costly, unproductive, and inflationary means of creating opportunities for capital accumulation, for the big corporations it is also the most profitable and least troublesome, since most of the costs and risks are assumed by the government.

The Department of Defense (commonly known as the Pentagon) is the largest, richest, most powerful unit of government. Its budget ($223 billion in 1982 and increasing to an estimated $377 billion by 1985) continues to grow in leaps regardless of whether there is war or peace. The Pentagon projects a five-year military build-up costing over $1.5 trillion, or 60 times the cost of the Vietnam war, as much as was spent in all the years since World War II.[15] It is estimated that the average family pays $3,000 a year to the Pentagon and each person in the nation works the equivalent of five years to pay for U.S. military expenses.[16]

For almost forty years the Pentagon has been conjuring up the specter of Soviet military supremacy in order to maintain its hold over the public purse. In 1956 Americans were alerted to a dangerous "bomber gap"; in 1960 it was a "missile gap," and in 1967 an "anti-

---

14. Sidney Lens, *The Military-Industrial Complex* (Philadelphia: United Church Press, 1970), p. 8. See Senator Russell Long's comments quoted in Richard Harris, "Annals of Politics: A Fundamental Hoax," *New Yorker*, August 7, 1971, p. 53. On antitrust enforcement, see *The Closed Enterprise*, study project directed by Mark Green (Washington, D.C.: Center for Study of Responsible Law, 1972).

15. *Washington Post*, January 8, 1982.

16. For overall critiques of the military establishment, see Lens, *The Military-Industrial Complex*; Richard F. Kaufman, *The War Profiteers* (New York: Bobbs-Merrill, 1971); Seymour Melman, *Pentagon Capitalism* (New York: McGraw-Hill, 1970); and Melman's *The Permanent War Economy* (New York: Simon and Schuster, 1974); Adam Yarmolinsky, *The Military Establishment* (New York: Harper & Row, 1973); Tom Gervasi, *Arsenal of Democracy* (New York: Grove Press, rev. ed. 1981).

SURVIVAL OF THE FATTEST

ballistic missile gap." In 1975 the Department of Defense announced we were falling behind the Russians in the development of multiple-warhead missiles. From 1977 through 1981, scare reports appeared in the business-owned press describing how the Soviets had moved ahead of the U.S. in conventional arms and were thereby posing a mortal threat to Western Europe. In 1981–1982 the Reagan administration repeatedly announced that the United States was alarmingly behind the Soviets in strategic nuclear missiles.

In each of these instances it was subsequently discovered that no such weaknesses existed and that U.S. and NATO capabilities in nuclear and conventional forces were equal or superior to those of the

Soviet Union and the Warsaw Pact nations. But these revelations came only after new multibillion-dollar allocations had been voted by Congress.[17]

The leading beneficiaries of defense contracts, the large corporations, have helped propagate the military's cause with skillful lobbying and mass advertising that stresses the importance of keeping America "strong." And as private industry became the supporter of defense preparedness, military men spoke more openly about the blessings of free enterprise. With 90 percent of the contracts awarded with no competitive bidding, relations between corporate and military personnel became an important determinant of who got what. Senior military officers and civilian Pentagon officials who promoted the right corporate contracts looked forward to early retirement and entrance into high-paying corporate jobs.[18]

As a result of the overall military-industrial partnership, enormous portions of American purchasing power have been siphoned off by the government through taxation and channeled into the major corporations. The twenty-five largest contractors receive over half the prime contracts for weapons production, thereby further centralizing corporate wealth in America.[19]

Profitable Waste

Waste and duplication are a standard part of the Pentagon's operations. The Army allocated $1.5 billion to develop a heavy-lift helicopter—even though it already had heavy-lift helicopters—while the Navy was building an almost identical one. At the cost of many hundreds of millions of dollars, the Air Force and the Navy simultaneously developed airborne warning systems.[20] A coalition of Congressmen discovered on one occasion that the Pentagon was unable to locate where half its procurement budget, a sum of $20 billion, was being spent, the money having gone to corporate subcontractors of whom no record was kept. It was also discovered that Pentagon offi-

17. See Senator William Proxmire's letter to the *New York Times*, January 30, 1979; also Richard Stubbing, "The Imaginary Defense Gap: We Already Outspend Them," *Washington Post*, February 14, 1982; see also *World Press Review*, October 1981, p. 51; *New York Times*, April 11, 1981, and September 27, 1981, on East-West balance of military forces.

18. Gordon Adams, *The Iron Triangle: The Politics of Defense Contracting* (New York: Council on Economic Priorities, 1981).

19. *Wall Street Journal*, October 30, 1978.

20. *New York Times*, July 4, 1969.

cials had lost track of $30 billion in weapons and other military equipment intended for foreign orders.[21]

The General Accounting Office (GAO) published a detailed report showing that the defense budget was regularly padded by billions to ensure against congressional cuts. Meanwhile, the Pentagon hands out huge sums to companies to compensate for losses and mismanagement and to save them from bankruptcy. Lockheed Corporation alone received a $1 billion loan guarantee from the federal government to keep it solvent.[22]

That certain firms suffer losses does not mean defense is a high-risk, low-profit industry. *Sales* profits may appear low, but since most of the costs are paid by the government, profits on the company's actual investments are usually astronomical.[23]

Many items in the military budget end up costing far more than the original bid. Often firms do not explain their cost overruns, even when requested to do so by the government. The C5A transport plane had a $4 *billion* cost overrun (and its wings kept falling off). In little more than a year a Navy antisubmarine weapon system almost doubled in cost from $3.6 billion to $7 billion. The Army's M1 supertanks initially were to cost $500,000 each but by 1982 each tank cost $2.6 million.[24] A study by the establishment-oriented Brookings Institution concluded that "virtually all large military contracts . . . ultimately involved costs in excess of original contractual estimates of from 300 to 700 percent."[25] In one decade, at least 68 weapons systems were scrapped as unworkable.[26] As weapons become more technologically complex (and more expensive and profitable to produce), they also become less functional and more prone to breakdowns, needing excessively elaborate maintenance and highly trained personnel.[27]

21. *New York Times*, May 23, 1977; *Business Week*, July 24, 1978.

22. *New York Times*, February 4, 1976, and February 8, 1971; and A. Ernest Fitzgerald, *The High Priests of Waste* (New York: Norton, 1972).

23. See Kaufman, *The War Profiteers*, and Adams, *The Iron Triangle*. Sales profit may be only 10 percent, but since the company puts up only, say, 20 percent of the capital (the rest comes from the government) and gets to keep all the profits, then the return on the private investment is 50 percent.

24. *Washington Post*, March 3, 1981.

25. Cited in Lens, *Military-Industrial Complex*, chapter 1; see also William Flannery, "Pentagon Spending," *New York Times*, February 27, 1979. Speaking of waste, one might consider the space program, which has consumed many billions of dollars otherwise better spent on domestic needs. Government probers have found that private companies have been inflating costs and padding expenses in the space program.

26. Lens, *Military-Industrial Complex*; also *Washington Post*, February 10, 1982.

27. Alexander Cockburn et al., "The Pentagon Spends Its Way to Impotence," *Village Voice*, February 18–24, 1981; also Adams, *The Iron Triangle*.

The rewards for all this waste and inefficiency have been high. In 1978 the GAO revealed that profits before taxes—and the big corporations pay almost no taxes—were 56.1 percent for defense contractors, while one company made a profit of 240 percent.[28] Two highly regarded scientists demonstrated after a painstaking study that the defense budget could be cut by 40 percent with no loss in military capability.[29]

Armaments and the Economy

It is not enough to condemn the waste and profligacy of the Pentagon; we must also understand its function in the existing capitalist society. For the millions of taxpayers who are deprived of essential domestic services because the military budget devours such a large chunk of the public treasure, defense spending is wasteful. But for the industrial empire that has grown rich by servicing the U.S. military, defense spending is wonderful. Consider the following:

1. The taxpayers' money covers all the risks and *most of the costs* of weapons development and sales. Unlike automobile manufacturers, who must worry about selling the cars they produce, the weapons dealer has a contracted market, complete with cost-overrun guarantees.

2. Almost all contracts are awarded without competitive bidding. Hence, a company can get a contract at just about whatever price it names, no matter how inflated. Indeed, the higher the negotiated contract, the more welcome it is, since both the contractor and the military want the largest possible operation.[30]

3. The overproduction of consumer products leads to a falling rate of profit. The company that keeps investing its earnings on refrigerators into making still more refrigerators eventually gluts the market and shrinks its per-unit profits. Instead, it can now invest

---

28. After these kinds of revelations by the GAO, a House committee launched an investigation—not of the Pentagon but of the GAO. See also James Barron, "Bad Weapons Never Die: Onward and Upward with the GBU-15," *Nation*, January 27, 1979.

29. See the report by Philip Morrison and Paul F. Walker in the October 1978 issue of *Scientific American*. In 1981 President Reagan's own budget director, David Stockman, admitted that the Pentagon was riddled with "blatant inefficiency, poor deployment of manpower, contracting idiocy" and "a kind of swamp" of $10 billion to $30 billion worth of waste that "can be ferreted out if you really push hard." *New York Times*, November 12, 1981. Instead of pushing, Reagan favored the military with the fattest budget in history.

30. Harold Freeman, "On Consuming the Surplus," *Progressive*, February 1977, p. 21. Upon his retirement in January 1982 Admiral Hyman Rickover said: "Defense contractors can do anything they want with nothing to hinder them."

its surplus funds in arms. The armaments market provides a whole new area of demand and investment that does not compete with the consumer market. Furthermore, it is a limitless market, since military products have a relatively brief life span. Technical innovations suggested by the corporate contractor or the military buyer, along with fearful and often exaggerated references to Soviet advances in weaponry, create a built-in obsolescence and an endless demand for more expensive and sophisticated weapons.

4. Given all this, the defense industry is the most lucrative business there is, with profits many times higher than in the private consumer market. Small wonder the military budget continues to expand. Its growth is a perfectly functional and profitable arrangement for many big corporations.

Taking into account the multiplier effect of a dollar spent and the network of subsidiary services that feed on the defense dollar, possibly a fifth of all economic activity in the United States is dependent on military expenditures. In 1974 Defense Secretary James Schlesinger defended an increase in the military budget on the grounds that it would provide a stimulus to a lagging domestic economy. More recently Defense Secretary Caspar Weinberger said the leap in military spending in the 1980s was "the second half of the administration's program to revitalize America." Thus U.S. leaders acknowledge that the arms budget is in part dictated by the needs of the corporate economy rather than by strictly military defense needs.[31]

Some people have defended military spending because it provides jobs. So do the heroin, prostitution, and pornography industries. Highway accidents provide employment for wreckers, repairmen, and hospital workers. The cigarette industry provides jobs, but that is no reason to encourage cigarette consumption. There are many needed things our labor and resources might be expended on, but these do not include the capacity to blow up the world a hundred times over or produce mountains of obsolete, death-dealing weapons. Furthermore, studies have found that arms spending creates fewer jobs than any other government expenditure except the space pro-

31. *New York Times*, February 27, 1974; James Cypher, "The Basic Economics of 'Rearming America,' " *Monthly Review*, November 1981, p. 15. Many expensive weapon systems, like the B-1 bomber, have little military justification and are being built to create contracts for the big firms. Senator Ted Stevens (R.–Alaska) said the CIA had told him that the existing B-52 would do as well in penetrating the Soviet Union with cruise missiles between now and about 1995 as would the B-1 bomber. Defense Secretary Weinberger admitted that the B-1, which would not be completed until about 1985, would not be able to survive against Soviet defenses any later than 1990. See *Washington Post*, November 10, 1981.

gram. A billion dollars spent on education, health care, public safety, or housing generates from two to three times more employment than the same money expended on defense programs.[32]

By draining off resources that would otherwise be available for civilian use, military spending increases the costs of civilian production and contributes heavily to inflation.[33] Huge military budgets have not brought prosperity but an increasing impoverishment of the civilian sector. The people of New York City, for instance, pay more in taxes to the Pentagon than to their city. What the people of Cleveland spend on armaments in two weeks would be enough to wipe out Cleveland's debt and end its financial crisis. The military establishment feasts on billions. The military brass enjoys without charge: luxury condominiums, riding stables, golf courses, private beaches, and house servants. The cost to human services is staggering. *One* M1 tank could pay for a dozen day-care centers and for the special national milk program for children, which Congress abolished in an economizing effort. The cost of one E-3A Airborne Warning plane ($123.5 million) could cover one year's Medicare benefits for a million women and children cut from the program in 1981. The $300 million that President Reagan saved by denying food aid to 700,000 undernourished infants, older children, and pregnant women in 1981 is equivalent to what the Pentagon spends in *ten hours*. The cost overruns on 45 weapons systems amounting to $38 billion could pay for a water-pollution abatement program for the entire nation.[34]

The Military Culture

Of the many agencies engaged in propagandizing the public, none is more active than the Pentagon. The armed services currently compose the strongest lobby in Washington, exerting more influence over Congress than that body exerts over the Defense Department. That it happens to be a federal offense to use the taxpayers' money to propagandize taxpayers seems not to have deterred the military. The Pentagon spends many millions a year on exhibitions, films, publications, and recruitment tours to schools and a flood of press releases, which,

32. See the studies done by Employment Research Associates (Lansing, Michigan) and Council of Economic Priorities (New York) summarized in *Washington Post,* January 13, 1982; *Daily World,* September 30, 1981; *Guardian,* December 16, 1981.

33. Seymour Melman, "Beating 'Swords' into Subways," *New York Times Magazine,* November 19, 1978, p. 48.

34. Seymour Melman, "Looting the Means of Production," *New York Times,* July 26, 1981; *Daily World,* May 7, 1981.

planted as "news reports" in the media, propagate the military's view of the world without identifying the military as their source.[35]

The military establishment heavily influences the academic community as well. While President Reagan was cutting the Student Loan program, the Department of Defense was handing out more and more ROTC scholarships (26,500 for 1983, up 23 percent from the previous year). Pentagon-financed research on college campuses has increased greatly in recent years. At least 90 universities are researching problems in weaponry, counterinsurgency, biological warfare, and other subjects of interest to the military.[36] As one researcher at MIT noted: "Our job is not to advance knowledge but to advance the military."[37]

Many social scientists have joined programs financed by the military, producing studies devoted to counterrevolutionary techniques and the manipulation of opinion at home and abroad. In hundreds of conferences and in thousands of brochures, articles, and books written by members of the academic community who are in the pay of the government, military propaganda is lent an aura of academic objectivity. Casting a shadow on their own integrity as scholars and teachers, such intellectuals transmit to an unsuspecting public the military view of reality and the Pentagon's sense of its own indispensability.

The proliferation of Pentagon-financed "independent" corporations such as RAND and the Hudson Institute—the "think tanks" that analyze technical military problems for a fee—testifies to the growing role played by nonmilitary persons. Progressively less able to provide the brainpower for all their needs, the armed services simply buy up such human resources from the universities, corporations, and planning institutions. The staggering fact is that over two-thirds of all the technical research in America is consumed by the military.

If we define "military state" as any polity that devotes the major portion of its public resources to purposes of war, then the United States is a military state, the biggest in history. Contrary to the conventional view, then, a civilian constitutional government is as capable of becoming a militarist power as is a dictatorship. The political system of a nation is of less importance in determining its military capacity than is the need to bolster capital accumulation and corporate

---

35. J. William Fulbright, *The Pentagon Propaganda Machine* (New York: Vintage, 1971); Lens, *The Military-Industrial Complex*, chapter 5.

36. See the special issue of *Science For the People*, July/August 1981, entitled "Militarism and Science."

37. Quoted in Bert Cochran, *The War System* (New York: Macmillan, 1965), p. 307.

profits, the need to guard against real or imagined foreign enemies, and the need to expand and defend overseas investment.

THE SWORD AND THE DOLLAR: TRAVELS ABROAD

The postwar growth of American corporations has been stupendous, but problems come with such success. Enormous profits remain after operational expenses are paid and even after the billions in yearly dividends are distributed—chiefly to the wealthiest 1 or 2 percent. The remaining undistributed profits must be invested somewhere. As noted earlier, the growth in profits intensifies the search for new profit-yielding opportunities, which, in turn, create more profit surplus and a still more strenuous pursuit of investment (i.e., profit) opportunities. In a word, profit abundance and profit hunger are but two sides of the same coin. Overseas investments—especially in underdeveloped countries—become increasingly attractive because of the cheap native labor, the high investment return, the absence of corporate taxes, the marketing of products at monopoly prices, and the opportunity to invest surplus capital, which—if invested at home—would only glut the domestic market and depress the profit rate, and—if invested in other industrialized nations—would bring a lower return.[38]

The federal government performs two major functions for capitalism overseas, roughly the same ones it performs at home: first, it subsidizes and finances corporate foreign investments with many billions of dollars yearly; and second, it provides a military force to protect private capital in its conflicts with labor. Consider each of these in turn:

The U.S. government spends from $8 billion to $10 billion yearly on foreign-aid programs ostensibly to help poorer nations help themselves, but these funds actually buttress the rule of wealthy and powerful Third World elites, who are friendly to U.S. corporate investors and U.S. policies. Most of the aid falls into the hands of the big landowners and top government and military officials of various "developing" nations. Thus $23 million supposedly slated for poor farmers in Honduras ended up helping rich ranchers, and $5.2 million for road construction for small farmers in Liberia instead helped Fire-

---

38. See Harry Magdoff, *The Age of Imperialism* (New York: Monthly Review Press, 1969); also Magdoff's *Imperialism: From the Colonial Age to the Present* (New York: Monthly Review Press, 1978).

stone transport its products from its huge rubber plantations.[39] Most of the highways, ports, dams, and utilities constructed in foreign lands with U.S. government funds are planned around the needs of American-owned companies. Abroad, as at home, it is the U.S. taxpayer who pays for the "social overhead capital" needed to service the multinational corporations.

The U.S. government subsidizes overseas business investments and exports. The government compensates corporations for losses due to war, revolution, insurrection, or confiscation by a foreign government, and refuses aid to any country that nationalizes without compensation assets owned by U.S. firms. U.S. funds were given to Latin American governments for the purpose of having them expropriate *unprofitable* U.S. firms at *above-market prices*. "In turn, U.S. corporations used the funds procured to invest in more profitable activities."[40] Thus American taxpayers help foreign governments bail out U.S. multinational corporations.

Many persons wonder why the gap between rich and poor nations grows wider despite the increase in Third World investments. The an-

---

39. Frances Moore Lappe, Joseph Collins, and David Kinley, *Aid As Obstacle* (San Francisco: Institute for Food and Development Policy, 1980); Teresa Hayter, *Aid as Imperialism* (Baltimore: Penguin Books, 1971).

40. James Petras, "U.S. Business and Foreign Policy," in Michael Parenti (ed.), *Trends and Tragedies in American Foreign Policy* (Boston: Little, Brown, 1971), p. 98; also Anne Jackson and Angus Wright, "Running Risks For IBM," *Progressive*, August 1981, pp. 44–45.

swer is that the gap widens *because* of such investments. Unless we assume that multinational corporations are philanthropic undertakings, it is clear that investments have the ultimate purpose of *extracting* wealth from other nations. Between 1950 and 1972, U.S. corporations showed a $50 billion overseas investment outflow and a $99 billion profit influx.[41] In Chile alone over the last several decades, U.S. copper companies extracted $3.8 billion in profits, leaving in their wake devastated mining lands and impoverished communities.

U.S. aid allows multinationals to exploit the recipient country's labor, monopolize its resources, control its politics, and influence its tastes, markets, and technical needs so that dependency on American products continues well after the aid program has ceased. The effect of foreign aid and private U.S. investment is to retard the productive capacity of the poorer country by limiting it to a few specialized extractive industries like oil, timber, tin, and copper, or cash crops like sugar, coffee, or cocoa. The labor and resources of the land are mobilized to fit the interests of U.S. corporations rather than the needs of the populace. The result is low wages, high illiteracy, and chronic poverty. In a country like Guatemala, while U.S. corporations own three-fourths of the arable land and extract enormous profits, the rural population has a smaller per-capita food supply today than during the Mayan civilization.[42]

U.S. aid and corporate investments leave Third World countries deeply indebted to U.S. banks. Debtor nations borrow increasingly larger sums at high interest rates to pay off an ever-growing debt, the temporary relief of each new loan only creates a heavier debt obligation for the future. Some Third World nations devote the major part of their export earnings to paying off their multibillion-dollar debts to American banks.[43]

The growth of American capitalism from a weak domestic position to a dominant international one has been accompanied by a similar growth in American military interventionism. Sometimes the sword has rushed in to protect the dollar, and sometimes the dollar has rushed in to enjoy the advantages won by the sword. To make the

---

41. Paul Sweezy, "Growing Wealth, Declining Power," *Monthly Review*, March 1974, pp. 6–7.

42. Magdoff, *Age of Imperialism*, pp. 129 ff; also "The U.S. Foreign Aid Program," *Dollars and Sense*, March 1979, p. 8; James Petras, *Critical Perspectives on Imperialism and Social Class in the Third World* (New York: Monthly Review Press, 1978).

43. Jonathan Aronson and Elliot Stein, Jr., "Bankers Milk the Third World," *Progressive*, October 1977, pp. 49–51; Isabel Letelier and Michael Moffitt, "Human Rights, Economic Aid and Private Banks" (Issue Paper, Institute for Policy Studies, Washington, D.C., 1978). As of 1982 the Third World debt to Western banks was a trillion dollars.

world safe for capitalism, the United States government has embarked on a global counterrevolutionary strategy, suppressing insurgent peasant and worker movements throughout Asia, Africa, and Latin America. But the interests of the corporate elites never stand naked; rather they are wrapped in the flag and coated with patriotic appearances. Knowing that the American people would never agree to sending their sons to fight wars in far-off lands in order to protect the profits of Gulf Oil and General Motors,[44] the corporate elites and their political spokesmen play upon popular fears, telling us that our "national security" necessitates American intervention wherever a colonial order is threatened by a popular uprising seeking to establish a socialist economic system.

By 1979–1982, after a decade of détente between the United States and the Soviet Union, the Carter and Reagan administrations revived the cold war anti-Soviet rhetoric of the 1950s, sounding alarms about the imminent threat of Soviet aggression. Moscow's intervention into Afghanistan and Soviet pressures on Poland were treated as certain evidence that the U.S.S.R. was bent on world conquest and was even planning a nuclear war against the U.S. And, as in previous decades, every popular insurgency against reactionary dictatorships, from Africa to Central America, was depicted as Soviet inspired—as if the indigenous peoples of these countries fought not for their own interests but because the Kremlin commanded them to do so. This view of the world was instrumental in winning ever fatter military budgets at home and buttressing U.S. intervention and protecting corporate investments abroad.[45]

To justify U.S. interventionism in other countries, our policymakers also claim they are defending democracy from communism. But closer examination shows they are defending the capitalist world from social change—even if the change be peaceful, orderly, and *democratic*. Guatemala in 1954, the Dominican Republic in 1962, and Chile in 1973 are cases in point. In all three countries popularly elected governments began instituting progressive changes for the benefit of the destitute classes and began to nationalize or threatened to nationalize U.S. corporate holdings. And in each instance, the United States was instrumental in overthrowing these governments

---

44. A Harris poll found that by lopsided majorities Americans opposed sending U.S. troops to aid countries under foreign attack, even if the attack came from a Communist nation. The only nation Americans supported sending troops to in case of invasion was Canada. See *Burlington* (Vt.) *Free Press*, March 25, 1975. Opinion polls in 1981–1982 showed overwhelming opposition to U.S. military involvement in El Salvador and elsewhere in Central America.

45. Cypher, "The Basic Economics of 'Rearming America.' "

and instituting right-wing regimes that accommodated U.S. investors and ruthlessly repressed the peasants and workers. Similarly, in Greece, the Philippines, Iran, Indonesia, East Timor, and at least ten Latin American nations, popular governments have been overthrown by military oligarchs—largely trained and financed by the Pentagon and the CIA—who prove themselves friendly to capitalism.[46]

For all their talk about "human rights," U.S. government leaders have been propping up fascist regimes throughout the world, using assassination squads, torture, and terror to support the allies of the corporate world order.[47] In many U.S.-supported states, strikes have been outlawed, unions destroyed, wages cut back, and dissidents murdered. Illiteracy, poverty, and hunger are the lot of the many, while wealth and power accumulate in the hands of a few rulers who prove themselves cooperative friends of the multinational corporations.

This policy of containing social change in order to make the world safe for capitalism has had its serious setbacks. In the post World-War-II era, successful national liberation movements in China, Cuba, Vietnam, Cambodia, Laos, Mozambique, Nicaragua, Grenada, and elsewhere have vanquished corporate social orders and have instituted popular socialist governments. If military-corporate America lost the war in Indochina, it was not for want of trying. The United States government, under the leadership of Democratic and Republican administrations, spent $150 billion and more than ten years prosecuting that war, dropping almost 8 million tons of bombs, 18 million gallons of chemical defoliants, and nearly 400,000 tons of napalm. The Vietnamese, Laotian, and Cambodian countrysides were desolated by saturation bombings; several million Vietnamese, Cambodians, and Laotians were killed, millions more were maimed or wounded, and almost 10 million were left homeless; about 58,000 Americans lost their lives and hundreds of thousands more were wounded or permanently disabled. But the war did bring benefits to a tiny segment of the American population: corporate defense contractors like DuPont, ITT, and Dow Chemical.[48]

---

46. See Stephen Schlesinger and Stephen Kinzer, *Bitter Fruit, The Untold Story of the American Coup in Guatemala* (Garden City, N.Y.: Doubleday, 1982); and James Petras and Morris Morley, *The United States and Chile: Imperialism and the Overthrow of the Allende Government* (New York: Monthly Review Press, 1975).

47. See Noam Chomsky and Edward Herman, *The Washington Connection and Third World Fascism* (Boston: South End Press, 1979); Penny Lernoux, *Cry of the People* (Garden City, N.Y.: Doubleday, 1980).

48. William Hoffman, "Vietnam: The Bloody Get-Rich-Quick Business of War," *Gallery*, November 1978, p. 42. Hoffman notes that the top ten defense firms grossed $11.6 billion in contracts during the Vietnam war.

If we define "imperialism" as that relationship in which one country dominates, through use of economic and military power and the land, labor, resources, finances, and politics of another country, then the United States is the greatest imperialist power in history. The American empire is of a magnitude never before equaled. More than 1.5 million American military personnel are stationed in 119 countries. The United States maintains 429 major military bases and 2,972 lesser bases in 30 countries, covering some 4,000 square miles and costing over $5 billion a year. The military has some 8,500 strategic nuclear weapons and 22,000 tactical ones deployed throughout the world. The U.S. Navy deploys a fleet larger in total tonnage than all the other navies of the world combined, consisting of missile cruisers, nuclear submarines, nuclear aircraft carriers, destroyers, and spy ships, which sail every ocean and make port on every continent. The United States has trained and equipped over 2 million troops and police in foreign lands ruled by military dictatorships; the purpose of this militarization has been not to defend these countries from outside invasion but to protect capital investments and the ruling oligarchs from the dangers of domestic insurgency.

With only 5 percent of the earth's population, the United States expends one-third of the world's military funds. Two-thirds of the discretionary portion of the federal budget (that is, the portion not obligated by Social Security) is spent on war preparation. Despite a nuclear "overkill" capacity that can destroy the entire world more than twenty-five times over, the U.S. nuclear arsenal continues to grow at the rate of three H-bombs each day. Since World War II, more than $90 billion in U.S. *military* aid has been given to some eighty nations.[49]

This American global expansionism is designed to prevent competing social orders from emerging, especially those having a non-capitalist way of using wealth and labor. The costs of empire are not paid by the business class, which derives most of the benefits but are carried by the working populace. The *profits* of empire flow into corporate hands, while the growing military and investment costs are largely borne by the U.S. taxpayer.

This is not to say that U.S. expansionism has been impelled by the profit motive alone, but that various other considerations—such as national security and patriotism—are defined in a way that serves the material interests of a particular class. Indeed, much of what passes

---

49. No one knows precisely how much goes for military aid. Congress exercises no effective oversight over the program. See "Curbing Arms Aid," *Progressive*, April 1971, p. 7.

for "the national interest" in capitalist America, not surprisingly, has been defined from the perspective of a capitalist social order. "A serious and explicit purpose of our foreign policy," President Eisenhower observed in 1953, "[is] the encouragement of a hospitable climate for investment in foreign nations."[50] Since American "security" is supposedly dependent on American power, and such power depends in part on American wealth (i.e., a "sound economy," "secure markets," "essential raw materials," etc.), then policies that are fashioned to expand U.S. corporate wealth abroad are presumed to be in the national interest. Thus we avoid any question as to whose interests are benefited by military-industrial global expansionism, at whose cost, and in pursuance of whose particular definition of "security" and "national interest."

TAXES: HELPING THE RICH IN THEIR TIME OF GREED

The corporate state uses taxation as well as public spending to redistribute income and wealth in an upward direction. Our tax structure is thought to burden the rich more than the poor, when actually the tax load falls more heavily on those least able to pay. Taking into account all local, state, and federal sales and excise taxes, as well as Social Security and income taxes, we find that lower-income people pay a higher percentage of their earnings than do upper-income people, while generally getting less for what they pay.[51] The law is written so that more than half of all tax savings go to the top 10 percent of taxpayers. The middle bracket usually benefits somewhat from the loopholes, but the true majority, the bottom 60 percent, get almost nothing.[52] The same inequality exists in regard to property taxes: the richer the family the lower the percentage of property taxes paid.[53]

The wealthier the person, the greater the opportunities to enjoy lightly taxed or nontaxable income from capital gains, expense accounts, tax-free municipal and state bonds, private retirement plans,

---

50. *New York Times*, February 3, 1953, quoted in Magdoff, *The Age of Imperialism*, p. 126.

51. Philip Stern, *The Rape of the Taxpayer* (New York: Random House, 1973); Herman P. Miller, *Rich Man, Poor Man* (New York: Crowell, 1971); Joseph Pechman, *Federal Tax Policy* (Washington, D.C.: Brookings Institute, 1966). These books provide the documentation for much of the above discussion on taxes.

52. *Dollars and Sense*, May–June 1980, pp. 14–15.

53. Thomas Bodenheimer, "The Poverty of the State," *Monthly Review*, November 1972, pp. 13–14.

"YOU HAD A VERY PROFITABLE YEAR. LET'S SEE— AFTER SPECIAL TAX BREAKS AND SUBSIDIES, WE OWE YOU..."

stock options, and various kinds of business and professional deductions. For the very rich, almost any investment can be turned into a tax shelter. Herds of cattle, baseball teams, orange groves, and office buildings can provide generous depreciation and maintenance write-offs. Potential income that does not materialize can be claimed as a loss so that one can have a big income yet show a loss and enjoy a hefty tax deduction. In 1976, 182 millionaires paid no income taxes at all. Billionaires like H. L. Hunt and J. Paul Getty, with annual incomes of $50 million and $100 million respectively, paid only a few thousand dollars a year. In contrast, a New York City dishwasher who earned $4,800 that year paid $1,213 in federal, state, and city income taxes plus another $200 in sales taxes, or the equivalent of four months' salary.[54]

It has been argued that if the wealthy were more heavily taxed this would make no appreciable difference in federal revenue since they are relatively few in number. In fact, it is estimated that in any one year from $77 billion to $91 billion is lost to the federal government in the form of tax preferences and write-offs, the largest share going to the uppermost brackets of the business community. According to the economist William Tabb, tax loopholes for the rich climbed to $277 billion in 1982. *If the top 100 corporations were taxed at the same rate as the average middle-income family, there would be more than enough to cover all federal expenditures for welfare, education, child care, occupational safety, housing, environmental protection, and medical care.*[55]

While the share of federal revenues coming from individual taxpayers has been rising, the portion paid by corporations has dropped from 50 percent in 1945 to 14 percent in 1979 to an estimated 9 percent in 1983. Nor do these tax cuts act as a spur to new investments, since most of the deductions are taken against investments that would have been made anyway. Past experience shows that tax windfalls to big companies neither ease unemployment nor trickle down to wage earners, but certainly do their share in feeding inflation and fattening profits.[56]

While corporations claim they need still more tax benefits in order to have sufficient capital for investment, the truth is that "major producers are engulfed by a massive cash flow and are casting about for interesting diversions for their money."[57] In 1977 the oil industry's cash flow amounted to more than $30 billion. Its return on invested capital jumped 30 percent, amounting to $10.7 billion after taxes. There was no capital shortage and there were more profits than ever. Yet the following year, Congress cut corporate taxes by yet another

---

54. An upper-income person like Ronald Reagan may pay as much as 33⅓ percent, say, $125,000 on his $375,000 "adjusted gross income" (income after allowable deductions). But his actual income *before* deductions is likely to be $1 million or more, so the tax is really closer to 12½ percent, about the same rate paid by the lowest wage earner who does not itemize. The poorer person also pays a higher percentage of income in sales taxes and other regressive taxes.

55. Tabb's estimates are from a talk he gave at the City University of New York, April 1982; see also *New York Times*, March 2, 1975, and Erwin Knoll, "It's Only Money," *Progressive*, March 1972, p. 25.

56. Paul Rosenstiel, "How Business Profits from Inflation," *Nation*, March 17, 1979, pp. 270–73.

57. See the statement by the New Jersey Department of Energy Commissioner in the *New York Times*, June 1, 1978.

$3.7 billion and capital gains by $2.2 billion.[58] While making billions in profits each year, the largest commercial banks and industrial firms like Chase Manhattan, Morgan Guaranty Trust, General Dynamics, ITT, AT&T, U.S. Steel, and Exxon pay little or no taxes.[59]

Many private utilities not only fail to pay their fair share of taxes but also pocket most of the tax dollars charged to their customers. Each year the largest utilities collect taxes on their monthly billings to customers, but by taking advantage of write-offs, they are able to keep the lion's share, amounting to billions, for themselves.[60] In addition, an estimated 350,000 companies are illegally withholding Social Security and income taxes from their employees' paychecks and then pocketing the money. Few of these delinquent firms have been prosecuted.[61]

As bad as things were, the 1981 tax law sponsored by the Reagan administration and obligingly passed by Congress made things worse. Massive new tax cuts were initiated, the greater share going to the top 5 percent of the population. Upper-bracket people were accorded income-tax savings of anywhere from $20,000 to $30,000 yearly. The lowest brackets had to make do with $50 to $150 cuts—which were more than offset by new increases in Social Security taxes. For those with income from investments (known accurately as unearned income or property income) the tax cuts were even more significant, amounting to over $17,000 for an unearned income of $200,000 and over $62,000 for an unearned income of $500,000. Inheritance taxes on the wealthiest estates were sharply reduced, allowing an estimated tax break in 1982–1985 of $15.6 billion for the beneficiaries of very large fortunes.[62]

---

58. Business enterprises owned by religious organizations—are free of tax obligations. The billions collected by churches from Sunday collection plates, bingo games, wills, and bequests and from investments in real estate, liquor, dairy farms, armaments, television, etc., go untaxed and are exempt by law from audit and disclosure. As churches accumulate more property, the tax base shrinks and the tax burden increases for wage earners and small-property owners. See Martin Larson and Stanley Lowell, *The Religious Empire* (Washington: Robert B. Luce, 1976).

59. *Tax Notes*, December 14, 1981, pp. 1448–61; also Rep. Charles Vanik's report in *Congressional Record*, June 27, 1980.

60. *Dollars and Sense*, September 1980, p. 18. One year Georgia Power Co. charged customers $108 million in taxes and paid nothing to the government. In 1980 customers paid $3.3 billion in federal taxes on their phone bills, but AT&T turned over only $566 million to the government.

61. *Moneysworth*, October 13, 1975.

62. *Washington Post*, July 30 and 31, 1981, and February 16, 1982. An advertisement by an aviation firm in a San Diego newspaper made clear who was helped by the cuts: there is a photograph of a smiling man pointing at his aircraft and saying: "Reagan's new tax law enabled me to buy my own airplane. . . . I paid for it with tax dollars! and I've virtually eliminated my taxes for 1981." Reported in the *Washington Post*, October 25, 1981.

The 1981 tax law showed unbounded generosity to banking and industry, granting them effective cuts of anywhere from 30 to 100 percent. The corporate tax rate was reduced to 46 percent but with new tax credits and deductions it can be reduced below zero, a negative tax rate amounting to a tax subsidy. Unprofitable firms could "sell" their tax breaks to more prosperous firms. The latter make a big tax savings while the "poorer" ones pick up large cash payments in return. In fact, it turns out that highly profitable firms, which are already paying little or no taxes and have no shortage of capital, began selling their tax deductions to other rich firms. The result has been a bonanza for the big companies.[63]

The tax law of 1981 brought a massive upward shift in income, along with a downward shift in the tax burden since every dollar not paid by the wealthy must be carried by wage and salary earners. While greatly increasing the federal deficit, the law showed no evidence of stimulating economic recovery. Even the establishment *New York Times* was moved to editorialize that the tax law gives "a bushelful of money to some of the richest individuals" while leaving "the Federal Budget deep in the red for the rest of the decade, guaranteeing high interest rates and recurring frantic battles to cut even more from Federal programs. . . . For the nation as a whole, there is virtually nothing to celebrate."[64]

DEFICIT SPENDING AND SUPPLY-SIDE ECONOMICS

One way government keeps business profits high is by spending more than it collects in taxes, a process known as "deficit spending." The government expends billions on behalf of business firms and defense contractors, yet cuts business taxes. To meet its deficits it borrows from financial institutions, wealthy individuals, and other creditors in the U.S. and abroad. Small wonder business people like *this* kind of deficit spending: it allows the federal government to use its immense borrowing powers to subsidize corporate profits and maintain capital accumulation.[65]

Small wonder also that conservative leaders who sing hymns to a balanced budget on Sunday are among the wildest deficit spenders

---

63. *Washington Post*, August 2, 1981; November 14, 1981; and February 20, 1982; *New York Times*, May 2, 1982.

64. *New York Times*, July 29, 1981.

65. Leo Huberman and Paul Sweezy, "The Kennedy-Johnson Boom," in Marvin Gettleman and David Mermelstein (eds.), *The Great Society Reader* (New York: Random House, 1976), p. 103.

during the rest of the week. The Nixon and Ford administrations produced record peacetime deficits, and President Reagan's budget deficits threatened to run off the charts, estimated at $120 billion for 1982 and $200 billion for 1983, a deficit rate several times higher than previous peacetime and *wartime* budgets.[66]

As government plays an increasingly active role in maintaining profit growth, it must spend greater and greater sums, borrowing from the future earnings of the people to shore up the present earnings of the wealthy. As with the debts incurred by our cities and by Third World nations, the U.S. national debt seems to grow at an increasingly greater rate. The more the government owes, the more it must borrow—which puts it still deeper in the hole. In 1940 the national debt was $43 billion; the costs of World War II brought it to $258.7 billion. By 1970 it climbed to $370 billion, but by 1982 it had ballooned to $1 trillion and may reach $1.5 trillion by 1985.[67]

As time goes on, the government not only borrows more, but does so at higher rates and on shorter terms; hence the interest paid on the national debt has been growing twice as fast as the budget itself. In 1978 the interest payment was $49 billion; in 1980, $75 billion; in 1981, $96 billion. This interest payment represents another huge hand-out to the wealthy. It is one of the largest single items in the federal budget each year, a sum *almost three times the amount spent on federal welfare payments to the poor.* The bulk of this money, drawn as taxes from the working public, constitutes an upward redistribution of wealth, another manifestation of the "siphoning-up" of income.

Deficit spending, then, serves the moneyed class not only by allowing the government to subsidize the corporate economy but by providing a relatively risk-free, high-yield place for investors who shy away from a depressed private market. By buying up government bonds and securities wealthy creditors can put their surplus capital into the federal deficit and watch it grow at public expense.

As noted above, the Reagan administration initiated massive tax cuts designed not to increase the spending power and consumption of the working populace but to increase the wealth of the wealthy. It

---

66. "Deficit Spending—A Hard Habit to Break," *U.S. News & World Report*, October 29, 1979; *Guardian*, February 17, 1982.

67. *New York Times*, September 30, 1981. There are also "off-budget" deficits, agency-sponsored obligations, and loan guarantees; these consist of low-interest loans made to business by government agencies. Some of these notes are then assumed by private banks at a higher interest rate, with the government covering the difference. Such debt obligations do not show up in the budget and are made without going through Congress, but they amount to goodly sums: an estimated $90 billion in 1981.

was anticipated that, with more money on their hands, business people would invest more; the economy would expand; employment would increase; tax revenues would climb back up as the tax base grew, and there would be prosperity for all. So argued proponents of supply-side economics (known previously as trickle-down economics). As of late 1982, however, business showed no inclination to risk investments in non-existent markets and simply pocketed the tax windfall.

At the same time the Reagan administration initiated a policy of limiting the money supply, thus causing interest rates to climb. High rates, in turn, curb credit by making borrowing more costly, and this supposedly slows down inflationary spending. Thus a monetary policy to decrease investment and contract the economy joined with a supply-side fiscal policy of increasing investment and expanding the economy. The result was the worst of both worlds: the economic recession deepened while inflation continued (albeit at a slightly slower rate given the sharp drop in home and automobile sales).

The policy was attacked as irrational "voodoo economics." But when one realizes that the Reagan administration's intent was not to achieve full employment but to ensure business profits, then "Reaganomics" does not seem all that irrational. It *has* succeeded in doing its part in the struggle between capital and labor by effecting a massive transfer of income from the working populace to the propertied class—which may well have been its original intent.[68]

To summarize the major points in this chapter: the outputs of the political system, as manifested by the services, subsidies, prices, protections, taxes, leases, credits, and market quotas established by public authority, affect the various areas of business enterprise and socioeconomic life mostly to benefit those who own the wealth of the nation and at the expense of the working populace. In almost every area of enterprise, government has provided business with unsurpassed opportunities for nonrisk investments, gainful inefficiency, monopolistic pricing, lucrative contracts, and huge profits. Government feeds capital surplus through a process of deficit spending, offers an endless market in the defense, space, and nuclear industries, and provides for the financial aid, global expansion, and military protection of modern multinational corporations. From ranchers to resort owners, from doctors to bankers, from auto makers to missile makers,

---

68. There remained the danger that Reaganomics was serving its friends *too* well and was destroying the economic base upon which the plutocracy rests. Thus by late 1981, some Wall Street representatives voiced concern about the pace and size of the tax cuts, military appropriations, and budget deficits (while generally still supporting Reagan's programs).

there prevails a welfarism for the rich of such stupendous magnitude as to make us marvel at the big businessman's audacity in preaching the virtues of self-reliance and private initiative whenever lesser forms of public assistance threaten to reach hands other than his own.

7

Health, Welfare, and Environment: The Sacrificial Lambs

In this chapter we will discuss the policies of what has been called the "welfare state." As we have seen, government plays a major role in sustaining the profits of capitalism. In addition, government must take care that the worst abuses of the economic system do not incite people to disrupt the system. The class struggles that won important gains during the Great Depression of the 1930s did not end then. Spearheaded by labor unions, minorities, the poor, environmental groups, women, and public-interest organizations, the country's democratic forces have continued to press their fight against economic and social injustice. Faced with such popular restiveness and with the inability of business to meet the needs of the people, the federal government began a series of face-saving human-services programs. Although these programs bettered the lot of many, they failed to reach millions, including many of the people most in need.

Herein, we will discuss various policy areas in some detail and offer an explanation of why human-services programs have been an inadequate and costly disappointment.

THE POOR GET LESS (AND LESS)

In the 1960s large sums were allocated for a "war on poverty" that brought no noticeable betterment to millions living in destitution, nor to millions of others who, although technically above the poverty

level, were still burdened by low wages, high prices, taxes, and economic insecurity.[1] After studying antipoverty programs in a dozen cities, one observer noted that funds were appropriated "in the name of the poor . . . without direct concern for, or serious attempts at, involvement of the poor."[2]

What was true of the inner cities was equally true of rural America. During the 1960s, $7 billion was invested by federal, state, and local governments in the Appalachia region, yet the bulk of the poor "remain largely untouched" by the expenditures.[3] Some Office of Economic Opportunity officials complained that the poverty program was "chiefly a boon for the rich and for the entrenched political interests," specifically Appalachia's suburban "Main Streeters"—merchants, bankers, coal-industry leaders, and road contractors.[4]

---

1. See Richard Parker, *The Myth of the Middle Class* (New York: Liveright, 1972).

2. The social psychologist, Kenneth B. Clark, quoted in the *New York Times*, November 9, 1969.

3. *New York Times*, November 29, 1970.

4. *Ibid.*

Here are other examples of federal assistance programs that do more for the haves than for the have-nots:

1. Under the federal school-lunch program, more lunches are distributed to middle-class children than to the poor. All federal food programs combined reach only about 18 percent of the indigent.
2. As with lunch, so with breakfast. Some 14 million low-income children are eligible for the school-breakfast program, yet most schools in poor areas do not have the program, while some upper-class schools like Phillips Exeter Academy do.[5]
3. Most state governments dispense aid through matching funds, giving larger sums to upper-income school districts and smaller sums to the poorer districts that have smaller budgets, thereby doing little to lessen and much to intensify inequities.[6]
4. In higher education the major beneficiaries of public aid have been in the upper-income brackets. In the mid-1960s the students who attended the University of California received an average subsidy of about $5,000 and were mostly upper- and upper-middle-class, while lower-middle- and working-class students were concentrated in the California junior colleges, where the per-capita subsidy was only about $1,000.[7] Educational opportunities are limited largely according to one's ability to pay. Every year hundreds of thousands of academically qualified working-class high school graduates do not go to college because of a lack of funds.[8]
5. The multibillion-dollar federal manpower training programs have been described as a "business bonanza" for corporations like GE, IBM, and AT&T that run them at considerable profit to themselves while generating relatively few jobs for the unemployed.[9]
6. Over the last decade there has been a shift from aid to the poor "to aid for more middle-class Americans in the suburbs and smaller towns."[10] Spending programs supposedly intended for the needy have been used for such things as tennis courts, convention

---

5. *Guardian*, October 26, 1977.
6. John Coons, William Clune, and Stephan Sugarman, *Private Wealth and Public Education* (Cambridge, Mass.: Harvard University Press, 1970).
7. W. Lee Hansen and Burton A. Weisbord, *Benefits, Costs and Finance of Public Education* (Chicago: Markham, 1969).
8. *Chronicle of Higher Education*, September 25, 1978, p. 3.
9. See Ivar Berg and Marcia Freedman, "The Job Corps: A Business Bonanza," *Christianity and Crisis*, May 31, 1965, pp. 115–19.
10. *New York Times*, September 26, 1975.

halls, parking garages, and private golf courses in affluent communities.[11]

One study shows that federal transfer payments, such as Social Security, workmen's compensation, unemployment benefits, and veteran's disability compensation, distribute $7 billion more to people earning above $10,000 than to those below, with a person under the $5,000 income level receiving only a third of the share available to someone in the $25,000–$50,000 bracket.[12] Social Security, better described as "social insecurity," provides benefits for aged individuals averaging several thousand dollars below the poverty level. As inadequate as it is, three-fifths of the elderly depend on Social Security for half their income, and for a quarter of them, it provides 90 percent of their support. Most of the elderly would be utterly destitute without this modest stipend.[13]

In 1981 and 1982, with the support of conservatives and some "moderates" of both parties in Congress, President Reagan implemented cuts amounting to $85 billion in domestic programs. Medicare was reduced, causing the elderly and the handicapped to pay more for medical services. Many poor persons lost Medicaid assistance. More rigid eligibility standards were imposed for disability insurance. Some ten percent of recipients became ineligible for food stamps, and most others received reduced benefits. The program to combat hunger and malnutrition for infants and older children was sharply curtailed. Unemployment insurance was reduced from 39 to 26 weeks in many states. Rents on public housing for low-income people were raised, and all new contracts for subsidized housing for the poor were eliminated for 1983. The Comprehensive Employment and Training Administration (CETA), employing hundreds of thousands of people (70 percent of them women) to staff day-care centers, libraries, and centers for the disabled and aged, was entirely abolished.

---

11. Ian Menzies, "Money for Poor Going to Suburbs," *Boston Globe*, September 29, 1976. Generally, the federal government spends more money in rich counties than in poor ones. See *Guardian*, October 5, 1977, and *New York Times*, February 3, 1978.

12. Taylor Branch, "The Screwing of the Average Man. Government Subsidies: Who Gets the $63 Billion?" *Washington Monthly*, March 1972, p. 22. Branch drew from a study by the Brookings Institution. About 22 million retired or disabled persons receive Social Security benefits. The regressive quality of Social Security funding should be noted. A corporate executive with a $200,000 salary pays little more Social Security tax than the janitor who cleans his office. Those in the lowest-paying jobs who are too poor to pay income taxes must still pay Social Security.

13. William Tabb, "Social Security Goes Private," *Nation*, January 30, 1982, p. 113.

Almost ten percent of all welfare recipients were cut from the rolls by 1983 and many others have received reduced benefits. The Summer Feeding Program, which provides meals for 1 million poor children, was to be eliminated by the summer of 1983.[14]

In addition, there were cuts in railroad services, legal services for the poor, neighborhood self-development, student loans, and remedial education. While President Reagan called for a "New Federalism"—which amounted to dismantling the federal government's social programs and letting the states take up the burden—most states and municipalities were caught in budget squeezes of their own and were making similar cuts in services, thus compounding the hardships of people of modest means.

Generally, those people with the fewest economic resources and the least political clout were made to bear the greatest austerity under Reaganomics. Translated from abstract figures to human experience, the cuts have meant more isolation, hunger, and malnutrition for infants, older children, and the elderly; more unattended illnesses; more homeless, jobless, and desperate people; more crime, pathology, unhappiness, and pain.[15]

The Reagan cuts were defended as a way of getting welfare "chiselers" off the dole. But half the people benefiting from food stamps were the children of low-income families. Of the 11 million recipients of Aid to Families with Dependent Children (AFDC or "welfare"), 9 million were children; 3 million were aged, disabled, or blind; most of the others were single mothers with no means of support; less than 1 percent were able-bodied men.[16] Most recipients were White. While there may be occasional instances of fraud, the AFDC program is one of the most strictly supervised, with the largest portion of its monies spent on administrative oversight and fraud investigation.[17]

---

14. *New York Times*, October 1, 1981; *Washington Post*, February 16 and 20, 1982, and June 10, 1982. In his 1983 budget Reagan proposed additional cuts in human services amounting to $26.2 billion; *Economic Notes* (New York), March 1982, p. 5.

15. For evidence of this see *New York Times*, October 17 and 21, 1981; *Washington Post*, February 16, and June 10, 1982; *The Human Cost of Reagan's Budget*, report of the Worker's League (New York: Labor Publications, 1981). Some 60 percent of the Reagan cuts were from entitlements and other programs assisting those below the poverty level: *Newsweek*, April 5, 1982; also Robin Herman, "Nutrition Watch Committee Finds Hunger in State Rising," *New York Times*, June 25, 1982.

16. Various studies indicate that about one out of every five or six unemployed women is jobless because she is unable to make satisfactory child-care arrangements. See U.S. Commission on Civil Rights booklet, *Child Care and Equal Opportunity for Women* (Washington, D.C., 1981).

17. A typical example is California's Alameda County, where to administer $16 million in payments, some $28 million was spent, out of which $7 million went to hunt "fraud." *Guardian*, January 18, 1978. Of the estimated $767 billion for fiscal 1983, $5.5 billion went for AFDC "welfare."

Even before the Reagan cuts, many welfare recipients suffered from overcrowded housing, chronic illnesses, and inadequate medical care. Approximately one-fourth of all welfare children aged 5 to 14 have never seen a dentist; at least half suffer from malnutrition.[18] The number of recipients has been markedly reduced even as needs have increased with the recession. One welfare expert estimated that for every two people receiving support, between two and three people did not get the assistance to which they were entitled, and this does not include persons who received payments smaller than they legally deserved.[19] Even before Reaganomics, millions of destitute Americans received no assistance at all. They found themselves too young for Social Security or otherwise not covered by it, too old for Aid to Families with Dependent Children, not disabled enough for Aid to the Totally Disabled, not covered by unemployment benefits or their benefits have run out, eligible for food stamps but unable to get a sufficient amount, and eligible for welfare but unable to collect it. Welfare is hardly an adequate solution to the economic problems of the poor, but, as Piven and Cloward note, "Eliminating welfare payments in the absence of other economic and social opportunities is . . . a worse solution."[20]

"URBAN REMOVAL" AND THE DEATH OF CITIES

American cities are among the prime victims of the profit system. Consider the housing crisis. By conservative estimates, one out of every five Americans lives in a substandard domicile lacking adequate plumbing, heat, and other facilities. Millions of people suffer from overcrowding or pay so much rent that they have insufficient income left for living expenses.[21] The scarcity of decent homes allows landlords to charge exorbitant rents. In places like New York City, landlords take ownership of a building and milk it ruthlessly, neglecting to

18. Department of Labor study reported in the *New York Times*, August 7, 1978; *Boston Globe*, March 6, 1977. The Reagan cuts will curb food programs that have reached some—but never all—of the neediest children. *New York Times*, January 1, 1982.

19. *New York Times*, December 12, 1977; also Homer Bigart, "Hunger in America: Stark Deprivation Haunts a Land of Plenty," *New York Times*, February 16, 1969. Between 1969 and 1981 the purchasing power of people on welfare declined by almost 30 percent, making their situation all that more difficult: *Newsweek*, April 5, 1982.

20. Frances Fox Piven and Richard Cloward, *The New Class War* (New York: Pantheon, 1982), p. 4.

21. *America's Housing Needs 1970–1980* (a report by the Joint Center for Urban Studies, Cambridge, 1977).

pay taxes and fuel bills, permitting violations to pile up without making repairs, but at the same time collecting rents from the tenants. The landlord eventually abandons the building in a ruined condition and disappears with thousands of dollars in excess of the initial investment. Yet no federal or state law makes such conduct criminal. "The economics of ghetto housing ensures that bad housing is profitable and that good housing cannot be maintained."[22]

Federal programs have done little to redress the inequities of housing-for-profits and much to worsen them. While new housing is beyond the means of 75 to 85 percent of the nation's families,[23] lavish assistance has been provided to upper-income homeowners in the form of low-cost credit, income-tax deductions, and other subsidies amounting to more than $5 billion a year. The wealthiest fifth of the population receives easily twice as much in housing subsidies as the poorest fifth.[24] As the *New York Times* reports, "the bulk of urban aid from Washington is targeted not at still festering poverty sections but at . . . well-to-do neighborhoods . . . and suburbs."[25]

Most of the billions spent by the Department of Housing and Urban Development (HUD) have been channeled into the private sector of the economy in response to the profit interests of developers, banks, and speculators, *thereby providing few homes for people who cannot afford market prices.* Speculators buy up large numbers of old houses, apply cosmetic improvements, then get an inflated appraisal of the property's worth, often at several times its actual market value. The houses are then sold to low-income families with a federal guarantee covering the mortgage. The families soon find their homes to be in unlivable condition. Unable to afford the major repairs, they abandon the houses. At this point HUD is obliged to pay off the mortgage holders at the inflated value and take possession of the houses. Speculators have made an average profit of more than 100 percent on HUD-guaranteed houses, according to Justice Department investigators.[26] Defaults on HUD mortgages have created hundreds of thou-

---

22. William Tabb, *The Political Economy of the Black Ghetto* (New York: Norton, 1970), pp. 13–14. Slum economics also makes arson profitable as buildings are put to the torch to collect the insurance and drive out low-income tenants. "Why It Pays to Burn," *Dollars and Sense*, January 1980, pp. 7–9.

23. *America's Housing Needs* . . . ; also the HUD study reported in the *Progressive*, May 1976.

24. William Proxmire, *Uncle Sam: The Last of the Bigtime Spenders* (New York: Simon and Schuster, 1972), pp. 196–97.

25. *New York Times*, April 19, 1976; also Hugh T. Miller, "Private Accumulation and Socialized Costs: The Side Effects of 'Easy Mortgages,' " unpublished monograph, American University, 1981.

26. G. C. Thelen, Jr., "Homes for the Poor: The Well-Insured Swindle," *Nation*, June 26, 1972, pp. 814–16; *Guardian*, June 16, 1976.

sands of abandoned domiciles in our cities and have been a major factor in the spread of urban blight.

Housing developments built with federal assistance are often rented to low-income people for a year or two in order to qualify for federal funds, then renovated or sold to other private owners who, not held to the original contract, evict the tenants and turn the units into high-priced rentals or condominiums. Many already sound houses are rehabilitated with federal funds so that landlords can then drive out the poorer residents and make a greater return on their investments.

At first glance we are confronted with a seemingly senseless state of affairs: HUD leaves blocks and blocks of empty shells standing while using funds to tear up and renovate inhabited, well-constructed buildings. Such a policy is irrational when measured against human and social needs, but the imperatives of the housing industry have less to do with *community* needs than with the *market* and *profit* needs of banks and developers. It is these latter considerations that guide the funding. In this sense, HUD's policy successfully serves the profit needs of the housing industry on its own terms.

Urban renewal is better described as "urban removal." By the power of eminent domain, the municipal or state government can do for investors what they could not do for themselves—namely, forcibly buy large tracts of residential areas from reluctant small owners and small businessmen, or from "far-sighted" speculators who, armed with inside information, buy up land in the "condemned" area for quick resale to the city at substantial profit. Then the city sells this land, often at less than the market value, to big developers, underwriting all investment risks on their behalf. The losses suffered by the municipality are usually made up by federal funds and constitute another multibillion-dollar public subsidy to private capital.[27]

The chairman of the National Commission on Urban Problems, former Senator Paul Douglas, concluded that "government action through urban renewal, highway programs, demolition on public housing sites, code enforcement and other programs has destroyed more housing for the poor than government at all levels has built for them."[28] Blacks, Latinos, and other minorities occupy a dispropor-

27. See Paul Baran and Paul Sweezy, *Monopoly Capital* (New York: Monthly Review Press, 1968), pp. 289–300; also Edward C. Higbee, *The Squeeze: Cities Without Space* (New York: Morrow, 1960).

28. Quoted in Michael Harrington, "The Betrayal of the Poor," *Atlantic*, January 1970, p. 72. The destruction continues: in 1981 the Michigan Supreme Court gave General Motors and the city of Detroit permission to demolish "Poletown," a stable working-class community of 3,400 inhabitants, in order to build a new Cadillac plant. Thus the power of the state is used to condemn the property of a weak private interest in order to serve a strong private interest. *Washington Post*, March 14, 1981.

tionate share of the nation's bad housing. According to one Senate report: "From 1960 to 1968, the percentage of non-whites occupying substandard housing actually increased from 22 to 33 percent."[29] Nor has that trend been reversed in the 1970s or 1980s.

The transportation system provides another example of how public resources are used to benefit the haves at the expense of the have-nots. High-income business air travelers are sumptuously subsidized while low-income persons, who "suffer from the most severe problems deriving from transportation," including pollution, congestion, and sheer lack of service, receive the least support.[30]

As mass-transit systems decline, a growing reliance is placed on the automobile, which in turn leads to a further decline in mass transit. The social costs of the automobile are staggering. About 45,000 people are killed on the highways each year and hundreds of thousands more are injured and maimed. More than 60 percent of the land of most U.S. cities is taken up by the movement, storage, and servicing of automobiles. Homes, schools, recreational areas, and whole neighborhoods are razed to make way for highways and parking lots. The single greatest cause of air pollution in urban areas is the automobile. As the number of cars grows, so do the revenues from the gasoline tax that go into the Highway Trust Fund. As more superhighways are built with these accumulated billions, the carnage, environmental devastation, and—just as significantly—the profits of the oil, auto, trucking, tire, cement, construction, and motel businesses increase. At the same time mass-transit systems—the most efficient, cleanest, and safest form of transporting large numbers of people—fall into further decay.

These developments are not a matter of stupidity or poor planning. In transporting people one railroad car can do the work of 50 automobiles. Railroads consume one-sixth the energy of trucks to transport goods. But these very efficiencies are what make railroads so *un*desirable to the oil and auto industries. For over a half-century the corporate response has been to undermine the nation's rail and electric-bus systems. For instance, in 1935 a once beautiful Los Angeles was served by one of the largest inter-urban railway systems in the

---

29. Senate Committee on Nutrition and Human Needs, quoted in "Rural Housing Famine," *Progressive*, April 1971, p. 8.

30. Robert Benson and Harold Wolman (eds.), *Counterbudget: A Blueprint for Changing National Priorities 1971–1976* (New York: Praeger, 1971), p. 157. In rural communities many low-income people and elderly "are isolated and immobile and face extreme difficulties in gaining access to jobs, health care and social services," according to a government study quoted in *Dollars and Sense*, October 1980, p. 18. One-third of all Americans are rural dwellers, but the government spends only 6 percent of its transportation dollars on rural areas.

world, covering a 75-mile radius with 3,000 quiet, pollution-free electric trains that carried 80 million people a year. But General Motors and Standard Oil of California, using dummy corporations as fronts, purchased the system, scrapped its electric transit cars, ripped up the tracks, tore down its power transmission lines, and placed GM diesel buses fueled by Standard Oil on Los Angeles's crowded streets. By 1955, 88 percent of the nation's electric-streetcar network had been eliminated by collaborators like GM, Standard Oil, Greyhound, and Firestone. In short time, city and suburban bus services were cut back and people had to rely increasingly on private cars. In 1949 General Motors was found guilty of conspiracy in these activities and fined the devastating sum of $5,000.[31]

Most municipal transit systems are funded by deficit spending with bond issues sold to wealthy individuals, banks, and business firms. In any one year, bondholders receive millions of dollars in interest, payments that force transit systems to cut services and raise fares as they go deeper into debt. What is called "public ownership" in transportation is really a system controlled by private bondholders, with tax-free, risk-free, high-yield dividends going to the rich, while the costs are paid by working people.[32]

What is true of public-transit systems is true of cities in general. Like the Third World debtor nations discussed in the previous chapter, cities are the victims of private "aid" and investment. Once in debt, a city must pay an increasingly large portion of its budget to service the debt. It has a difficult time finding adequate sources of revenue and must borrow still more. Speaking of New York City, Jack Newfield observed, "The banks acted like a drug dealer, and the city became a junkie. The banks made a pusher's profits, and the city got addicted."[33] New York City pays out more than 20 percent of its annual budget to service its debt. The further the city falls into debt, the greater the bargaining power of the banks to exact ever higher interest rates for each successive loan. In 1975 New York City faced bank-

31. Bradford Snell, "The Right to Travel," in Marcus Raskin (ed.), *The Federal Budget and Social Reconstruction* (New Brunswick, N.J.: Transaction Books, 1978), pp. 344–46.

32. A good example is the Chicago Transit Authority, which has a history of purchasing highly inflated bonds to buy up bankrupt private transit companies, after the companies have been milked by their investors. (The New York City subway system came under municipal ownership in the same way.) About $300 million will eventually be returned to bondholders who originally paid $138 million, a 220-percent profit from a "public, nonprofit" transit authority. See *Workers World*, September 26, 1975; also Si Gerson, "Politics of the Subway Fare," *Daily World*, June 27, 1981, p. 11.

33. Jack Newfield, "Who Killed New York City?" *New Politics*, Winter 1976, pp. 34–38.

ruptcy when it could not sell a half-billion-dollar bond issue needed to pay off earlier debts that had fallen due. The city was put in receivership by large creditors, led by David Rockefeller, who eventually formed the Emergency Finance Control Board to exercise final authority over all city expenditures.

In addition, most large municipalities pay much more in federal taxes than they receive in federal funds. This situation, plus an ever increasing debt burden, has a devastating impact on their economies. To "rescue" the cities from their plight, the federal government and the banks had a plan, first applied to New York and later used against other major urban centers: drastically cut services to the people. New York closed down day-care and drug-rehabilitation centers, health clinics, every venereal-disease clinic, senior-citizen centers, and summer park services for children; 43,000 city employees, including hospital workers, sanitation workers, firemen, and teachers, were laid off; hundreds of millions in new taxes were introduced; free tuition at City University was abolished; and the subway fare was raised again and again.[34]

This dreary story has been repeated in other municipalities where the question no longer is how the mayor will govern but whether the mayor can govern at all, now that banks and other businesses can directly dictate city programs. Sharing in none of the hardships suffered by ordinary citizens, the moneyed interests have profited handsomely from the crises of the cities, enjoying new tax abatements, greater public subsidies, and high-interest bonds that are virtually default-proof because they are backed by taxes drawn from a municipal budget that bankers themselves now control.[35]

At present, every indicator suggests that the urban crisis will deepen. The cities are caught in the squeeze of a capitalist system working its inexorable effect. The juxtaposition of private wealth and public poverty so frequently found in the United States is no mere curiosity. The two go together and reinforce each other. The profit imperatives of the private sector create maldistribution, want, and social dislocation. Confronted with these problems, the government works through the same private sector that is creating them, thereby doing little to prevent, and sometimes much to augment, the process of social disintegration.

---

34. *Ibid.*; and *New York Times*, May 26, 1976.
35. Ronald Berkman and Todd Swanstrom, "A Tale of Two Cities," *Nation*, March 24, 1979, pp. 297–99; David Moberg, "Unions Tackle 'Bankers' Budget," *In These Times*, June 4–17, 1980.

HEALTH AND SAFETY FOR NOBODY

Consumer protection is another area in which government efforts seem designed to advance the interests of private producers at the expense of the public. Adulterated products, unsafe additives, false advertising, overpricing, planned obsolescence, and shoddy and dangerous commodities are common evils of the consumer market.[36] The Food and Drug Administration (FDA) tests but 1 percent of the millions of yearly shipments of marketed drugs and foods, yet issues reassuring pronouncements on the safety of numerous products whose effects are highly suspect. One study found that the FDA approved drugs for public use on the basis of "inaccurate and unreliable" data supplied by the drug industry itself.[37]

Drug companies spend $1 billion a year to promote sales—three times more than they spend on research and development. Physicians admit that drug salespeople, who know almost nothing about medicine, are their first source on the uses of new drugs. The World Health Organization reports that one-fourth of all people who die in hospitals are killed by drugs and that this is probably because physicians are unfamiliar with the dangers of the new drugs they freely prescribe.[38]

FDA claims that it has not enough staff to police the food, drug, and cosmetics industries, but its agents spend much time investigating, prosecuting, and stigmatizing as "faddists" health-food innovators whose ideas about nutrition and medicine are critical of established drug and food enterprises.[39]

Given the way health care is organized, money often makes the difference between life and death. Many sick people die simply because they are poor and cannot afford medical assistance. Millions live in areas where treatment is unavailable except at substantial fees,

---

36. David Sanford (ed.), *Hot War on the Consumer* (New York: Putnam, 1969); Jacqueline Verrett and Jean Carper, *Eating May Be Hazardous to Your Health* (Garden City, N.Y.: Doubleday, 1974).

37. Hundreds of hair dyes, food additives, cosmetics, and drugs marketed for years without FDA testing have been linked to cancer and birth defects. *New York Times*, July 22, 1973, and March 18, 1975; Verrett and Carper, *Eating May Be Hazardous* . . . p. 18; Alan Anderson, "Neurotoxic Follies," *Psychology Today*, July 1982, pp. 30–42.

38. Amanda Spake, "The Pushers," *Progressive*, April 1976, p. 18; T. A. Vonder Haar, "Cures That Can Kill," *Progressive*, April 1977, pp. 40–43. According to a Senate subcommittee about 30,000 people die each year from adverse reactions to medical drugs. Other studies place the toll as high as 100,000. See Bernard Winter, M.D., "Health Care: The Problem is Profits," *Progressive*, October 1977, p. 16.

39. Omar Garrison, *The Dictocrats' Attack on Health Foods and Vitamins* (New York: Arco, 1971); Richard Harris, *The Real Voice* (New York: Macmillan, 1964).

or where public hospitals are closing down for lack of funds.[40] Doctors' fees have more than doubled in recent years, and hospital bills have been rising five times faster than the cost of living; yet people are not receiving better care, only more expensive care, and in some areas the quality of care has deteriorated.[41]

Doctors organize their practices as would any entrepreneur, incorporating themselves to avoid taxes, selling services to customers at a price the market will bear. Some physicians have cheated Medicaid and Medicare of hundreds of millions of dollars by consistently overcharging for services and tests, by fraudulently billing nonexistent patients or charging for services not rendered or unneeded.[42] An estimated two million unnecessary operations are performed yearly, costing about $4 billion and leading to the death of some 10,000 patients and an undetermined number of disabilities.[43]

Senator Edward Kennedy found during his Senate investigation of health care that throughout the nation people were denied emergency treatment because they could not show proof of ability to pay, others were ejected from hospitals in the midst of an illness because they were out of funds, others were bankrupted by medical bills despite supposedly "comprehensive" insurance coverage, and still others suffered iatrogenic illness and death in hospitals that were below minimal standards of cleanliness, safety, and staffing.[44]

Medical care, much like agriculture, housing, and transportation, is organized as a publicly subsidized private enterprise whose purpose

---

40. Ellen Cantarow, "Always Too Little, Sometimes Too Late," *In These Times*, May 13–19, 1981, pp. 8–9, 15.

41. "Doctors' Incomes Are Still Going Up—And Up," *New York Times*, March 26, 1978; *Washington Post*, December 6, 1981; John Ehrenreich, "Where the Health Dollar Really Goes," *Nation*, May 15, 1982, pp. 586–89. Another exploitative enterprise is the nursing-home business, a highly profitable, government-subsidized industry guilty of widespread mistreatment of the elderly. See Mary Adelaide Mendelson, *Tender Loving Greed* (New York: Knopf, 1974); also Bruce Vladeck, *The Nursing Home Tragedy* (New York: Basic Books, 1980).

42. *New York Times*, June 25, 1976, and April 16, 1978. A Ralph Nader task group estimates that surgeons overcharge about $3 billion a year. The group found differences of as much as $1,560 for the same surgical procedures in the Washington, D.C., area: *Washington Post*, March 30, 1979; see also Marcia Millman, *The Unkindest Cut: Life in the Backrooms of Medicine* (New York: Morrow, 1976).

43. *New York Times*, January 26, 1976; also the report of the House Subcommittee on Interstate and Foreign Commerce in the *Guardian*, January 10, 1979. Surgeons are more likely to operate on a patient if the latter has medical insurance. For a critique of standard medical practice see Ivan Illich, *Medical Nemesis* (New York: Pantheon, 1976).

44. Edward Kennedy, *In Critical Condition* (New York: Simon and Schuster, 1972). For good analyses of how medicine is shaped by capitalism see Lesley Doyal, *The Political Economy of Health* (Boston: South End Press, 1980); and E. Richard Brown, *Rockefeller Medicine Men* (Berkeley, Calif.: University of California Press, 1979).

is to make a profit for those who control it. Dr. Bernard Winters points out:

> Just as our defense budget has little to do with actually defending the United States, so our health budget has little to do with maintaining the health of the American people. It is a costly, wasteful mechanism for funneling money to a sprawling medical industry that encompasses not only physicians and hospitals but equipment manufacturers, pharmaceutical corporations, banks and insurance companies. The impulse that drives this industry is the same that drives every industry—the maximization of profit.[45]

As past efforts have shown, unless medical service is reorganized on a nonprofit basis, additional public monies poured into the medical system will only lead to more profits for the few, not better services for the many.[46]

One cannot talk about the health of America without mentioning the awesome problem of occupational safety. Every year more than 14,000 workers are killed on the job; another 100,000 die prematurely and 400,000 become seriously ill from work-related diseases, such as black lung, brown lung, and cancer. All told, one out of every four workers suffers from occupationally connected diseases. Five million on-the-job injuries occur each year.[47] The daily casualties suffered by working people are many times higher than what Americans sustained during the Vietnam war, yet no one is organizing mass protests against this industrial slaughter.

Industrial work may always carry some degree of risk, but the present rate of attrition is due less to unavoidable happenstance than to inadequate safety standards, speed-ups, and lax enforcement of codes. Thus almost all coal-mine accidents could be avoided if proper safeguards were employed. Work conditions in U.S. mines are among the worst in the world. In Poland, a large exporter of coal, accidents

---

45. Winter, "Health Care: The Problem is Profit."

46. A conservative organization like the American Medical Association (AMA) opposes government regulation of medicine and calls for "free individual choice." Yet the AMA uses the coercive powers of government to maintain a monopoly control over medical practice. Thanks to AMA political pressure, in many states people are forbidden by law to choose alternative forms of treatment such as osteopathy, homeopathy, and naturopathy.

47. Jeanne Stellman and Susan Daum, *Work Is Dangerous to Your Health* (New York: Pantheon, 1973); Rachel Scott, *Muscle and Blood* (New York: Dutton, 1974); Daniel Berman, *Death on the Job* (New York: Monthly Review Press, 1978); Joseph Page and Mary Win O'Brien, *Bitter Wages* (New York: Grossman, 1973); Joel Makower, *Office Hazards* (Washington, D.C.: Tilden Press, 1981).

are rare because of good safety measures. This same emphasis on worker safety is found in other noncapitalist countries.[48]

The overriding imperative of capitalist production is to maximize profits. One way is by cutting the costs of maintaining safe conditions. Accidents produce even greater costs in the form of lost income, hospital bills, and disability support. But these losses are shifted onto the government or onto the workers themselves. Company money spent not on production for profit but on safety for the worker is money spent in the worker's interest rather than the owner's. Describing the conditions on a big commercial farm in California, one farm worker testifies:

> I began to see how everything was so wrong. When growers can have an intricate watering system to irrigate their crops but they can't have running water inside the houses of workers. Veterinarians tend to the needs of domestic animals but they can't have medical care for the workers. They can have land subsidies for the growers but they can't have adequate unemployment compensation for the workers. They treat him like a farm implement. In fact, they treat their implements better and their domestic animals better.
>
> . . . Stoop labor is very hard on a person. Tuberculosis is high. And now because of the pesticides, we have many respiratory diseases. The University of California at Davis has government experiments with pesticides and chemicals, to get a bigger crop each year. They haven't any regard as to what safety precautions are needed.[49]

For years labor has fought for laws to protect workers. In 1970 Congress finally created the Occupational Safety and Health Administration (OSHA). In the chemical industry alone, OSHA regulations brought a 23-percent drop in accidents and sickness, averting some 90,000 illnesses and injuries at a yearly cost to industry of $140 per worker. Yet the agency's resources are vastly insufficient for the task it is supposed to do. OSHA has only enough inspectors to visit each workplace once every 80 years; workplace standards to control the tens of thousands of toxic substances are issued at the rate of less than three a year.[50]

---

48. According to the *New York Times*, October 26, 1974; also the report of a West Virginia miner who visited the Soviet Union, *United Mine Workers Journal*, November 1, 1974.

49. Quoted in Studs Terkel, *Working* (New York: Pantheon, 1972), p. 12; see also Paula DiPerna, "Pesticides' High Cost: Maimed Farmworkers," *Guardian*, July 1, 1981, p. 7.

50. Matt Witt and Steve Early, "The Worker As Safety Inspector," *Working Papers*, September/October 1980, p. 21; also Ruth Ruttenberg and Randell Hudgins, *Occupational Safety and Health in the Chemical Industry* (New York: Council on Economic Priorities, 1981).

Even this modest effort was too much for business. Under the Reagan administration OSHA began removing protections, exempting 75 percent of all firms from routine safety inspections, and weakening safety standards and the worker's right to see company medical records.[51] As coal-mine safety inspections decreased under the new policy and mine owners paid less in fines, mining accidents increased. In 1981, 153 miners were killed, the highest death rate in six years.[52]

Under existing workers compensation laws only about 10 percent of the millions of injured and disabled workers actually get any benefits, and the average compensation is less than half the amount specified by state laws. The law usually places the burden of proof on the injured worker, provides no penalties when industry withholds or destroys evidence, and allows long delays in procedure that work against the unemployed and the penurious. The law also imposes a statute of limitation, which makes it difficult to collect on diseases that have a long latency period.[53] And recipients of workers compensation forfeit their right to sue a negligent employer. The workers compensation program is "a parody of its name. Rather than compensating those maimed on the job, the system shields industry from financial liability for its workplace practices and its promiscuous use of hazardous chemicals and thereby undermines the country's efforts to improve worker safety and health."[54]

ON BEHALF OF POLLUTION AND RADIATION

When it comes to pollution, everyone is at fault—or so we have been repeatedly told by commentators who fail to distinguish between littering (a nuisance and an eyesore) and pollution (a lethal chemical assault on all forms of life). These same commentators fail to distinguish between the few who actually do the polluting and the many of us who suffer the effects. Like sin, pollution is regularly denounced but vigorously practiced. Strip mining and deforestation by coal and timber companies continue to bring ruination to millions of acres. For the sake of short-term profits, the ecological balance of our rivers and seas is being systematically destroyed by the dumping of industrial wastes and by spills from tanker accidents and offshore drillings amounting to about 1.3 billion gallons of oil each year. Agribusiness

51. Report by the AFL-CIO Department of Labor, reprinted in *AFL-CIO News*, May 1, 1982.
52. *Washington Post*, February 15 and 20, 1982.
53. Mark Reutter, "Workmen's Compensation Doesn't Work or Compensate," *Business and Society*, Fall 1980, pp. 39–44.
54. *Ibid.*, p. 39.

sprays tons of poisonous herbicides and pesticides onto our land—with little control exercised by government. Industry introduces some one thousand new chemicals into the marketplace annually, adding to the 70,000 already there, few of which are covered by safety regulations. *Over 1 billion pounds of chemicals are released into the environment each day*, causing one government study to conclude that the air we breathe, the water we drink, and the food we eat are now perhaps the leading cause of death in the United States.[55]

Consider also the newly discovered dangers of ground pollution. Some 77 billion pounds of toxic chemical wastes, produced yearly by the manufacturers of plastics, pesticides, and other such commodities, are buried in makeshift sites—only to leach over wide areas and contaminate billions of gallons of ground water. Whole residential areas, such as the Love Canal neighborhood in Niagara County, New York, have suffered contamination as the underground toxins percolate into homes and play areas, causing a startling number of cases of birth defects, miscarriages, headaches, liver and kidney abnormalities, epilepsy, and cancer. At least 51,000 sites across the country pose serious health hazards to communities, farmlands, and livestock.[56]

Then there is kepone, an insecticide more poisonous than DDT that destroyed a multibillion-dollar fishing and seafood industry after being dumped into the James River and Chesapeake Bay by Allied Chemical, putting 3,000 people out of work and threatening premature death to hundreds of contaminated workers and their families. There is dioxin, one of the deadliest of all chemicals, used as a defoliant in Vietnam and as a herbicide in the United States, sprayed on American pasture lands and forests, and even used as a weed killer in residential areas and an additive in certain laundry solutions, causing birth deformity, miscarriage, and cancer. There is acid rain, a deadly combination of pollutants, resulting from the industrial and automobile combustion that rises into the atmosphere and deposits itself over much of North America and Scandinavia, damaging farm crops, for-

---

55. Michael Brown, *Laying Waste: The Poisoning of America by Toxic Chemicals* (New York: Pantheon, 1980); James Ridgeway, *The Politics of Ecology* (New York: Dutton, 1970). For accounts on pesticides and oil spillage see *New York Times*, July 31, 1975, and January 2 and 5, 1977; Dorothy McGhee, "The Secret Killers," *Progressive*, August 1977, p. 26; *Washington Post*, September 12, 1980, contains a summary of the U.S. Surgeon General's report on toxic chemicals in the environment. Evidence is accumulating that human-made carcinogens could be the cause of almost all cancer. See Lewis Regenstein, *America the Poisoned: How Deadly Chemicals Are Destroying Our Environment, Our Wildlife and Ourselves* (Washington, D.C.: Acropolis, 1982).

56. Brown, *Laying Waste*; David Weinberg, "Breakdown: Love Canal's Walking Wounded," *Village Voice*, September 9–15, 1981; *New York Times*, November 16, 1980, and January 2, 1981; *Washington Post*, June 23, 1980.

ests, lakes, and buildings, endangering wildlife and human life. There are carcinogenic plastic products, dyes and cosmetics, lead and mercury poisoning, microwave radiation, PCB, and DES.[57]

Pollution continues unabated because it is profitable for the polluters. Production costs are cheaper when industrial wastes can be dumped into the environment. Rather than instituting costly controls and safety tests of products, industry passes the social and human costs on to the public in the form of ecological devastation, illness, and death. The expense of alleviating the effects of this destruction is taken up by the government and the public. The costs of cleaning up rivers, lakes, and land, the costs of disposing of industrial effluents (which compose 40 to 60 percent of the loads treated by municipal sewage plants), the costs of developing new water sources (while industry and agribusiness consume 80 percent of the nation's daily water supply), the costs of maintaining public recreational facilities, and the costs of seeking to restore individual health do not enter the accounts of industrial firms but are taken out of the earnings of working people in the form of taxes.[58]

In response to the growing public outcry, government has been forced to take some action on environmental issues. In 1970 Congress passed the Clean Air Act, which has saved an estimated 14,000 lives a year and over $21 billion in health, property, and vegetation damage, compared with the $17 billion in compliance costs. Similarly, the Clean Water Act of 1972 has brought improvements to a number of our rivers and lakes. Nevertheless, the government's overall record is dismal. Congress voted to allow the Environmental Protection Agency (EPA) to put chemical compounds on the market before their safety is proved. In July 1982 the government finally set up waste disposal and storage standards, which, while better than nothing, were still criticized by environmental groups as "weak" and insufficient.[59]

---

57. *New York Times*, May 6 and December 27, 1977; Daniel Zwerdling, "Chemical Catastrophes," *Progressive*, February 1977, pp. 15–18; Barry Weisberg, *Beyond Repair* (Boston: Beacon Press, 1972); Barry Commoner, *The Politics of Energy* (New York: Knopf, 1979). Increased use of pesticides often *causes* serious infestations of pests by eliminating their natural enemies and creating generations of insects more resistant to chemical controls. In the last 30 years pesticide use in the United States has increased twelvefold and crop losses to insects have almost doubled. See Robert Van Den Bosch, *The Pesticide Conspiracy* (Garden City, N.Y.: Doubleday, 1978). Some farmers have come to realize the enormous expense and destructive effects of pesticides and chemical fertilizers (which harden the soil and diminish the yield) and are getting better-than-average yields with organic farming. *Washington Post*, April 16, 1982.

58. See Robert Howard, "The Killing Ground," *In These Times*, September 9–15, 1981.

59. Quoted in the *New York Times*, January 2, 1981.

Conservatives within the Reagan administration, in eager alliance with big-business interests, sought to weaken or abolish almost all environmental protections because they were supposedly too costly to industry. A study done by the EPA, however, reveals that government and industry regularly exaggerated the costs of complying with environmental rules by anywhere from 137 to 200 percent.[60]

In 1971 the President's Council on Environmental Quality estimated that the cost of cleaning up the nation's air, water, and ground pollution would amount to some $105 billion, less than military appropriations for one year.[61] Business claims that environmental protection means a loss of jobs. In fact, the recently spawned pollution-clean-up industry has created more jobs than have been eliminated.

Government's approach to pollution, as with its approach to most other problems, hews closely to three principles: (1) pollution control must not compete with the basic profit interests of business and must be accommodated to the capitalist production system rather than developing alternative systems; (2) most of the costs of pollution control are to be borne by the public rather than by the plutocracy; and (3) the companies that pollute the most get the most; hence, the 1969 Tax Reform Act gives the big corporate polluters the big clean-up subsidies and big tax credits. In sum, at times the polluter is rewarded rather than punished.[62]

Another menace to health and safety is nuclear power. A major accident at a nuclear plant could kill as many as half a million people and contaminate an area the size of California—and there have been some frightfully close calls.[63] Reactors employed by the military are even more dangerous than commercial reactors and account for half

---

60. The report is summarized in the *Guardian*, July 2, 1980. For Reagan's assault on environmental regulations see *Washington Post*, May 26, 1981, and *New York Times*, May 1, 1981. Consider the case of Gulf Resources and Chemical Co., which made $25 million in profits in 1980 but refused to spend $880,000 to clean up a smelting plant. When the company threatened to close the plant, EPA and OSHA granted 5-year delays on worker safety and emission standards. *Guardian*, October 7, 1981.

61. *Newsweek*, August 16, 1971.

62. As of 1982, companies could buy "pollution credits" from other firms in the same way they could buy tax credits. Thus Borden Chemical paid B. F. Goodrich to let it put 25 tons of hydrocarbons into the air in Goodrich's name and at a great savings to Borden. Since Goodrich is cleaner than the law requires, Borden's dirt became Goodrich's and no one had to clean up the toxic emissions. *In These Times*, June 2–15, 1982, citing a report from *Forbes*.

63. Such as the near disasters in Idaho Falls, Idaho; Detroit; Hanford, Wash.; Brown's Ferry, Ala.; Rochester, N.Y.; and other places. The accident at Three Mile Island in Pennsylvania was distinctive in that it received national press coverage; see *New York Times*, April 8–13, 1979; also John Fuller, *We Almost Lost Detroit* (New York: Crowell, 1976); Ralph Nader and John Abbotts, *The Menace of Atomic Energy*, rev. ed. (New York: Norton, 1979), pp. 94–96. On the construction errors of the Diablo Canyon reactor see *New York Times*, October 1, 1981.

of all radioactive waste and 99 percent of all high-level wastes.[64] Contaminating leakages and breakdowns are common occurrences, there having been some 4,000 mishaps in 1981, according to the Nuclear Regulatory Commission (NRC).[65] The radioactive emissions resulting from the mining, milling, storage, and shipment of nuclear materials are far in excess of "permissible" levels established by the NRC. No one has ever demonstrated there *is* such a thing as a "permissible" level of radioactive leakage. The best scientific evidence indicates that *any* amount of emission can damage health and genetic structure.[66] Extraordinarily high rates of cancer, birth deformities, and deaths have been found among populations residing within 15 miles of nuclear plants.[67]

Nuclear wastes, some of which remain radioactive for 250,000 years, are building up in the soil and in the silt of rivers. The nuclear industry has no long-term technology for safe waste disposal. Millions of gallons of corrosive wastes are buried at sites throughout the country in tanks that have a life expectancy of less than fifteen years, and much waste has already leaked into surrounding areas. Hence, the Cheyenne River in South Dakota now contains "tons of radioactive material," much of which contaminates the ground water in local communities.[68]

Nuclear plants built in the 1970s are already deteriorating dangerously because of corrosion and embrittlement, and, like the Three Mile Island reactors, they may have to be shut down permanently. As of now no safe technology exists for entombing or decontaminating old nuclear plant sites.[69]

---

64. "Military Nuclear Wastes: The Hidden Burden of the Nuclear Arms Race," *Defense Monitor*, report by the Center for Defense Information (Washington, D.C., 1981).

65. *Nation*, February 6, 1982; John Gofman and Arthur Tamplin, *Poisoned Power* (New York: Signet, 1971); Anna Gyorgy et al., *No Nukes* (Boston: South End Press, 1979), pp. 99 ff. Nuclear plants are so hazardous that insurance companies refuse to handle them.

66. Nader and Abbotts, *Menace of Atomic Energy*, pp. 72–81. A White House Task Force estimated in 1979 that over one million Americans have already become victims of "low-level" radiation: *Potomac Alliance Newsletter* (Washington, D.C.), October 1979.

67. *New York Times*, April 10, 1979; Ernest Sternglass, "The Three Mile Island Fallout," *In These Times*, March 12–25, 1980, p. 19.

68. *Progressive*, August 1980, p. 11; *New York Times*, July 12, 1978; *Washington Post*, October 26, 1981.

69. Fred J. Cook, "The Case of the Nuclear Turkeys," *Nation*, January 2–9, 1982; Virginia Witt, "What To Do With Old Nuke Power Plants?" *Guardian*, February 24, 1982. There is not even a safe system of transporting wastes. During the next 20 years as many as 300,000 truck shipments of contaminated wastes will pass over U.S. highways close to populated areas and other vehicles, vulnerable to leakage and accident: *Washington Post*, February 4, 1982.

The nuclear industry is dominated by a few corporate giants who draw billions from the federal treasury for production costs and uranium price supports. The more expensive things get, the more the contractors rake in. And nuclear energy is the most expensive and least efficient large-scale method of producing electricity.[70] The federal government has spent millions promoting nukes, publicizing the false notions that nuclear energy is safe and cheap, and repeatedly suppressing findings by its own scientists that demonstrate to the contrary.[71] While cutting back on other energy and conservation programs, the Reagan administration in 1983 scheduled a 6-percent increase, to $1.7 billion, in the nuclear-industry budget for 1983.

The government spends almost nothing on alternative fuel sources such as solar, geothermal, and tidal energies. Much of the federal money for solar-energy development has gone to Westinghouse and General Electric, the two major nuclear-reactor builders, who, not surprisingly, announced that solar-energy technology is not yet commercially viable—although hundreds of thousands of people around the world are already relying on solar heating devices.[72]

In the energy field as elsewhere we discover the basic contradictions between our human values and our economic system: the social need to conserve energy and use it rationally as opposed to the corporate need to get people to consume expensive forms of energy in greater quantities in order to maximize profits; the human need for safe, clean energy sources versus the corporate need for profitable energy markets, no matter how lethal they may be. We can expect a continued deterioration in the quality of our environment until (1) the drive for profits is curbed and capital is invested for social purposes, (2) a comprehensive energy conservation program is developed for industrial society, and (3) alternative forms of production like solar energy and organic farming are developed.

To conclude this chapter: a large part of the domestic budget appears to be spent on worthwhile things; indeed, *some* of these monies reach the needy; some clinics, food programs, and child-care centers help the have-nots. But despite the expenditure of large sums, most government programs are designed to maintain private capital accumulation even at a cost to human life and ecology. At great cost to the working populace in the form of high taxes and neglected services, the government absorbs all or most of the expenses and financial risks of

---

70. David Moberg, "Nuclear Power Costs Too Much," *In These Times*, May 13–19, 1981, summarizes a report by Komanoff Energy Associates.

71. *New York Times*, November 10, 1974; Gyorgy et al., *No Nukes*, pp. 92–94.

72. Gyorgy et al., *No Nukes*, pp. 225–95.

various programs, while the private contractor or creditor pockets all the profits. When financial crises intensify because of economic recession, the burdens of austerity are shifted more heavily onto those at the bottom who are least able to defend their interests.

8

Law and Order: The Double Standard

In response to decades of struggle by democratic forces, government has been obliged to expend billions for social programs, the bulk of which is concentrated in a few large but insufficient services like Social Security, Medicare, and welfare payments to the poor. (The other human services programs, while vast in number, remain minuscule in size and funding by federal standards. The primary function of these expenditures is to ameliorate the conditions of want—so as to take the edge off popular discontent and avoid more serious challenges to the politico-economic system. But government does not rely solely upon spending programs to keep people quiescent. There are sterner measures. Besides the carrot, there is the stick. Behind the welfare bureaucracy, there stand the police, courts, and prisons.

Since we have been taught to think of the law as an institution serving the entire community and to view its representatives—from the traffic cop to the Supreme Court justice—as guardians of our rights, it is discomforting to discover that laws are often written and enforced in the most tawdry, racist, class-oriented, and sexist ways.

THE PROTECTION OF PROPERTY

Far from being a neutral instrument, the law belongs to those who write it and use it—primarily those who control the resources of society. It is no accident that in most conflicts between wealth and

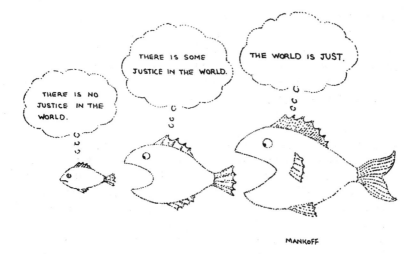

MANKOFF

worker the law intervenes on the side of the former. The protection of property is deemed tantamount to the protection of society itself and of benefit to all citizens, presumably even the propertyless. Those who equate the interests of property with the common interest seldom distinguish between (a) large corporate capital used for the production of profit and (b) consumer-use possessions like homes and personal articles. Most political conflicts are concerned with the distribution and use of (a), not (b).

The very definition of what is and is not lawful contains a class bias. Hence, the theft of merchandise from a neighborhood store is unlawful, while the theft of the store itself and the entire surrounding neighborhood by investment speculators, bankers, and public officials is hailed as an act of civic development.

The law's proximity to capital and its distance from labor can be seen in the curriculum of the average law school: one learns corporate, tax, insurance, and realty law; torts and damages; and even labor law chiefly from the perspective of those who own the property. Owners, trustees, and landlords have "rights," but workers, students, consumers, and tenants have troublesome "demands." In most instances, crime is defined by law as something that the have-nots commit against the haves. Under the law, management may call in the police to lock out workers, but workers cannot call in the police to drive out management. University trustees may bring in the police to suppress striking students, but students cannot call on the police to control unaccountable trustees. Landlords can have the police evict rent-striking tenants, but tenants cannot demand that police arrest rent-gouging landlords. Low-income residents soon learn that laws dealing with the collection of rents, eviction of tenants, and protection of property are swiftly enforceable, while those dealing with flagrant violations of building and safety codes, rent overcharging, and the protection of people go unenforced.[1]

The biases written into the law, which reflect the often unjust property relations of the society, are compounded by the way the law is enforced. Even when the letter of the law is on their side, working people have little else going for them. Although they are in greatest need of legal protection, they are least likely to seek redress of grievances through the courts, having neither the time nor the money. And when they find themselves embroiled in court cases, it is almost always at the initiative of bill collectors, merchants, or landlords, who regularly use the courts as a means of asserting their property interests.

The law does little to protect us from business crime even though it is socially as damaging as other crimes, since it involves the health, safety, and earnings of millions of workers.[2] Ralph Nader estimated that each year orange-juice companies steal more money from the public by watering down their product than bank robbers steal from banks.[3] White-collar crimes like embezzlement, fraud, commercial theft, and business-related arson add 15 percent to the price of all goods and cost over $40 billion a year, or five times the cost of street crimes like robbery, burglary, and auto theft, according to U.S. Chamber of Commerce estimates. This figure excludes antitrust violations, which may add as much as $160 billion.[4] The U.S. Treasury loses up to $100 billion yearly in tax revenues from the unreported income of criminal operations and legal businesses, the worst offenders in the latter category being doctors.[5] Fraud in federal aid programs costs the public an additional $12 billion or more, most of which is pocketed by "relatively well-to-do doctors, pharmacists and businessmen who have contracted with the Government to provide services and then set out to defraud it intentionally and systematically."[6]

---

1. Stuart Nagel, "The Poor, Also, Want Law and Order," *Chicago Daily Law Bulletin*, April 26, 1968.

2. See the report *Corporate Crime* by the House Judiciary Subcommittee on Crime, 96th Congress, 2nd session (Washington, D.C.: U.S. Government Printing Office, 1980).

3. "Nader Report: Consumers Lose Billions to Invisible Bilk," *Crime and the Law* (Washington, D.C.: Congressional Quarterly, 1971), p. 21.

4. See statement by Rep. John Conyers (D.-Mich.) in the *Guardian*, December 20, 1978, p. 8; also *New York Times*, May 23, 1977.

5. Tristam Coffin reporting the comments of a Commissioner of Internal Revenue in the *Washington Spectator*, March 1, 1982.

6. *New York Times*, April 16, 1978.

The criminality of corporations, Edwin Sutherland concludes, is persistent, "like that of professional thieves."[7] Looking at seventy large corporations in the United States, he found that in several decades they had been convicted of an average of ten criminal violations each (a figure that greatly underestimates the actual amount of corporate crime, since most violations go unchallenged). Any ordinary citizen with such a conviction record would be judged a "habitual offender" deserving of heavy punishment. Yet the guilty companies were provided with special stipulations and negotiated settlements or were let off with light penalties.

Often companies are not even obliged to appear in court. They can file "consent decrees," which, in effect, say that the firm has done nothing wrong and promises never to do it again. Then the government's files are made confidential and all the evidence against the company is locked away. Persons seeking damages in civil suits must try to uncover the evidence on their own. Wealthy corporate criminals are separated administratively from ordinary offenders, facing "a far gentler disciplinary system composed of inspectors, hearing examiners, boards and commissions. . . . For the affluent, the loopholes are so abundant that it takes determination to avoid them."[8]

The law has been harsh toward labor and tender toward business. Courts will impose injunctions and massive fines to break strikes and cripple unions. A federal judge fined the United Mine Workers $5 million for failing to contain a wildcat strike by its rank and file over safety violations in the mines. A Teamster local was fined $5.8 million for a wildcat strike. Leaders of public-employment unions, including health workers and teachers, have been jailed up to one year for strikes deemed illegal.[9] In contrast:

1. A group of oil companies were indicted for fixing prices and creating artificial scarcity. The evidence compiled by the Justice Department was detailed and devastating, but Federal Judge Royce Savage dismissed the case as based on "hearsay" without bothering to hear the defense. A year later Savage became a top executive at one of the indicted companies.

---

7. Edwin Sutherland, *White Collar Crime* (New York: Holt, Rinehart & Winston, 1949), pp. 210–22. Sutherland found three-fourths of all banks were violating the banking laws. See also Sarah Carey, "America's Respectable Crime Problem," *Washington Monthly*, April 1971. A *Fortune* (December 1980) survey finds a "surprising number" of major corporations involved in criminal conduct, with more than one in ten convicted or admitting guilt in cases involving price fixing, criminal fraud, illegal political contributions, antitrust violations, bribery, and kickbacks. The violators include ITT, U.S. Steel, Pepsi, Allied Chemicals, and DuPont.

8. Senator Philip Hart, "Swindling and Knavery, Inc.," *Playboy*, August 1972, p. 156.

9. *Guardian*, June 14, 1978.

2. Gulf Oil, the principal party in another price-fixing cartel that cost utility customers millions of dollars, was allowed to plead no contest to a misdemeanor and fined $40,000.

3. The average fine against companies with serious workplace safety violations, according to Representative George Miller (D–Cal.) is $239, a figure not likely to terrorize Wall Street.

4. By making false representations about its financial standing and by pleading poverty, U.S. Steel for years cheated the government, the public, and its own workers out of millions of dollars in wages, tax write-offs, depreciations, subsidies, and import protections. Then in 1981, the supposedly impoverished company came up with a $6-billion kitty to buy Marathon Oil. The government made no investigation.

5. A Justice Department inquiry into mine-safety regulations revealed a consistent pattern of nonenforcement by federal judges, who regularly postpone civil penalty cases that would force mine owners to pay fines for safety violations.[10]

Nonenforcement of the law is common in such areas as price fixing, restraint of trade, tax evasion, occupational safety, environmental and consumer protection, child labor, and minimum wages. In the early 1960s, when liberals took hold of the Justice Department, the government started making an effort at prosecuting such white-collar crimes as overseas bribery and security fraud. But given the high-powered legal defense that business can buy, convictions have been difficult. Furthermore, federal judges are usually drawn from the same social strata as businessmen and are reluctant to treat them as common criminals, relying instead on mild sanctions and admonitions. So penalties have remained light, a typical sentence being one year of unsupervised probation and a six-month suspended sentence. Meanwhile, price fixing and other monopolistic practices remain everyday occurences, adding heavily to both business profits and inflation.[11]

"Crime in the suites" may be due less to the venality of executives and more to the nature of the profit system. Many business people have argued that their illegal actions were not designed to line their pockets with someone else's money but were done "under pressure to

---

10. On the cases above see Burton Wolfe, "The Judge Who Saved the Oil Companies," *San Francisco Bay Guardian*, January 9–16, 1975; *Washington Post*, September 17, 1979; *Workers World*, December 4, 1981; *Guardian*, December 1, 1976.

11. Joe Sims, "The Prosecution of Price-Fixing," in Mark Green and Robert Massie, Jr. (eds.), *The Big Business Reader* (New York: Pilgrim Press, 1980), p. 51.

get their profits up, or because the competition forced them to it."[12] In any case, the decision in 1981 by the conservative Attorney-General William French Smith to concentrate Justice Department efforts on "street crime" and give little or no attention to organized rackets and white-collar crime should help make life easier for both the underworld and the upper class.[13]

CRIMINAL ENFORCEMENT: UNEQUAL BEFORE THE LAW

Looking at the criminal-law enforcement process, we find that various racial, sexual, political, and class factors help determine the kind of treatment accorded an individual from the time of arrest to the time of imprisonment.

Arrest

An arrest is not only the first step in the enforcement process, it is often a punishment in itself, leading to incarceration, legal expenses, psychological intimidation, and sometimes loss of job. Many people arrested are never charged or convicted of anything—which indicates that frequently the purpose of arrest is to intimidate and immobilize persons who have broken no law (e.g., political demonstrators and inner-city residents). Police have the power to jail anyone for up to three days without pressing charges.

The class and racial prejudices of society and police can help determine who gets arrested and who does not. "If you are stopped by the cops for weaving boozily through late-night traffic, you will be far wiser to be a Congressman in a large new car than an unemployed hod carrier in a 1950 Chevrolet with one fender missing."[14] A study of 1,700 persons weighted toward the upper-income brackets found that 91 percent admitted (after being guaranteed anonymity) to having committed at least one felony or serious misdemeanor including car

---

12. *Ibid.*, pp. 50–51. At the same time, the boys at the top *do* line their pockets: the systemic pressures *for* corporate crime rarely work *against* personal interests.

13. Dan Moldea, "Reagan Administration Officials Closely Linked to O.C.," *Organized Crime Digest*, February 1982, pp. 1, 5–11; Tim Wheeler, "Reagan 'Crime War,' " *Daily World*, September 30, 1981.

14. Russell Baker's column, *New York Times*, September 14, 1974; also Robert Lefcourt (ed.), *Law Against the People* (New York: Random House, 1971).

theft and burglary. None had ever been arrested.[15] The notion that crime is the special practice of the poor is false.

Charges

Every arrest situation has enough ambiguity to allow authorities some discretion in determining charges. Whether a situation is treated as "disorderly conduct" or "mob action," "aggravated battery" or "attempted murder," depends somewhat on the judgment of the law enforcers, both police and prosecutors, and their feelings about the suspect.

A factor sometimes determining the seriousness of the charges is the degree of injury *sustained*, not inflicted, by the arrested person. Police are inclined to bring heavier charges against someone they have badly beaten—if only to justify the beating and further punish the "offender." The beating itself is likely to be taken as evidence of guilt. "I cannot believe a state trooper would hit anyone for no reason," announced one judge in a trial involving a college professor who had been repeatedly clubbed by troopers while participating in an antiwar demonstration.[16]

Bail and Legal Defense

After being charged and booked, the suspect is held in jail to await arraignment. At arraignment the judge has the option of doing anything from releasing the defendant on his own recognizance to imposing a bail high enough to keep him in jail until his trial date—which might come a couple of years later—as was the fate of numerous Black Panthers[17] arrested and held on bonds of $100,000 and $200,000. Even if found innocent—as was the case of the New York and New Haven Panthers—the defendant will have suffered the immense costs and anxieties of a trial and an extended imprisonment. This "preventive detention," commonly employed against large numbers of people rounded up during urban disturbances, allows the state

---

15. Jessica Mitford, *Kind and Usual Punishment: The Prison Business* (New York: Vintage, 1974). The *victims* of street crime are overwhelmingly poor people, particularly inner city Blacks and Latinos, according to a Law Enforcement Assistance Administration study discussed in the *Guardian*, June 7, 1978.

16. Michael Parenti, "Repression in Academia: A Report from the Field," *Politics and Society*, 1, August 1971, pp. 527–37.

17. The Black Panthers are a Black leftist group that advocated socialist revolution during the late 1960s and early 1970s.

to incarcerate and punish individuals without having to convict anyone of a crime.[18]

One study found 73 percent of all indigent people arrested were denied pre-trial release as opposed to 21 percent of "respectable," middle-class persons.[19] Most of the people held in county and municipal jails have been convicted of no crime but are awaiting either a trial or hearing.[20] Brought into court directly from jail, a defendant is more likely to be convicted and more likely to be sentenced to a longer term than someone free on bail, whose lawyer can point to his law-abiding life since the original arrest.[21] Poor people also are more likely to be persuaded to plead guilty to reduced charges (plea bargaining).[22] Ninety percent of all defendants plead guilty without a trial; of the other 10 percent, more than half are convicted of something. This statistic hardly fits with the image of "coddled" criminals and "softhearted" courts propagated by the get-tough advocates.

Lawyers, Juries, and Judges

Like medical service, legal service in our society best serves those who can pay for it. The corporate executive who has the $400,000 for top legal assistance experiences a different treatment from the law than the poor person with a court-appointed lawyer who will have little time for the defendant, sometimes seeing him for the first time on the day of his trial. Public defenders often provide able legal service, but because of insufficient funds, disproportionate numbers of arrests in low-income areas, and other problems, they are overworked, understaffed, and often demoralized. Many indigents, especially in the lower courts, are deprived of a lawyer, being encouraged by judges to waive their right to counsel.[23]

---

18. See Jerome Skolnik, "Judicial Response in Crisis," in Theodore Becker and Vernon Murray (eds.), *Government Lawlessness in America* (New York: Oxford University Press, 1971), p. 162; also Herman Schwartz, "Bad Time in the Bail Jail," *Nation*, June 30, 1979, pp. 782–84.

19. Stuart Nagel, "Disparities in Criminal Procedure," *UCLA Law Review*, 14, August 1967, pp. 1272–1305.

20. 1970 National Census, statistics reproduced in *Crime and the Law*, p. 12.

21. Ralph Blumenfeld, "The Courts: Endless Crisis," *New York Post*, May 15, 1973; also Nagel's "Disparities in Criminal Procedure."

22. Contrary to the belief that plea bargaining gives the criminal an easy way out, most defendants end up with sentences as severe as any they would have received had they stood trial; so finds a Washington, D.C., study of street-crime convictions. *Morning Union* (Springfield, Mass.), August 21, 1978.

23. Jeffrey Reiman, *The Rich Get Richer and the Poor Get Prison* (New York: Wiley, 1979); also Jerold Auerbach, *Unequal Justice* (New York: Oxford University Press, 1976).

In most states, prospective jurors are chosen from voter registration rolls or county tax lists, which underrepresent racial minorities, women, young people, and low-income people. Officials do not pick randomly but usually choose a jury pool from street lists and neighborhoods they favor. The few cultural or political nonconformists who might survive this process and get called for jury duty are usually weeded out at selection time by the peremptory challenges of the prosecutor.[24]

As portrayed in the media, judges are distinguished-looking persons possessed of a wise and commanding air, calming courtroom passions with measured admonitions, showing fear and favor toward none, yet capable of a certain compassion for the accused. Turning from Hollywood to reality, we discover that judges are often arrogant, corrupt, self-inflated persons. After observing courtroom procedures for two years, Jack Newfield concluded that along with "personal venality" many judges were marked "by cruelty, stupidity, bias against the poor, short tempers or total insensitivity to civil liberties."[25] Investigations by a special prosecutor in 1975–76 in New York found widespread sale of judgeships to moneyed persons. Once on the bench, these individuals commonly sold "not guilty" verdicts to businessmen, crime-syndicate bosses, and corrupt politicians brought before them.[26]

A study of state courts found that judges were more inclined to send poorly educated, low-income persons to prison and less likely to give them suspended sentences or probation than better educated, higher-income persons convicted of the same crimes.[27] A study of courts in Seattle, Washington, found that persons who convey the appearance of a middle-class status are treated by judges as more worthy of leniency than those who by dress or attitude do not seem to value "the same things which the court values."[28] One study found that persons convicted of burglary, auto theft, and small-time drug dealing

---

24. Persons called for jury duty have been subjected to secret background checks by IRS agents as U.S. prosecutors have sought to exclude those with "antigovernment biases": *New York Times*, April 19, 1976.

25. Jack Newfield, "The Next 10 Worst Judges," *Village Voice*, September 26, 1974, p. 5; also Charles Ashman, *The Finest Judges Money Can Buy* (Los Angeles: Nash, 1973). A majority of federal judges in the South and in major cities outside the South belong to all-White segregated clubs: *Washington Post*, September 20, 1979.

26. The special prosecutor, Maurice Nadjari, launched 500 investigations and got 79 convictions and 296 indictments against judges and other officials. His efforts proved so troublesome to the powers that be that he was eventually fired by Governor Carey.

27. Nagel, "Disparities in Criminal Procedure."

28. The study is reported in Ray Bloomberg, "Court Justice Tied to Middle-Class Values," *Quaker Service Bulletin*, 54, Spring 1973, p. 8. This and other studies have found that both poverty and race are the big factors in court bias.

received harsher sentences than persons convicted of security fraud, bribery, and embezzlement.[29] One judge imposed a small fine on a stockbroker who had made $20 million through illegal stock manipulations and, on the same day, sentenced an unemployed Afro-American to one year in jail for stealing a $100 television set from a truck shipment.[30]

One observer of New York City courts concluded: "Favoritism to the prosecution is the rule among most judges here."[31] Judges not only identify with the prosecutor, they frequently *are* former prosecutors, having made their way to the bench via the office of district attorney or state attorney or via the Justice Department. The image we have of an orderly, even-handed system of justice does not coincide with the picture drawn by Newfield:

> Routinely, lives are ruined and families broken by 30-second decisions. Some judges quit work at 2:00 P.M. to play golf, while some 8,000 men and women presumed innocent under the Constitution wait months for trials in the city's overcrowded detention jails. . . . Legal Aid lawyers defend 50 poor clients a day with not a second for preparation. . . . Civil cases almost always get decided in favor of the landlord or businessman, or city agency.[32]

Penalties and Prisons

Echoing a favorite conservative theme, President Nixon once complained of "softheaded judges" who showed more concern for "the rights of convicted criminals" than for innocent victims.[33] But an American Bar Association study found that, far from coddling criminals, American judges imposed much severer sentences than jurists in Western European countries. Sentences of over five years for felony convictions are rare in Europe but common in the United States, where jail terms sometimes have an eighteenth-century quality about them. In Norfolk, Virginia, a man received ten years for stealing eighty-seven cents; a youth in Louisiana got fifty years for selling a few ounces of marijuana, and another in Virginia got forty years for

---

29. *Guardian*, October 18, 1972; also Whitney North Seymour, Jr., *Why Justice Fails* (New York: Morrow, 1973).

30. Leonard Downie, Jr., *Justice Denied* (New York: Praeger, 1971).

31. Ralph Blumenfeld, "The Courts: Endless Crisis," *New York Post*, May 15, 1973.

32. Jack Newfield, "New York's Ten Worst Judges," *New York*, October 1972, p. 32.

33. See the response by Marvin Frankel, "An Opinion by One of Those Soft-headed Judges," *New York Times Magazine*, May 13, 1973, p. 41. Judge Marvin Frankel describes judges as "arbitrary, cruel and lawless" in the ways they determine sentences; see his *Criminal Sentences* (New York: Hill and Wang, 1973).

doing the same.[34] When a five-time petty offender stole $73, a Dallas court gave him 1,000 years in prison. And a New Orleans judge gave a four-time petty offender life imprisonment for possession of a stolen television set.[35]

If any criminals are coddled, they are likely to be of the white-collar variety. Thus the notorious Dr. Bernard Bergman, convicted of swindling people out of millions of dollars in the nursing-home business, was sentenced to four months. And two wealthy contractors, who received $1.2 million in phony government contracts for work they never did, were ordered to pay $5,000 in fines and do 200 hours of "community service."[36] Likewise, a major heroin dealer, with previous arrests and important mob connections, was given a conditional discharge. A big-time racketeer had felony charges against him dismissed by a compassionate judge known for his stern rulings against counterculture youths and Blacks.[37]

Consider how the law was applied in these cases:

1. A White, unemployed farm worker, Thomas Boronson, and his family were eating one meager meal a day from money earned by selling their blood. Boronson and a friend, Lonnie Davis, took over a welfare office in a desperate attempt to get the several hundred dollars owed by the state to the Boronsons. The youngest of Boronson's six children was a sick infant who had been denied medical care because the family could not pay. Boronson and Davis were arrested and convicted of kidnapping, assault, and robbery, even though the welfare workers refused to press charges. They were sentenced to nine and seven years respectively.[38]

2. A Black student, Philip Allen, joined a small crowd watching a drunk smash a store window. When the police arrived, they jumped Allen with drawn pistols, according to witnesses. The police claim that Allen, who is 5' 3" and weighs 135 pounds, overpowered several of them, seized one of their guns, shot three of

---

34. *Washington Star*, April 29 and 30, 1975.

35. Gary Cartwright, "The Tin-Star State," *Esquire*, February 1971, p. 100; Reiman, *The Rich Get Richer* . . .

36. *Washington Post*, May 30, 1979; see also Herbert Jacob, *Justice in America*, 2nd ed. (Boston: Little, Brown, 1972).

37. Herbert Mitgang, "The Storefront Lawyer Helps the Poor," *New York Times Magazine*, November 10, 1968. The leniency and neglect with which influential mobsters are treated by the law help explain why organized crime continues to be a growth industry. See Jonathan Kwitny, *Vicious Circles: The Mafia in the Marketplace* (New York: Norton, 1979).

38. *Guardian*, May 26, 1976.

them—killing one—without leaving any fingerprints on the gun and then was captured by the other two. No witnesses saw Allen holding a gun at any time. The police most likely shot each other in the scuffle. Allen was convicted and given a life sentence.[39]

3. A bus carrying Black children was attacked by a White mob. According to the bus driver, a gun was fired from the crowd; it missed the bus but killed a White youth. The Black students were forced out of the bus by police. One of them, Gary Tyler (age fifteen at the time), was arrested for "interfering with an officer" when he objected to the deputy sheriff's putting a gun to the heads of students. The police "found" a gun in the bus, which turned out to be a police revolver with no fingerprints. Tyler was charged with murder, convicted by an all-White jury, and sentenced to die. The prosecution's case rested on two witnesses, both of whom later recanted, charging that police had coerced them into fingering Tyler. The police had threatened to take one witness's child away from her and charge her as an accessory to the murder. The judge refused to grant a new trial.[40]

Those convicted of crimes must then face our "correctional institutions." American prisons are overcrowded, unhealthy places, breeding violence, rape, and disease. Prisoners who protest the inhumane conditions are likely to be subjected to extreme forms of harassment and retribution. At Atmore and Holman prisons in Alabama, forty-five of the inmates who organized for better prison conditions were indicted on charges. In a year and a half, five of the leaders had been killed by prison guards.[41] The prison population in America is about 50 percent White, 47 percent Black, and 3 percent other. *Blacks tend to get substantially longer prison terms than Whites convicted of the same crimes, even when the Black person is a first-time offender and the White person a second- or third-time offender.*[42]

---

39. Communiqué from the Philip Allen Defense Committee of the First Unitarian Church, Los Angeles, California, April 1976.

40. *Workers World*, May 21, 1976. Tyler's death sentence was commuted to life imprisonment. He exhausted all appeals and is serving his time. On the problem of justice for Blacks, see Haywood Burns, "Can a Black Man Get a Fair Trial in This Country?" *New York Times Magazine*, July 12, 1970, pp. 5, 38–46; also the case of Earl Charles in Marc Levinson, "Like a Checker on a Checkerboard," *Nation*, December 16, 1978; and the case of Eddie Morant in *Washington Post*, November 27, 1981.

41. *Ithaca* (N.Y.) *New Times*, February 1, 1976. On prison conditions see Mitford, *Kind and Usual Punishment*; also Alan Dershowitz, "Let the Punishment Fit the Crime," *New York Times Magazine*, December 28, 1975.

42. Frank L. Morris, "Black Political Consciousness in Northern State Prisons," paper presented at the National Conference of Black Political Scientists, New Orleans, May 1973; also *Denver Post*, May 1, 1977. On racial breakdowns see the 1974 and 1978 surveys by the National Prison Statistics Branch, U.S. Bureau of the Census.

During times of economic hardship, as poverty and crime increase, the corporate state has to operate more repressively. While unable to build enough decent housing for those it leaves impoverished, the plutocracy is building new prisons at the federal, state, and local levels. The U.S. government spends more money imprisoning one person for a year than the cost of a year's education at Harvard. The U.S. imprisons more people per capita than any industrial country in the world except South Africa.[43] By the early 1980s the Federal Bureau of Prisons was working hard to wipe out prison reforms won in the previous two decades of struggle for prisoners' rights.[44]

With a deepening recession, most states have reinstituted the severest of all punishments—the death penalty. Numerous arguments have been posed against the death penalty:

1. There are no data to support the idea that it is a deterrent to capital crimes.
2. It leaves no room for redress should the wrong person be convicted and executed; in effect, it assumes the infallibility of a very fallible enforcement process.
3. The state should not commit premeditated institutionalized murder.
4. The overwhelming majority of those on death row did not have effective legal assistance; most were represented by inexperienced, overburdened, and poorly financed court-appointed lawyers or public defenders.
5. The death penalty has been applied almost exclusively against poor Whites and racial minorities. "I don't know of a wealthy person ever executed in the United States," observes a former longtime warden of San Quentin prison.
6. The penalty is also arbitrarily applied. Some child-killers and cold-blooded "contract" murderers are paroled after doing ten or fifteen years of a life sentence, while a low-income White like John Spenkelink is executed for killing a man who had robbed, beaten, and raped him.[45]

---

43. Diane Feinberg, "Economic Crisis Fuels Prison Uprisings," *Workers World*, June 12, 1981.

44. Newsletter, National Committee to Support the Marion Brothers (St. Louis, Missouri), June 1982.

45. Hugo Adam Bedau (ed.), *The Death Penalty in America*, 2nd ed. (Chicago: Aldine, 1967); Ramsey Clark, "Rush to Death: Spenkelink's Last Appeal," *Nation*, October 27, 1979, pp. 400–403; the San Quentin warden is quoted in Peter Ross Range, "Will He Be the First?" *New York Times Magazine*, March 11, 1979. There are over 1,000 people on death row; 52 percent are White, 42 percent Black, 6 percent from other racial groups; almost all are low-income: *Washington Post*, June 13, 1982.

To sum up, poor and working-class persons, the uneducated, and the racial minorities are more likely to be arrested, less likely to be released on bail, more likely to be induced to plead guilty, more likely to go without a pretrial hearing even though entitled to one, less likely to have a jury trial if tried, more likely to be convicted and receive a harsh sentence, and less likely to receive probation or a suspended sentence than are mobsters, businessmen, and upper- and middle-class Whites in general. "The rich have little reason to fear the system and the poor have little reason to respect it."[46]

Women of upper-class social background are more likely to receive favored treatment at the hands of the law than are low-income or impoverished people of either sex, and in many cases White women receive better consideration than Black men. But race and class aside, women suffer legal injustices of their own.[47] In some states wives still have not achieved equality with their husbands in regard to consent in contracts and sharing of property. Incarcerated women are subjected to sexual exploitation by male guards and trustees. In one women's prison in Alabama there were eight births in one year, most of them the result of sexual assault by male guards.[48]

Every year thousands of women are hospitalized because of beatings from their spouses, yet the law is seldom enforced against husbands who batter their wives. The law also has yet to prove effective in protecting women from sexual harassment on the job or breaking down discriminatory employment and wage practices. Some of the largest corporations have admitted to a policy of paying women less for doing the same work as men.[49] Along with immigrant workers and child workers, women historically have served as a reserve army of labor, paid less so as to keep wage rates down for all workers. Women who have agitated for equal pay, prison reform, day care, lesbian rights, and legalized abortion have been the object of FBI and CIA surveillance.[50]

After years of struggle, working women have made some important gains, organizing themselves into unions as nurses, clerical workers, and factory employees. In noticeable numbers women are moving into professions and occupations previously thought "unsuitable" for them. Women have won maternity leave from several hundred

46. Hart, "Swindling and Knavery, Inc.," p. 162.
47. Karen De Crow, *Sexual Justice* (New York: Random House, 1974).
48. *Workers World*, March 5, 1976; Ann Jones, "Sex Exploitation Behind Bars," *Nation*, April 17, 1982, pp. 456–59.
49. Betty Friedan, *The Second Stage* (New York: Summit, 1981).
50. Letty Cottin Pogrebin, "The FBI Was Watching You," *Ms.*, June 1977, pp. 37–44.

corporations. And as women challenge traditional roles, more men are learning to share in child-rearing and family chores. These changes, however, have invited attacks from right-wingers who resist any form of gender and class equalization.

For homosexuals, also, the oppression practiced in the wider society is reflected and reinforced in the law and courts. In 36 states homosexual love is still punished under "sodomy" or "unnatural acts" laws, and gays who love each other can find themselves hustled off to jail or a mental institution for "treatment." In 1976 the Supreme Court ruled that states may prosecute consenting adults who commit homosexual acts in private. And in 1978 the Court upheld lower-court decisions that a teacher could be fired for no other reason than being a homosexual.[51]

---

51. *Doe* v. *Commonwealth's Attorney*, 425 U.S. 901 (1976); also *Gish* v. *Board of Education of Paramus, N.J.*, 434 U.S. 879 (1978); and *Gaylord* v. *Tacoma School Dis-*

In recent years "manly" thugs have assaulted and murdered gays in Arizona, Texas, New York, and California, to name a few places. In none of these cases did the killers serve time.[52] Both men and women have been discharged from the armed services because they were gay. Mothers have been denied custody of their children on the grounds that their lesbian preferences made them unfit parents.[53] Gay-rights organizers have been beaten and arrested by law officers in Detroit, Houston, New York, Seattle, and elsewhere, and gay bars have been raided by police.

Many of the gains won by homosexuals have come under attack by the "Christian" Right. Nevertheless the organized struggles launched by gays in recent years have succeeded in changing homophobic attitudes among many non-gay people, and progress has been made against discriminatory housing and employment practices.

POLICE TERROR: KEEPING THE OPPRESSED IN THEIR PLACE

No discussion of law and order would be complete without some mention of the police. Law enforcement represents the largest budget item of many local governments, yet the crime rate continues to rise. If the police have been largely unsuccessful against organized crime, they have not been idle in regard to workers, poor people, youth, racial minorities, and other elements that might prove troublesome to the interests of property and propriety. Studies show that racial minorities and low-income Whites have many more personal encounters with police brutality than middle-class White "respectables."[54] Consider these instances:

A 10-year-old Black boy walking with his foster father in Queens, N.Y., is killed by a plainclothes policeman who leaps from

---

trict, 434 U.S. 879 (1978). In states like Oklahoma any school employee can be fired merely for speaking in favor of gay rights.

52. Doug Ireland, "Open Season On Gays," *Nation*, September 15, 1979, pp. 207–10.

53. Clifford Guy Gibson and Mary Jo Risher, *By Her Own Admission* (Garden City, N.Y.: Doubleday, 1977); *New York Times*, November 22, 1979.

54. David H. Bayley and Harold Mendelsohn, *Minorities and the Police* (New York: Free Press, 1971), p. 122; Paul Jacobs, *Prelude to Riot* (New York: Random House, 1968), pp. 29–30. In one year in Houston 14 Chicanos—all unarmed—were murdered by the police under highly questionable circumstances, and in Los Angeles 28 people, mostly unarmed Blacks and Chicanos, were shot to death by police. *Guardian*, November 2, 1977, and February 22, 1978. The number of deaths at the hands of police increased in the 1970s by over 20 percent. Some 40 percent of the instances in which police discharged a weapon involved misdemeanors or even more minor offenses: see the various studies summarized in Brian Hudson, "Police Abuse and National Unrest," *Guardian*, June 25, 1980, p. 6.

his unmarked car without identifying himself, shouts, "Hey niggers!" and opens fire.

A Black teenager in Miami urinating against a factory wall is shot dead by an off-duty policeman who first claims self-defense, then says his gun went off accidentally.

A White man, finding his home surrounded by armed, unidentified men in Humboldt County, California (who turn out to be county police and narcotic agents raiding the wrong place), flees in terror out the back door and is shot dead.

A 12-year-old Chicano boy in Dallas, arrested as a burglary suspect, is shot through the head while sitting handcuffed in a patrol car.

A White, working-class youth is beaten to death by police in a paddy wagon in Cambridge, Massachusetts.

A Black, shell-shocked Vietnam veteran is killed by two police on a Houston street as he reaches into his pocket to take out a Bible.

A Chicano youth in Houston is taken to a secluded spot by police, beaten until unconscious, then thrown into a bayou to drown.[55]

Nor is police terror merely a matter of just "a few bad apples" on the force. Investigations of police departments in Philadelphia, Houston, Los Angeles, Milwaukee, Mobile, Miami, Newark, and elsewhere reveal that brutality is widespread and is often tolerated by department commanders.[56] The victims are almost always from low-income groups.[57] Few of the officers involved in fatal cases of brutality have ever been indicted for murder. Some have been suspended from the force, and a few have been tried for "justifiable homicide" or "manslaughter" and acquitted or given light sentences.[58]

The history of the labor movement in the United States reveals a pattern of police harassment and violence. From the earliest days of

---

55. For accounts of these and similar incidents see "Homicide Squad," *Inquiry*, July 7–21, 1980, p. 4; Joan Walsh, "Police Brutality Divides Milwaukee," *In These Times*, September 9–15, 1981, p. 6; Murray Kempton, "The Harlem Policeman," in Becker and Murray (eds.), *Government Lawlessness in America*, pp. 47–49; and issues of the *Guardian*, *Workers World*, and *Daily World*. Atrocities like these are seldom reported in the business-owned press.

56, *Guardian*, May 19, 1976; *New York Times*, March 2, 1975, and April 15, 1979; *Newsweek*, July 4, 1977; *In These Times*, September 9–15, 1981, and citations in previous two footnotes.

57. Albert Reiss, "How Much 'Police Brutality' Is There?" in Stephen David and Paul Peterson, *Urban Politics and Public Policy* (New York: Praeger, 1973), p. 282.

58. Sara Blackburn (ed.), *White Justice* (New York: Harper & Row, 1972). For recent cases: *Guardian*, March 18, 1981, and November 11, 1981; *Workers World*, May 22, 1981, August 28, 1981, and December 4, 1981; *Daily World*, December 16, 1981, and July 1, 1982.

industrial conflict to today, agents of the law have sided with the propertied and powerful, either looking the other way or actively co-operating when goons and vigilantes attacked union headquarters and pickets.[59] In recent years throughout the country, police in riot gear have attacked striking construction workers, factory workers, farm workers, truckers, and miners, arresting and badly injuring hundreds. Many workers have been imprisoned for resisting court injunctions against strikes and pickets. In Harlan County, Kentucky, a striking coal miner was shot to death by a scab, as was a farm worker in Texas. In Elwood, Indiana, within a period of a few months, seven strikers were shot by company goons. In all these instances police apprehended no one despite eyewitness evidence of the identity of the killers.[60]

The law and its enforcement agents do many worthwhile things. Many laws enhance public safety and individual security. The police sometimes protect life and limb, direct traffic, administer first aid, assist in times of community emergency, and perform other services with commendable dedication and courage.[61] But aside from this desirable *social-service* function, the police serve a *class-control* function—that is, they must protect those who rule from those who are ruled. And they protect the interests of capital from those who would challenge the inequities of the system. The profiteering corporate managers, plundering slumlords, swindling merchants, racist school boards, self-enriching doctors, special-interest legislators, and others who contribute so much to the scarcity, misery, and anger that lead to individual crimes or mass riots leave the dirty work of subduing these outbursts to the police. When the police charge picket lines—beating, gassing, and occasionally shooting workers—they usually are operating with a court injunction that allows them to exert force in order to protect the interests of the corporate owners.

The police confront dangers and social miseries of a kind most of us can only imagine. They deal with the waste products of an affluent, competitive corporate society: corpses in the street, back-alley muggers, pimps, child molesters, winos, heroin pushers, psychopaths, the ill-fed, the ill-housed, the desperate, and the defeated. The slums are not the problem, they are the *solution*; they are the way capital-

---

59. Richard Boyer and Herbert Morais, *Labor's Untold Story*, 3rd ed. (New York: United Electrical, Radio, and Machine Workers, 1972), *passim*.

60. For an analysis of the class function of the police see *The Iron Fist and the Velvet Glove: An Analysis of the U.S. Police*, 2nd ed., written and published by the Center for Research on Criminal Justice (Berkeley, Calif., 1977).

61. See Jill Freedman, *Street Cop* (New York: Harper & Row, 1981) for a compassionate photographic essay on the struggles of police at the street level to keep the victims of society from victimizing each other.

ism deals with the surplus people of a market economy. And for all they cost the taxpayer in crime, police, and welfare, the slums remain a source of profit for certain speculators, arsonists, realtors, big merchants, and others. But they do present problems of violence and social pathology that need to be contained. And that is the job of the police: to sweep protest and poverty under the rug—even if it takes a club or gun. Repressive acts by police are not the aberrant behavior of a few psychotics in uniform but the outgrowth of the kind of class-control function that law officers perform and rulers insist upon—which explains why the police are able to get away with murder.

Some police are aware of the class function they serve. Former Boston Police Commissioner Robert DiGrazia summed it up:

> We are not letting the public in on our era's dirty little secret: that those who commit the crime which worries citizens most—violent street crime—are, for the most part, the products of poverty, unemployment, broken homes, rotten education, drug addiction and alcoholism, and other social and economic ills about which the police can do little, if anything.
>
> Rather than speaking up, most of us stand silent and let politicians get away with law and order rhetoric that reinforces the mistaken notion that police—in ever greater numbers and with more gadgetry—can alone control crime. The politicians, of course, end up perpetuating a system by which the rich get richer, the poor get poorer, and crime continues.[62]

---

62. Quoted in *Parade*, August 22, 1976. Perhaps even in the best of circumstances there is a "criminal element" who will resort to violent and unlawful means to get what they want. Not all crime is a direct reaction to social deprivation. But a great deal of it is—which is why crime rates usually increase with poverty and unemployment.

9

Law and Order: The Repression of Dissent

Among those whom the law treats repressively are persons and organizations who oppose capitalism and advocate alternative economic orders. According to the view propagated by purveyors of the established ideology, capitalism is an essential component of Americanism and democracy. It follows that anticapitalists are antidemocratic, unAmerican, and a "subversive threat" to the national security, thus fair game for repression. The repression is directed against communists and other anticapitalists and eventually against anyone else who shows an active interest in progressive causes. Under the guise of defending democracy, security agencies often impose severe limitations on democratic rights.

REPRESSION FOR THE MANY

When directed toward social reforms that might benefit the working populace, the law usually proves too weak for effective change. But when mobilized against political dissenters, the resources of the law appear boundless, and enforcement is pursued with a punitive vigor that itself becomes lawless. Dissident groups have had their telephones tapped, their offices raided, and their records and funds stolen by law officers. Members of these groups have been threatened, maligned, beaten, murdered, or arrested on trumped-up charges, held on exorbitant bail, and subjected to costly, time-consuming trials that, whether won or lost, paralyze their leadership, exhaust their funds, and consume their energies. With these kinds of attacks, the government's message comes across loud and clear: people are not as free as they think. They may organize against government policies, but their public utterances and private behavior will be watched by one or more of the many security agencies. If they persist, they may encounter the repressive legal mechanism of the state. The law is a weapon used against people who challenge the class and social relations of the society.[1]

Consider some specific cases: the Black socialist Martin Sostre, long an opponent of heroin traffic in the ghetto, was convicted and sentenced to 30 years for dealing in heroin—on the sole testimony of a convict who subsequently admitted in a sworn statement that his testimony had been fabricated. The trial judge refused to believe his recantation. Sostre served nine years, mostly in solitary confinement. After much protest from progressive and humanitarian groups, the governor of New York granted Sostre amnesty.[2]

Then there was George Jackson. Sentenced as a youth to a long, indeterminate prison term for a relatively minor crime, Jackson became radicalized while in the penitentiary. He began organizing inmates and writing books about his revolutionary creed. For this he was placed in solitary for long periods and repeatedly beaten. Eventually he was shot dead by guards. At the trial of surviving Soledad brothers, an undercover FBI agent described the successful plans of the police to kill Jackson during what was to appear as an "escape attempt."[3]

Frank Shuford, a Black community activist and a socialist in Santa Ana, California, was organizing people to oppose poverty, drug pushers, and police complicity with the drug traffic until he was arrested for the shooting of two store clerks. At the time of the crime Shuford was home with family and friends. Neither clerk identified him as the gunman and no material evidence was presented against him. At his trial Shuford was branded a "revolutionary troublemaker" by the prosecution. His own lawyer conducted a strangely lackadaisical defense, neglecting to object to any of the district attorney's tactics. The lawyer later was appointed a district attorney immediately after Shu-

---

1. Note how the law was used against the antiwar movement; see Jessica Mitford, *The Trial of Doctor Spock* (New York: Knopf, 1969); and Jason Epstein, *The Great Conspiracy Trial* (New York: Vintage, 1971).

2. *New York Times*, December 25, 1975.

3. See George Jackson, *Soledad Brother* (New York: Bantam, 1970); also Eric Mann, *Comrade George: An Investigation into the Life, Political Thought and Assassination of George Jackson* (New York: Harper & Row, 1974); *Guardian*, April 21, 1976.

ford was found guilty by an all-White jury and sentenced to 30 years. In prison Shuford was drugged, beaten, denied medical care, and scheduled for a lobotomy. Only community pressure on his behalf prevented the operation from taking place.[4]

When a White mob invaded the Black community in Wilmington, North Carolina, setting fire to several buildings, police did nothing to stop them. But a year later, in connection with these fires, the Reverend Ben Chavis, along with nine other community activists, was arrested on charges of arson. (Chavis had been previously arrested on 78 separate trumped-up charges over a 3-year period and acquitted on all.) The "Wilmington Ten" were found guilty on the testimony of three persons, including two who were themselves facing long jail terms for an unrelated crime. All three subsequently recanted their testimony. Chavis was sentenced to 34 years, while the others received sentences of 29 to 34 years.[5]

Eddie Carthan was the first Afro-American mayor elected in Tchula, Mississippi, in a century and the first mayor to buck the local White plutocracy. He refused to appoint cronies of the big planters, refused bribes, and investigated the corruption of previous administrations. Carthan also started doing things for the poor Black majority; he began a nutrition program for the elderly and handicapped, a health clinic, day-care centers, and a housing rehabilitation program. In response, the Board of Aldermen, dominated by planter interests, cut his salary from $600 to $60 a month and barred him from his City Hall office. The governor had all federal funds to Tchula cut off, ending most of the mayor's programs. When Carthan retook City Hall with five auxiliary police, he was charged with assault, convicted on the testimony of a witness who later recanted, and sentenced to three years. After an exhaustive FBI investigation of Carthan, he was convicted of fraud (for authorizing an assistant to sign his name to a delivery receipt for day-care equipment) and sentenced to an additional four years. Then, almost a year after a Black alderman was robbed and murdered and the murderer caught and convicted, Carthan was charged for the same crime (supposedly he had plotted the whole thing). Facing seven years in the state penitentiary and a trial for

---

4. *Guardian*, September 24, 1975; Shuford Defense Committee *Newsletter*, January 1978. Shuford is serving the 30 years. The community youth organization he developed to deal with drug and employment problems and to administer breakfast programs has fallen apart.

5. Buffy Spencer, "North Carolina: Laboratory for Racism and Repression," *Outfront* (Amherst, Mass.), August 1976, p. 9. As of 1980 all ten were out on parole; Chavis was the last released after serving five years.

murder and robbery, the reform mayor of Tchula was sent to prison in 1982.[6]

Sostre, Jackson, Shuford, Chavis, and Carthan—dramatic instances from among numerous similar cases—all had much in common. They were Black progressives who wanted to make changes in the existing structure of wealth and power and who were subjected to legal lynchings. Their cases demonstrate how the law can be used in the class struggle by the class that writes and controls it—against the most oppressed elements of the working populace, the racial minorities.

The guardians of the law are quick to use unlawfully violent measures in the repression of dissent. This account of a police attack against a peace demonstration in New York in 1969 is typical of incidents that occur throughout the United States during political protests and labor conflicts:

> A number of policemen came charging into the crowd, many, but not all, with their clubs in hand raised to the levels of their heads. . . . I saw other people being beaten. Some were arrested and others were not. It appeared to me that the police were just beating people at random with no clear indication that the people they were attacking had committed an illegal act. I saw none of the people being attacked fight back or attempt to hit the police. Most attempted to protect themselves by covering their heads or tried to run.[7]

Of the one hundred or so murders of persons associated with the civil rights movement during the 1960s, almost all were committed by police and White vigilantes. Few of the murderers were caught; none was convicted of murder. From 1968 to 1971 police wrecked Black Panther headquarters in more than ten cities, stealing thousands of dollars in funds and arresting, beating, and shooting the occupants in well-planned, unprovoked attacks. More than forty Panthers were killed by police in that period. More than three hundred were arrested and many were imprisoned for long periods without bail or trial.[8]

In Orangeburg, South Carolina, three Black students were killed and twenty-seven wounded when police fired into a peaceful campus

---

6. John Wojcik, "The Incredible Frameup of Mayor Eddie Carthan," *World Magazine*, May 6, 1982, pp. 10–11.

7. Peggy Kerry, "The Scene in the Streets," in Theodore Becker and Vernon Murray (eds.), *Government Lawlessness in America* (New York: Oxford University Press, 1971), p. 61.

8. For the FBI's role in instigating and assisting in these police attacks see *Chicago Tribune*, April 20, 1976, and June 12, 1976.

demonstration. No guns had been seen among the students, and many students were shot in the back while fleeing.[9] In antidraft demonstrations in 1970, unarmed Black students at Jackson State were murdered by police. At Kent State University in Ohio, four White students were murdered and two maimed by National Guardsmen. In the latter two instances, the evidence gathered by government agencies clearly indicated that the lives of the law-enforcement officers and Guardsmen were never in danger. In both cases, state grand juries refused to indict the murderers but did indict demonstrators, including several who had been wounded.[10]

The list of killings could go on, but the pattern remains the same: law-enforcement agents have used lethal weapons against strikers, protesters, and political radicals, none of whom were armed, a few of whom were reported to be hurling rocks or making "obscene gestures." In almost every instance, an "impartial investigation" by the very authorities responsible for the killings exonerated the uniformed murderers and their administrative chiefs.

Political dissenters in the military are often meted out harsh treatment; they have been denied access to radical publications, confined to quarters, physically threatened, framed on trumped-up charges, courtmartialed, and incarcerated in the stockade.[11]

Similarly, persons who become politically active and rebellious in prison run serious risks. The rebellion at Attica State Penitentiary in 1971 against inhumane conditions demonstrates the point. Asserting that the uprising was the work of "revolutionaries," Governor Nelson Rockefeller (who had more to lose from a revolution than most people) ordered an armed assault. Blasting their way into the prison yard, troopers killed 34 inmates and 9 prison guards who were being held as hostages and wounded more than 100 other inmates. Not a

---

9. *New York Times*, December 12, 1968; also Jack Nelson and Jack Bass, *The Orangeburg Massacre* (New York: World, 1969). A federal grand jury refused to indict the highway patrolmen involved in the action.

10. I. F. Stone, "Fabricated Evidence in the Kent State Killings," *New York Review of Books*, December 3, 1970, p. 28. After much public pressure, the Justice Department indicted the Guardsmen involved in the Kent State killings. However, the judge threw the case out, arguing that the prosecution had proven excessive and unjustified force but had not shown the Guardsmen had acted with premeditation: *New York Times*, November 9, 1974. Guardsmen who admitted to having lied under oath in earlier grand jury investigations were never tried for perjury: *New York Times*, May 4, 1976, and May 7, 1978.

11. See Robert Sherrill, *Military Justice Is to Justice as Military Music Is to Music* (New York: Harper & Row, 1970). In contrast, American Nazis in the U.S. Army are treated well. Army regulations do not prohibit soldiers from joining the Nazi party and wearing the Nazi uniform when off duty. *New York Daily News*, October 26, 1977. (Regulations, however, do provide up to five years in prison and $10,000 fine for any soldier who joins a union.)

single gun was found among the prisoners. A Special Commission declared the assault to be "the bloodiest attack by Americans on Americans" since the 1890 U.S. Army massacre of Indians at Wounded Knee.[12]

Among those singled out for special oppression have been members of the American Indian Movement (AIM), a group that has persistently challenged the injustices accorded Native Americans. The case of Russell Means, AIM leader, is instructive. Within a five-year period, Means was pistol-whipped by a sheriff while getting out of a car; assaulted and arrested by tactical squad police because, as a spectator in court, he refused to stand when the judge entered; convicted of "rioting" and sentenced to four years because of the courtroom incident; faced with four other trials with threatened sentences of more than 110 years; shot in the back by a police agent while a candidate for election on an Indian reservation; shot again by a sniper as he rode in a car; arrested and charged with murder after visiting a bar to buy a six-pack of beer even though the dying victim told police that Means had not been in the bar when the shooting occurred; and forced out of a house he was visiting by unidentified armed men who shot and wounded him and another AIM activist "at close range in an execution attempt," as one witness put it. (These incidents occurred while he was under 24-hour FBI surveillance.) While serving the four years for the courtroom incident, Means was stabbed close to the heart by a White inmate in another unsuccessful assassination attempt.[13]

The state also has more subtle instruments of oppression than the club and the gun. One of these is the grand jury. Supposedly intended to weigh the state's evidence and protect the innocent from unjustifiable prosecution, the grand jury has usually been turned into its opposite—doing what the prosecution wants. A common device is to suspend the Fifth Amendment right against self-incrimination by granting witnesses immunity from prosecution. If they then refuse to testify, they can be imprisoned for contempt. The upshot is to turn people into involuntary informers regarding any conversation or activity to which they have been privy. The grand jury is often used to

---

12. Annette T. Rubinstein, "Attica Now," *Monthly Review*, January 1976, pp. 12–20.

13. *Workers World*, July 4, 1975, May 14, 1976, and February 9, 1979; *News and Observer* (Raleigh, N.C.), July 17, 1975. Numerous other Native American activists have been subjected to similar attacks and imprisonments. See *Milwaukee Courier*, May 28, 1981; *Seven Days*, April 11, 1977. Another AIM member, Dick Marshall, was convicted in the same barroom shooting involving Means by an all-White jury on the testimony of an FBI informer and several witnesses who have since changed their testimony. The shooting victim had not identified Marshall as the attacker. He is serving a life sentence at hard labor.

carry out "fishing expeditions" against dissenters to intimidate persons engaged in radical political activities and jail those who refuse to cooperate. People have been required to appear without benefit of counsel and without being told the nature of the investigation. They can be forced to answer any question about political ideas and associations with friends, neighbors, or relatives or face up to eighteen months in prison for refusing to do so.[14]

The powers of government have been applied against the opponents of capitalism in other ways. For years "loyalty and security" tests were used to deny public employment to people of leftist persuasion. Under the name of protecting the Constitution, lawmakers have tried to repeal First Amendment guarantees of free speech.[15] Anticapitalist dissenters encounter oppression within the private sector of society as well. Employees who agitate for better working conditions or enunciate unpopular opinions risk loss of job. At most universities students seldom get the opportunity to investigate the world from an anticapitalist viewpoint, since the bulk of their readings and almost all their instructors are either ignorant of, or hostile to, information and analysis that might reflect such a perspective. As has been the case in academia for over a century, socialist teachers are frequently not hired or are purged from faculty ranks.[16]

The government also protects us from ideas imported from abroad. In recent years scores of Marxist scholars, novelists, artists, performers, and union leaders have been denied visas and prevented from entering the United States to participate in cultural events and conferences to which they had been invited by private groups. Aliens who are "anarchists" or advocates of the "economic and global doctrines of communism" are banned by the McCarran-Walter Act.[17]

---

14. John Conyers, Jr., "Grand Juries: The American Inquisition," *Ramparts*, August/September 1975, p. 15; also Marvin Frankel and Gary Naftalis, *The Grand Jury* (New York: Hill and Wang, 1977); "Crime Victims," *Nation*, June 12, 1982, p. 706.

15. For recent attempts by Congress to deny employment to radicals see *Nation*, January 3–10, 1981, p. 6.

16. Ellen Schrecker, "Academic Freedom and the Cold War," *Antioch Review*, 38, Summer 1980, pp. 313–27; Michael Miles, "The Triumph of Reaction," *Change, The Magazine of Higher Learning*, 4, Winter 1972–73, p. 34; Michael Parenti, "Political Bigotry in Academe," *Chronicle of Higher Education*, January 21, 1980, p. 56.

17. Many thousands are prevented from visiting or emigrating to the United States each year because of these restrictions. John Rosenberg, "The Chaos of Immigration Policy," *Nation*, September 2, 1978; *New York Times*, March 10, 1977; Charles Mann, "The Dario Fo Affair," *Attenzione*, September 1980, p. 14. Americans are periodically prevented from visiting communist countries. For the latest restrictions on travel to Cuba see *New York Times*, April 20, 1982. Aliens such as Salvadoreans, Haitians, Northern Irish, and Filipinos, who have resisted and fled repressive regimes, have been deported back to their countries, often to face jail or death: *Washington Post*, January 31, 1982; *Los Angeles Times*, July 13, 1980.

When U.S. Ambassador to the United Nations Andrew Young remarked that "hundreds, perhaps thousands" of persons were in U.S. prisons because of their political beliefs and activities and not because of the crimes they were charged with, he was quickly silenced by President Carter. Indignant officials and media pundits assured the public that in the United States, unlike many other countries, there is no such thing as a political prisoner. In truth, considering only widely known cases, there has been a long history of American political prisoners: Eugene Debs and many hundreds of other socialists and radical IWW organizers were imprisoned during the First World War and in the Palmer raids immediately afterward. Then there were Sacco and Vanzetti, the anarchists executed for a crime they did not commit, and the mass arrests of socialists and pacifists who opposed both World War II and the Korean War, plus the scores of others jailed under the Smith Act, or those jailed for refusing to cooperate with congressional witch hunts during the McCarthy era.[18] During the Vietnam War, almost every New Left antiwar activist who occupied a position of national or even local leadership, and many who did not, were arrested at one time or another. Many stood trial or were jailed or went into exile or went underground.

At the time of Ambassador Young's remark in 1978, at least several hundred persons were incarcerated because of their political activities, many of them serving life sentences, including some twenty-five members of the Black Liberation Army; almost fifty AIM leaders; two dozen Black Panthers; a dozen Republic of New Africa persons (a radical Black separatist group); about twenty anti-Vietnam war resisters, including the Camp Pendleton 14; scores of Chicano, Black, and Puerto Rican activists, nationalists, and radicals, and a lesser number of White ones; and dozens of prison inmates who had been given additional sentences for their work with prisoners' rights groups.[19] As of 1982 most of the above were still in prison and others had joined them, such as the nine members of a Black anticapitalist group, MOVE, who were given 30 to 100 years for the slaying of a policeman during a predawn police assault on their commune,[20] and the

---

18. In 1950 an obscure Republican Senator Joseph McCarthy of Wisconsin began to make speeches charging that the State Department and other government agencies were infiltrated by communists. He helped generate an atmosphere of intimidation and hysterical red-baiting. Thousands of persons were hounded from their jobs in trade unions, the press, the universities, and the government. In late 1954, after McCarthy started attacking the leadership of the Republican party itself, the U.S. Senate censured McCarthy.

19. For a partial list see Peter Biskind, "Political Prisoners U.S.A.," *Seven Days*, September 8, 1978, pp. 22–25.

20. The defendants maintained that the slain policeman was killed by other police

ten members of the FALN, a Puerto Rican revolutionary group, who were given 55- to 90-year terms for "seditious conspiracy," weapons charges, and illegal interstate travel—although no evidence was presented linking them to any violent act.[21] Contrary to the image cultivated by officialdom, political prisoners are as American as apple pie.

AGENTS OF NATIONAL INSECURITY

At least twenty well-financed federal agencies (of which the FBI and the CIA are only the best publicized) and hundreds of state and local police units actively engage in the surveillance and suppression of dissenting groups. The Army employs an estimated 1,200 agents for *domestic* spying. Counterinsurgency methods developed by the government for use in other lands have been applied at home to combat racial minorities, student radicals, and striking workers.[22] The Justice Department's Law Enforcement Assistance Administration has poured more than $10 billion into research and law-enforcement hardware for state and local police, providing such things as wall-penetration surveillance radar, night-vision devices, television street-surveillance systems, SWAT squad assault training, and riot equipment.[23] The unrestricted adoption of surveillance technology by police moved one Rand Corporation engineer to speculate that "we could easily end up with the most effective, oppressive police state ever created."[24]

Police devote more time to radical groups than to mobsters. According to Illinois Police Superintendent James McGuire, there are more law officers throughout the country "on political intelligence assignments than are engaged in fighting organized crime."[25] Street gangs that confine their activities to robbery and rape have relatively

---

during the raid. The prosecution never established which, if any, of the nine fired the fatal shot. *Guardian*, August 26, 1981.

21. *Guardian*, March 11, 1981.

22. Frank Donner, *The Age of Surveillance* (New York: Knopf, 1980); Theodore Becker and Vernon Murray (eds.), *Government Lawlessness in America* (New York: Oxford University Press, 1971); *New York Times*, March 5, 1972.

23. Les L. Gapay, "Pork Barrel for Police," *Progressive*, March 1972, pp. 33–36.

24. Quoted in Robert Barkan, "New Police Technology," *Guardian*, February 2, 1972.

25. Quoted in Frank Donner, "The Theory and Practice of American Political Intelligence," *New York Review of Books*, April 22, 1971, p. 28*fn*. Some of these units, less active after the antiwar movement ended, have been reactivated to deal with the growing antinuclear movement and the supposed growth in "terrorist" organizations. However, FBI officials have admitted that terrorism in the United States by radical groups is not a big problem and is declining: *Washington Post*, February 21, 1981.

little trouble with the law. But should they become radicalized, as did the Devil's Disciples and the Young Lords in Chicago and New York during the late 1960s, they find themselves threatened and attacked by police. Perhaps one reason law officers cannot win the "war against crime" is they are too busy trying to contain the class struggle.

Making the world safe for capitalism is a massive enterprise. Government security agencies expend approximately $10 billion a year on intelligence and covert action at home and abroad. This is, at best, a rough estimate, since Congress has no exact idea how much money organizations like the CIA are spending or for what purposes.[26] A Senate subcommittee revealed that federal agencies maintain a total of 858 data banks containing about 1.25 *billion* files, mostly on individuals suspected of harboring unorthodox political views. Data on political dissenters are shared by federal, state, and local intelligence units and are sometimes fed to the press and to employers, landlords, and others who might have opportunity to harass the persons under surveillance.[27]

"Justice," said the late FBI director J. Edgar Hoover in 1970, "is merely incidental to law and order . . . but not the whole of it." Indeed, the whole of it, Hoover demonstrated on many occasions, is the preservation of the plutocratic status quo. In pursuance of that goal, the FBI launched a Counterintelligence Program (COINTELPRO) designed, in Hoover's words, "to expose, disrupt, misdirect, discredit, or otherwise neutralize" members and supporters of Black nationalist and radical groups.[28] Under COINTELPRO, initiated in the 1950s with White House authorization, the FBI has conducted hundreds of illegal burglaries against political organizations and individuals, stealing private files and documents, while denying any knowledge of such crimes.[29] Undercover agents have attempted to sabotage the legal operations of dissident groups and have fomented ideological divi-

---

26. See the House Select Committee report on the CIA, excerpted in *Village Voice*, February 16, 1976. CIA officials questioned by the committee refused to state the size of their budget.

27. *New York Times*, October 3, 1975. For a chilling case study of illegal and sinister attacks on a noted radical entertainer see Paul Robeson, Jr., and Gil Noble, *Of Malice Toward One: The Secret War Against Paul Robeson* (forthcoming).

28. Quoted in the *Village Voice*, September 9–15, 1981, p. 25.

29. *New York Times*, March 29 and June 24, 1976. FBI agents continued their illegal break-ins even after being ordered to stop by FBI director Kelly: *New York Times*, August 11, 1976. Despite disclosures of widespread criminal behavior by upper-level FBI officials, the Justice Department failed to take action: "Selective Prosecution: The Blind Eye of the U.S. Department of Justice," *Freedom*, May 1979, pp. 13–14. In 1980 two agents were finally prosecuted, fined $3000 and $5000 respectively, and pardoned by President Reagan the following year.

siveness and personal conflict within and among them.[30] As the *New York Times* noted: "Radical groups in the United States have complained for years that they were being harassed illegally by the Federal Bureau of Investigation and it now turns out that they were right."[31] Liberal organizations such as the Southern Christian Leadership Conference and Americans for Democratic Action have also been infiltrated and targeted for disruption.

The FBI has collected secret dossiers, conducted wiretaps, and carried out physical surveillance of White House political opponents,

30. *New York Times*, January 29, 1975, September 4, 1976, and November 22, 1977; *Chicago Tribune*, February 5, 1976; *Guardian*, June 24, 1981.
31. *New York Times*, November 24, 1974; also William Kunstler, "FBI Letters: Writers of the Purple Page," *Nation*, December 30, 1978, pp. 721, 735–40.

journalists, congressional representatives, and members of congressional staffs. The Bureau has infiltrated and spied on various labor unions in an attempt to brand them as "communist controlled" and has carried out, in cooperation with management, secret surveillances of union strike activities.[32] The FBI keeps a "security index" of some 15,000 persons, mostly members of anticapitalist groups, who are slated for arrest and detention in case of a "national emergency"—although the law authorizing this practice was declared unconstitutional.[33]

In 1982, to assure us that little had changed since J. Edgar Hoover's reign, FBI director William Webster denounced the National Lawyers Guild and other progressive and civil-rights organizations because they "produce propaganda, disinformation and legal assistance [that] may be even more dangerous than those who actually throw the bomb."[34]

In contrast to the way they treat the left, the FBI and the police have given a free hand to or have actually assisted right-wing extremists. The bureau provided information and encouragement to organizations like the Minutemen and the John Birch Society in their harassment campaigns against progressive groups. In San Diego, the FBI financed a crypto-fascist outfit called the Secret Army Organization (SAO), whose members were heavily armed with automatic weapons and explosives. All SAO activities, ranging from burglary and mail theft to bombings, kidnapping, assassination plots, and attempted murder, were pursued under the supervision of the FBI.[35]

Violence as such has never bothered the FBI or the police; it depends on who is using it against whom. Bureau agents infiltrated the Ku Klux Klan and took part in acts of racist terrorism and violence, including the killing of two civil-rights activists and the Birmingham, Ala., church bombing that took the lives of four Black children.[36] According to Justice Department documents, the FBI rarely acted to head off violent Klan attacks against Afro-American and civil-rights workers despite advance notice.[37]

---

32. *New York Times*, February 24, 1975. The FBI used its agents to break a Teamsters strike in San Francisco: *Guardian*, July 5, 1978. On the surveillance of journalists and congressmen see *New York Times*, December 4, 1975.

33. *New York Times*, August 3 and October 25, 1975. On political surveillance and repression consult issues of *The Public Eye* (P.O. Box 3278, Washington, D.C.), and *Rights*, publication of the National Emergency Civil Liberties Committee, New York.

34. Quoted in the *Daily World*, July 3, 1982.

35. *San Francisco Examiner*, January 11, 1976.

36. *New York Times*, February 17 and 18, 1980.

37. *Ibid.*; also *New York Times*, December 3, 1975; Patsy Sims, *The Klan* (New York: Stein and Day, 1978).

In 1974 when two Chicano socialists were killed by bombs planted in their respective cars, the FBI made no arrests. A powerful bomb wrecked the offices of several progressive and civil-liberties groups in New York, injuring three people; the police made only a perfunctory investigation. When a Cuban-American, who had led an organization seeking normalized relations between the U.S. and Cuba, was murdered in Puerto Rico and another who advocated closer ties with Cuba was murdered in Union City, N.J. (right-wing Cuban exiles had threatened the lives of both), the police and FBI took no action.[38] A right-wing Cuban exile group, Omega 7, claimed credit for some 21 bombings between 1975 and 1980 and for the murder of a Cuban diplomat in New York; the group escaped arrest in all but two of the bombing attacks.[39] When shots were fired into Socialist Workers Party headquarters in Pittsburgh, almost killing one person, the police did not even bother to investigate.[40] The Unidos Bookstore in the East Los Angeles Chicano community was bombed twice. An American Nazi group publicly claimed credit for the first attack, but police failed to arrest anyone. A progressive bookstore in Venice, California, was the target of a fire bomb. Police arrived a half hour after being called. No arrests were made.[41] After a series of threats, an antinuclear organizer was shot dead in Houston and an assistant was seriously wounded; police came up with not a clue.[42] On her way to a meeting with a *New York Times* reporter, union activist Karen Silkwood was killed in a mysterious car crash; evidence suggested that her automobile had been forced off the road by another vehicle. The papers she had in the car exposing Kerr-McGee for radiation safety negligence were never recovered. Silkwood had been subjected to previous threats and dangers, but police said her death was just another auto accident.[43]

In 1979 Klan and Nazi members fired upon a nonviolent rally organized by the Communist Workers Party in Greensboro, North Carolina, killing five and wounding several others. The attack was recorded on videotape by a television crew covering the rally. The murderers were found not guilty by an all-White jury. The five victims had all been active in community and union organizing in the area.

---

38. *Miami Herald*, May 3, 1979; Jeff Stein, "Inside Omega 7," *Village Voice*, March 10, 1980, pp. 1, 11–14.
39. Stein, "Inside Omega 7"; *Cuba Update* (publication of the Center for Cuban Studies), October 1980, p. 3.
40. *Guardian*, February 4, 1981.
41. *Guardian*, December 12, 1973, and March 12 and May 21, 1975.
42. *New Age*, July 1979, p. 10.
43. Howard Kohn, *Who Killed Karen Silkwood?* (New York: Summit, 1981).

Further investigation revealed that the massacre could not have occurred were it not for the undercover federal and local police agents who recruited the Klan and Nazis for the attack, provided automatic weapons, and directed the group to the site of the rally.[44]

In addition to the FBI there are local police "red squads" operating throughout the country. Investigations of red squads in cities like Detroit, Chicago, New York, Washington, Indianapolis, and Baltimore reveal the same dismal record of unlawful burglaries and wiretapping, infiltration of groups engaged in no illegal activity, aid to right-wing terrorist organizations, and attacks against the left.[45]

Federal, state, and local police collaborate with security forces employed by corporations to spy on and harass union organizers and strikers. There are one million police in the United States, only half of whom are sworn to uphold the law; the rest are employed by private companies and are engaged in the surveillance and harassment of organized labor, peace, environmental, minority, and civil-liberties groups that might prove troublesome to business.[46] Secret files on over 100 million Americans are kept by private firms.[47]

Then there is the Central Intelligence Agency. With a legal mandate to act only as an overseas intelligence-gathering agency and prohibited from domestic spying, the CIA nevertheless has been heavily involved in extensive domestic activities, including wiretapping and break-ins, against Americans engaged in protest activities. In addition:

1. For 20 years the CIA opened the mail of private citizens. (When the FBI found out about this illegal practice, it became an active participant.)
2. The CIA admitted to maintaining surveillance on members of Congress and infiltrating congressional campaign organizations.

---

44. Michael Parenti and Carolyn Kazdin, "The Untold Story of the Greensboro Massacre," *Monthly Review*, November 1981, pp. 42–50. Hundreds of Nazi war criminals have lived unmolested by the law in the United States, some of them employed by U.S. security agencies: see Howard Blum, *Wanted: The Search for Nazis in America* (New York: Quadrangle, 1977).

45. *Progressive*, April 1977; *Guardian*, March 30, 1977, and April 8, 1981; *People*, June 11, 1979, pp. 89–94 for the interview with ACLU investigator Linda Valentino. Among the sinister organizations the Chicago police "Red Squad" has kept under surveillance are the World Council of Churches, the League of Women Voters, and the Parent-Teachers Association: *Atlanta Journal*, January 9, 1981.

46. George O'Toole, *The Private Sector: Rent-a-Cops, Private Spies and the Police-Industrial Complex* (New York: Norton, 1978); Jim Hougan, *Spooks: The Haunting of America* (New York: Morrow, 1978).

47. James Rule, *Private Lives and Public Surveillance* (New York: Schocken, 1974).

3. The CIA has given sums of money to private corporations but has refused to disclose the purpose of such payments. The agency owns a complex of companies whose profits are invested or used as it sees fit.

4. The CIA has conducted surveillance of news reporters to determine their information sources regarding government practices. It has infiltrated various news services and admits that at least forty overseas American correspondents are in its pay.

5. The CIA has worked closely with right-wing Cuban exiles and notorious foreign intelligence agencies of such countries as Chile, South Korea, and Iran (under the Shah), allowing them to terrorize and even murder exiles from these countries residing in the U.S.

6. The CIA propagates its cold-war, counterinsurgency view of the world in the groves of academe, keeping hundreds of college professors on its payroll, conducting its own intern and resident-scholar programs, and having hundreds of its agents participate in academic conferences.

7. The CIA has infiltrated and financed student, labor, scientific, and peace groups, has secretly financed the writings of "independent" scholars, and has subsidized publishing houses and periodicals. It has financed research programs on mind-control drugs conducted at leading universities.

8. The CIA has equipped, trained, and supported local police forces even though the National Security Act of 1947 states that the CIA "shall have no police, subpena, law enforcement powers or internal security functions."[48]

It has been revealed that the White House and the Treasury and Commerce departments were infiltrated by CIA agents, that the CIA was involved in the Southeast Asia heroin trade, that it used notorious mobsters to assist in CIA assassination plots, that it routinely provided (and continues to provide) covert aid to foreign politicians and politi-

---

48. For documentation of the above points see David Wise, *The American Police State* (New York: Random House, 1976); Victor Marchetti and John Marks, *The CIA and the Cult of Intelligence* (New York: Knopf, 1974); Morton Halperin et al., *The Lawless State* (New York: Penguin, 1976); John Hanrahan, "Foreign Agents in Our Midst," *Progressive*, November 1977, pp. 31–35; Stein, "Omega 7"; John Dinges and Saul Landau, *Assassination on Embassy Row* (New York: Pantheon, 1980); *New York Times*, June 4 and July 1, 1977, and May 9, 1978; John Marks, *The Search for the Manchurian Candidate* (New York: Times Books, 1979). The CIA spent over $25 million experimenting with mind-control drugs, often on unsuspecting persons, and was responsible for the death of at least one government employee.

cal parties even though U.S. law prohibits the practice, and that it re-tained a stockpile of poisonous gas despite a presidential order to de-stroy it.[49]

The CIA's crimes against the peoples of other nations are too nu-merous to record here in any detail. In various Latin American coun-tries, the agency has used military force, terror, and sabotage to bring down democratically elected governments and install reactionary dic-tatorships friendly to American corporate interests. It has infiltrated and fractured the trade-union movements of other nations. It has funded and trained secret armies, torture squads, death squads, and "destabilization" campaigns. It has been involved in the assassination of labor, peasant, and student leaders in various nations.[50]

Public exposure of CIA illegal actions in the U.S. led to several in-vestigations of the agency but no indictments of any CIA officials. A 1978 executive order by President Carter designed to discourage un-lawful CIA acts was countermanded in December 1981 by President Reagan's executive order that, in direct violation of existing law, (1) permits the CIA and FBI to carry out domestic covert operations, in-cluding the infiltration and disruption of organizations and individ-uals "believed" to have links or sympathies with foreign groups or powers, (2) gives the CIA more leeway for spying on U.S. citizens, (3) allows the CIA to equip, train, and support local police, and (4) au-thorizes intelligence agencies to enter secret contracts with corpora-tions, academic institutions, other organizations, and individuals for the provision of services and goods.[51] The Reagan order gave a green light to renewed and expanded unlawful COINTELPRO-type do-mestic operations against groups involved in the labor movement and other progressive causes.

It has been argued that a "strong intelligence community" is needed to gather information essential for government policymakers. But the CIA has been involved in *covert actions* including economic, political, and military sabotage; terror; and disruption—activities

---

49. *New York Times*, June 11 and 20, 1975; July 9 and 10, 1975; April 13, 28, and 29, 1976; August 2, 1977; June 11, 1982; *Newsweek*, June 7, 1982; Alfred McCoy, *The Politics of Heroin in Southeast Asia* (New York: Harper and Row, 1973).

50. Wise, *The American Police State*; Philip Agee, *Inside the Company* (London: Allen Lane, 1975); Philip Agee, Louis Wolf et al., *Dirty Work: The CIA in Western Europe* (Secaucus, N.J.: Lyle Stuart, 1979); also past and present editions of *Covert Action Information Bulletin* (Washington, D.C.). Jesse Leaf, an ex-CIA agent active in Iran, reported that CIA operatives instructed the Shah's secret police on interrogation "based on German torture techniques from World War II" and that the torture project was "all paid for by the U.S.A." *New York Times*, January 7, 1979.

51. *New York Times*, December 5, 1981.

that go beyond intelligence gathering and beyond the CIA's lawful mandate.

WATERGATE—AND BEYOND

In June 1972, a group consisting of ex-CIA agents were caught breaking into the Democratic party headquarters in the Watergate building in Washington. Subsequent investigations revealed that the burglary was part of an extensive campaign involving political espionage, electoral sabotage, wiretapping, theft of private records, and illegal use of campaign funds—planned and directed by members of Nixon's campaign staff and White House staff. Testimony by persons close to the president alleged that Nixon withheld evidence of a break-in at the office of Daniel Ellsberg's psychiatrist and may have even ordered it, that he tampered with the judge presiding over the "Pentagon Papers" trial of Ellsberg and Russo by offering him the directorship of the FBI while the trial was still in progress, that he failed to respond to warnings of cover-up efforts by White House staff members, and that he himself engaged in cover-up activities.

Nixon denied the charges, and there the matter might have stood: the president's word against those of several underlings. Most likely he would have survived in office, albeit as a weakened president. But then it was discovered that tapes of all Oval Office conversations had been maintained, and these revealed that Nixon had been engaging in cover-up activities and had been lying to the public. In August 1974, facing impeachment proceedings in the House of Representatives, Nixon resigned from office. Vice-President Gerald Ford succeeded to the presidency and promptly pardoned Nixon for all crimes relating to Watergate, including any that might come to light at some future time.[52]

Not long after Nixon retired with his presidential pardon and presidential pension, many opinion makers were announcing with satisfaction that "the system worked." Apparently they believed the tapes would be there again next time. But how did the system work? It was not only Nixon and his aides who attempted to limit the Watergate

---

52. Other high-placed persons found guilty in the Watergate affair were given relatively light sentences. Former Attorney General Richard Kleindienst, who committed perjury regarding his role in related matters, was allowed to plead guilty to a misdemeanor count of "failing to testify fully," was given a thirty-day suspended sentence and a $100 fine, and won praise from the judge for being an outstanding public servant.

crisis to save their necks; Congress and even the press, which is credited with exposing the scandal, played a part in downplaying Watergate, first by making no investigation for half a year after the break-in, then by emphasizing Nixon's personal role and defining the events in narrow ways. The press and Congress focused on Nixon's failure to pay his income taxes, his personal corruption in appropriating funds for his estate, and his attempts at cover-up. Little attention was given to the president's repeated violations of the Constitution, his unlawful, massive bombing of Cambodia, his role in the assassination of foreign leaders, his unlawful campaign to destroy radical groups, and the unlawful cover-up role played by the entire intelligence community, including the FBI and CIA.

Congress and the press used Watergate to legitimate the system by treating it as a unique and unprecedented instance of government lawlessness. In fact, for many decades these same tactics have been and continue to be employed against political heretics. What shocked the establishment politicians was that in this instance the crimes were committed against a segment of the establishment itself—specifically, the Democratic party and mass-media newsmen. (To the very end Nixon claimed he had the "inherent executive power" under the Constitution to commit even criminal acts when impelled by considerations of national security. And "national security" seemingly embraced every conceivable area of political activity.)[53]

In 1982, at the urging of the Reagan administration, Congress passed a law that made it a crime to publish any information that might lead to the disclosure of the identities of present or former intelligence agents and informers, even if the information came from published sources. Under the law, most news reports and articles about CIA and FBI unlawful covert activities become illegal.

The trend toward greater secrecy and less accountability is not likely to reverse itself without a great deal of popular agitation and mass protest. As economic conditions worsen and popular discontent deepens, the necessity for tighter controls becomes more urgent. Unable to do two contradictory things: pursue its class interests and satisfy the needs of the people, the ruling class must suppress or neutralize popular pressures. As the crisis of capitalism deepens and austerity is shifted onto the shoulders of the working populace, the people become more restive; they mobilize to defend their standard of living through popular democratic protest. The plutocracy must then find

---

53. Nixon reiterated this position in a television interview, May 19, 1977: "When the President does it, that means that it is not illegal." Scratch a president and you find a divine-rights monarch.

ways of discrediting and undermining these democratic forces, denying them access to critical information, using covert action and police repression, weakening popular controls over government security agencies, and making it more difficult to hold power wielders accountable for their actions.

The increasing repression denotes the weakness, rather than strength, of the existing politico-economic system, for it is a manifestation of the declining legitimacy of the dominant plutocratic interests and of the growing need to rule by fear and force.

It is difficult to have a nice repression. If it is the unenviable task of police to keep a lid on the angry victims of racial and class oppression—a task assigned to them by those in power—then criminal acts by law officers inevitably occur. If it is the job of law officers to suppress radical political ideas and organizations and keep surveillance on every imagined political "troublemaker," then it is not long before the police, the FBI, the CIA, Army Intelligence, and other such units begin to see the Constitution as little more than an obstacle to be circumvented or brushed aside. In time, the state's security forces become a law unto themselves.

By now, it should be apparent that what is called "law and order" is a system of authority and interest that does not and usually *cannot* operate with equitable effect. The laws are themselves *political* rulings and judgments, the outcome of a process that is most responsive to the pressures of the politically stronger, as we shall see. Rather than being neutral judgments, laws are the embodiment of past political victories and therefore favor the interests of the victors. The law is inevitably an outgrowth of the established order that produced it, and by its nature it serves the established interests far better than the unestablished ones. When discussing law and order, then, it is imperative to ask *whose* law and *whose* order we are talking about. While the courts, the security forces, and the lawmakers claim to be protecting order as such, they really are protecting a particular kind of class order.

MIND CONTROLS FOR LAW AND ORDER

In their never-ending campaign to contain the class struggle and control behavior unacceptable to the existing order, authorities have moved beyond clubs, bullets, and eavesdropping devices and are resorting to such things as electroshock, mind-destroying drugs, and psychosurgery. Since the established powers presume that the present social system is virtuous, then those who are prone to violent or disruptive behavior, or who show themselves to be manifestly disturbed about the conditions under which they live, must be suffering from *inner* malfunctions that can best be treated by various mind controls. Not only are political and social deviants defined as insane, but sanity itself has a political definition. The sane person is the obedient one who lives in peace and goes to war on cue from his leaders, is not too much troubled by the inhumanities committed against people, is capable of fitting into one of the mindless job slots of a profit-oriented hierarchical organization, and does not challenge the established rules and conventional wisdom. If it happens that he actually has been victimized by class conditions—if, for instance, he cannot find decent housing or employment and sees his children go hungry and his family and his life falling apart—then he must be able to handle these distresses without resorting to aggressive, "abnormal" behavior. Most individuals treated by mind-control methods are selected because of their socially deviant and "disturbed" (i.e., disturbing) attitudes and behavior.

What is called sane or insane, normal or abnormal, in many cases is a *political* judgment made by privileged medical and other institutional authorities loyal to the status quo. Seldom do they manifest any awareness of the class, racial, sexual, and political biases influencing their supposedly scientific diagnoses. Since they accept the present politico-economic system as a good one, then anything that increases its ability to control dissident and unhappy persons—whose rebellion is rarely thought of as a justifiable response to an unjust social system— is also seen as good.[54]

Among the mind-control methods employed, probably the most inhumane is psychosurgery, better known as lobotomy, an operation that modifies behavior by destroying brain cells. Between 600 to 1,000 such operations are reported in the nation each year, with an unknown number going unreported. Advertised as a cure for anger, anxiety, depression, espousal of unpopular political opinions, and refusal to take orders, psychosurgery has been used on rebellious prison inmates, old people, mental patients, incarcerated political dissenters, "hyperactive" children, and, most commonly, women. In most cases, drastic personality changes result: individuals become compliant, emotionally dulled, and less able to cope with new situations and show a striking deterioration in memory and intelligence.[55] One leading psychosurgeon noted that lobotomized men find it diffi-

54. Bruce Ennis, *Prisoners of Psychiatry* (New York: Avon, 1972); Philip Brown (ed.), *Radical Psychology* (New York: Harper & Row, 1973).

55. Lani Silver et al., "Surgery to the Rescue," *Progressive*, December 1977, p. 23.

cult to get a decent job and lobotomized women find it easier doing routine housework.[56]

Psychosurgeons at the Harvard Medical School received funds from the Law Enforcement Assistance Administration to study the possibilities of using "corrective treatment" on "violent slum dwellers" who participate in urban uprisings. Of painful interest is the case of a 27-year-old Black man arrested in one of the very slum riots that so disturbed the Harvard lobotomists. He was declared unfit for trial and committed to a mental hospital. His psychiatrist found that much of his mental trouble stemmed from head injuries suffered when police beat him after he was arrested. Proving a difficult patient, he was lobotomized.[57]

There are many weapons in the arsenal of the American mind-control state. Some 200,000 people each year are subjected to electro-shock treatment, which injures the brain and nervous system. And a $15 billion-a-year "mental health" industry dispenses to over 30 million Americans annually such psychoactive drugs as Thorazine and Stelazine, sometimes called "chemical straitjackets."[58]

Prison inmates who propagate revolutionary or Black nationalist ideas or who engage in prison protests have been singled out for mind-control programs. Prisoners like the socialist Stephen Kessler, charged with disrupting a federal penitentiary by "promoting racial unity, collectivizing the inmate population, attempting to secure legislative inquiries . . . into prison conditions and being involved with outside radical groups," are placed in "behavior modification" units to be subjected to mind-altering drugs, beatings, forced rectal searches, prolonged shackling, isolation, and other tortures.[59] In the words of one Oklahoma prisoner: "As long as prisoners confine themselves to gambling, shooting dope, running loan rackets and killing each other, everything is fine. Let them pick up a book on Marx's theory of dialectical materialism and they are immediately branded a communist agitator and locked in solitary confinement."[60]

In a class-action suit against the behavior-modification program

56. Dr. Walter Freeman quoted in *Liberation*, July/August 1976, p. 39. A congressionally authorized commission endorsed psychosurgery, changing its status from "experimental" to "therapeutic," thus making it easier to bypass legal protections for prisoners and mental patients: Silver et al., "Surgery to the Rescue."

57. "Behavior Control: Psychosurgery Widespread," *Guardian*, April 28, 1976.

58. At least 5,000 mental patients are killed each year by mind-control drug treatments: Morton Silverman and Phillip Lee, *Pills, Profits and Politics* (Berkeley, Calif.: University of California Press, 1974); Ennis, *Prisoners of Psychiatry*.

59. *New York Times*, February 20, 1974; *Guardian*, January 21, 1976.

60. Letter from Chuck Stotts, inmate in Oklahoma State Prison, *Liberation*, February 1975, p. 5.

in Marion Federal Penitentiary, Warden Ralph Aron testified: "It [the program] is necessary because of the revolutionary attitudes acting throughout our country." Asked by one of the inmates' lawyers, "Is the control unit used to control prisoners with revolutionary attitudes and tactics?" Aron replied: "That is correct."[61] Federal Judge James Foreman agreed, noting in *Bono* v. *Saxbe* that the control unit had been used "to silence prison critics . . . religious leaders . . . [and] economic and philosophical dissidents. Often no showing was made of how these persons disrupted the orderly running of the institution."[62]

Behavior-modification programs use several approaches. One technique is to put the prisoner in solitary confinement under excruciating conditions of filth, cold, insufficient food, and sensory deprivation and make piecemeal improvements in each of these conditions as a reward if he develops the kind of attitude and behavior patterns desired by the authorities. The conversion must be a "sincere" one. "Reformed" prisoners are then forced to harass and inform upon their fellow inmates and engage in marathon sessions to help break other prisoners. Those who refuse to cooperate are once more subjected to behavior-modification torture themselves.[63]

Another method is "aversion therapy." By the use of electric shock, a prisoner is made to associate pain with whatever the authorities consider bad. In Vacaville, California, inmates accused of homosexuality are shown erotic gay films and shocked whenever a polygraph indicates the prisoner is sexually aroused. Drugs that induce a death panic by paralyzing one's breathing for a couple of minutes are sometimes used.[64] A group of prisoners in one behavior-modification program wrote: "Anyone who has spent any amount of time in [Dannemora State Hospital] must know at least one person who was sent for punishment, and returned with the mind of a vegetable or moron if he returned at all."[65] Eddie Sanches, who became a socialist while in prison, wrote from the behavior-modification unit at the federal penitentiary in Marion, Illinois: "Since I've been confined here on and off since 1971, I've personally seen over two dozen men driven insane. . . . Others have been driven to suicide or attempts at suicide."[66]

61. Phyllis Roa, correspondence in *New York Review of Books*, March 9, 1978.

62. Quoted in Chuck Nowlen, "A Prison on Trial," *Progressive*, April 1980, p. 28.

63. Mark Kleiman, "Drugs Replace Clubs in Nation's Prisons," *Guardian*, May 29, 1974.

64. Joel Meyers, "Electrode Torture and Starvation: Legal 'Therapy' in U.S. Prisons," *Workers World*, May 25, 1973, p. 6.

65. Letter by Dannemora inmates in *Workers World*, May 25, 1973, p. 15.

66. Letter to *Workers World*, November 15, 1974; also *Workers World*, May 20, 1977.

More than a million children are kept in orphanages, reformatories, and adult prisons. Most have been arrested for minor transgressions or have committed no crime at all and are jailed without due process. Ninety percent of the children brought into juvenile court are impoverished and of those incarcerated, a majority are Black or a member of some other minority. Many are subjected to beatings, sexual assault, prolonged solitary confinement, mind-control drugs, and, in some cases, psychosurgery.[67]

Hyperkinetic or hyperactive children run some of the same risks. Coming to school hungry, physically ill, and under emotional stress from growing up in impoverished home and neighborhood conditions, low-income children are regularly treated with powerful mind-control drugs "whose safety has never been documented and whose efficacy has never been proved."[68] Among the ninety-nine symptoms of hyperactivity or minimal brain dysfunction listed by the "experts" are such categories as: awkwardness, slowness in finishing work, foot tapping, wriggling, insistent questioning, and interest in sexual matters.[69] Nearly a million youngsters are treated with drugs, at a yearly profit of many millions for the drug industry and with side effects like weight loss, growth retardation, and acute psychosis for the children.[70]

Other kinds of medical aggression perpetrated against poor people, especially racial minorities, include the sterilization of women without their knowledge or consent. One of every four Native American women of childbearing age is sterilized. One of every three women in Puerto Rico has been sterilized, most of them involuntarily. In Los Angeles and parts of the Southwest, Chicano women have been forcibly sterilized. And in parts of the South, Black girls whose mothers are on welfare are routinely sterilized when they turn fifteen.[71] While the federal government limits funding for Medicaid abortions, thus depriving low-income women of access to medically

---

67. Thomas Cottle, *Children in Jail* (Boston: Beacon Press, 1977); Kenneth Wooden, *Weeping in the Playtime of Others* (New York: McGraw-Hill, 1976).

68. "Minimal Brain Dysfunction (MBD): Social Strategy or Disease?" report by the Medical Committee for Human Rights, New York, n.d.

69. Peter Schrag and Diane Divoky, *The Myth of the Hyperactive Child* (New York: Pantheon, 1975). Much hyperactivity in children has recently been traced to artificial flavorings and colorings in foods. Often hyperactivity disappears miraculously when children leave school, suggesting that school is not just the setting but the cause.

70. *Ibid.*

71. For these and other instances see Claudia Dreifus, "Sterilizing the Poor," *Progressive*, December 1975, pp. 13–18; *New York Times*, June 28 and August 1, 1973; *Guardian*, April 23, 1980. Evidence of massive involuntary sterilization of American Indians was unearthed by a GAO study: *East West Journal*, March 1977, p. 10.

safe abortions, the government continues to fund sterilization operations for low-income people.[72]

Among the institutions devoted to repression and control is the
mental hospital. Ninety percent of all mental patients are confined involuntarily—on the testimony of hostile relatives, school authorities,
social workers, psychiatrists, employers, or police—without benefit of
counsel, trial, or other procedural safeguards. Many are brought in
for having committed culturally taboo acts, including using marijuana. Others are confined for their politically unorthodox beliefs and
practices. The supposedly scientific medical considerations that guide
the psychiatric priesthood often betray a marked bias.[73] A worker in a
New York mental hospital reports:

> One Black woman was admitted . . . because she began screaming at
> the landlord who had come to evict her and her several children. . . .
> The Bureau of Child Welfare took her children. This upset her even
> more. She came to the Admissions Committee, crying, hysterical and an-
> gry. Obviously a "paranoid schizophrenic. . . ." The comfortable mid-
> dle-class psychiatrist said so, and after all he *knows*. . . .
>
> Patients [upon release] are often secured jobs working for companies
> which pay them considerably less than other workers. Social workers ad-
> vise the patient not to join unions and "make trouble" or they will be re-
> turned to the hospital.[74]

Almost all mental patients are forced to take mind-altering drugs,
which have damaging side effects. Many patients who are quite rational upon arrival begin to deteriorate. Many, incarcerated for trivial reasons, are kept for long, sometimes lifelong, durations.

To be sure, some people are mentally dysfunctional or gravely retarded and need institutional help. But because of meager funding,
understaffing, and inadequate facilities, public mental hospitals are
designed to fail them. During the 1970s the public outcry against the

---

72. Federal regulations designed to protect low-income Medicaid patients from involuntary sterilizations are regularly ignored by the states: *Washington Post*, July 17,
1981.

73. Thomas Szasz, *Law, Liberty and Psychiatry* (New York: Macmillan, 1963);
Ronald Leifer, *In the Name of Mental Health* (New York: Science House, 1969); Seymour Halleck, *The Politics of Therapy* (New York: Science House, 1971).

74. "Mental Hospitals and the Poor," *Workers World*, December 25, 1970. For the
horrifying story of how an independent, progressive Hollywood actress was railroaded
into an asylum, tormented, raped, drugged, electroshocked, and finally lobotomized
into submission see William Arnold, *Frances Farmer: Shadowland* (New York: Mc-
Graw-Hill, 1978). See also the documentary film "Hurry Tomorrow" about a California state mental hospital (distributed by Tricontinental Film Center, New York and
Berkeley, Calif.); also Frederic Wiseman's documentary on a Massachusetts state mental hospital, "Titicut Follies."

treatment accorded mentally ill persons provided fiscally pressed states with an excuse to close down facilities so that the 535,000 mentally ill or mentally retarded or senile patients in state facilities in 1960 were reduced to 281,000 by 1981. Once again, when a public service failed to deal with a problem correctly or sufficiently, the conservative response was to diminish the public service. What occurred, however, was not a "deinstitutionalization" but a "privatization" and a "reinstitutionalization," as large numbers of former inmates were dumped into private-profit nursing homes, boarding houses, and flophouse hotels—places gravely deficient in medical care, recreational facilities, and health and safety standards. "If the old institutions were 'warehouses,' the new institutions are deathtraps."[75] The condition for most non-affluent mental patients has gone from bad to worse.

Police, judges, FBI and CIA agents, drug-pushing school authorities, prison guards, behavior-modification experts, psychiatrists, and psychosurgeons—all have one thing in common: they work to make the world safe for those on top by exercising arbitrary power over those below. They help the capitalist class protect itself from its own people, all in the name of peace and security, normality and well-being, law and order.

---

75. Mary Ellen Schoonmaker, "Home, Home on the Curb," *In These Times*, April 28–May 4, 1982, p. 16; *Washington Post*, May 21, 1981; Robert McGarrah and David Kusnet, "Where Have They All Gone?" *In These Times*, December 16–22, 1981, p. 11.

10

The Mass Media: By the Few, for the Many

Many of the values and practices of our culture do not evolve randomly and innocently. Rather they are cultivated by the dominant interests of society. As noted in chapter 3, one of the most important purveyors of plutocratic culture is the mass media (newspapers, magazines, radio, and, above all, television). The media help propagate and shape established myths and images. They select most of the information and misinformation that we use to define sociopolitical reality. We experience almost all political life through the media. How we view issues and events, even what we define as an issue or event, what we see and hear, and what we do *not* see and hear are largely determined by those who control the communications world. By enlarging our vision through technology, we have actually surrendered control over much of our own sensory experience.[1] Even those of us who are often critical of news distortions are inclined to accept what we see, hear, or read in the media.

HE WHO PAYS THE PIPER

Who controls the mass media? Five New York banks (Chase Manhattan, Morgan Guaranty Trust, Citibank, Bankers Trust, and the Bank of New York) own controlling shares in the three national television

---

1. Robert Cirino, *Don't Blame the People* (New York: Vintage, 1972), pp. 30–31; Herbert I. Schiller, *The Mind Managers* (Boston: Beacon Press, 1973).

and radio networks (NBC, CBS, and ABC) and are powerful share-owners of the *New York Times, Time,* Columbia Pictures, and Twentieth Century–Fox. The networks themselves exercise a controlling interest over publishing houses and film companies. They own television stations located in key urban areas, reaching a lion's share of the national audience.[2]

Of the "independent" television stations, 80 percent are network affiliates. Practically the only shows these "independents" produce are the local evening newscasts; the rest are network programs. Most of the remaining "independents" are affiliated with NET, the "educational" network, which receives almost all its money from the Ford Foundation (controlled largely by the Morgan and Rockefeller banks) and a few allied foundations. The Ford Foundation picks NET's board of directors and reserves the right to inspect every program produced with Ford money.

Newspapers show the same pattern of ownership, with most of the large-circulation dailies owned by chains like Knight-Ridder and Gannett. The trend in ownership concentration continues unabated, as the large chains buy not only independent papers but also other chains. Less than 4 percent of American cities have competing newspapers under separate ownership; and in cities where there is a "choice," the newspapers offer little variety in editorial policy, being mostly mainstream conservative. Most of the "independents" rely on the wire services and big-circulation papers for syndicated columnists and for national and international coverage. Like television stations, they are independent more in name than content.[3]

Although declining in number, newspapers are doing quite well as business ventures. Through mergers, packaged news service, and staff cutting, the larger conglomerates are big moneymakers. The same is true of television and radio networks, which earn high profits from advertising revenues.[4] Like most of corporate America, control of the media is principally in the hands of the Morgan and Rockefeller financial empires. And like other businesses, the media corporations are diversified and multinational, controlling film, television, and radio outlets throughout Latin America, Asia, and the Middle East—as

---

2. See Peter Brosnan, "Who Owns the Networks?" *Nation,* November 25, 1978, pp. 561, 577–79. Brosnan notes that "an incredible 77.29% of ABC common stock is held by a tight circle of financial institutions, comprising less than 1% of all ABC stockholders."

3. *New York Times,* February 15, 1977; James Aronson, *Packaging the News* (New York: International Publishers, 1971).

4. Desmond Smith, "Mining the Golden Spectrum," *Nation,* May 26, 1979, p. 595. *New York Times,* December 12, 1977.

well as Europe and North America.[5] In recent years, independent publishing houses have been bought up by the giant corporations, who place a great emphasis on mass-market books and profits; thus, Bobbs-Merrill is owned by ITT, Simon & Schuster by Gulf & Western, and Putnam by MCA. "Is it beyond belief that most of the books in the racks a few years hence may be chosen for you, like television programs, by Mobil, Exxon and the rest?"[6]

The primary function of the media is not to keep the public informed but, like any business, to make money for their owners, a goal seldom coinciding with the need for a vigilant, democratic press. This is not to imply that those who control the media are indifferent to its political content. Quite the contrary. The media are given over to trivialized "features" and gossip items. Coverage of national and local affairs is usually scant, superficial, and oriented toward "events" and "personalities," consisting of a few short "headline" stories and a number of conservative or simply banal commentaries and editorials.[7] One group of scholars noted after a study: "Protection against government is now not enough to guarantee that a [person] who has something to say shall have a chance to say it. The owners and managers of the press determine which person, which facts, which version of the facts, and which ideas shall reach the public."[8]

Unions have few opportunities in the business-owned media to present programs on the needs and struggles of labor, but corporations, led by the oil companies, underwrite an estimated 75 percent of prime-time shows—both on public and commercial television. The business-owned media have little to say about the relationship of the capitalist system to pollution and poverty, the cozy relations between political and business leaders, and the role of the multinational corporations in shaping American interventionist policy abroad. No positive exposure is given to the socialist or anti-imperialist alternatives emerging throughout the world or the socialist critique of capitalism at home.

Many interesting documentaries made by independent film producers, dealing with racism, women's oppression, nuclear energy, conditions in prisons and mental hospitals, labor struggles, poverty,

---

5. Herbert Schiller, *Mass Communication and American Empire* (New York: Augustus Kelley, Publishers, 1969); and Schiller's *Communication and Cultural Domination* (New York: Pantheon, 1978).

6. Leonard C. Lewin, "Publishing Goes Multinational," *Nation*, May 13, 1978; also *New York Times*, May 18, 1977.

7. For a critique of local news shows see Ron Powers, *The Newscasters* (New York: St. Martin's Press, 1977).

8. Report by the Commission on Freedom of the Press, quoted in Cirino, *Don't Blame the People*, p. 47.

the FBI, and U.S. imperialism, reveal a side of reality highly critical of the established order. Few of them have been shown in commercial movie houses or on the major television networks. A documentary critical of nuclear power, "Paul Jacobs and the Nuclear Gang," was not shown on many PBS affiliates because of pressure from the nuclear industry. A film, "The Battle of Chile," was deemed too controversial for public television and was never even considered for commercial stations. A documentary on the Vietnam war, "Hearts and Minds," won an Academy award, yet its producer, Columbia Pictures, refused to give it mass circulation and its director had trouble getting financial backing for another film. And a documentary on the working and living conditions of farm workers was not shown on Florida educational television after a few powerful orange growers interceded.[9]

Reporters, columnists, and telecasters who occasionally report facts troublesome to the established interests have had their copy censored by superiors.[10] Relying on institutional authorities for much of their information, newspersons are disinclined to be critical of these sources. News reports on business developments rely mostly on business and allow little space for the views of organized labor or consumers. Reports about State Department or Pentagon policies rely heavily on State Department and Pentagon releases. Media coverage of the space program uncritically accepts the government's claims about the program's desirability and seldom gives exposure to the arguments made against it. In general, most of what is reported as "news" is nothing more than the transmission of ruling-elite views to an unsuspecting public.[11]

Far from being vigilant critics, most newspersons share the counterrevolutionary, anticommunist assumptions and vocabulary of the ruling class, which employs them. For years the press has propagated support for cold-war policies and attitudes, including hatred and fear of the Soviet Union and of socialism, and support for the domestic witch hunting and red-baiting that culminated in McCarthyism, loyalty oaths, the Korean war, and U.S. involvement in Southeast Asia.[12]

Consider how the Vietnam war was covered. From 1945 to 1954

9. Ralph Nader in the *Washington Star*, March 17, 1979; also the *Progressive*, July 1977, p. 11; Andrew Kopkind, "Hollywood Politics: Hearts, Minds and Money," *Ramparts*, August/September 1975, p. 46.

10. For examples see James Aronson, *The Press and the Cold War* (Boston: Beacon Press, 1970); also my *Inventing Reality* (forthcoming).

11. For good overall critiques see John Downing, *The Media Machine* (London: Pluto Press, 1980); David Paletz and Robert Entman, *Media—Power—Politics* (New York: Free Press, 1981).

12. Aronson, *The Press and the Cold War*.

the United States spent several billion dollars supporting French colonialism in Vietnam, but the American public was never informed of this. In the following decade the United States assumed full responsibility for the maintenance of the South Vietnamese right-wing dictatorship, but the public neither read nor heard a word of debate in the media about this major policy commitment. In 1965 the United States began a massive buildup of ground forces in Vietnam, but Americans were told that the troops were merely a small support force. The *New York Times* and other major news agencies knew the real nature of the buildup but felt it was in the "national interest" to keep this information from the public.[13] Reporters who covered the Vietnam war were expected to "get on the team"—that is, to share the military's view of the war and its progress—and most of them did. From at least 1965 on, American forces engaged in massive destruction of the Vietnamese countryside, resorting to indiscriminate saturation bombings, defoliation, and the wholesale killing of civilians. Yet it took years before these facts became widely known. Stories by journalists describing how American soldiers slaughtered hundreds of defenseless women, children, and old people in the village of My Lai were turned down by the wire services, several national magazines and news weeklies, one network, and major newspapers in New York and Boston.[14]

Throughout the Vietnam war, the insurgent forces were described as the "enemy," although it was never explained why they deserved to be so considered. Reporters who pride themselves on their objectivity saw cities "fall" to the "enemy" when they might have as easily viewed them as "liberated," or merely changing hands. Communists "nibbled" and "gobbled" territory and engaged in "terror" attacks, but the war of terror waged by U.S. forces was never labeled as such. During April 1975, as insurgent forces achieved a final victory in Vietnam, the U.S. public was bombarded with stories of refugees fleeing from the "invading communists." But a story buried in the back pages of the *New York Times* noted that most refugees reported they were fleeing because they feared the return of U.S. bombings or they simply wanted to get away from the fighting. Almost none mentioned fear or hatred of communism as a cause for flight.[15] Yet the

13. Robert Cirino, *Power to Persuade* (New York: Bantam, 1974), p. 63.

14. More than a year and a half after My Lai, the story was finally broken by Dispatch News Service. See Cirino, *Power to Persuade*, pp. 61–62.

15. *New York Times*, March 26, 1975. For a superb and monumental study of U.S. policy in the Third World and how the press has misrepresented that policy see Noam Chomsky and Edward Herman, *The Washington Connection and Third World Fascism* (Boston: South End Press, 1979), and Chomsky and Herman, *After the Cataclysm: Postwar Indochina and the Reconstruction of Imperial Ideology* (Boston: South End Press, 1979).

media continued to give the American public a contrary impression. During this period the press talked constantly of the impending "blood bath" that would supposedly occur when the communists took over in Vietnam. Subsequent reports by Westerners who remained in that country revealed that the massacres never materialized. But this fact also was buried in the back pages of newspapers, if reported at all.[16]

Within a couple of years after the Indochina war, the U.S. press began to circulate stories of mass atrocities in Cambodia, claiming that the poorly equipped Khmer Rouge, numbering not more than 35,000 cadres, seized by mysteriously wanton impulses, had somehow managed to slaughter one, two, three, or sometimes even four million of their eight million compatriots. How they accomplished this feat was never explained. A series of photographs, purportedly showing grisly executions in Cambodia but declared by U.S. State Department intelligence sources to be fake pictures taken in Thailand, were nevertheless widely circulated in major publications like *Time*, *Newsweek*, and the *Washington Post*. The press made no mention of the dreadful destruction of life, land, and property; the forced urbanization; and the starvation caused by the massive U.S. saturation bombings of Cambodia.[17]

The U.S media ignored the slaughter by the right-wing Indonesian military of some 500,000 Indonesians, just as it ignored the genocidal campaign waged by this same military in East Timor and the massive repression, torture, and murder of progressives in Uruguay, Guatemala, Argentina, Paraguay, Brazil, Zaire, the Philippines, and other U.S.-supported pro-corporate regimes.[18] For twenty-five years, the Shah of Iran, a friend of the U.S. oil companies and a product of the CIA, maimed and murdered tens of thousands of dissident workers, students, peasants, and intellectuals. For the most part, the U.S. press ignored these terrible happenings and portrayed Iran as a citadel of stability and the Shah as an enlightened modernizer. However, when the Polish government cracked down on the Solidarity union in

---

16. *Newsweek*, August 18, 1975, and February 16, 1976; and the two volumes by Chomsky and Herman cited in the previous footnote.

17. Douglas Foster, "$20,000 Profit on Faked Photo," *Pacific Sun*, February 24–March 2, 1978, p. 15; Chomsky and Herman, *After the Cataclysm*, pp. 139–294. In Cambodia, as in every revolution including our own, there were violent acts of retribution, but the scope of these has never been documented, or, more accurately, the documentation we do have would account for the death of thousands, not millions.

18. After ignoring the Indonesian genocide for 12 years, the *Times* quoted in its back pages the Indonesian chief of security who proudly announced that "500,000 Communists" were slaughtered after the right-wing takeover in 1965: *New York Times*, December 21, 1977; also Chomsky and Herman, *The Washington Connection*, pp. 41–204; Paletz and Entman, *Media—Power—Politics*, pp. 213–35.

Poland in December 1981, resulting in the death of several miners and the incarceration of several thousand other people, every network, newspaper, and news magazine gave these events top-story play for weeks on end. During this very same period, a fascist government in Turkey executed thousands of workers and dissenters and jailed tens of thousands, yet this brutal repression went largely unmentioned.

The business-owned media treats the atrocities of U.S.-sponsored rightist regimes with benign neglect while casting a stern, self-righteous eye on popular revolutions, as in Nicaragua. Generally the press defames leftist movements and governments and supports those right-wing pro-capitalist dictatorships that are clients of the multinational corporations.[19] The view from the newsroom is essentially the view from the Pentagon and the CIA, which in turn is the view from the boardrooms of Exxon and First National Bank.

The workings of the capitalist political economy remain another area uncharted by the news media. The need to invest surplus capital; the falling rate of profit; the drive toward profit maximization; the tendency toward instability, recession, inflation, and underemployment—these and other such problems are treated superficially, if at all, by newspersons and commentators who have neither the knowledge nor the permission to make critical analyses of multinational corporatism. Instead, economic adversity is ascribed to innocent and unavoidable causes, such as "hard times." One television commentator put it this way: "Inflation is the culprit and in inflation everyone is guilty."[20] When economic news *is* reported, it is almost always from management's viewpoint. Each evening the network news programs faithfully report the Dow Jones stock-exchange averages, but stories deemed important to organized labor are scarcely ever touched upon, according to a study made by union members.[21] Reporters fail to enlist labor's views on national questions. Unions are usually noticed only when they go on strike, but the issues behind the strike, such as job security, occupational and public safety, and resistance to loss of

---

19. Even nonrevolutionary democratic governments are treated poorly by the press if they have socialist leanings; see Roger Morris, "Through the Looking Glass in Chile: Coverage of Allende's Regime," *Columbia Journalism Review* (November/December 1974), pp. 15–26; John C. Leggett et al., *Allende, His Exit and Our "Times"* (monograph, Livingston College, Rutgers University, New Jersey, 1978). For a critique of how the U.S. press distorted the news about the leftist movement in Portugal, see Michael Parenti, "Portugal and the Press," *Progressive*, December 1975, pp. 43–45; for other countries consult sources cited in previous footnotes, especially the Chomsky and Herman books.

20. Garner Ted Armstrong, Channel Nine News, Ithaca, N.Y., February 11, 1976.

21. International Association of Machinists and Aerospace Workers, *Network News and Documentary Report* (Washington, D.C.), July 30, 1980.

benefits are seldom acknowledged. The misleading impression is that labor simply turns down "good contracts" because it wants too much for itself.[22]

There are few progressive and no socialist commentators in the mass media. In contrast, reactionaries, militarists, and ultrarightist elements have a multimillion-dollar yearly propaganda budget donated by business firms, and each week across the country they make over 17,000 television and radio broadcasts—with much of the air time donated by sympathetic station owners.[23]

On the infrequent occasions when liberals muster enough money to buy broadcasting time or newspaper space, they still may be denied access to the media. Liberal commentators have been refused radio spots even when they had sponsors who would pay. A group of scientists, politicians, and celebrities opposing the Pentagon's antiballistic missile program was denied a half hour on television by all three major networks, even though they had the required $250,000 to buy time. On various occasions the *New York Times* would not sell space to citizens' groups that wanted to run advertisements against the war tax or against the purchase of U.S. Savings Bonds. A *Times* executive explained that the advertisements were not in the "best interests of the country."[24]

Denied access to the media, the political left has attempted to get its message across through little magazines and radical newspapers, but from New England to California these publications suffer chronic financial difficulties and harassments from police and rightist vigilantes.[25] Needless to say, affluent donors and big advertisers usually eschew the radical media, leaving small leftist publications and the several existing progressive radio stations constantly on the edge of insolvency.

Dissenters also attempt to make themselves heard by mobilizing great numbers of people in public protest. But popular demonstrations against official policies are often trivialized, undercounted, and accorded minimal coverage by the business-owned media. The September 1981 march on Washington, in which a half million working people protested Reagan's policies, was the largest ever to take place in that city. In June 1982 upwards of a million people marched in New York to protest nuclear armaments in the largest demonstration

---

22. *Ibid.*
23. Report by In the Public Interest; statistics by Group Research, Inc., Washington, D.C., n.d.
24. Cirino, *Don't Blame the People*, pp. 90, 302.
25. Geoffrey Rips, *The Campaign Against the Underground Press* (San Francisco: City Lights Books, 1981). On the censorship and repression of student publications see *New York Times*, May 6, 1979.

in U.S. history. However, neither historic event received direct coverage (unlike the marriage of England's Prince Charles or the funeral of Monaco's Princess Grace). The networks preferred to concentrate on sporting events on those days, giving but a few minutes of evening news to these massive expressions of popular sentiment.

This is not to say that the press is entirely immune to mass pressures. If, despite the media's misrepresentation and neglect, a well-organized and persistent public opinion builds around an issue or set of issues, the press eventually feels compelled to acknowledge its existence. If the popular opinion is strong and widespread and *if it does not attack the capitalist system as a system*, it can occasionally break through the media-controlled sound barrier, albeit with selected images.

It is said that a free and independent press is a necessary condition for democracy, and it is frequently assumed that the United States is endowed with such a press. While the news in "totalitarian" nations is controlled, we Americans supposedly have access to a wide range of competing sources. In reality, the controls exerted in the United States, while more subtle than in some other countries, leave us with a press that is far from "free" by any definition of the word. When it comes to getting the other side of the story, Americans are a rather deprived people. U.S. programs can be heard throughout Eastern Europe via Voice of America. U.S. films are regularly shown in socialist countries. Twenty percent of the television shows in Poland come from the United States. American novels and other books are translated and widely read in the Soviet Union and Eastern European countries. Cubans can watch Miami television and listen to a half dozen U.S. radio stations and to Spanish-language Voice of America programs. But how many Americans are exposed to the media and literature of socialist countries? More importantly, how many Americans get information about their *own* country, from *within* their own country, that is contrary to the capitalist orthodoxy? Perhaps we Americans should think more of ourselves and worry less about others. We should want the same good things for ourselves that we so fervently desire for Soviets and Cubans, namely the opportunity to hear and express iconoclastic, anti-establishment views in our national media without fear of censorship and reprisal.

THE POLITICS OF ENTERTAINMENT

While the entertainment sector of the media, as opposed to the news sector, supposedly has nothing to do with politics, entertainment programs in fact undergo a rigorous political censorship. Shows that treat controversial, antiestablishment subjects have trouble getting sponsors and network time.[26] Songs containing references to drugs, prison conditions, junk foods, the draft, and opposition to U.S. military interventions have been cut from entertainment shows.[27] When David Susskind submitted five thousand names of people he wished to have appear on his talk show to the advertising agency that represented his sponsor, a third of the candidates were rejected because of their political viewpoints. The censorship code used by Proctor and Gamble for shows it sponsored stated in part: "Members of the armed forces must not be cast as villains. If there is any attack on American custom, it must be rebutted completely on the same show."[28]

While political critiques are censored out of entertainment shows, there is plenty of politics of another sort. In the media world, adversities are caused by ill-willed individuals rather than by the economic and social system in which they live, and problems are solved by individual effort within the system rather than collective effort against it. Demonstrators, radicals, revolutionaries, and foreign agents are seen as menacing our land, and the military and police as protecting it.[29] In an episode of "Kojak" on CBS, the tough cop was pitted against a terrorist Puerto Rican organization whose members were characterized as violent fanatics and assassins. The organization's name was "El Comite," the same as a Puerto Rican group founded in 1970 and committed to socialism. Not to be outdone by Kojak, the ever-alert FBI began a series of harassing raids on the homes of real-life members of El Comite shortly after the Kojak show was aired. This is more than just a matter of life imitating art. By conditioning the public to accept authoritarian law-and-order solutions, the television crime shows may be helping to create the very climate of opinion that allows for repressive police actions against dissenters.[30]

In the world of Hollywood and television, establishment figures like judges, businessmen, doctors, and police are fair and competent—never on the take, never on the make, never corrupt, bigoted, or oppressive. If there *are* a few bad ones, they are soon set straight by their more principled colleagues.[31] Various kinds of aggressive behav-

---

26. Eric Barnouw, *The Television Writer* (New York: Hill and Wang, 1962), p. 27.

27. See Cirino, *Don't Blame the People*, pp. 305–6, for various examples.

28. Murray Schumach, *The Face on the Cutting Room Floor*, quoted in *ibid.*, pp. 303–4.

29. Downing, *The Media Machine*; Parenti, *Inventing Reality*.

30. " 'Kojak' Attacks El Comite on CBS," *New American Movement*, February 1975. See also footnote 33.

31. Not always. The 1980–81 television season brought a new kind of evening soap opera, such as "Dallas" and "Dynasty," which depicted a corporate world of ruthless tycoons engaged in an amoral pursuit of wealth, power, and women. But the audience is invited to identify with, rather than reject, it all.

ior are indulged in and even glorified. Conflicts are resolved by generous applications of violence. Nefarious violence is met with righteous violence, although it is often difficult to distinguish the two. The brutal and sometimes criminal behavior of law officers is portrayed sympathetically as one of those gutsy realities of life. One study of "cop and crime" shows found that police actions habitually violate the constitutional rights of individuals: "The message communicated is that evil may be subdued by state-sponsored illegality."[32] The profound importance of the concept of due process is lost as TV police carry out illegal searches and break-ins, coerce suspects into confessing, and regularly use homicidal violence against suspected criminals in shoot-em-up endings. Violence on television and in Hollywood films is omnipresent, often linked to sex, money, dominance, self-aggrandizement, and other attributes that represent "manliness" in the male-chauvinist, capitalist American culture.[33]

In the media, women appear far less often than men and primarily in supportive roles as housewives, secretaries, and girlfriends. They usually are incapable of initiating actions of their own; they get into difficulties from which they must be extricated by their men. When not treated as weak and scatterbrained, women are likely to be portrayed as devious, dehumanized sex objects, the ornaments of male egoism. In media advertisements, women seem exclusively concerned with being cheery, mindless handmaidens who shampoo a fluffy glow into their hair, wax floors shiny bright, make yummy coffee for hubby, and get Junior's grimy clothes sparkling clean. There have been a few programs featuring women as lawyers, police officers, and other such lead characters, but even these women play predominantly sexist roles, operating in a male-defined world devoid of feminist values and usually oblivious to the oppressions of women.[34]

Perhaps most repugnant of all is daytime television, consisting

---

32. Stephen Arons and Ethan Katsh, "How TV Cops Flout the Law," *Saturday Review*, March 19, 1977, pp. 11–18.

33. The typical hour of TV network programming contains 7.43 violent episodes. Forty people are murdered every week; the wounded and assaulted are too numerous to contemplate. Saturday morning television, expressly designed for children, averages one violent act every three-and-a-half minutes: Media Action Project report in the *Guardian*, October 15, 1975; also *Liberation*, July/August 1976, p. 39; and Joseph J. Seldin, "The Saturday Morning Massacre," *Progressive*, September 1974, pp. 50–52. Studies show that adults become more belligerent after large doses of TV violence and more fearful of racial minorities, cities, and criminal attack: Richard Saltus, "The Research Shows Cop Shows Make Us Violent," *Leisure*, February 21, 1976, p. 22; George Gerbner's report in *Psychology Today*, April 1976, finds that heavy TV viewers are more convinced that more police repression is needed to control crime.

34. Gaye Tuchman et al. (eds.), *Hearth and Home: Images of Women in the Mass Media* (New York: Oxford University Press, 1978).

largely of two types of programs. (1) Soap operas portray a White, middle-class world of young professionals who spend most of their waking hours wrestling with a never-ending succession of personal crises in a world devoid of politico-economic oppression and social injustice. (Rape, alcoholism, unemployment, and wife battering make their appearance, but as personal rather than social problems.) (2) Quiz shows present contestants who are encouraged to divest themselves of every shred of dignity and privacy in a greedy, frenetic effort to win money, a new refrigerator, or some other goody.

There have been a number of "quality programs," dramatizations or series like "Lou Grant" or "Kaz," which have touched on important sociopolitical issues. While sometimes directing our attention to questions of injustice and oppression, these shows fall short of any systemic critique. Having little to say about economic power, capitalism, class structure, and other such issues that would horrify sponsors and networks, "quality programs" are mostly engaged in lukewarm criticisms of establishment abuses.[35]

The mass media are also the White media. For years characters that were Black or members of other racial minorities were allowed no appearance on television or radio except in such shows as "Amos 'n' Andy," which specialized in Negro dialect stereotypes, or "Beulah," the Black maid in a White family "who looked as though she'd been taken off a package of pancake mix."[36] Blacks have been appearing in TV commercials living in make-believe integrated suburbs, in "superstud" detective movie roles, and in comedy series like "Sanford and Son," an updated, slicker version of "Amos 'n' Andy." Of the some sixty lead and supporting performers in twenty-one new television shows in the 1978-79 season, two were Black and one was Puerto Rican. Minorities do make frequent appearances in cop shows—as crooks, pimps, informers, or persons in need of assistance from White professionals. What is missing is any treatment of life as lived by the great mass of ordinary Black, Chicano, and other minority peoples in rural and urban areas. The few programs about Blacks are created by

35. As mild as it was, "Lou Grant" was canceled in 1982. Claiming that the show's ratings had declined, CBS replaced it with a program with an even lower rating. (In fact, "Lou Grant" had one of the higher ratings when it closed in September 1982.) More likely the show was eliminated because of the controversial content of some of its programs and because its star, Ed Asner, was politically active raising money for medical aid to insurgents in El Salvador and speaking out in support of organized labor. Ultra-right groups targeted "Lou Grant" for a boycott, Kimberly-Clark Corporation withdrew sponsorship, and CBS obligingly imposed its censorship.

36. Bob Ray Sanders, "Black Stereotypes on TV: 25 Years of 'Amos 'n' Andy,' " *New American Movement*, February 1975, p. 9.

middle-class Whites who are guided by their own stereotyped notions of how minorities live and feel.[37]

As mentioned earlier, working-class people in general, be they White, Black, Chicano, or whatever, have little representation in the entertainment media except as uncouth, ignorant persons, hoodlums, buffoons, servants, and other stock characters. The tribulations of working-class people in this society—their struggle to make ends meet, the specter of unemployment; the lack of decent recreational facilities; the machinations of unscrupulous merchants and landlords; the loss of pensions and seniority; the battles for unionization and better wages and work conditions; the dirty, noisy, mindless, dangerous quality of industrial work; the lives wrecked and cut short by work-connected injury and disease—these and other realities are given no dramatic treatment in the business-owned media.[38]

One-fifth of all television time is taken up with commercials that often characterize people as loudmouthed imbeciles whose problems are solved when they encounter the right medication, cosmetic, or cleanser. In this way industry confines the social imagination and cultural experience of millions, teaching people to define their needs and life styles (and those of hubby, wifey, and baby) according to the profit dictates of the commodity market.[39]

Not all air time is given to commercial gain. The Federal Communications Commission requires that broadcasters devote about 3 percent of air time, worth a half-billion dollars, to public-service announcements. Like the free space donated by newspapers and magazines, this time is monopolized by the Advertising Council, a group composed of representatives from the networks and big busi-

---

37. Of the nine Blacks portrayed in one year of episodes of "Hawaii Five-O," a detective adventure show, five were pimps, two prostitutes, and two students. The eleven Hawaiians and Polynesians in the show included two pimps, two assassins, and three mobsters, according to a study by the U.S. Civil Rights Commission, which charged the television industry with perpetuating racial and sexual stereotypes; see *New York Post*, August 16, 1977. On stereotypes of White ethnic minorities, see Randall M. Miller (ed.), *Ethnic Images in American Film and Television* (Philadelphia: Balch Institute, 1978); Michael Parenti, "The Media Are the Mafia: Italian-American Images and the Ethnic Struggle," *Monthly Review*, March 1979, pp. 20–26.

38. Prime-time entertainment shows offer a warped distribution of occupational roles: prostitutes outnumber factory workers by 12 to 1; there are twice as many witch doctors as welfare workers, 8 times more butlers than miners. On the infrequent occasions that union activities are a significant part of the plot, the portrayal is likely to be a negative one. Generally unions are presented as selfish, violent organizations that are likely to do their members no good. Ralph A. Johnson, "World Without Workers: Prime Time's Presentation of Labor," *Labor Studies Journal*, 5, Winter 1981, p. 203.

39. For a provocative study of how advertising has been used to create the kind of consumerism needed by capitalism, see Stuart Ewen, *Captains of Consciousness* (New York: McGraw-Hill, 1976).

ness. No public-interest groups are represented. While supposedly "nonpolitical," the Council's "public service" commercials laud the blessings of free enterprise and falsely claim that business is "doing its job" in hiring veterans, minorities, and the poor. Workers are exhorted to take pride in their work and produce more for their employers—but nothing is said about employers paying more to their workers. The ads blame pollution on everyone (but not on industry) and treat littering as the major environmental problem. In general, social and political problems are reduced to individual failings or evaded altogether, and the air time that could be used by conservationists and labor, consumer, and other public-interest groups has been preempted by an Advertising Council that passes off its one-sided ads as noncontroversial and nonpartisan.[40]

REPRESSING THE PRESS

On those rare occasions when the news media expose the murky side of official doings, they are likely to encounter serious discouragements from public authorities. Government officeholders treat news that places them in an unfavorable light as "slanted" and criticize reporters for not presenting the "accurate" and "objective" (that is, uncritical and supportive) viewpoint. These kinds of attacks allow the media to appear as defenders of free speech against government pressure, instead of supporters of the established order as they more commonly have been.[41]

The federal government has used the FBI to harass and arrest newspersons who persist in writing troublesome news reports.[42] The Justice Department won a Supreme Court decision requiring reporters to disclose their information sources to grand-jury investigators, in effect reducing the press to an investigative arm of the courts and the prosecution—the very officialdom over whom it is supposed to act as a watchdog. Dozens of reporters have since been jailed or threatened with long prison terms on the basis of that decision.[43] On repeated occasions the government has subpoenaed documents, tapes, and other materials used by news media. Such interference imposes a

---

40. Bruce Howard, "The Advertising Council: Selling Lies," *Ramparts*, December/January 1974–1975, pp. 25–32.

41. See Cirino, *Don't Blame the People*; William E. Porter, *Assault On the Media* (Ann Arbor: University of Michigan Press, 1977).

42. Porter, *Assault On the Media*.

43. *United States* v. *Caldwell*, 33 L. Ed. 2d 626 (1972); also *New York Times*, September 4, 1976, and November 19, 1978.

"chilling effect" on the press, a propensity—already evident in news reports—to slide over the more troublesome aspects of a story and censor oneself in order to avoid censorship by those in power. One might recall how the president of CBS offered to cooperate more closely on news stories about the White House in return for government assistance in quashing a congressional contempt citation against CBS for its mildly critical documentary about the Pentagon.[44]

Most American presidents and other top officials have attempted to slant the news, winning the cooperation of the press in killing "sensitive" stories and planting favorable ones. Members of the press knew our government was flying U-2 planes over Soviet territory; they knew our government was planning an invasion of Cuba at the Bay of Pigs; they knew there were facts about the Tonkin Bay incident in Vietnam that differed from the official version; they knew the United States was engaged in a massive, prolonged saturation bombing of Cambodia. But in each instance they chose to act "responsibly" by not informing the American public. "The old blather about 'responsibility' to keep secrets instead of exposing abuses has begun to creep back into press parlance," complained columnist Jack Anderson.[45] "Journalistic responsibility" should mean the unearthing of true and significant information. But the "responsibility" demanded by government officials and often agreed to by the press means the opposite—the burying of some piece of information precisely because it is troublesomely true and significant.

The relationship between the CIA and much of the press offers another example of how the media have been anything but independent of the official viewpoint. More than four hundred American journalists, including nationally syndicated columnists, have carried out secret assignments for the CIA over the last three decades. Publishers and top executives from the networks, news services, and leading newspapers and magazines have actively cooperated with the agency.[46] The CIA has had two principal objectives in developing its media network. One is to use journalists to gather intelligence and do espionage throughout the world. The other is to get journalists to write the kind of stories that create a climate of opinion supportive of the government's policy objectives.

From what has been said so far it should be clear that one cannot talk about a "free press" apart from the economic and political reali-

---

44. *Ithaca* (N.Y.) *New Times*, January 18, 1976.
45. Columnist Jack Anderson, quoted in *Ramparts*, July 1975, p. 8.
46. *New York Times*, December 25, 26, and 27, 1977; Carl Bernstein, "The CIA and the Media," *Rolling Stone*, October 20, 1977.

ties that determine who owns and controls the media. Freedom of speech means not only the right to hear "both" sides of a story (Republican and Democratic) but the right to hear *all* sides. It means not only the right to *hear* but the right to *be heard*, to talk back to those in government and in the network offices and newsrooms, something few of us can do at present.

There is no such thing as unbiased news. All reports and analyses are selective and inferential to some inescapable degree—all the more reason to provide a wider ideological spectrum of opinions and not let one bias predominate. If in fact we do consider censorship to be a loathsome danger to our freedom, then we should not overlook the fact that the media are *already* heavily censored by those who own and control them. Creative, imaginative, progressive, working-class, socialist, antiimperialist, communalist, radical-feminist, and Third World themes are consistently programmed out of the media, while violent, competitive, sexist, authoritarian, trivial, tasteless, individuated, privatized, consumeristic, capitalist, racist, progovernment themes are programmed in. The very process of selection allows the cultural and political biases and class interests of the selector to operate as a censor. Some measure of ideological heterodoxy could be achieved if public law required all newspapers and broadcasting stations to allot substantial portions of space and time to a diverse array of political opinion, including the most progressive and revolutionary. But given the interests the law serves, this is not a likely development.

Ultimately the only protection against monopoly control of the media is ownership by community people themselves, with legally enforceable provisions allowing for the maximum participation of conflicting views. As A. J. Liebling once said, freedom of the press is guaranteed only to those who own the presses. In Europe some suggestive developments have taken place: the staffs of various newspapers and magazines like *Der Stern* in Germany and *Le Figaro* in France have used strikes to achieve greater editorial control of the publications they help produce. And *Le Monde's* management agreed to give its staff a 40 percent share in the profits and a large share in managerial decisions, including the right to block any future sale of the paper.[47]

While they point to alternative forms of property control, these developments are themselves not likely to transform the property relations of a capitalist society and its mass media. With few exceptions, those who own the newspapers and networks will not relinquish their

---

47. Aronson, *Packaging the News*, p. 99.

hold over private investments and public information. Ordinary citizens will have no real access to the media until they come to exercise direct community control over the material resources that could give them such access, an achievement that would take a different kind of economic and social system than the one we have. In the meantime, Americans should have no illusions about the "free press" they are said to enjoy.

11

The Greatest Show On Earth: Elections, Parties, and Voters

As noted earlier, most institutions in America are ruled by self-appointed business elites who are answerable to no one. Presumably the same cannot be said of *government*, since a necessary condition of our political system is the popular election of those who govern, the purpose being to hold officeholders accountable to the people who elect them. But does it work that way? Not usually.

In truth, the American two-party electoral system, with its ballyhoo and hoopla, its impresarios and stunt artists, is the greatest show on earth. Campaign time is show time, a veritable circus running for 6- to 12-month periods, brought into our living rooms via television as a form of evening entertainment. The important thing is that the show must go on—because it is more than just a show. The two-party electoral system performs the essential function of helping to legitimate the existing social order. It channels and limits political expression, exhausts political energies, and blunts class grievances. It often leaves little time for the real issues because it gives so much attention to the contest *per se*: who will run? who is ahead? who will win the primaries? who will win the nomination? who will win the election? It provides the form of republican government with little of the substance. It covers the plutocratic system with a democratic facade, giving an appearance of popular participation while being run by and for a select handful of affluent contestants.

But people are tiring of the show. They complain of the quality of the candidates, the lack of real choice, the absence of real issues, the endless primaries, and the vast expenditures of campaign funds. As they watch the parade of clowns and acrobats, elephants and don-keys, they feel something urgent is being trivialized.[1] This public dis-enchantment is a worrisome development for faithful allies of the ex-isting politico-economic system, who engage in concerned discussions about "a party system in decline."[2] They understand it is a serious matter when one of the crucial legitimating institutions of the estab-lished order, the two-party electoral system, finds its *own* legitimacy waning.

THE SOUND AND THE FURY: "DEMOPUBLICANS"

For generations, the electoral circus was run by professional party politicians who enjoyed a class and ethnic familiarity with the com-mon voters and who were sufficiently occupied by the pursuit of of-fice and patronage to remain untroubled by questions of social justice. Alan Altshuler describes the machine politicos:

> Though they distributed favors widely, they concentrated power tightly. Though their little favors went to little men, the big favors went to land speculators, public utility franchise holders, government contrac-tors, illicit businessmen, and of course the leading members of the ma-chines themselves. . . .
>
> The bosses were entrepreneurs, not revolutionaries. They provided specific opportunities for individual representatives of deprived groups, but they never questioned the basic distribution of resources in society. Their methods of raising revenue tended toward regressivity. On the whole, the lower classes paid for their own favors. What they got was a *style* of government with which they could feel at home. What the more affluent classes got, though relatively few of them appreciated it, was a form of government which kept the newly enfranchised masses content without threatening the socio-economic status quo.[3]

Old-fashioned political machines can still be found in a number of cities, but they seldom exercise influence beyond the local level.[4] To-

1. In 1980 a Gallup poll found that voters most disliked the length of campaigns, the amount of mudslinging, the lack of issue discussion, and the high campaign costs, in that order. See *Washington Post*, November 23, 1980.

2. For example: Everett Ladd, Jr., *Where Have All the Voters Gone?* (New York: Norton, 1978), an expanded version of articles by a political scientist written on assign-ment for *Fortune* magazine.

3. Alan Altshuler, *Community Control* (New York: Pegasus, 1970), pp. 74–75.

4. For accounts of old-time political bosses who operate today see Carol Polsky, "Portrait of a Politician," *Attenzione*, October 1980, pp. 72–74; Nicholas Acocella, "Pancake House Politicking," *Attenzione*, November 1980, pp. 72–77.

11.12

1980 Sentinel Star
Field Newspaper Syndicate

"I'M HAVING SECOND THOUGHTS ABOUT THE
ELECTION... I'M NOT SURE I VOTED AGAINST
THE RIGHT PERSON."

day most candidates hire their own professionals, rely on media experts, and assiduously court rich backers. Now that television can reach everyone at home, no one needs the precinct captain to canvas the neighborhood. Now that more and more states have adopted the direct primary, candidates no longer seek out the political boss for a place on the ticket but instead must independently pursue the nomination through the ballot box. The outcome is a decline in party apparatus, an increase in free-for-all primary contests, and an ever greater dependency on big contributors to pay for individualized staffs and costly media campaigns.[5]

This fracturing of party organizations, however, has not fostered any new diversity of political viewpoints and ideological perspectives. If anything, the fractionalization has made for less party cohesion, less accountability to the voters, and an ever greater emphasis on is-

---

5. Sidney Blumenthal, *The Permanent Campaign* (Boston: Beacon Press, 1980).

sueless politics and candidate image appeal. Electoral contests, supposedly providing democratic heterodoxy, have generated a competition for orthodoxy. In politics, as in economics, competition is rarely a safeguard against monopoly and seldom a guarantee that the competitors will offer the consumer a substantive choice.

This is not to say there are no differences between (and within) the major parties or that one party is not preferred by some people over the other. Generally the racial minorities, union workers, lower-income urban groups, and more liberal professionals support the Democratic party, while the White Protestant, rural, upper-income business-oriented, and conservative elements of the electorate tend to make their home in the Republican party.[6] These differences are sometimes reflected in the voting records of Democratic and Republican legislators, albeit within a narrow range of policy alternatives.

When magnified by partisan rhetoric, the differences between the parties appear worrisome enough to induce millions of citizens to vote—if not *for* then *against* someone. While voters have no great hope that the incumbent will do much for them, they persistently fear that the challenger might make things even worse. Or conversely, they may dislike the challenger but reluctantly vote for him only because the incumbent has become unbearable. It has been said in jest that the only reason Ronald Reagan won the presidency in 1980 was because he was running against the incumbent Jimmy Carter. Had he been running unopposed, he would have lost.

The two-party system is a marvelous ruling-class device. You offer the people a candidate who violates their interests and who is dedicated to the preservation of plutocracy, then you present them with another candidate who promises to be even worse. Thus you not so much *offer* them a choice as *force* them into a choice. It is another example of how, under capitalism, the monopoly market prefigures our consumer decisions. This lesser-of-two-evils appeal is the single most effective inducement to voter participation.[7]

It is not quite accurate to characterize the Republicans and Democrats as Tweedledee and Tweedledum. Were they exactly alike in image and posture, they would have even more difficulty than they do in maintaining the appearances of choice. Therefore, it is preferable

---

6. Delegates to the 1980 Republican national convention were mostly White, middle-aged men with a median income of $47,000: *Washington Post*, July 27, 1980.

7. CBS News/*New York Times* polls found that voters participating in 1980 presidential primary contests most frequently cited "the lesser of evils" as the determinant of candidate choice: *New York Times*, June 4, 1980; also Murray Levin, *The Alienated Voter* (New York: Holt, Rinehart and Winston, 1960), pp. 37–39.

that the parties be fraternal rather than identical twins. From the perspective of those who advocate a fundamental change in our national priorities, the question is not, "Are there differences between the parties?" but, "Do the differences make a difference?" For the similarities between the parties in organization, funding, ideological commitment, and policy loom so large as frequently to obscure the differences. The Democratic and Republican parties are both committed to the preservation of the private corporate economy; huge military budgets; the use of subsidies, deficit spending, and tax allowances for the bolstering of business profits; the funneling of public resources through private conduits, including whole new industries developed at public expense; the concoction of palliatives for the less fortunate segments of the population; the use of repression against opponents of the existing class structure; the defense of the multinational corporate empire; and intervention against social-revolutionary elements abroad. In short, Republicans and Democrats are dedicated to strikingly similar definitions of the public interest, at great cost to the life chances of underprivileged people at home and abroad.

The lack of real differences between the major parties is evident to the corporate business elites:

> Top executives may still be Republican, but they are no longer *partisan*. Professional managers who deal with the big world, most of them have come to think it does not usually make all that much difference which party wins, and indeed that business and the country often fare better under the Democrats. Observes Rawleigh Warner, Jr., the chairman of Mobil: "I would have to say that in the last ten to fifteen years, business has fared equally well, if not better, under Democratic administrations as under Republican administrations." Other top executives echo Warner's sentiments.[8]

So, in a different tone, do labor leaders like William Winpisinger, president of the International Association of Machinists:

> What separates the Democrats from the Republicans is the windowdressing—the Democrats want it and the Republicans don't. . . . We don't have a 2-party system in this country. We have the Demopublicans. It's one party of the corporate class, with two wings—the Democrats and Republicans. They both say the other can't do the job for working people, and they're both right.[9]

---

8. Ladd, *Where Have All the Voters Gone?* p. 17.
9. *Guardian* Special Report, Fall 1981.

Supposedly the emergence of GOP right-wing conservatism under Ronald Reagan in 1980 demonstrated a difference between the two parties. But actually, Reaganism strikingly revealed the conservative consensus among "Demopublicans." In 1981–1982, in response to the Reagan program, both parties in the 97th Congress sought to curb inflation with fiscally conservative policies that deepened the recession; both supported massive tax cuts favoring the upper-income brackets; both advocated huge increases in military spending and a more intensive arms race; both voted cuts in social programs and supported an easing of government regulations of business.[10]

From a progressive point of view, the problem with the Democrats is not that they are worse than or as bad as the Republicans, but that they are *perceived* as being far less conservative than they really are. They are seen as the party of labor, the poor, and the minorities, when they have been the party of the business subsidies, tax breaks, and big military budgets about as much as the GOP. The upshot is that popular constituencies do not mount any serious campaign against the conservative Democratic party. Time and again they settle for the empty shell, the "windowdressing," as Winpisinger said, and decide that the Democrats have their hearts in the right place and are doing the best they can under the circumstances.[11] They forget that the Democrats are a major force in creating those circumstances.

The similarities between the parties do not prevent them from competing vigorously for the prizes of office, expending huge sums in the doing. The very absence of significant disagreement on fundamentals makes it all the more necessary to stress the personalized features that differentiate oneself from one's opponent. As with industrial producers, the merchants of the political system have preferred to limit their competition to techniques of packaging and brand image. With campaign buttons and bumper stickers, television commercials and radio spots, sound trucks and billboards, with every gimmick devoid of meaningful content, the candidate sells his image as he would a soap product to a public conditioned to such bombardments.[12] His family and his looks; his experience in office and devo-

---

10. *New York Times*, November 6, 1980. This is not to deny there is a small left-liberal faction within the Democratic party composed of the Black Caucus and some other legislators in the House and the Senate who have consistently opposed the Reagan program and have drawn up a progressive alternative budget.

11. These points are made by Skipper Canis, "Better a Wolf in Wolf's Clothing," *Progressive*, October 1980, p. 32; see also Michael Kinsley, "The Shame of the Democrats," *Washington Post*, July 23, 1981.

12. Blumenthal, *The Permanent Campaign*; Joe McGinnis, *The Selling of the President 1968* (New York: Simon & Schuster, 1970).

tion to public service; his sincerity, sagacity, and fighting spirit; his
military record, patriotism, and ethnic background; his determination to limit taxes, stop inflation, improve wages, and create new jobs
by attracting industry into the area; his desire to help the worker,
farmer, and business person, the young and old, the rich and poor,
and especially those in between; his eagerness to fight poverty but
curb welfare spending while ending government waste and corruption and making the streets and the world itself safe by strengthening
our laws, our courts, and our defenses abroad, bringing us lasting
peace and prosperity with honor, and so forth—such are the inevita-
ble appeals that like so many autumn leaves, or barn droppings, cover
the land each November.

THE TWO-PARTY MONOPOLY

The two major parties cooperate in various stratagems to maintain
their monopoly over electoral politics and discourage the growth of
progressive third parties. All fifty states have laws, written and enforced by Republican and Democratic officials, regulating party representation on the ballot. Frequently the provisions are exacting
enough to keep smaller parties from participating. In order to win a
place on the ballot, minor parties are required to gather a large number of signatures on nominating petitions, an expensive, time-consuming task. In some states they must pay exorbitant filing fees
($5,000 in Louisiana for an independent candidate) and observe ex-
acting deadlines when collecting and filing nominating petitions. In
Pennsylvania third-party candidates for statewide office had to obtain the signatures of 36,000 registered voters within a three-week period; while in Maryland independent candidates were required to collect 55,517 signatures in a short period of time. Sometimes a 5 percent
requirement for signatures of registered voters has been interpreted to
mean 5 percent of voters from every district within the state—an impossible task for a third party whose base might be confined to a few
urban areas.

Persons who sign nominating petitions for unpopular third parties
sometimes find their names publicized by town clerks in an effort to
embarrass them into withdrawing their names, as happened in Vermont in regard to Communist party petitions. In some states voters
who are registered with the major parties are not allowed to sign or
circulate minor-party nominating petitions. Petitions are often
thrown out by hostile officials on trivial and sometimes unlawful

technicalities, compelling minor parties to pursue court battles that further strain their financial resources.[13]

To get on the ballot in all 50 states, a third party would have to expend an estimated $750,000 in filing fees and other expenses and collect 1.2 million signatures, a feat accomplished in 1980 only by the richly financed independent John Anderson and the affluent right-wing anarchist Libertarian party. But what low-budget progressive party can do it?[14]

It has been argued that such ballot requirements are needed to screen out frivolous candidates. But who decides who is "frivolous"? And what is so deleterious about allegedly frivolous candidates that the electorate must be protected from them by all-knowing Democratic and Republican officials? In any case, the few states that allow an easy access to the ballot—such as Iowa and New Hampshire where only 1,000 signatures are needed and plenty of time is allowed to collect them—have suffered no invasion of frivolous or kooky candidates.

The Federal Election Campaign Act of 1974 finances the major parties (giving each about $30 million for their 1980 presidential campaigns), but the minor parties can obtain federal funds only after an election, if they glean 5 percent of the vote (about 4 million votes), something nearly impossible to achieve without generous funds and regular mass-media access. "It's a classic Catch-22 situation: you don't get the money unless you get the 5 percent of the vote; you don't get the 5 percent unless you get the money."[15] The act also created the Federal Election Commission (FEC), designating that it be composed of three Republican and three Democratic commissioners. Thus two private parties have been endowed with public authority to regulate the activities of other parties whose existence is ignored by the law. No wonder FEC auditors spend most of their time looking for delinquencies in the accounts of smaller parties, and no wonder most FEC civil suits are filed against independent candidates and minor parties.[16]

---

13. Richard Walton, "The Two-Party Monopoly," *Nation*, August 30–September 6, 1980, p. 176. In 1932 Communist party candidates ran in 38 of the 48 states; in 1972, mostly because of legal restrictions, the Communist party got on the ballot in only 13 of the 50 states: Simon Gerson, "To Put a Red on the Ballot, Cross a 'Legal Mine Field,' " *New York Times*, July 17, 1976. In 1978, after much tenacity and hard work, the party achieved ballot status in 19 states and the District of Columbia.

14. Simon Gerson, "Does the U.S. Have 'Free Elections'?" *Political Affairs*, December 1981, p. 13.

15. Walton, "The Two-Party Monopoly," p. 177.

16. *Ibid*; also Gerson, "Does the U.S. Have 'Free Elections'?"

Even the Postal Service does its bit to protect the two-party monopoly by granting lower rates (3.4 cents per letter) to the Republicans and Democrats while denying the same privilege to other parties.[17]

According to one survey, half the nation's 13-year-olds believe it is against the law to start a third party.[18] In a sense they are correct: the electoral law is so written and applied by and for the major parties as to accord them something of an official status. We Americans would balk at seeing any particular religious denomination designated *the* state religion, to be favored by the law over all other religions; indeed, the Constitution forbids it. Yet we have accepted laws that, in effect, make the Democrats and Republicans *the* official state parties. At a time when they are less popular and less accepted than in a century, "this status serves to sustain them."[19]

The system of representation itself limits the opportunities of third parties. The single-member-district elections used throughout most of the United States tend to magnify the strength of the major parties and the weakness of the smaller ones, since the party that polls a plurality of the vote, be it 40, 50, or 60 percent, wins 100 percent of a district's representation with the election of its candidate, while smaller parties, regardless of their vote, receive zero representation. This is in contrast to a system of *proportional representation*, existing in many western countries, which provides a party with legislative seats roughly in accordance with the percentage of votes it wins, assuring minor parties of some parliamentary presence. Duverger notes that under the winner-take-all system "the party placed third or fourth is underrepresented compared with the others: its percentage of seats is lower than its percentage of votes, and the disparity remains constantly greater than for its rivals. By its very definition proportional representation eliminates this disparity for all parties."[20]

---

17. Walton, "The Two-Party Monopoly"; Gerson, "Does the U.S. Have 'Free Elections'?"

18. *Progressive*, March 1977, p. 14.

19. Walton, "The Two-Party Monopoly."

20. Maurice Duverger, *Political Parties* (New York: Wiley, 1955), p. 248, and the discussion on pp. 245–55; E. E. Schattschneider, *Party Government* (New York: Holt, Rinehart and Winston, 1960), pp. 74–84. In 1947 Benjamin Davis and Peter Cacchione, Communists elected to the city council in New York, lost their seats when the city shifted from proportional representation to single-member districts. The change was explicitly intended to get rid of the Communists and discourage the growth of other dissident parties. Proposals were introduced to abolish proportional representation in local elections in Cambridge, Massachusetts, in 1972 after victories by a few radically oriented candidates.

The winner-take-all, single-member-district system deprives the minority parties not only of representation but eventually of voters too, since not many citizens wish to "waste" their ballots on a party that seems incapable of achieving legislative representation. Some political scientists argue that proportional representation is undesirable because it encourages the proliferation of "splinter parties" and leads to legislative stalemate and instability. In contrast, the present two-party system muffles rather than sharpens ideological differences and allows for the development of a consensus politics devoid of fragmentation and polarization. But one might question why the present forms of "stability" and "consensus" are to be treated as sacred. Stability is often just another word for "keeping things as they are." Whose stability and whose consensus are we talking about? And one might wonder whether stalemate and fragmentation—with their consequent ill effects on the public interest—do not characterize the *present* political system in many policy areas. The muting effects of the two-party system so thoroughly limit the arena of political choice and action as to manufacture a "stability" and "consensus" that violate the needs of the populace.

The monopoly electoral system is rigged in other ways so as to thwart challenges from *within* as well as without the two-party system. A common device is *redistricting*, changing the boundaries of a constituency to guarantee a preferred political outcome. Consider this report on Jackson, Mississippi:

> While Blacks make up 47 percent of the population of this Mississippi capital city, they have about as much political clout as their slave ancestors . . . Black leaders say.
>
> No Black has been elected to city office here since 1912. . . . Henry Kirksey, a Black state legislator vying to become the first Black mayor . . . didn't expect to win the election. Since 1960, White suburbs have been annexed three times, each time substantially diluting Black voting strength just as it appeared Blacks were about to become a majority. And each election, like this one, has been characterized by racial bloc voting and increasingly apathetic Black voters.
>
> "Many Blacks in Jackson have just given up," Kirksey said.[21]

In various states over the last five decades, redistricting has been used to weaken or eliminate the electoral base of radical or progressive members of Congress, state legislatures, and city councils.

---

21. *Washington Post*, June 19, 1981.

A well-known form of redistricting is the *gerrymander*.[22] The "salvage" form of gerrymander is indicated in Figure 1, which shows how New York City Congressional districts 8, 19, and especially 17 are drawn in contorted ways to gather in noncontiguous White, middle-income neighborhoods, thereby preventing the numerically dominant lower-income areas in the Bronx and Manhattan from having a majority in all the districts of both boroughs.

The second form of gerrymander is the "divide and conquer." Figure 2 shows how the predominantly Black Delta district, which had been politically intact since 1882, was chopped into three pieces in 1966 and absorbed by White majorities—when substantial numbers of African-American people began to register. Similarly, in 1981 the new city council district in Queens, N.Y., with the approval of Mayor Koch, who was not known for his friendliness toward Blacks, split the 50,000 working-class Black voters in the Corona and East Elmhurst communities into three different city council districts, making them a numerical minority in all three.[23]

If, despite rigged rules and official harassments, radical groups continue to prove viable, then authorities are likely to resort to more violently coercive measures. Almost every radical group that has ever managed to gain some grass-roots organizational strength has become the object of official violence. The case of the American Socialist party is instructive. By 1918 the Socialist party held 1,200 offices in 340 cities including seventy-nine mayors in twenty-four different states, thirty-two legislators, and a member of Congress. In 1919, after having increased its vote dramatically in various locales, the Socialists suffered the combined attacks of state, local, and federal authorities.[24] Their headquarters in numerous cities were sacked by police, their funds confiscated, their leaders jailed, their immigrant members deported, their newspapers denied mailing privileges, and their elected candidates denied their seats in various state legislatures and in Congress. Within a few years the party was finished as a viable political force. While confining themselves to legal and peaceful forms of political competition, the Socialists discovered that their opponents were burdened by no similar compunctions. The guiding

22. Named after an early practitioner of the method, Governor Elbridge Gerry of Massachusetts, who employed it in 1812, and *salamander*, from the odd shape of the district.

23. *Daily World*, July 30 and June 12, 1981; on the struggle within state legislatures to control redistricting see *New York Times*, November 6, 1980.

24. James Weinstein, *The Decline of American Socialism* (New York: Monthly Review Press, 1967).

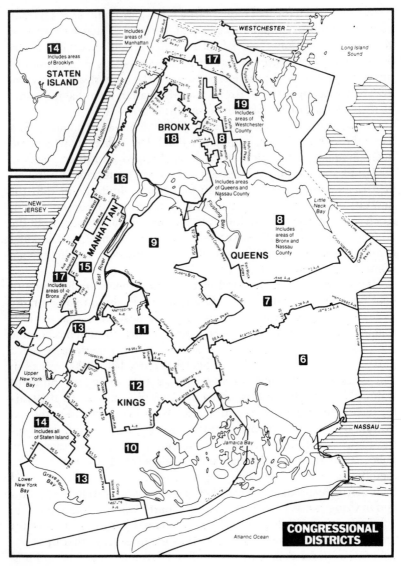

Figure 1.

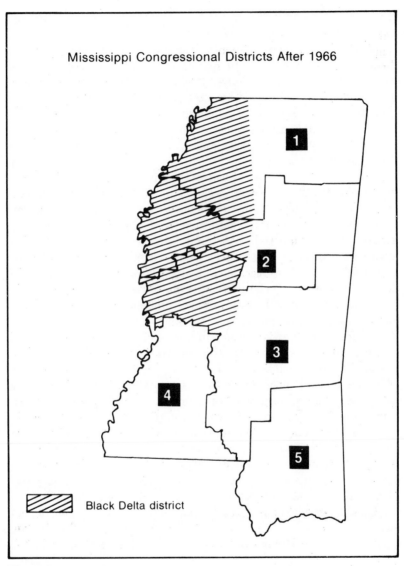

Mississippi Congressional Districts After 1966

Black Delta district

Figure 2.

principle of the establishment was (and still is): *When change threat-ens to rule, then the rules are changed.*

Another example is the case of radical judge Justin Ravitz, elected to Detroit's criminal court in 1972. Ravitz had won a good deal of support from the Black community, the peace movement, and some labor unions. The day after his election, the Detroit Bar Association called for the elimination of popularly elected judges and for the ap-pointment of all judges by the governor. A spokesman for the bar ad-mitted that this proposal was designed to prevent people like Ravitz from gaining office.[25]

Money is the lifeblood of electoral politics, helping to determine the availability of manpower, organization, mobility, and media visi-bility. Without money, the politician's days are numbered. Com-menting on the plight of reformers in Congress, Representative Charles Vanik observed: "As things are now, the public-interest members here have no reward except personal satisfaction. In the long run most of them face defeat by the big-money people. Many of the best men who come here lose after one or two terms."[26]

Besides coping with severe money problems, progressive candi-dates must try to develop a plausible image among a citizenry condi-tioned for more than a century to hate socialists, communists, and other leftists. They find themselves dependent for exposure on mass media that are owned by the conservative interests they are attacking. They see that, along with the misrepresentations disseminated by a hostile press, the sheer paucity of information and haphazard report-age can make any meaningful campaign dialogue nearly impossible. The dissenters compete not only against well-financed opponents but also against the media's many frivolous and stupefying distractions. Hoping to "educate the public to the issues," they discover that the media allow little opportunity for the expositions needed to make their position understandable to voters who might be willing to listen.

Candidates who hope to reach a mass electorate are largely depen-dent on mass media. For most voters "the campaign has little reality apart from its media version."[27] Since the media do not cover a third

---

25. Margaret Borys, "Detroit Judge Is a Radical," *Guardian*, December 13, 1972, p. 6.

26. Quoted in Richard Harris, "Annals of Politics," *New Yorker*, August 7, 1971, p. 59. Harris also quotes Senator Charles Mathias: "The fundamental problem is that the ability to raise money starts the screening-out process. If you don't get the money, you don't get the nomination." (p. 54) Money is no guarantee of victory but it is some-thing of a necessary condition. It is not certain you will win an important office if you have millionaires on your side, but it is quite likely you will lose if you don't.

27. Political scientist Thomas Patterson quoted in *New York Times*, April 6, 1980.

party's campaign, most people remain unaware of its existence.[28] During presidential campaigns the television networks give the Democratic and Republican candidates 10 to 15 minutes of prime-time coverage every evening, while minor-party presidential candidates receive but a few minutes' exposure, if that, in their *entire* campaign. By withholding coverage from minor-party candidates while bestowing it lavishly on major-party ones, the media help perpetuate the two-party monopoly.

> It is ironic that while more and more Americans are withdrawing their allegiance from the major parties—and the polls show the number of independents at around 40 percent and growing—the major parties have steadfastly continued to enjoy unchallengeable preeminence in American politics. It is not necessarily because they are valued and respected, but rather because of the biases built into the system.[29]

On those infrequent occasions when progressive dissenters win office as mayors, governors, or federal or state legislators, they often find themselves burdened by administrative duties or relegated to obscure legislative tasks. If they attempt changes, they run into the opposition of other elected and bureaucratic officials and of economic interests larger and more powerful than they.[30] They frequently decide that "for now" they must make their peace with the powers that be, holding their fire until some future day when they can attack from higher ground. To get along they decide to go along. Thus begins the insidious process that lets a person believe he is still opposing the ongoing arrangements when in fact he has become a functional part of them. There are less subtle instances of cooptation, as when reformers are bought off with favors by those who hold the key to their survival. Once having won election, they may reverse their stands on fundamental issues and make common cause with established powers, to the dismay of their supporters.

In sum, of the various functions a political party might serve—(1) selecting candidates and waging election campaigns, (2) articulating

---

28. When the Socialist Workers party candidate for president, Peter Camejo, was accorded a half-hour on nationwide television at 1:30 A.M. (the "Tomorrow Show"), his party headquarters was deluged by thousands of pieces of mail from people requesting more information, sending small donations, and asking questions like, "Why haven't I heard about you before?"

29. Jim McClellan and David Anderson, "The Making of the Also-Rans," *Progressive*, January 1977, p. 29.

30. See the shocking case of Mayor Carthan of Tchula, Miss., discussed in chapter 9; also the struggles of Mayor Hatcher of Gary, Ind., described in Edward Greer, *Big Steel* (New York: Monthly Review Press, 1979).

and debating major issues, (3) formulating coherent and distinct programs, and (4) implementing a national program when in office—our
parties fulfill none of these functions with any distinction. The parties
are loose conglomerations organized around one common purpose:
the pursuit of office. For this reason, American parties have been
characterized as "nonideological." And indeed they are—in the sense
that their profound ideological commitment to capitalism at home
and abroad and to the ongoing class structure is seldom made an explicit issue. The major parties have a conservative effect on the consciousness of the electorate and on the performance of representative
government. They operate from a commonly shared ideological perspective that is best served by the avoidance of iconoclastic politico-
economic views and by the suppression or cooptation of dissenters. In
their common effort to blur and pass over fundamental issues, the
major parties prevent class divisions from sharpening and serve a
valuable function of maintaining a noisy, apolitical politics, distracting us from the real problems and narrowing the scope of participation while giving an appearance of popular government.

According to democratic theory, electoral competition keeps political leaders accountable to their constitutents. Politicians who wish to
remain in office must respond to voter preferences in order to avoid
being replaced by their rivals in the next election. But do the conditions of electoral competition actually exist? As noted earlier, legal,
political, and moneyed forces so limit the range of alternatives as to
raise serious questions about democratic accountability.

About one out of every ten Representatives are elected to Congress
with no opposition in either the primary or the general election. During the 1970s, from 90 to 96 percent of incumbents who sought congressional office were reelected.[31] Death and voluntary retirement
seem to be the important factors behind the turnover in representative
assemblies. In this respect, legislative bodies bear a closer resemblance
to the nonelective judiciary than we would imagine. One study of
municipal governments found that upwards of half the members of
city councils anticipated their own voluntary retirement after one
term and about one-fourth held nonelective appointments to fill unex-
pired terms. Many of the council members admitted that they paid
little heed to constituent complaints. They entered and left office "not
at the whim of the electorate, but according to self-defined sched-

---

31. See the study by Americans for Democratic Action, UPI report, November 14,
1977. Of late, the increasing work load and the lure of more lucrative careers have
caused a rise in voluntary retirements in the House of Representatives, usually after
four or five terms.

ules," a procession of like-minded persons of similar social background.[32]

NONVOTING AS A POLITICAL RESPONSE

Much has been written about the deficiencies of ordinary voters, their prejudices, lack of information, and low civic involvement. More should be said about the deficiencies of the electoral-representative system that serves them. It has long been presumed that since the present political system represents the best of all worlds, those who show an unwillingness to vote must be manifesting some failing in themselves. Seldom is nonparticipation treated as a justifiable reaction to a politics that is lacking in its electoral content and disappointing in its policy results.

In addition to the undemocratic features of the electoral system noted earlier, voters face other discouragements, such as the false claims that politicians propagate to cover their actual performance. With good reason people complain: "Politicians tell us one thing to get our votes and then do another thing once they are elected to office." If so many politicians are dissemblers and half-truth artists, it is not because they are all morally flawed in their personalities. Rather they are caught in the systemic contradiction of having to be both a "candidate of the people" and—if they want to survive and advance—a servant of the powerful.[33]

Given all these negative factors, it is not surprising that the percentage of nonvoters continues to increase, running as high as 65 percent in congressional and gubernatorial contests. In the 1978 off-year elections roughly two-thirds of the eligible electorate stayed home. In the presidential primaries of some states, the participation rate may be as low as 15 to 20 percent of the registered voters. In many local elections, voter participation is so low as to make it difficult to speak of "popular" representation in any real sense. Observing that in a municipality of 13,000 residents, an average of 810 voters elected the city council, Prewitt comments:

> Such figures sharply question the validity of thinking that "mass electorates" hold elected officials accountable. For these councilmen, even if

---

32. Kenneth Prewitt, "Political Ambitions, Volunteerism, and Electoral Accountability," *American Political Science Review*, 64, March 1970, p. 10. Prewitt presents data on eighty-two municipal governments.

33. See Chapter 14 for numerous examples of how presidents have vowed support of popular interests during campaigns, then pursued contrary policies once in office.

serving in relatively sizable cities, there are no "mass electorates"; rather there are the councilman's business associates, his friends at church, his acquaintances in the Rotary Club, and so forth which provide him the electoral support he needs to gain office.[34]

Presidential contests over the last 20 years reveal a similar decline in percent of eligible voters who voted—from 62.8 (1960), to 61.9 (1964), to 60.9 (1968), to 55.5 (1972), to 54.4 (1976), to 52.3 (1980). In 1980, elected in what was proclaimed a "landslide," Reagan actually won support from less than 27 percent of the eligible voters.

Low participation has a political significance in that nonvoters are disproportionately concentrated among the poor, the young, low-income and nonunion workers, and racial minorities.[35] As fewer among these groups vote, politicians pay less attention to them in their campaigns and policy decisions, giving the dispossessed even less reason to go to the polls, thereby intensifying the vicious cycle of powerlessness. (Thus more than 3 million of the 9.6 million Blacks who voted in 1976 stayed home in 1980, rejecting both Carter and Reagan, representing about a 33-percent decline in the Black vote.)

Residency requirements and the registration of voters at obscure locations and inconvenient hours during the political off-season discriminate against the less established community elements, specifically the poor, the unemployed, and transient laborers.[36] Working long hours for low pay, deprived of the kind of services and material security that the well-to-do take for granted, made to feel personally incapable of acting effectively, and living in fear of officialdom, low-income people frequently are reluctant to make political commitments of any kind. As Kimball describes it:

> Tenements, rooming houses, and housing projects—the dormitories of the ghetto electorate—provide . . . a shifting, changing human environment instead of the social reinforcements that encourage political involvement in more stable neighborhoods. And the immediate struggle for subsistence drains the reservoirs of emotional energy available for the dis-

---

34. Prewitt, "Political Ambitions, Volunteerism, and Electoral Accountability," p. 9. In some western regions of the U.S., where district boards administer land and water resources and most other local government functions, voting is limited to property owners, who may cast one vote for each dollar's worth of land they possess in the district, in effect giving control to a few big corporations and rich individuals. Where this is the case, voter turnout is as low as 8 percent, and most district supervisors run unopposed or are appointed by the existing governing board: Merril Goodall and James Jamieson, "Property Qualification Voting in Rural California's Water Districts," *Land Economics*, 1, August 1974, pp. 292–94.

35. Penn Kimball, *The Disconnected* (New York: Columbia University Press, 1972).

36. Steven Rosenstone and Raymond Wolfinger, "The Effect of Registration Laws on Voter Turnout," *American Political Science Review*, 72, March 1978, pp. 22–45.

tant and complex realms of politics. . . . Elections come and go, and the life of poverty goes on pretty much as before, neither dramatically better nor dramatically worse. The posturing of candidates and the promises of parties are simply irrelevant to the daily grind of marginal existence.[37]

Many of the procedural discouragements to voting have been removed in the last two decades: the poll tax was outlawed as a voting requirement; polling-place racial discrimination has lessened; linguistic, literacy, and residency requirements were eased or abolished; stringent registration requirements were discarded; and young persons between 18 and 21 were enfranchised. The conventional wisdom of the 1960s predicted that these reforms would increase election-day turnout, but the trend toward declining voter participation continues. Difficult electoral procedures may discourage voting, but an easing of these conditions does not guarantee an increased turnout, especially if other discouragements continue to work their effect. For behind much nonvoting is the belief that the promises of politicians are part of a grand deception. The skepticism and cynicism that many people feel may be summarized as follows:

1. The progressive challenger, who calls for sweeping reforms, is still a politician and therefore as deceptive as the others.
2. Even if sincere, the progressive challenger does not have a chance of defeating the better-financed establishment candidates.
3. Even if the progressive wins, he or she is eventually bought off by the powers that be.
4. Even if not bought off, the progressive once in office can do little against those who really run things.[38]

It has been argued that if nonvoters tend to be among the less informed, less educated, and more apathetic, then it is just as well they do not exercise their franchise. Since they are likely to be swayed by prejudice and demagogy, their activation would constitute a potential threat to our democratic system.[39] Behind this reasoning lurks the du-

---

37. Kimball, *The Disconnected*, p. 17.
38. Michael Parenti, "Power and Pluralism: A View From the Bottom," *Journal of Politics*, 32, August 1970, p. 515; Kimball, *The Disconnected*, pp. 61–62.
39. A typical example of this view: Seymour M. Lipset, *Political Man* (Garden City, N.Y.: Doubleday, 1960), pp. 215–19. Occasionally there is an admission by the well-to-do that voting should be limited not to protect democracy but to protect themselves. A letter to the *New York Times* (December 6, 1971) offered these revealing words: "If . . . everybody voted, I'm afraid we'd be in for a gigantic upheaval of American society—and we comfortable readers of the *Times* would certainly stand to lose much at the hands of the poor, faceless, previously quiet throngs. Wouldn't it be best to let sleeping dogs lie?"

bious presumption that the better-educated, upper-income people who vote are more rational, less compelled by narrow self-interests, and less bound by racial and class prejudices, an impression that itself is one of those comfortable prejudices upper- and middle-class people (including social scientists) have of themselves.

Drawing on opinion surveys from six presidential elections, V. O. Key concludes that voters do try to make sense of political campaigns by trying to pick candidates who seem closest to their views: "To be sure, many individual voters act in odd ways indeed; yet, in the large, the electorate behaves about as rationally and responsibly as we should expect, *given the clarity of the alternatives presented to it and the character of the information available to it.*"[40] The "clarity of the alternatives" and the forthright enunciation of issues that interest the working populace often are the very things missing from political campaigns. For instance, a 1968 study found that voters were not to blame for their lack of issue-oriented responses to the Vietnam war since the presidential candidates, Richard Nixon and Hubert Humphrey, offered indistinguishably vague positions on the war. When presented with distinct choices on Vietnam by presidential primary candidates like Eugene McCarthy and George Wallace, the voters did respond in accordance with their policy preferences. The elitist notion that ordinary people are incapable of making rational election choices, while sometimes true, puts too much blame on the electorate and overlooks the fact that from among the major-party candidates there often is no rational choice to be made.[41]

Some writers argue that low voter turnout in the United States is symptomatic of a "politics of happiness": people do not bother to participate because they are fairly content with the way things are going.[42] But the 40 to 50 million adult Americans outside the voting universe are not among the more contented but among the less affluent and more alienated, displaying an unusual concentration of socially deprived characteristics.[43] The "politics of happiness" may be nothing more than a cover for the politics of discouragement. The nonpartici-

---

40. V. O. Key, Jr., with Milton Cummings, Jr., *The Responsible Electorate* (Cambridge, Mass.: Harvard University Press, 1966). Italics added.

41. Benjamin Page and Richard Brody, "Policy Voting and the Electoral Process," *American Political Science Review*, 66, September 1972, pp. 979–96. When deprived of a choice, many people vote merely out of civic obligation. See the next section of this chapter.

42. Heinz Eulau, "The Politics of Happiness," *Antioch Review*, 16, 1956, pp. 259–64; Lipset, *Political Man*, pp. 179–219.

43. Walter Dean Burnham, "The Changing Shape of the American Political Universe," *American Political Science Review*, 59, March 1965, p. 27. Kimball, *The Disconnected, passim*.

pation of many people often represents a feeling of powerlessness, a conviction that it is useless to vote or demonstrate, useless to invest precious time, energy, and hope, because nothing changes. For many ordinary citizens, nonparticipation is not the result of contentment, apathy, or lack of civic virtue but an understandably negative response to the political realities they experience.[44]

VOTING AS A DUTIFUL ACT

As we have just noted, voters do try to make rational choices in accordance with what they perceive to be their interests. But what is it that motivates them when no rational choice presents itself—as is usually the case? Millions just stay home, but what of the millions who vote?

The question is especially compelling when we realize that *many regular voters share the disillusionment of alienated nonvoters*. According to one survey, 57 percent of those who participated in the 1978 elections reported they did not think their candidates believed their own campaign statements. Another study found that of those who "didn't care at all" about the election outcome, 52 percent voted. In the 1980 presidential campaign, 51 percent of the voters said there were no "important differences" between the candidates and parties.[45]

Political leaders and educators usually characterize nonvoters as "slackers" and seldom as people who might be justifiably cynical about the electoral system. Conversely they portray voters as conscientious citizens performing their civic responsibility. Certainly many voters seem to agree. Studies show that many people participate not because of the substantive issues (since these are so often lacking) but out of a feeling of civic obligation.[46] For them the vote is an exercise more of civic virtue than of civic power. This raises the interesting question of who really is the deadwood of democracy: the "apathetic"

---

44. A similar conclusion can be drawn from Studs Terkel, *Division Street: America* (New York: Pantheon, 1967); Kimball, *The Disconnected*; Levin, *The Alienated Voter*; Harold V. Savitch, "Powerlessness in an Urban Ghetto: The Case of Political Biases and Differential Access in New York City," *Polity*, 5, Fall 1972, pp. 17–56; Parenti, "Power and Pluralism"; Lewis Lipsitz, "On Political Belief: The Grievances of the Poor," in Philip Green and Sanford Levinson (eds.), *Power and Community* (New York: Pantheon, 1969), pp. 142–72.

45. *New York Times*, November 16, 1980; Christopher Dodd, "We Have to Decide Why We Are Democrats," *American*, Winter 1982, pp. 16–17; Angus Campbell et al., *The American Voter* (New York: Wiley, 1960), pp. 103–6.

46. Campbell et al., loc. cit.

or the "civic minded," those who see no reason to vote or those who vote with no reason?

There are, of course, other inducements to voting besides a sense of civic obligation. The tendency to vote for the lesser, or lesser known, of two evils has already been noted. The location of undesirable traits in one party suggests the relative absence of these traits in the other and sometimes becomes enough reason for partisan choice. Thus the suspicion that Democrats might favor Blacks and labor unions leads some middle-class Whites to assume that the Republican party is devoted to their interests, a conclusion that may have no basis in the actual performance of Republican officeholders. Similarly, the identification of Republicans as "the party of big business" suggests to some working-class voters that, in contrast, the Democrats are *not* for business but for the "little man," a conclusion that may be equally unfounded.

Nowadays citizens are more inclined to identify themselves as "independents" and to look with distrust on both political parties.[47] Yet they continue to vote for major-party candidates, even if in split-ticket fashion, usually because no real independent is running. They are "independent" voters largely within the confines of the two-party monopoly.

Some people vote because it is "the only thing the ordinary person can do."[48] Not to exercise one's franchise is to consign oneself to total political impotence, an uncomfortable condition for those who have been taught they are self-governing. Voting not only induces a feeling of efficacy, it often *results* from such a feeling. Persons with a high sense of political efficacy are the more likely to vote. High efficacy is related to a citizen's educational and class level: better-educated people of comfortable income who feel most efficacious in general also tend to feel more politically efficacious than lower-income persons. But while many studies relate sense of political efficacy to voting, there is almost nothing relating sense of political efficacy to actual efficacy. In fact there may be little relationship between the two.[49]

The argument is sometimes made that if deprived groups have been unable to win their demands from the political system, it is be-

---

47. Norman H. Nie, Sidney Verba, and John R. Petrocik, *The Changing American Voter* (Cambridge, Mass.: Harvard University Press, 1976).

48. Robert Lane, *Political Ideology* (New York: Free Press, 1962), p. 166; Gabriel Almond and Sidney Verba, *The Civic Culture* (Boston: Little, Brown, 1963), p. 131.

49. See Robert R. Alford and Harry M. Scoble, "Sources of Local Political Involvement," *American Political Science Review*, 62, December 1968, pp. 1192–1206. Alan Wertheimer, "In Defense of Compulsory Voting," in J. Roland Pennock and John Chapman (eds.), *NOMOS XVI: Participation in Politics* (New York: Lieber-Atherton, 1975).

cause they are numerically weak compared to White, middle-class America. In a system that responds to the democratic power of numbers, a minority poor cannot hope to have its way. The representative principle works well enough, but the poor are not numerous enough. Therefore, the deficiency is in the limited numbers of persons advocating change and not in the representative system, which operates according to majoritarian principles. What is curious about this argument is that it is never applied to more select minority interests—for instance, oilmen. Now oilmen are far less numerous than the poor, yet the deficiency of their numbers, or of the numbers of other tiny minorities like bankers, industrialists, and millionaire investors, does not result in any lack of government responsiveness to their wants. On most important matters government policy is determined less by the majoritarian principle and more by the economic strength of private interests. The fact that government does little for the minority poor does not mean that it operates according to majoritarian principles, for it does very little for the working majority.[50]

THE DEMOCRATIC INPUT

There are two sweeping propositions that might mistakenly be drawn from what has been said thus far: (1) It does not matter who is elected. (2) Elected officials are indifferent to voter desires and other popular pressures. Both these notions are far from being the whole picture.

As already mentioned, many people reject voting not only because they feel there is no choice but because they see politics itself as something that cannot deliver anything significant even if a dedicated anti-establishment candidate is elected. And given the plutocratic dominance of the two-party monopoly, they are not too far wrong. Yet it should be noted that even within the confines of capitalist public policy, people's lives can be affected for better or worse by what happens within the electoral realm. Having correctly observed that two-party elections are a rigged charade designed to blur real issues, some people incorrectly conclude that what Democrats and Republicans do once elected to office is also inconsequential and farcical. In truth, major-party policies can have an important effect on our well-being—as the previous chapters on what government does in the realm

---

50. In any case, the poor are not the only people who want change. A 1980 postelection survey found that 51 percent of the voters in general and 58 percent of nonvoters agree with the statement, "The country needs more radical change than is possible through the ballot box." *New York Times*, November 16, 1980.

of health, education, the environment, taxation, and foreign and military policy testify.

In western Europe, benefiting from the far more democratic system of proportional representation, left-wing parties have established a viable presence in parliaments, even ruling from time to time. While this has never proven sufficient to bring the structural changes needed for socialism, the left parties have helped create labor conditions superior to those found in the U.S. Contrary to common belief, American workers have less protection and fewer benefits than their French, German, and Benelux counterparts, including paid vacations, family allowances, safety conditions, protection from speed-ups, the right to collective bargaining, and job security. Who is elected, then, *can* make a difference within a limited but important range of policy options.

In addition, there is ample evidence indicating that elected representatives are not totally indifferent to voter demands, since—along with money—votes are still the means to office and a source of power. The non-electoral pressures of demonstrations, civil disobedience, strikes, riots, and other uprisings and agitations were the crucial factors in the popular gains made in the 1930s and the civil-rights and antiwar struggles of the 1960s. Yet elections should not be entirely discounted. To the extent that many voters are concerned with the issues, so must the elected officeholders be, or pretend to be. When an issue wins broad, well-organized support and receives prominent attention in the media, then officeholders cannot remain supremely indifferent to it for long. Most often they respond with deceitful assurances. For instance, dozens of members of Congress who pledged to vote against draft registration in 1978 voted for registration in 1980. The heaviest applause line in President Carter's 1977 Inaugural Address was his vow to "move this year a step towards our ultimate goal—the elimination of all nuclear weapons from this Earth." But his administration then went on to build two or three more bombs a day.[51]

Politicians regularly make false assurances and empty promises, but the pressures of democratic opinion sometimes force them to place limits on how singlemindedly they may serve the moneyed powers and how unresponsive they may remain to the needs of ordinary people.

Still, whatever democratic responsiveness exists within the monopolistic confines of the two-party system, it is felt by growing num-

---

51. Sidney Lens, "The Irrelevant Ballot Box," *Progressive*, September 1980, p. 40.

bers of people to be insufficient in dealing with the problems that beset this country. So, in scores of towns and cities across the nation—despite every discouragement from the two-party monopoly—progressive third parties or independent candidates are gaining support and visibility, building coalitions, and reaching people who have previously been inactive.[52]

To summarize some of the observations offered in this chapter: important structural and material factors so predetermine the range of electoral issues and choices as to raise a serious question about the representative quality of the political system. Mass politics requires mass resources. Being enormously expensive affairs, elections are best utilized by those interests endowed with the resources necessary to take advantage of them. Politics has always been largely "a rich man's game." Ironically enough, the one institutional arrangement that is ostensibly designed to register the will of the many serves to legitimize the rule of the privileged few. The way people respond to political reality depends on the way that reality is presented to them. If people have become apathetic and cynical, including many of those who vote, it is at least partly because the electoral system and the major-party organizations resist the kind of creative involvement that democracy is supposed to nurture. It is one thing to say that people tend to be uninvolved, ill-informed, and given to impoverished and stereotyped notions about political life. It is quite another to maintain a system that propagates these tendencies with every known distraction and discouragement. Elections might better be considered a symbol of democratic governance than a guarantee of it, and voting often seems to be less an exercise than a surrender of sovereignty.

Still, in the face of all discouragements, third-party challenges continue to arise among people who seek a democratic alternative—bringing to mind the observation made years ago by the great American socialist Eugene Victor Debs: "I would rather vote for what I want and not get it than vote for what I don't want and get it."

---

52. Richard Walton, "Citizens Party," *Nation*, May 16, 1981, p. 589.

12

Who Governs?
Leaders, Lobbyists,
or Labor?

Tocqueville once said that the wealthy have little interest in governing the working people, they simply want to use them.[1] Yet members of the capitalist class seldom have been slow in assuming the burdens of public office. Not every important political leader is rich but many are, and those who are not are usually beholden to moneyed interests. Not all wealthy persons are engaged in ruling; some prefer to concentrate on other things. The ruling class, or plutocracy, consists largely of the politically active members of the wealthy class.

THE RULING CLASS

While the less glorious tasks of vote harvesting have often fallen to persons of modest class and ethnic origins, the top state and federal leadership positions, to this day, have remained largely in the hands of White, Protestant, middle-aged, upper-income males of conventional political opinion, drawn from the top ranks of corporate management, from the prominent law firms and banks of Wall Street, and, less frequently, from the military, the elite universities, the foundations, and the scientific establishment.

From the beginning of the American Republic to modern times, the great majority of those who have occupied the top political offices

---

1. Alexis de Tocqueville, *Democracy in America*, vol. 2 (New York: Vintage, 1945), p. 171.

"The Duke and Duchess of A.T. & T., the Count and Countess of Citicorp, the Earl of Exxon, and the Marchioness of Avco. The Duke of Warnaco . . ."

of the nation—including the presidency and vice-presidency, the cabinet and Supreme Court—have come from wealthy families (the upper 5 or 6 percent of the population), and most of the remainder have come from well-off, middle-class origins (moderately successful businessmen, commercial farmers, and professionals).[2] Of those who went to college, more than one-third attended the elite Ivy League

2. C. Wright Mills, *The Power Elite* (New York: Oxford University Press, 1956), pp. 400–2; C. William Domhoff, *Who Rules America?* (Englewood Cliffs, N.J.: Prentice-Hall, 1967), especially chapters 3 and 4; Domhoff, *The Higher Circles* (New York: Vintage, 1970); Domhoff, *The Powers That Be* (New York: Vintage, 1979); John C. Donovan, *The Cold Warriors* (Lexington, Mass.: Heath, 1973); Martin Weil, *A Pretty Good Club: The Founding Fathers of the U.S. Foreign Service* (New York: Norton, 1978); John Schmidhauser, *The Supreme Court* (New York: Holt, Rinehart and Winston, 1960).

schools. Since World War II, bankers, industrialists, and military men, in that order of frequency, have occupied almost all the top government positions. The men who ran the nation's defense establishment between 1940 and 1967 "were so like one another in occupation, religion, style and social status that, apart from a few Washington lawyers, Texans and mavericks, it was possible to locate the offices of all of them within fifteen city blocks in New York, Boston and Detroit."[3]

The wealthy carry into public life many of the class interests and values that shape their business careers. Be they of "old families" or newly arrived, liberal or conservative, they do not advocate the demolition of the economic system under which they prosper. The few rich persons who adopt leftward leanings are not usually invited into positions of power. Conversely, persons from modest class background such as Richard Nixon, Lyndon Johnson, and Ronald Reagan attract the financial backing that enables them to rise to the top by showing themselves to be—at a fairly early stage of their political careers—faithful and effective guardians of the privileged circles. Some politicians, academic advisors, and journalists are coopted into the ruling ranks, but for the most part, the plutocracy recruits its top members from its own social class. In any case, the crucial factor is not the class origin of leaders but the class interest they serve and the class they inhabit while serving. The question is not only "who governs?" but "who benefits and who doesn't?"—which is why so much attention is given in this book to policy outputs.

Government and business elites are linked by institutional, financial, and social ties and move easily between public and private leadership posts.[4] It takes a good deal of organization to wield and coordinate economic wealth and political power. So there are organizations like the Council on Foreign Relations, a private advisory group that plays an unofficial but crucial role in shaping American policy and recruiting elites for leadership posts. It is composed, like the ruling class itself, of corporate directors, military chiefs, White House and cabinet officers, influential members of Congress, and a few key pub-

---

3. Richard Barnet, *Roots of War* (New York: Atheneum, 1972), pp. 48–49.

4. Regarding their social ties: many elites go to the same schools, work in the same firms, play at the same vacation spots, intermarry, and dine together; (see the guest list for a dinner given in honor of President Reagan, *Washington Star*, February 28, 1981.) The elites even go to summer camp together: for almost a century the top decision-makers in business, government, the military, and media have gathered every summer for a week or two at Bohemian Grove, a 2,700-acre male-only retreat in California, for recreation and confabulation: Rick Clogher, "Weaving Spider, Come Not Here," *Mother Jones*, August 1981, pp. 28–35.

lishers, news commentators, and academics. In one year the major oil companies had thirty of their top executives on the council. Its members have included Rockefellers, DuPonts, and Morgans and various acolytes like Henry Kissinger. President Ford appointed fourteen council members to positions in his administration. When one council member, Robert McNamara, a former secretary of defense, retired as president of the World Bank in 1981, a dinner was given on his behalf by David Rockefeller. The corporate and political leaders who attended were described by the *Washington Post* as "the country's informal council of elders for most of two decades. . . . As Democrats and Republicans, the men . . . had quibbled over the years on the details of American foreign policy, but seldom over the broad outlines. The policy was based on an enlightened partnership between Washington and Wall Street. On this there was agreement."[5]

Of prominence has been the Trilateral Commission, a private assemblage of business and political luminaries from the major capitalist countries, initiated by David Rockefeller for the purpose of coordinating and protecting international capitalism in a changing world. Its members have included seventeen top members of the Carter administration, including the president and vice-president, and every member of the National Security Council, the nation's highest official policy-making body.[6]

Some observers see the Reagan administration as representing a new Sun Belt elite in conflict with the eastern Establishment. In fact, five of Reagan's first eight cabinet appointments held degrees from Yale or Harvard. At least ten of the seventeen Reagan cabinet officers admitted to being millionaires, rather like the "millionaire cabinets" of previous administrations.[7] This new group initiated policies that were largely beneficial to the military and big business and detrimental to the working populace. There were serious differences over degree and timing regarding particular policies between Eastern Ivy League and New Right Sun Belt millionaire policymakers. But no great ruling class schism occurred. If anything, by the end of 1982 Reagan was showing signs of abandoning some of his New Right pos-

---

5. *Washington Post*, March 23, 1981.

6. Holly Sklar (ed.), *Trilateralism* (Boston: South End Press, 1980).

7. *New York Times*, December 12, 1980; *Daily World*, February 14, 1981. To avoid the appearance of conflict of interest, wealthy persons who assume government posts place their assets into "blind trusts" administered usually by a close associate. The U.S. Comptroller-General reviewed 26 blind trusts of former top federal officials and found none of them met Civil Service standards: Henry Bretton, *The Power of Money* (Albany, N.Y.: State University of New York Press, 1980), pp. 191–200. On the Reagan plutocracy see Ron Brownstein and Nina Easton, *Reagan's Ruling Class* (Washington, D.C.: Center for the Study of Responsive Law, 1982).

tures and making concessions to the mainstream conservatives on tax policies and budget deficits.

The policies that plutocrats pursue in office frequently are connected to the corporate interests they represent in their private lives. Thus Attorney-General William French Smith, who is responsible for enforcing antitrust laws, is himself something of a walking trust, having served as counsel or director for companies that are interlocked with top firms in banking, defense, oil, and some 35 other industries. Similarly the decision makers involved in the U.S. armed intervention against the worker-student uprising in the Dominican Republic in 1965 consisted of Ellsworth Bunker, Averell Harriman, and others who were financially linked to large sugar companies that depended on Dominican sugar for their operations. "Even without these direct economic interests, it would be difficult for these gentlemen in their 'neutral' decision-making roles to escape the assumptions, inclinations and priorities inculcated by their economic and social milieu."[8]

The Things Money Can Buy

One of the many ways the ruling class exercises its influence over the democratic process is by expending large sums of money to influence elections. A small number of big donors pay the bulk of congressional, state, and local campaign expenses.[9] In 1972 ninety-five wealthy individuals donated $47.5 million to the Nixon reelection campaign.[10] Electoral spending figures confirm the maxim that the better financed candidate usually wins: thus in 1978, 1980, and 1982 the bigger spenders won in over 80 percent of the House and Senate races and in most of the gubernatorial contests.[11] In 1981 alone, Republican national and congressional party committees raised $73.6 million, while their Democratic counterparts garnered $9.9 million.[12]

---

8. Fred Goff and Michael Locker, *The Violence of Domination: U.S. Power and the Dominican Republic*, quoted in James Petras, "U.S. Business and Foreign Policy," *New Politics*, 6, Fall 1967, p. 76.

9. An excellent study is David Nichols, *Financing Elections: The Politics of an American Ruling Class* (New York: Franklin Watts, 1974); Herbert Alexander, *Money in Politics* (Washington, D.C.: Public Affairs Press, 1972); Herbert Alexander, *Financing Politics* (Washington, D.C.: Congressional Quarterly Press, 1976); G. William Domhoff, *Fat Cats and Democrats* (Englewood Cliffs, N.J.: Prentice-Hall, 1972).

10. In 1978 Congressional candidates spent almost $150 million on their primary and election contests; by 1980 the figure had jumped to $239 million, according to a statement from the Federal Elections Commission to me, August 31, 1981, and *Washington Post*, February 21, 1982.

11. National Committee for an Effective Congress, "Save This House" bulletin, Washington, D.C., 1982. *Washington Post*, November 7, 1982.

12. *Washington Post*, January 17, 1982.

However, money knows no firm party lines, only class lines: Democrats with strategic committee positions are often generously funded by business interests that seek favors from those already in power, regardless of party label.[13] Thus in a successful effort to defeat legislation that would have limited hospital costs, the American Medical Association poured more than $3.2 million into the campaign coffers of both Democrats and Republicans who were on committees dealing with medical and hospital proposals.[14] Similarly, banking, defense, real estate, oil and gas, private utility, and other special interests contribute huge sums to candidates at all levels of government to help ensure that laws are written in ways pleasing to them.[15]

While politicians insist that campaign contributions do not influence them, few are inclined to go against those who support them financially. A former assistant to two prominent Democratic senators made the following observation:

> Any member of Congress who says donations don't influence him is lying. All of them are corrupt. The only question is the degree of corruption. One reason members of Congress insist that money doesn't influence them is that they . . . often become convinced of the rightness of their backers' causes without admitting it even to themselves. In time, they come to really believe that the guy who gives the big dough is the best guy and that helping him is in the public interest. But campaign money *has* to influence even the most incorruptible men here, because most people don't give away large sums of money for nothing.[16]

The bipartisan influence of big-business contributors is so pronounced as to move one Democratic senator to remind his party colleagues that they were neglecting to keep up appearances as "the party of the people." In a speech on the Senate floor urging that the scientific patents of the $25 billion space program not be given away

---

13. Everett Ladd, Jr., *Where Have All the Voters Gone?* (New York: Norton, 1978), p. 15.

14. *New York Times*, January 11, 1973; Common Cause Report (Washington, D.C., 1978).

15. *Washington Post*, May 26, 1981, for industry's contributions to influence environmental legislation. Defense contractors have the largest campaign funds of all corporations. Gordon Adams, *The Iron Triangle: The Politics of Defense Contracting* (New York: Council on Economic Priorities, 1981).

16. A congressional aide quoted in Richard Harris, "Annals of Politics: A Fundamental Hoax," *New Yorker*, August 7, 1971, p. 54. In the words of Senator Russell Long: "When you are talking in terms of large campaign contributions . . . the distinction between a campaign contribution and a bribe is almost a hair's line difference."

to private corporations but applied for public benefit, Russell Long (D-La.) made these candid remarks:

> Many of these [corporate] people have much influence. I, like others, have importuned some of them for campaign contributions for my party and myself. Nevertheless, we owe it to the people, now and then, to save one or two votes for them. This is one such instance. . . . We Democrats can trade on the dubious assumption that we are protector of the public interest only so long if we permit things like these patent giveaways.[17]

In 1976 the Supreme Court removed most of the limits on campaign spending imposed by federal law. The Court reasoned that limitations on expenditures were an infringement of the First Amendment right to free speech. Individuals are now allowed to expend any amount in an "independent" effort to elect or defeat any candidate, and candidates themselves may spend as much as they desire of their personal or family fortunes on their own campaigns, a decision greatly favoring the wealthy. The Court also upheld the use of public money to fund major-party presidential candidates.[18]

Public financing of presidential campaigns was originally advocated by big donors who complained that campaigns were costing them too much and by reformers who thought publicly funded candidates would no longer be obligated to private interests. In fact, the law has amounted to a splendid feed for Democrats and Republicans. In 1980 a sum of $120 million in tax money was paid for the primaries, national conventions, and presidential electoral expenses of the Republican and Democratic parties. And conservative fat cats still contributed an additional $12.2 million to Reagan's campaign and lesser sums to Carter through "independent" committees.[19]

The 1974 Federal Election Campaign Act, backed by subsequent court decisions and Federal Election Commission rulings, allows corporations to form political action committees (PACs) that can solicit contributions from stockholders and from all company employees— from managers on down—and can spend as much as they please on candidates of their choice. PAC operating expenses now can be paid out of corporate funds. The result has been an explosion of corporate PACs—776 in 1978, 954 in 1980, 1,327 in 1982—and a dramatic in-

---

17. *Congressional Record*, vol. 112, part 9, June 2, 1966.
18. *New York Times*, January 31, 1976.
19. Mary Meehan, "How the Donkey and the Elephant Turned Into Pigs," *Inquiry*, July 7 and 21, 1980, pp. 11–15.

crease in big-business contributions, especially to conservatives of both parties.[20]

LOBBYISTS AND THEIR SPECIAL INTERESTS

Lobbyists are persons hired by interest groups to influence legislative and administrative policies. Some political scientists see lobbying as essentially a "communication process." They argue that the office-holder's perception of a policy is influenced primarily by the information reaching him. The lobbyist provides that information. By this view, the techniques of the "modern" lobbyist consist mostly of disseminating data and "expert" information and making public appearances before legislative committees rather than the obsolete tactics of secret deals and bribes.[21]

Those who propagate this image of the influence system overestimate the changes that have occurred within it. The development of new lobbying techniques has not brought an end to the older, cruder ones. Along with the slick brochures, expert testimony, and technical reports, corporate lobbyists still have the succulent campaign contribution; the "volunteer" campaign workers; the fat lecture fee; the stock award; the high-paying job offer in private industry; the lavish parties and prostitutes; the meals, transportation, housing, and vacation accommodations; and the many other hustling enticements of money. "Many a financial undertaking on Capitol Hill," writes Washington columnist Jack Anderson, "has been consummated in cold cash—that is, with envelopes or briefcases stuffed with greenbacks, a curious medium for honorable transactions."[22]

From the lowliest city councilman to the White House itself, officeholders accept money and favors from lobbyists in return for favored treatment. The late Wright Patman (D.-Tex.) former chairman of the House Banking and Currency Committee, complained:

> Members [of the committee] have been offered hugh blocks of bank stocks free of charge and directorships on bank boards. Freshmen members have been approached within hours of their arrival in Washington

---

20. *Washington Post,* January 19, 1982; *New York Times,* January 20, 1982.

21. Lester Milbrath, *The Washington Lobbyists* (Chicago: Rand McNally, 1963), p. 185 and *passim*. See also Douglass Cater's comparison of the "new" with the "old" NAM in his *Power in Washington* (New York: Random House, 1964), p. 208.

22. *Washington Post,* August 7, 1980; also Robert Winter-Berger, *The Washington Pay-Off* (New York: Dell, 1972).

and offered quick and immediate loans. In one instance that was reported to me, the bank told the member, 'Just write a check, we will
honor it.'[23]

"Everyone has a price," Howard Hughes once told an associate
who later recalled that the billionaire handed out about $400,000
yearly to "councilmen and county supervisors, tax assessors, sheriffs,
state senators and assemblymen, district attorneys, governors, congressmen and senators, judges—yes, and vice-presidents and presidents, too."[24]

Many large corporations have a special division dedicated to performing favors for officeholders. The services include everything from
free Caribbean trips on private jet planes to loans, private contacts,
and illegal gifts. An employee at ITT's congressional-liaison section
publicly complained about the way congressmen continually called
her office for favors "on a big scale." This situation "shocked" her, she
said, even though "very little in Washington would shock me."[25]

The American Petroleum Institute, an organization of oil, gas,
and petrochemical companies, spends $75 million a year in lobbying
efforts in Washington and has a dozen full-time lobbyists. The oil industry employs over 600 people to pressure Congress and government
agencies.[26] The Chamber of Commerce, with its 89,500 corporate
members, $20 million annual budget, and 1,200 local "Congressional
watch committees," can bring down a snowstorm of mail and a
mountain of pressure on the lawmakers and is regarded as "very effective" on Capitol Hill.[27] Of special note is the Business Roundtable, the
"trillion-dollar voice" of big business, considered by many to be the
most powerful lobby in Washington. The Roundtable is composed of
190 chief executives of the nation's blue-chip corporations, one or another of whom are always in contact with key figures in the White
House, the cabinet, and Congress. Credited with thwarting or water-

---

23. Robert Cirino, *Don't Blame the People* (New York: Vintage, 1972), p. 144. Not
long before a crucial vote on commodity trading in the House Ways and Means Committee, commodity-industry PACs passed out money contributions to 22 committee
members, 19 of whom then voted special tax exemptions for professional commodity
speculators: *Washington Post*, August 8, 1981.
24. Howard Kohn, "The Hughes-Nixon-Lansky Connection," *Rolling Stone*, May
20, 1976, p. 44.
25. *New York Times*, March 31, 1972. For a fascinating eyewitness account of corruption and special influence in Washington see Winter-Berger, *The Washington Pay-
Off*; see also Lawrence Gilson, *Money and Secrecy* (New York: Praeger, 1972).
26. Jack Newfield, "Oil: The Imperial Lobby," *Village Voice*, November 5, 1979,
p. 1.
27. Jack Anderson, "Lobbyists: The Unelected Lawmakers in Washington," *Parade*,
March 16, 1980, p. 4.

ing down antitrust, environmental, pro-labor, pro-consumer, and tax-reform measures, the Roundtable exercises an influence over government eclipsing even that of the National Association of Manufacturers and the U.S. Chamber of Commerce. Much of the Roundtable's effectiveness stems from the powerful economic positions its members occupy in heavy industry, mining, and banking.[28]

Summing up the power of lobbyists, Speaker of the House Tip O'Neill said: "The grab of special interests is staggering. It will destroy the legislative process."[29] It has certainly destroyed much legislative integrity. The case of Claude Wild, Jr., is instructive. As a vice-president of Gulf Oil and a lobbyist over a 12-year period, Wild had the full-time job of passing out about $4.1 million of Gulf's money to more than one hundred U.S. senators and representatives, eighteen governors, and scores of judges and local politicians. His gift list included Lyndon Johnson, Richard Nixon, Gerald Ford, and Jimmy Carter (when he was governor of Georgia). Over a ten-year period, four oil companies paid out $8 million in illegal payments to 45 members of Congress.[30] None of the above recipients was ever prosecuted.

In addition to the sums distributed at home, the multinationals have paid out many millions in bribes and political contributions to reactionary governments, militarists, and conservative leaders in countries like South Korea, Bolivia, Iran (under the Shah), Taiwan, Japan, and Italy.[31] The international influence system works both ways: there also are about 15,000 persons employed as foreign lobbyists, spending $100 million a year to influence U.S. lawmakers and other public officials.[32]

The big-time Washington lobbyists are usually attorneys or business people who have proven themselves articulate representatives of their firms, or ex-legislators or former bureaucrats with good connec-

---

28. The Roundtable's chief executive officers "have immediate access to many legislators just because they are the heads of their corporations"—according to "Business Battles Back," *Environmental Action*, December 2, 1978, p. 13; also Mark Green and Andrew Buchsbaum, *The Corporate Lobbies* (Washington, D.C.: Public Citizen, 1980); Philip Burch, Jr., "The Business Roundtable," *Research in Political Economy*, vol. 4 (JAI Press), pp. 101–127.

29. Anderson, "Lobbyists: The Unelected Lawmakers . . ."

30. According to SEC investigators: *Washington Post*, March 22, 1976; *New York Times*, September 9, 1976. On Claude Wild and the Gulf payments see *Wall Street Journal*, November 17, 1975; *Philadelphia Bulletin*, November 12, 1975; *Washington Post*, June 24, 1979.

31. *New York Times*, February 5, 1976; Anthony Sampson, "How the Oil Companies Help the Arabs Keep Prices High," *New York*, September 22, 1975, p. 48; "Profits of Crime," *Nation*, June 30, 1979, p. 772.

32. Russell Warren Howe and Sarah Hays Trott, *The Power Peddlers* (Garden City, N.Y.: Doubleday, 1977).

tions. Whatever their varied backgrounds, the one common resource lobbyists should have at their command in order to be effective is money. Money buys what one House aide called that "basic ingredient of all lobbying"—*accessibility* to the officeholder and, with that, the opportunity to shape his or her judgments with arguments of the lobbyist's own choosing. But this takes more than just accessibility. As Woodrow Wilson once pointed out:

> Suppose you go to Washington and try to get at your Government. You will always find that while you are politely listened to, the men really consulted are the men who have the big stake—the big bankers, the big manufacturers, and the big masters of commerce. . . . The masters of the Government of the United States are the combined capitalists and manufacturers of the United States.[33]

It is, then, something more than "information flow" that determines influence, the decisive factor being not just the message but the messenger. Even if information does play a crucial role in shaping the officeholder's awareness of the problem, the ability to disseminate information to decisionmakers, to cultivate liaisons, and to propagate one's cause itself presumes access to organization, expertise, time, and labor—things money can buy. In addition, the mere possession of great wealth and the control of industry and jobs give corporate interests an advantage unknown to ordinary working citizens, for business's claims are paraded as the "needs of the economy" and, as it were, of the nation itself. Having the advantage of pursuing their interests within the framework of a capitalist system, capitalists predetermine and control the range of solutions.[34]

The business-dominated pressure system also operates at the state and local levels. The influence exercised on state legislatures by big-money interests "is so widespread in this country it appears endemic."[35] The state legislatures are "the willing instrumentalities of an array of private corporate entities."[36] While most of the public has no idea what their state representatives are doing, the banks, land developers, utilities, and manufacturers carry on a regular liaison with

---

33. Quoted in D. Gilbarg, "United States Imperialism" in Bill Slate (ed.), *Power to the People* (New York: Tower, 1970), p. 67.

34. For a discussion of how power is used not only to *pursue* interests but to *define* them, see my *Power and the Powerless* (New York: St. Martin's Press, 1978).

35. Martin Waldron, "Shadow on the Alamo," *New York Times Book Review*, July 10, 1972, p. 2.

36. "The Sick State of the State Legislatures," *Newsweek*, April 19, 1965, p. 31; *Boston Globe*, September 8, 1976.

them, showering them with campaign contributions, legal retainers, special-term "loans," and investment tips. Subservience to business is so pervasive as to make it sometimes difficult to tell the lawmakers from the lobbyists. State legislators usually work only part-time at their tasks, devoting the better part of their days to their private businesses, which often benefit from their legislative efforts. About half the New York legislators are attorneys who also service businesses with direct interests in state laws. A sizable number of the legislators are trustees or directors of banks.[37]

Surveying the organized pressure groups in America, E. E. Schattschneider notes: "*The system is very small.* The range of organized, identifiable, known groups is amazingly narrow; there is nothing remotely universal about it."[38] The pressure system, he concludes, is largely dominated by business groups, the majority of citizens belonging to no organization that is effectively engaged in pressure politics. Almost all organized groups, even nonbusiness ones such as religious, educational, and professional associations, "reflect an upper-class tendency,"[39] not surprisingly, since ordinary working people rarely have the time and money that would enable them to participate.

The pressure system is "small" and "narrow" only in that it represents a highly select portion of the public. In relation to government itself, the system is a substantial operation. Some 15,000 lobbyists prowl the Capitol's corridors and lobbies (whence their name).[40] Others seek favorable rulings from agencies within the vast bureaucracy. Still others are engaged in public relations. Lobbyists are so helpful that members of Congress sometimes rely on them to perform tasks normally done by congressional staffs. Lobbyists will draft legislation, write speeches, and plant stories in the press on behalf of cooperative lawmakers. Lobbyists "put in millions of hours each year" to make the world a better place for their clients, "and they succeed on a scale that is undreamed of by most ordinary citizens."[41] A favorable adjustment in rates for interstate carriers, a special tax benefit for a family oil trust, a high-interest bond issue for big investors, a special charter for a bank, a tariff protection for auto producers, the leasing of public

---

37. *Times-Union* (Albany, N.Y.), January 19, 1974. This same story quotes a prominent banking official as saying; "I don't buy legislators dinners, I buy legislators." For an account of how the nuclear industry influences state and local politicians see Lonnie Rosenwald and Rod Gramer, "So What If the Water's Nuked?" *Progressive*, October 1980, p. 41.

38. E. E. Schattschneider, *The Semi-Sovereign People* (New York: Holt, Rinehart and Winston, 1960), p. 31. Italics in the original.

39. *Ibid.*, pp. 33–34, and the studies cited therein.

40. Anderson, "Lobbyists: The Unelected Lawmakers . . ."

41. Harris, "Annals of Politics," p. 56.

lands to a lumber company, emergency funding for a faltering aero-nautics plant, a postal subsidy for advertising firms, the easing of safety standards for a food processor, the easing of pollution controls for a chemical company, a special acreage allotment for peanut growers and tobacco growers, an investment guarantee to a housing developer, a lease guarantee to a construction contractor—all these hundreds of bills and their thousands of special amendments and the tens of thousands of administrative rulings, which mean so much to particular interests and arouse the sympathetic efforts of legislators and bureaucrats, will go largely unnoticed by a public that pays the monetary and human costs and has not the means to make its case— or even to discover it has a case.

Public-interest groups, professing to speak for the great unorganized populace, make many demands for reform but have few of the resources that could move officeholders in a reformist direction. The relative sparsity of power resources available to them within the existing politico-economic system limits their worthwhile efforts. Congressional subcommittee counsel Peter Kinzler explains it this way: "There's the 23-year-old consumer lobbyist and the businessman who gives you $5000. Whom are you going to listen to?"[42]

"Grass-Roots Lobbying"

Pressure-group efforts are directed not only at officeholders but also at the public. Corporations and trade associations spend nearly one billion dollars a year on this "grass-roots lobbying," whereas environmental, consumer, and other public-interest groups spend three-tenths of one percent of that amount.[43] Grant McConnell offers one description of a grass-roots campaign:

> The electric companies, organized in the National Electric Light Association, had not only directly influenced Congressmen and Senators on a large scale, but had also conducted a massive campaign to control the substance of teaching in the nation's schools. Teachers in high schools and grammar schools were inundated with materials. . . . Each pamphlet included carefully planted disparagement of public ownership of utilities. The Association took very active, if inconspicuous, measures to insure that textbooks that were doctrinally impure on this issue were withdrawn from use and that more favorable substitutes were produced and used. College professors . . . were given supplemental incomes by the Associa-

42. "Business Battles Back," p. 14.
43. *Ibid.*, p. 12.

tion and, in return, not infrequently taught about the utility industry
with greater sympathy than before. . . . Public libraries, ministers, and
civic leaders of all kinds were subjected to the propagandistic efforts of
the electric companies.[44]

Consider also business's campaign against a consumer-protection
agency in the late 1970s. Trade associations got thousands of their local business members throughout the country to send letters to their
representatives and senators. The Business Roundtable hired a public-
relations firm to produce editorials and editorial cartoons opposing
the consumer agency and sent them free of charge to small daily and
weekly newspapers—over 800 of which reproduced them without
mention that they were political announcements from the Roundtable. "The use of such 'canned' editorial material from special interest groups is a routine practice among small newspapers."[45]

Business grass-roots lobbying often targets not "the people" in general, but the *right* people, the ones the legislator might find especially
persuasive: the radio-station owner, newspaper editor, franchise op-
erator, store manager, and Rotary Club officer in the lawmaker's
home district, and the campaign contributor who may live in *any* district.[46]

Some grass-roots lobbying is intended to build a climate of opinion
favorable to the corporate giants rather than to push a particular
piece of legislation. The steel, oil, and electronics companies do not
urge the public to support the latest tax-depreciation bill—if anything, they would prefer that citizens not trouble themselves with
thoughts on the subject—but they do "educate" the public, telling of
the many jobs the companies create, the progress and services they
provide, the loving care they supposedly give to the environment, etc.
This kind of "institutional advertising" attempts to place the desires of
the giant firms above politics and above controversy—a goal that is itself highly political.

In 1976 and in 1980 progressive groups in various states were able
to place referenda on the ballot pertaining to nuclear safety, state tax
reforms, public ownership of utilities, rent control, environmental
protection, and other issues. In response the business community
launched a multimillion-dollar media blitz to defeat most of these ini-

---

44. Grant McConnel, *Private Power and American Democracy* (New York: Knopf,
1966), p. 19.
45. "Business Battles Back," p. 13.
46. Now that election laws require candidates to reveal their contributors, business
pressure groups are able to contact these donors to assist in persuading a member of
Congress.

tiatives. In some states opinion polls showed that the defeated referenda had been supported by large margins in the early stages of the campaign, only to be rejected by the voters after massive propaganda assaults were launched by the corporations.[47]

DOES LABOR HAVE TOO MUCH POWER?

A 1982 survey found that more than two out of three Americans approve of labor unions and want them to thrive, yet many are concerned that unions exercise too much power in public life.[48] How powerful are unions? Certainly their material resources and political influence do not compare to those of business. Union busting is now a major industry, with more than a thousand consulting firms doing a $500 million yearly business teaching companies how to prevent workers from organizing and how to break existing unions. More than in most western industrial nations, unions in the United States are severely constrained by right-to-work laws and legal restrictions on strikes, boycotts, and organizing activities. The result is that union organizing is often arduous, and unions are declining in membership and losing more and more National Labor Relations elections.[49] During the 1980–1982 recession various industries used the threat of plant closings to extract benefit and wage concessions from unions "amounting to billions of dollars."[50]

Through much of their history unions have been the target of government repression. During the "McCarthy Era," press attention was focused on the famous and professional personages who were brought before congressional committees to account for their political associations and opinions. Less well remembered are the more numerous blue-collar victims, who were systematically purged from unions and fired from their jobs by bosses working in tandem with the FBI, congressional investigators, and conservative union factions. It was not the politics of union radicals as such that bothered business; it was that radical leaders and members were often more dedicated and effective in winning gains for labor. "The purge of labor, in that sense,

---

47. Corporations and trade assocations spent $2 million to defeat referenda in Massachusetts and $4 million to defeat a tax-reform initiative in Ohio that had the support of 30 statewide civic, farm, and labor groups. Nuclear interests spent close to $47 million around the country. See "Referenda Lessons," *Progressive*, March 1977, p. 11; *Boston Globe*, November 4, 1976; *In These Times*, January 14–20, 1981.

48. *Washington Post*, February 7, 1982.

49. Sidney Lens, "Disorganized Labor," *Nation*, February 24, 1979.

50. *New York Times*, June 13, 1982.

wasn't ideological at all: it was designed to weaken the labor movement by weakening its most militant leadership and rank and file."[51]

In a few cases, the more complacent and corrupt union leaders become union dealers, often powerful and undemocratic in relation to their own membership but tame junior partners of management, inclined to take on the boss's perspective, to emphasize labor's common stakes with capital, and to cooperate in speed-ups and in the surrender of union demands and benefits. On foreign-policy issues, they are usually conservative cold-war anticommunists who seek confrontations with the U.S.S.R. and support U.S. and CIA interventions in the Third World. In the worst instances, they turn the union organization into a personal empire, misusing funds and voting munificient salaries for themselves and their cohorts. A few union locals are infiltrated by racketeers who resort to gangland thuggery to intimidate the rank-and-file into submission, keeping wages low and doing nothing to assist the membership. In return, they win management's ready acceptance as a union.[52]

Far from having too much power, honest and progressive unions are fighting for their lives against hostile laws, court rulings, NLRB decisions, government harassment, congressional witch-hunting, corporate union busting, and negative images propagated by the business-owned media.[53]

To juxtapose Big Labor with Big Business in the manner of some American government textbooks is to overlook the fact that pro-business persons have a near monopoly on the top decision-making positions of successive administrations and of most other political and social institutions. Also, while labor can be an effective and important lobby on social security, health, education, job safety, the minimum wage, and other issues, it does not come close to matching the spending and lobbying powers of business in Washington and the state capitals and at the grass roots. In the 1980 campaign, corporate and New Right PACs outspent labor and liberal groups 4 to 1, or $100 million to $25 million. If we add the millions business gave to lawmakers between elections, the millions it spends on grass-roots and referenda campaigns, and the millions spent directly by wealthy individuals

---

51. Howard Rodman, "Working Over the Workingman," *Rights* (special report of the National Emergency Civil Liberties Committee, New York, n.d., circa 1981), p. 11; also Richard Boyer and Herbert Morais, *Labor's Untold Story* (New York: United Electrical, Radio and Machine Workers, 1972), pp. 340–80.

52. For one account of crime in the Teamster's union see Jack Newfield, "This Felon Controls the Most Corrupt Union in New York," *Village Voice*, November 6, 1978, pp. 1, 11–14.

53. See chapters 2 and 10 for statements on media stereotyping of unions and working people.

and candidates, the ratio is closer to 10 to 1.[54] This is not to discount organized labor as a political force, but to indicate the insufficiency of its political strength, especially when measured against the needs and numbers of the working class it attempts to represent.

To the extent that working people have any mass democratic organization in the United States it is in the unions, which reach large numbers of people through their publications and donate substantial, if often insufficient, funds to more progressive candidates. The AFL-CIO played a vital role in the passage of the 1963 and 1964 civil-rights bills and has supported national health insurance, low-income housing, mass-transit systems, consumer protection, price controls on natural gas, and the Equal Rights Amendment and has opposed repressive measures like emergency detention. Many unions have backed pollution and environmental controls and anti-nuclear measures in coalitions with other organizations. Some of the biggest unions broke with the militaristic cold-war mentality of the AFL-CIO (sometimes called the AFL-CIA) and supported peace in Vietnam and nonintervention in El Salvador.[55]

CORRUPTION AS A WAY OF LIFE

In recent years there have been reports of corruption involving federal, state, and local officials in every state of the Union. In Congress, "corruption is so endemic that it's scandalous. Even the honest men are corrupted—usually by and for the major economic-interest groups and the wealthy individuals who together largely dominate campaign financing."[56] "In some states—Louisiana, for instance—scandals are so prolific that exposure of them has absolutely no impact."[57] In a six-year period, the number of public officials convicted in federal courts included a vice-president, three cabinet officers, three governors, thirty-four state legislators, twenty judges, five state attorneys general, twenty-eight mayors, eleven district attorneys, and 170 police officers—and this included only those unlucky or clumsy

---

54. *Guardian*, February 18, 1981; *Washington Post*, February 21, 1982; Tim Wheeler, "$100 Million for Right-Wing Campaigns," *Daily World*, October 3, 1978.

55. Andrew Levison, *The Working-Class Majority* (New York: Penguin Books, 1974); Mark Hertsgaard, "Energy Week Inc." *Nation*, March 21, 1981, p. 325.

56. George Agree, director of the National Committee for an Effective Congress, quoted in Harris, "Annals of Politics," p. 62.

57. Waldron, "Shadow on the Alamo," p. 2. See also Peter Cowen, "Graft Held Fact of Life in Boston," *Boston Globe*, October 2, 1972; and Paul Simon, "The Illinois State Legislature," *Harper's*, September 1964, p. 74.

enough to get caught.[58] Widespread corruption has been found in the police forces of New York, Chicago, Philadelphia, Indianapolis, Cleveland, Houston, Denver, and numerous smaller cities where police were protecting narcotics dealers and gamblers, accepting bribes, burglarizing stores (or covering up burglaries), looting parking meters, shaking down prostitutes, and intimidating witnesses who attempted to testify against police crime.[59] Meanwhile FBI leaders have used bureau funds for personal purposes; and FBI agents, supervisors, and inspectors considered it "accepted procedure" to pocket money officially reported as having been paid to "informers."[60]

On a still grander scale, the Nixon administration was implicated in major scandals involving the sale of wheat, an out-of-court settlement with ITT, price supports for dairy producers, corruption in the Federal Housing Administration, stock-market manipulations, and political espionage—the Watergate affair. Vice-President Spiro Agnew resigned from office because of charges of bribery, extortion, and corruption.[61] And a Senate investigation revealed that fraud, theft, and waste throughout the government might be costing the taxpayers as much as $25 billion annually.[62]

The career of Nelson Rockefeller provides an impressive example of the legal and illegal uses of money in politics. The Rockefeller family spent over $10 million on Nelson's successful campaign for governor of New York and another $12 million on his tries for the presidency in 1964 and 1968. At the time he was being considered for appointment to the vice-presidency to replace Spiro Agnew, Rockefeller admitted to having given nearly $1.8 million in gifts and loans to 18 public officials since 1957, including $50,000 to Henry Kissinger (an erstwhile Rockefeller employee) three days before Kissinger became special advisor to President Nixon, and $625,000 to the chairman of the Port Authority of New York. (David Rockefeller's Chase Manhattan Bank has large bond holdings in the Port Authority.) Various other associates received lavish cash gifts while they held state

---

58. For accounts of corruption in states like West Virginia, Maryland, and New Jersey see the articles published under the title "Revenue Sharing with the Rich and the Crooked," *Washington Monthly*, February 1972, pp. 8–38; also Bill Prochnau, "Corruption in Massachusetts: 'A Way of Life,' " *Washington Post*, January 1, 1981; and *Washington Post*, December 10, 1981.

59. *Time*, May 6, 1974; *New York Times*, March 11, 1974, March 2, 1975, and April 15, 1979; *Newsweek*, July 4, 1977.

60. *New York Times*, January 15 and December 6, 1978.

61. Agnew pleaded guilty to income-tax evasion, was fined $10,000, and was given three years' probation. In return for his guilty plea and resignation from the vice-presidency, the Justice Department dropped the other charges.

62. Common Cause Bulletin (Washington, D.C., 1979).

jobs—despite the fact that New York law prohibits public employees from accepting any gift greater than $25. At a Senate hearing, Rockefeller insisted that these payments were simply manifestations of his esteem for the recipients. "Sharing has always been part of my upbringing," he told the senators, none of whom doubled over with laughter.[63] Neither the House nor Senate committees investigating Rockefeller's nomination wondered aloud whether a "gift" to public officials who make decisions affecting one's private fortune might not better be called by its more forthright name, a "bribe." Despite these revelations, Congress confirmed Nelson Rockefeller as vice-president of the United States.

Campaigning for president in 1976, Jimmy Carter made a plea for honesty in government at a $100-a-plate dinner in Miami, while beside him on the dais sat a mayor recently imprisoned for tax evasion, a couple of Florida state senators who had just pleaded guilty to conflict of interest, a commissioner facing trial for bribery, and three other commissioners charged with fraud.[64]

In the 1980 campaign Ronald Reagan promised to return "honesty and decency" to public life. When elected president he appointed high-ranking officers like CIA director William Casey, Attorney-General William French Smith, Secretary of Labor Raymond Donovan, and others who soon came under fire because of allegedly false financial disclosures, involvement in investment swindles, and other questionable practices. While Secretary Donovan was being investigated for links to organized crime in 1982, two witnesses in the inquiry were murdered gangland style. There is published evidence indicating that members of the Reagan administration, including Attorney-General Smith, presidential aide Ed Meese, and President Reagan himself, have close links with underworld figures like Sidney Korshak—described by the California Organized Crime Commission as a "senior advisor" to organized-crime groups.[65]

The public looks upon the widespread corruption in America with growing cynicism, uttering jokes about the habits of politicians and sometimes failing to appreciate how the corrupt officeholder is a pow-

---

63. *Newsweek*, October 21, 1974; *New York Times*, October 7, 1974.

64. *Workers World*, May 7, 1976.

65. *Miami Herald*, January 25, 1981; *New York Times*, March 6, 1981, and May 19 and July 22, 1982; *Washington Post*, January 5, 1982; David Wise, "Why the President's Men Stumble," *New York Times Magazine*, July 18, 1982, pp. 14–17, 44–46. The most revealing article on Reagan is Dan Moldea, "The Mafia and The Right," *City Paper* (Washington, D.C.), March 12, 1982, pp. 1, 6–7. Wise notes that President Reagan and his wife Nancy "have been criticized for the more than $30,000 in gifts they have accepted since coming to the White House"; *op. cit.*, p. 16.

erbroker in a larger, financially venal politico-economic system. Rather than being a violation of the rules of the game, corruption is the name of the game. It is not so much a matter of finding a few bad apples as noting that the barrel itself is rotten.

Some observers see corruption as a more or less acceptable fact of life. Passing a little money under the table is just another way of oiling the wheels of government and getting things done. But corruption has gone beyond the petty bribe to reach momentous proportions. Corruption in government promotes policies that lead to permanent public indebtedness, inefficiency, and waste; it drains the public treasure to feed the private purse; it converts constructive social power into destructive private power.[66] Corruption vitiates laws and regulations that might otherwise safeguard occupational, health, environmental, and consumer interests; it undermines equal protection of the law, producing favoritism for the few who can pay and injury and neglect for the many who cannot.

Besides denouncing corruption we should understand the politico-economic system that makes it ubiquitous. The temptation for corporate interests to use large sums of money to win decisions that bring in vastly larger sums is strong; indeed, it is a temptation that promises grand rewards and relatively few risks, especially since those who would be the guardians of the law themselves have their palms out or are in other ways beholden to the corrupting powers. Politicians too face a competitive market, and their campaign expenses are burdensome. To avoid yielding to the special interests, to refuse to take from the haves, is to turn oneself into a have-not and lower one's chances of political survival.

In sum, if the powers and resources of the social order itself are used for the maximization of private greed and gain, and if the operational ethic is "looking out for number one," then corruption will be chronic rather than occasional, a systemic product rather than an outgrowth of the politician's flawed character.

---

66. Bretton, *The Power of Money*, pp. 186–206.

13

Congress: The Pocketing of Power

As noted earlier, the framers fashioned a Constitution with the intent of deflecting the popular will. In order to guard against democratic "excesses" and ensure that men of their class and convictions held the reins of government, they separated the functions of state into executive, legislative, and judicial branches and installed a system of checks and balances. These measures were designed to forestall popular action and prevent fundamental changes in the class order. The framers understood what some theorists today seem to have forgotten: in a society in which private wealth is in the hands of a few, the *diffusion* of power among the various segments of government does not necessarily mean the *democratization* of power but more likely the opposite. Confrontations between concentrated private wealth and fractured public power do not usually yield democratic results. Fragmented power is more readily pocketed by specialized, well-organized, entrenched private interests and is thereby less responsive to the mass public.

Looking specifically at the United States Congress, one is struck by how the diffusion of power has led to undemocratic results. The deficiencies of Congress have been documented by journalists, political scientists, and members of Congress themselves.[1] Without attempting

---

1. The best of recent critical studies is Mark Green and Michael Calabrese, *Who Runs Congress?* 3rd edition (New York: Bantam Books, 1979); see also Joseph Clark, *Congress: The Sapless Branch* (New York: Harper and Row, 1964); Drew Pearson and Jack Anderson, *The Case Against Congress* (New York: Simon and Schuster, 1968).

to cover everything that might be said about the legislative branch, let us consider some of the more important points.

RULE BY SPECIAL INTEREST

For some years power in Congress has rested with the 20 or so standing (i.e., permanent) committees in each house that determine the destiny of bills, rewriting some, approving a few, and burying most. The committees have been dominated by chairpersons who rise to their positions by seniority, that is, by being repeatedly reelected—a feat best accomplished by winning the campaign support of powerful interests. And one is more likely to win such support by gaining prominent positions within the more important committees.[2] So seniority increases a legislator's influence within Congress and thereby attracts an increasing amount of outside moneyed support, and moneyed support helps assure reelection and seniority.[3]

The commitment to seniority has been a pervasive unwritten norm of Congress, determining not only the choosing of chairpersons but the assigning of members to committees and the selection of subcommittee chairpersons. Although seniority has remained the rule in both houses, the House Democratic Caucus has instituted a number of changes to weaken the hold of committee chairpersons, removing several from their positions and expanding the powers of subcommittees.[4] No longer can chairpersons arbitrarily select subcommittee chairpersons, nor can they stack a subcommittee with members of their own choice or cut its budget. Totaling over 350 in the House and Senate, the subcommittees have staffs of their own and fixed legislative jurisdictions. Advancement within the subcommittees, as within the full committees, is still mostly by seniority. In both the House and Senate, the party with a majority controls the committee and subcommittee chairmanships of that house.

---

2. The four most powerful committees are the ones that deal with taxing and spending: House Ways and Means, House Appropriations, Senate Finance, and Senate Appropriations.

3. Seniority also accumulates if one comes from a district or state where one party consistently dominates, which explains why Southern Democrats monopolized the chairmanships for years. With two-party competition growing in the South, committee chairpersons have increasingly come from non-Southern states and less conservative urban and suburban districts.

4. The Democratic Caucus is the meeting of all House Democrats. When composed of the majority party, it can shape the rules under which the House operates.

THE MADISON PRESS CONNECTION

KONOPACKI

ROTHCO

"SORRY, I DON'T CATER TO SPECIAL INTERESTS!"

Some of the power taken from the committees was slated to shift to the elected leadership of the House—the Speaker's office—which supposedly would have been in a position to develop broad policy initiatives. But that part of the Democratic Caucus reforms was never completed, since many House members preferred the system of divided authority offered by subcommittees. Furthermore, as legislators rely less on party leaders for campaign funds and a place on the ballot, the leadership exercises less leverage over them. The atomized campaign system makes for an increasingly atomized legislative process.

The committee system in Congress has been replaced by "the subcommittee system," in which every organized interest has, in the words of one congressman, "a port of entry into Congress."[5] What is missing is a countervailing central leadership to garner support for issues that affect interests other than the privileged ones. "More than mere specialization, the subcommittee permits development of tight little cadres of special interest legislators and gives them great leverage."[6] In agriculture, for instance, cotton, corn, wheat, peanut, tobacco, and rice producers compete for federal support programs; each interest is represented on the various subcommittees of the Senate and House Agricultural Committees by senators and representatives ready to do battle on their behalf.[7] The fragmentation of power within the subcommittees simplifies the lobbyist's task of controlling legislation. *It offers the special-interest group its own special-interest subcommittee.* To atomize power in this way is *not* to democratize it.[8] The separate structures of power tend to monopolize decisions in specific areas for the benefit of specific groups. Into the interstices of these substructures fall the interests of large segments of the unorganized public.

Whether Congress is organized under a committee system, a subcommittee system, or a strong centralized leadership—and it has enjoyed all three in its history—it seems unchanging in its dedication to business interests. In recent years Congress has received more special-interest money than ever and it has responded with abandon. A few examples from the first session of the 96th Congress:

> A Senate reclamation law revision exempts the big irrigators in the West from acreage limitations, continuing hefty tax subsidies. A House committee relieves asbestos producers of sharing the cost of removing their cancer-causing insulation from schoolhouses. A 2-year-old strip mine control law is dealt a stunning blow in the Senate under pressure from coal companies.
>
> Hospital cost-containment legislation is bottled up by a powerful hospital-doctor lobby that contributed more than $1.6 million to campaigners in 1977–1978. Sugar producers are voted a 15.8 cents-a-pound price

---

5. Representative David Obey (D.–Wisc.) quoted in the *New York Times*, November 13, 1978.

6. Douglass Cater, *Power in Washington* (New York: Random House, 1964), p. 158. The subcommittee system has been a long time developing. The House Democratic Caucus reforms did not create it but advanced and legitimized it.

7. *Washington Post*, April 20, 1981.

8. Grant McConnell, *Private Power and American Democracy* (New York: Knopf, 1966), p. 193 and *passim*. According to an auto-industry lobbyist: "It's down here in the subcommittees where you've really got to do your work." Green and Calabrese, *Who Runs Congress?* p. 63.

increase and milk producers' price supports are extended by a House committee.

Sand and gravel and limestone pit operators win an exemption from safety training requirements. The House waters down a windfall profits tax proposed on the affluent oil industry, whose PACs spent better than $1 million in the last two congressional elections.[9]

Congress produces an array of grants, subsidies, leases, franchises, in-kind supports, direct services, noncompetitive contracts, loan guarantees, loss compensations, and other forms of public largesse to private business. Every few years Congress engages in a bipartisan stampede to sustain the same (or an increasingly inequitable) system of tax deductions for capital gains, accelerated depreciation, investment credits, business expenses, tax-free income, and corporate foreign royalties. Every year there is another stampede to vote hundreds of billions for bloated military budgets and hundreds of millions for right-wing dictatorships throughout the Third World.

But Congress also knows how to save money. The 97th Congress in 1981–1982 refused to provide $9 million for a disease-control center dealing with tuberculosis, even though some 15 million Americans have TB. It cut 5 million doses out of the federal immunization program for children, for a grand saving of $10 million, and reduced venereal-disease programs by 25 percent despite severe increases in that disease. To teach people rugged self-reliance, that same Congress cut food programs for infants and senior citizens, assistance programs for the disabled, home-care and therapy programs for the infirm and handicapped, and medical care, job, and housing programs for the poor and elderly.[10]

What has failed to appear on Congress's agenda is any notion of major, progressive structural changes in class and power, of moving the economy toward nonprofit forms of production for social use rather than production for corporate profit. As an integral part and product of the existing politico-economic system, Congress is not likely to initiate a transformation of that system. Thus it tends to treat the economic problems of society either as insoluble or as worthy of little more than the spending programs of the past or the spending cuts of the present. Congress cannot try a new recipe because it is too committed to slicing up the existing pie.

On occasions when public opinion is aroused, Congress is likely to respond by producing legislation that appears to deal with the prob-

---

9. *Washington Post*, September 23, 1979.
10. *Washington Post*, July 9, 1982; *Daily World*, August 20, 1982.

lem but that lacks substance: thus we are treated to a lobbyist-registration act that does little to control lobbyists and an occupational-safety act that has grossly insufficient enforcement provisions. Or Congress will take sympathetic note of the public sentiment without making any substantive response to it. So after several years of intensive public demonstrations against the Vietnam intervention and with polls indicating that a majority of the people favored withdrawal from Vietnam, Congress was still voting huge appropriations for the war by lopsided majorities.[11] In 1973, in the face of a nationwide consumer meat boycott, demonstrations, and a deluge of letters and calls protesting inflation, Congress chose to listen to "cattlemen, banking and business interests and food merchants" and voted down all proposals for price freezes and price rollbacks.[12] In 1982 a massive grassroots movement for a freeze on nuclear weapons swept the country, yet Congress continued to vote for major escalations in nuclear-weapons systems.[13]

At other times, Congress will heed an aroused public opinion—especially as election time approaches. In September 1982 both the Democratic-controlled House and the Republican-controlled Senate overrode President Reagan's veto of a $14.1 billion spending bill. The president felt the bill allocated too much for human services and not enough for the military. With congressional elections less than two months away, Congress felt otherwise.[14]

The unorganized public, composed of ordinary working people, exercises an influence over Congress that is more episodic than durable. Given the demands made on his or her time by job and family, and the superficial and often misleading coverage of events by the media, the average wage earner has little opportunity to give sustained, informed attention to more than a few broad issues, if that. But throughout the legislative process, the organized interests remain actively engaged in shaping the details of legislation. Thus the final bill usually will be sufficiently diluted or transformed to accommodate powerful groups.

Worse still, Congress is inclined to remove itself from scrutiny whenever the people get too interested in its affairs. The Senate Armed Services Committee responded to the public's growing concern about military spending by increasing its percentage of secret hearings from 56 percent to 79 percent. The House Appropriations

---

11. Garrison Nelson, "Nixon's Silent House of Hawks," *Progressive*, August 1970, pp. 13–20.
12. AP report in the *Schenectady Gazette*, April 17, 1973.
13. *Washington Post*, November 23, 1981.
14. *New York Times*, September 10 and 11, 1982.

Committee held 92 percent of its meetings behind closed doors one year. Most other committees hold at least one-third of their sessions in secret.[15] Business interests enjoy a ready access to committee reports while newspersons and public-interest advocates are kept in the dark. "The thing that really makes me mad is the dual standard," complained a Senate committee staff member. "It's perfectly acceptable to turn over information about what's going on in committee to the auto industry or the utilities but not to the public."[16]

Sometimes secrecy envelops the entire lawmaking process: a bill cutting corporate taxes by $7.3 billion was (a) drawn up by the House Ways and Means Committee in three days of secret sessions, (b) passed by the House under a closed rule after only one hour of debate with (c) about thirty members of the House present for the (d) non-roll-call vote.[17] Under such conditions even the experienced journalist or academic specialist has difficulty ascertaining what is going on.

Many members of Congress allow their offices to be used as bases of operation for lobbying activities. One influential lobbyist, Nathan Voloshen, regularly worked out of Speaker John McCormack's office, paying McCormack a substantial "rent" along with a percentage of the take in return for use of the speaker's name and influence on behalf of Voloshen's business clients.[18] According to Winter-Berger, the lobbyist's main job is to circumvent existing laws and get preferential treatment "for clients who have no legal rights to them." To achieve this the lobbyist pays cash to "one or more members of Congress—the more influential they are, the fewer he needs," who make the contacts with the executive agency handling the matter. "Most lobbying is underground, because more than opinions are exchanged. Money is exchanged: money for favors, money for deals, money for government contracts, money for government jobs."[19] It is "a very common occurrence" for members of Congress to telephone or write the Justice Department on behalf of business interests, according to former Attorney-General Richard Kleindienst, who added: "We have a responsibility to permit that kind of thing to occur."[20]

---

15. *Washington Monthly*, September 1972, p. 17.
16. Green et al., *Who Runs Congress?* (2nd edition), p. 56.
17. *Washington Monthly*, April 1972, p. 18.
18. See Robert Winter-Berger, *The Washington Pay-Off* (New York: Dell, 1972). Winter-Berger was a lobbyist who worked closely with Voloshen and McCormack. He offers astonishing eyewitness testimony in his book. Voloshen was eventually convicted of fraud and given a suspended sentence. At his trial, McCormack professed to be ignorant of Voloshen's doings and everyone believed him.
19. *Ibid.*, pp. 14, 38.
20. Quoted in Martin Gellen, "ITT: The Tentacles of Power," *Guardian*, March 29, 1972, p. 3.

There are those who believe money has only a limited impact on the political process, since other factors, such as cultural norms and popular sentiment, exert a counterinfluence. That other factors exist, however, is no certain evidence that they work *against* the power of money. Many of our cultural norms, for instance, are shaped by a plutocratic culture that supports rather than restrains the moneyed interests. Furthermore, big contributors may be "limited" in their power in that they do not *always* get their way, but they *usually* get what they want. And they almost always can stop what they don't want.[21]

If money were not very effective, why would corporations and others spend so much of it on politics? Certainly corporate heads do not feel contributions are wasted. William May, chairman of the American Can Corporation, comments on his company's PAC contributions: "I've got to admit the money does have an impact. There is no doubt about it."[22]

The humorist Will Rogers once observed: "Congress is the best money can buy." The average senator or representative is an influence peddler, doing favors not only for ordinary folks back home but more often for special folks with special demands. Senator Jesse Helms (R–N.C.), for instance, argued successfully against cutting subsidies to peanut and tobacco growers because, as he put it, such monies affect "human beings." In contrast, Helms fought hard to cut school lunches and food stamps because, you see, school lunches are just inert lumps of food on trays and food stamps are only little pieces of paper. In any case, the peanut and tobacco producers are not just human beings but very *special* ones who contribute handsomely to Helms's campaign coffers, whereas the low-income recipients of federal nutrition programs are of little use to the senator and are thereby judged to be unduly reliant on government hand-outs.[23]

Looking Out for Themselves

Frequently members of Congress act without benefit of prodding by any pressure group, either because they are so well attuned to its in-

---

21. "Recent evidence, indeed, supports the view that major business lobbies appear to be able to exercise a de facto veto over measures they oppose. If business lobbies don't object, reform measures can become law; if they do, they can't." Green and Calabrese, *Who Runs Congress?*, p. 28.

22. Mark Green and Jack Newfield, "Who Owns Congress?" *Washington Post Magazine*, June 8, 1980, p. 12.

23. See *Washington Post* editorial, September 18, 1981; also Howie Kurtz, "Congress' Budget Cutters Protect the Home Folks," *Washington Post*, January 25, 1982.

terests or have lucrative holdings of their own in the same industry. Thus some members have large farm holdings and sit on committees that shape the farm subsidy programs that directly enrich them. Fully a third of the senators and representatives hold outside jobs as lawyers or officers of corporations, banks, and other financial institutions that closely link them "with the very industries they were elected to oversee."[24] More than a third of the senators make money every time the military budget increases, for they have interests in firms that rank among the top defense contractors. Almost half of all senators are either on boards or among the stockholders of federal banks. Over a hundred House members have interests in banking, including many who sit on the House Banking Committee and House Ways and Means Committee, both of which deal with banking legislation.[25] What is called "conflict of interest" in the judiciary and executive is defined as "expertise" in Congress by lawmakers who use their public mandate to legislate for their private interests.

Plutocracy—rule for the rich *by* the rich—prevails in Congress. More than a third of the U.S. Senate is made up of millionaires. Almost all the senators and representatives have annual incomes over $100,000, which puts them in the top one-percent bracket, somewhat beyond the concerns and problems of most wage and salaried workers. Our rulers experience a vastly different life from those over whom they rule. Transportation policy is made by people who fly in heavily subsidized private planes and who never have to search for a parking space or endure the suffocation of a rush-hour bus. Agricultural policy is shaped by legislators who never tried keeping a family farm going. Safety legislation is devised by lawmakers who never worked in a factory or mine. Medical policies are made by persons who never have to wait in a doctor's office or a crowded clinic. The legislators who impose austerity programs on working people vote themselves an unlimited outside-income ceiling, a guaranteed pay-raise procedure, and a tax-free income.[26]

24. *Washington Post*, September 5, 1979.
25. Members of Congress are now required to disclose their financial holdings. But many file "incomplete, misleading or useless" statements, according to the *Congressional Quarterly*, September 2, 1978. More thorough disclosures would likely reveal more millionaires: *Washington Post*, May 21, 1982. Millionaire representatives are a phenomenon found at the state level as well. In a poor state like West Virginia, an estimated half of the state legislators are millionaires, many of them coal-mine owners; almost none are environmentalists. Jean Callahan, "Cancer Valley," *Mother Jones*, August 1978, p. 40.
26. In 1981 members of Congress voted enough new tax breaks for themselves so as to avoid paying *any* income taxes: *Washington Post*, January 14, 1982; also Philip Green, *Political Equality* (unpublished manuscript), pp. 5–6, for a discussion of the unrepresentative lives of representatives.

Some members of Congress pilfer from the public treasure. Among their bad habits, the most common are:

1. Junketing—traveling for fun at government expense under the guise of conducting overseas committee investigations
2. Placing relatives on the payroll and pocketing their salaries
3. Taking salary kickbacks from staff members
4. Keeping unspent travel allocations for personal use
5. Double billing—charging both the government and a private client for the same expense
6. Using their franking privilege for mailing campaign literature
7. Using committee staff workers for personal campaign purposes
8. Keeping persons on the staff payroll whose major function is to perform sexual favors
9. Using unspent campaign contributions for personal living and recreational expenses[27]

Venality takes on more serious forms. Mark Twain once said, "There is no distinctly American criminal class except Congress." Since World War II more than 60 members of Congress or their aides have been indicted or convicted of bribery, influence peddling, extortion, and other crimes.[28] And these were only the ones unlucky enough to get caught. In 1980 eight members of Congress, including one senator, were indicted for accepting bribes from FBI agents posing as Arab businessmen in what became known as "Abscam." In addition, numerous other members have retired from office to avoid criminal charges. All in all, Capitol Hill seems to have a higher crime rate than inner-city Detroit.

While harboring some of the most fervent proponents of "law and order" Congress has shown no inclination to apply the law to itself. In 1976 at least 19 senators were implicated in a multimillion-dollar slush fund run by oil companies. Because of the publicity given the case, the Senate Ethics Committee, which had not investigated a senator's ethics in 10 years, finally initiated an inquiry—which it dropped a short time later without calling any corporate witnesses (including oil lobbyists who were willing to name names).[29] The

---

27. Green and Calabrese, *Who Runs Congress?* pp. 156–205; "Ethics on Capitol Hill," *Progressive*, August 1977, pp. 8–10; *New York Times*, May 26, 1976; *Washington Post*, August 13, 1982.

28. Green and Calabrese, loc. cit.; *Washington Post*, February 10, 1980, and July 15, 1982.

29. *Boston Globe*, September 22, 1976. One reason legislators are reluctant to investigate their colleagues is that they themselves are often vulnerable. The chairman of the Ethics Committee was Howard Cannon (D.–Nev.), who himself was said to be the recipient of illegal gifts from Northrup Corporation: *The American Sentinel*, July 1, 1975, p. 3.

House Ethics Committee has suffered from a similar sluggishness. When a member of the Korean CIA, testifying before the committee, named 30 congresspersons to whom he had given almost $1 million in bribes in exchange for votes in Congress in support of his government, the Ethics Committee responded by indicting only two ex-members of Congress.[30]

THE LEGISLATIVE LABYRINTH

As intended by the framers of the Constitution, the very structure of Congress has a conservative effect on what the legislators do. The staggered terms of the Senate—with only one-third elected every two years—are designed to blunt any mass sentiment for a sweeping turnover. The division of the Congress into two separate houses makes legislative action all the more difficult, giving an advantage to those who desire to prevent reforms. With bicameralism, lobbyists have more opportunities to exert pressure and more places to set up roadblocks; legislation that gets through one house can often be buried or mutilated in the other house.

A typical bill before Congress might go the following route: after being introduced into, say, the House of Representatives, it is (1) committed to a committee, where it is most likely summarily ignored, pigeonholed, or gutted by the chairperson, or (2) parceled out to various subcommittees for extensive hearings, where it might then meet its demise, or (3) reported out of subcommittee to full committee, greatly diluted or completely rewritten to suit influential lobbyists and their clients, some of whom sit on the committees as members of Congress. In the unlikely event that it is reported out of the full committee, the bill (4) goes to the Rules Committee, where it might be buried forever or subjected to further changes or replaced entirely by a bill of the Rules Committee's own preference. Upon reaching the floor of the House (5) it might be further amended during debate or voted down or referred back to committee for further study. If passed, *it must repeat essentially the same process in the Senate*, assuming the Senate has time for it.

If the bill does not make it through both houses before the next congressional election, it must be reintroduced and the entire process begun anew. Not surprisingly, the House and Senate frequently fail to

---

30. An earlier probe had disclosed that 115 members of Congress had taken bribes from South Korean agents. Executive officials, including Henry Kissinger, were implicated as well. *New York Times*, July 11, 1977; *Workers World*, June 2, 1978.

pass the same version of a bill; differences then have to be ironed out in ad hoc conference committees composed of several senior members from each house. More than one conference committee has rewritten a bill to better suit special interests. So in 1970 when the House voted $290 million for the supersonic transport plane (SST) and the Senate voted to *abolish* the program, the conference committee, stacked with Senate SST supporters, agreed on a $210 million "compromise" bill.[31]

The bill that survives the legislative labyrinth and escapes an executive veto to become an *act* of Congress, and the law of the land, may be only an *authorization* act—that is, it simply brings some program into existence. Congress then must vote *appropriations* to finance the authorized policy; hence, *the entire legislative process must be repeated for the appropriations bill.* Not infrequently legislation authorizing the government to spend a certain amount for a particular program is passed, but no appropriations are subsequently voted. Congress's task is made no easier by the duplication of bills and overlapping committee jurisdictions. In one session seventy bills were introduced to change the date of Veterans Day back to the traditional November 11. There are twenty-two House committees and subcommittees dealing—none of them very successfully—with the problems of the aged.[32]

Bills that benefit special corporate interests seldom get caught in the congressional labyrinth; generally when the big companies want action, they get it. But legislation designed to serve the politically weak, the low income, and the unorganized is treated with painfully slow deliberation, if at all. Without pause, Congress voted $6.75 million for a market news service to furnish timely reports on major agricultural commodities to enable agribusiness to better determine when to sell and how to price its products. But this same Congress debated at great length the passage of a minor pilot project supplying breakfast in school for hungry children, a program that would reach only a tiny number of millions of malnourished American children.[33] In almost everything Congress does, the pattern remains the same. Multibillion-dollar tax breaks for big business are passed in a matter of days with little debate, while reform bills languish in committee. When moving *against* human services Congress is able to act with dispatch. In 1981, in only three days, the Senate Budget Committee slashed $36

---

31. Green and Calabrese, *Who Runs Congress?* p. 67.

32. Roger Davidson and Walter Oleszek, *Congress Against Itself* (Bloomington: Indiana University Press, 1977); Morris Fiorina, *Congress: Keystone of the Washington Establishment* (New Haven: Yale University Press, 1977).

33. *Hunger, U.S.A.*, a report by the Citizens' Board of Inquiry into Hunger and Malnutrition in the United States (Boston: Beacon Press, 1968), p. 80.

billion from social programs and sent their work on to the full Senate for passage. In all, the 97th Congress reduced domestic services by $87 billion in a few months, undoing legislative programs that had taken years of struggle to achieve. Conservative interests have the fast track in Congress.

For all their activity, 100 senators and 435 representatives cannot produce an integrated national program. The subcommittee system with its fragmented power works against a coherent, nationally oriented program. In addition, members of Congress have neither the time nor the staff to inform themselves in any comprehensive way about the myriad problems of the nation or the vast undertakings of the executive branch. *The Defense Department has more people preparing its budget than Congress has for all its functions combined.* For most of its technical information and legislative initiatives Congress relies on the executive departments or on lobbyists from private industry, who often write the bills that friendly congressmen later introduce as legislation.

Congress "is at best a collection of well-intentioned people who have fallen back on a service role while making a great deal of noise about larger issues."[34] A member of Congress spends the bulk of his time performing minor ombudsman services for constituents, making calls to public agencies on behalf of private interests, and answering the huge quantity of mail he receives. In the time left for legislative tasks, he devotes himself to several specialized subcommittees, trying to build up some expertise in limited areas, in effect making himself that much more of a special-interest lawmaker who defines legislation in terms of distinct "problems" (e.g., tariffs, defense contracts, taxes, forestry) and who focuses little attention on the interrelatedness and *systemic* nature of politico-economic problems. On matters outside his domain he defers to his other special-interest colleagues.

With its fragmented pockets of special power, Congress is not just bicameral, it is "multicameral." These various special-interest congressional factions achieve working majorities through various trade-offs and mutual accommodations, a "logrolling" process that is not the same as compromise. Rather than checking one another as in compromise situations, and thus blunting the selfish demands of each—possibly with some benefit to the general public—interest groups end up supporting one another's claims, at the expense of those who are without power in the pressure system. Thus the oil lobby will

---

34. Sanford Ungar, "Bleak House: Frustration on Capitol Hill," *Atlantic*, July 1977, p. 38. Ungar was referring to the House, but his description applies to the Senate as well.

back farm supports in exchange for agribusiness support of oil leases. In both cases the ordinary consumers and taxpayers bear the costs. *Logrolling is the method by which the various haves reconcile their differences, usually at the expense of the have-nots.* The net effect is not a *check* on competing claims but a *compounding* of claims against the interests of the unorganized public.

This array of special interests has led some political scientists to the mistaken conclusion that Congress is a pluralistic arena, composed of shifting fluid coalitions that vary greatly from issue to issue, offering no discernible pattern of class and ideological cleavage. But a recent study has found fairly consistent liberal-conservative ideological divisions in such issue areas as domestic spending, foreign policy, race, and civil liberties.[35] The conflicts between the "special interest" legislators and the "public interest" ones are not resolved by logrolling but by a show of strength—with the results commonly favoring the conservatives who represent the business community, the medical association, and the suburban well-to-do rather than the liberals who sometimes represent blue-collar workers, racial minorities, and consumer groups.

CONGRESS: A PRODUCT OF ITS ENVIRONMENT

While Congress is a body supposedly dedicated to a government of laws, not of men, its procedures "are founded all too much on unwritten, unspoken, and largely unnoticed informal agreements among men."[36] The norms and customs that are so much a part of life in the House and Senate are generally conservative in their effect. The emphasis on elaborate forms of courtesy and on avoiding public remarks that might be construed as personally critical of colleagues discourages a good deal of discussion of things that are deserving of criticism. "The Senate is . . . the biggest mutual admiration society in history," observes a congressional intern. "How heated can debate get when every four seconds you're referring to your so-called rival as 'the honored gentleman from Illinois'? And that's not just a game; it's the whole spirit of the place."[37] The tendency to minimize differences

---

35. See the excellent study by Jerrold Schneider, *Ideological Coalitions in Congress* (Westport, Conn.: Greenwood Press, 1979).

36. Joseph Clark et al., *The Senate Establishment* (New York: Hill and Wang, 1963), p. 15. Clark was describing the Senate but his observations apply to both houses.

37. Quoted in Melvin Eli, "Most Interns Find D.C. Insulated and Elitist," *Valley Advocate* (Amherst, Mass.), September 15, 1976.

usually works to the advantage of those who prefer to avoid the confrontations needed to effect change.

In addition, there are various parliamentary devices, from time-consuming quorum calls to filibusters, which make it easier for entrenched interests to thwart action. The rule of unlimited debate in the Senate allows a small but determined number of senators to filibuster a bill to death or kill it by exercising the *threat* of filibuster. Over the years the filibuster has been used extensively by Southern senators against civil-rights bills and to a lesser degree by conservatives against measures deemed harmful to big business. On still rarer occasions liberals have resorted to the filibuster.[38]

The freshman legislator is socialized into a world of cronyism that makes mobilization around issue-oriented programs difficult to achieve. He learns not to give too much attention to issue politics—since issues can be divisive—and he develops personal loyalties to senior members, defers to their judgments, avoids exacerbating debates, and becomes a reliable member of the club. He soon realizes that opportunities for choice committee assignments and other favors are extended to him by senior members in accordance with his willingness to go along with things. In recent years this pattern has changed somewhat as junior members have manifested a marked inclination to challenge the seniority system and carve out a piece of the action for themselves through the subcommittee system.

---

38. In September 1982, Senate liberals successfully used the filibuster to defeat an anti-abortion bill: *New York Times*, September 16, 1982.

Members of Congress now may have greater "independence," but it is independence from their party leadership and from older colleagues, not from the moneyed lobbyists and well-organized pressure groups that work so effectively on the Hill and back home. In addition, lawmakers are restrained by a host of forces that threaten to make it too costly for them to embark upon a preferred course of action. Hence, they often act in a way contrary to their own political proclivities, operating in a state of anticipatory response to larger influences. The "law of anticipatory response," as Schneider notes, works with persistent effect,[39] and, I would add, in a society of concentrated wealth and power, it works largely with *conservative* effect, teaching caution to the maverick. Members of Congress anticipate the powerful interest groups, the president, the other chamber, certain executive officials and agencies, state and local political and governmental groups, the electorate, and the press. "All of these will constrain what congressmen believe worth an investment of time and effort and what they believe must be written off as desirable but infeasible."[40]

In recent years many members of Congress have been finding their jobs more demanding and less rewarding. The work load has greatly increased. Campaign costs have escalated, and fund raising takes up more and more time, especially for the less affluent and more progressive lawmakers who do not easily win the favors of wealthy contributors. Special-interest groups are more numerous and more demanding. The erosion of the seniority system has diminished the rewards of political longevity. The inability "to get things done" and "make a difference" frustrates the more idealistic legislators, and the attractions of highly lucrative jobs in private industry lure the less idealistic ones. Hence, record numbers of lawmakers are voluntarily retiring, at almost a 10-percent annual rate in recent years. Congress is less often a place where one settles in for life.[41]

Although the legislative branch is inhabited by special interests, it is not quite accurate to call it "unrepresentative." In a way, Congress is precisely representative of the power distributions of the wider society in that "power goes to those . . . legislators who service powerful interests, while isolation goes to those who merely represent powerless people."[42] And as long as Congress reflects the distribution of economic power in the wider society, it is not likely to change much even if liberals in both houses manage to gain control of the major commit-

---

39. Schneider, *Ideological Coalitions in Congress*, p. 8.
40. *Ibid.*
41. *New York Times*, March 27, 1978, and November 13, 1978.
42. Ralph Nader, "Making Congress Work," *New Republic*, August 21–28, 1971, p. 19.

tees, even if the cloture rule is changed to enable the Senate to rid itself of the filibuster, and even if seniority is done away with. For what remains is the entire system of organized corporate power with its hold over the economic life of the nation and the material resources of the society; its control of the media and mass propaganda; its dominance of most cultural and social institutions; its organized pressure groups, high-paid lobbyists, influence-peddling lawyers, big-money contributions, and bribes—all of which operate with such telling effect on legislators, including many professedly liberal ones.

To be sure, a representative system *should* be a pressure system, enabling constituents to influence their lawmakers. But what is usually missing from the lawmaker's own view is any real appreciation of the one-sidedness of the pressure system. For many in Congress, as in the state legislatures,[43] the existing pressure system *is* the representative system; that is to say, those groups having the money, organization, visibility, and expertise to *take* an interest in legislative affairs are presumed to be the only ones that *have* an actual interest. The muted levels of society are too often left out of the picture.

---

43. For an excellent study of political influence at the state level see James LaMare, *Texas Politics* (St. Paul, Minn.: West, 1981).

14

The President: Guardian of the System

In this chapter our task is to take a nonworshipful look at what presidents do and why they do it.

THE CORPORATE POLITICIAN

The president, we are told, plays many roles. He is not only chief executive, he is "chief legislator," commander-in-chief, head of state, and leader of his party. Seldom mentioned is his role as guardian and spokesman of capitalism. Far from being an opponent of big business, the president is the embodiment of the executive-centered political system that defends American corporate interests at home and abroad.

As authoritative figures whose opinions are widely publicized, presidents do their share to indoctrinate the American people into the ruling-class ideology. Every modern president has had occasion to warn the citizenry of the "dangers of radicalism" and the "tyrannies of communism." All have accepted and praised the "free enterprise system" and denounced its alternatives. President Carter proclaimed himself "an engineer, a planner and a businessman" who understood "the value of a strong system of free enterprise" with its "minimal intrusion of government in our free economic system."[1] One description

---

1. Carter's acceptance speech at the 1976 Democratic National Convention; *Seattle Post-Intelligencer*, July 16, 1976.

of President Ford could easily apply to any number of other presidents:

> [He] follows the judgment of the major international oil companies on oil problems in the same way that he amiably heeds the advice of other big businesses on the problems that interest them. . . . He is . . . a solid believer in the business ideology of rugged individualism, free markets and price competition—virtues that exist more clearly in his mind than they do in the practices of the international oil industry.[2]

The president is the top salesman of the system. He conjures up reassuring images about the state of the union. He lets us know he is guiding the ship of state with a firm hand. He would have us believe that our social problems and economic difficulties can be solved with enough "vigor" and "resolve," as John Kennedy used to say; or with "hard work" and "toughing it out," as Richard Nixon put it; or with a return to "self-reliance" and a "spiritual revival," as Ronald Reagan urged. Prosperity, our presidents tell us, is here or not far off—but so is the Red Menace, which we must guard against with huge military budgets and a strong internal security system.

---

2. William Shannon, *New York Times*, July 22, 1975.

Whether Democrat or Republican, liberal or conservative, the president tends to treat capitalist interests as synonymous with the nation's well-being. He will describe the overseas investments of giant corporations as "*United States* investments abroad," part of "*America's* interests in the world," to be defended at all costs—or certainly at great cost. He will speak of "our" oil in the Middle East and "our" markets in Latin America (to be defended by *our* sons) when what he is referring to are the holdings of a small, powerful segment of the population. Presidents have presented their multibillion-dollar spending programs on behalf of private industry as necessary for "*America's* growing needs" and have greeted the expansion of big business and big profits as manifestations of "a healthy *national* economy" and as good for the "*national* interest."

At the Constitutional Convention, the wealthy planter Charles Pinckney proposed that no one qualify for the presidency who was not worth at least $100,000—a most handsome sum for 1787. While the proposal was never written into the Constitution, it seemingly has been followed in practice. The men who have occupied the highest office, with a few notable exceptions, have come from the highest income brackets. Since World War II, almost all presidential candidates on the Democratic and Republican tickets have been millionaires either at the time they first campaigned for the office or by the time they departed from it. In addition, presidents have drawn their top advisors and administrators primarily from industry and banking and have relied heavily on the judgments of corporate leaders.[3]

Like other politicians, the men who run for president procure vast sums from the rich to defray their campaign costs. Big contributors may disclaim any intention of trying to buy influence with their gifts, insisting that they give freely because they "believe" in the candidate

---

3. See the discussion in Chapter 12 on the plutocracy. While in office the president lives like a multimillionaire in surroundings that might make it difficult for him to remember the economic difficulties faced by millions of other Americans. The president inhabits a rent-free, 132-room mansion called the White House, with a $2 million maintenance budget and a domestic staff of 83, including six butlers; a well-stocked wine cellar; a private movie room; a gymnasium; tennis courts; a bowling alley; and a heated outdoor swimming pool. In addition, he has the free services of a private physician, a dozen chauffeured limousines, numerous helicopters and jets, including Air Force One—which costs $5,221 an hour to fly—access to country retreats, frequent free vacations, a $50,000 yearly expense allowance—and for the few things he must pay for himself, a $200,000 annual salary. Journalists and political scientists have described the presidency as a "man-killing job." Yet presidents live well and generally live long, usually longer and better than the average American male. And after leaving office, they can count on a $69,000 yearly pension.

and think he will pursue policies beneficial to the national interest. That they view the national interest as something often indistinguishable from their own financial interests does not make their support hypocritical but all the more sincere. Their campaign contributions are not merely for a better personal deal but for a better America. And their image of a better America is a product of their own class experiences and life values.

If it should happen, however, that after the election the big contributor finds himself or his firm burdened by a problem that only the White House can handle, he sees no reason why he shouldn't be allowed to exercise his rights like any other citizen and ask his elected representative, who in this case happens to be his friend, the president of the United States, for a little help. Big interests have big problems, often national and international in scope, which require the attention of no one less than the president. Large donors to President Nixon's campaign, including certain insurance moguls, dairymen, bankers, railroad tycoons, and managers of giant conglomerates like ITT, benefited many times over from White House intercessions on their behalf. In the case of ITT, the Nixon administration helped settle a multibillion-dollar antitrust suit against that corporation in return for a promised $400,000 donation.[4] One of President Reagan's first acts was to deregulate heating-oil and gasoline prices—a $50 billion gift to the oil companies in return for the more than $200 million they kicked in for his 1980 campaign.[5]

There is a view—made popular about the time Harry Truman was president—that the greatness of the office lends greatness to its occupants; even those persons of mediocre endowment supposedly grow in response to the presidency's great responsibilities and powers. Closer examination shows that most White House occupants have been just as readily corrupted as ennobled by the power of the office, inclined toward self-righteous assertion, compelled to demonstrate their macho toughness and decisiveness, intolerant of, and irritated by, public criticism, and not above using their power in unlawful ways against political opponents. Thus at least six presidents employed illegal FBI wiretaps to gather incriminating information on rival political figures. The White House tapes, which recorded the private Oval Office conversations of President Nixon, revealed him to be a petty, vindictive, bigoted man who manifested a shallowness of

4. *New York Times*, June 15, 1973; also Anthony Sampson, *The Sovereign State of I.T.T.* (New York: Stein and Day, 1973); Ben A. Franklin, "Milk Aide Says a Lawyer for Nixon Sought Funds," *New York Times*, January 11, 1973.

5. Noel Reroff, *Daily World*, May 8, 1981.

spirit and mind that the majestic office could cloak but not transform.[6]

THE TWO FACES OF THE PRESIDENT

Presidents have made a show of concern for public causes, using slogans and images intended to enhance their popular appeal; thus Franklin Roosevelt had his "New Deal," Harry Truman his "Fair Deal," John Kennedy his "New Frontier," and Lyndon Johnson his "Great Society." Behind the fine-sounding labels one discovers much the same record of service to the powerful and neglect of the needy. Consider John Kennedy, a liberal president widely celebrated for his devotion to the underdog. In foreign affairs, Kennedy spoke of international peace and self-determination for all peoples, yet he invaded Cuba after Castro nationalized the holdings of U.S. corporations. He drastically increased military expenditures, instituted new counterinsurgency programs throughout the Third World, and sent troops to Vietnam.

In domestic matters Kennedy presented himself as a champion of civil rights yet did little to create job opportunities for Afro-Americans. He refrained from taking legal action to support antidiscrimination cases or to prevent repeated attacks against civil-rights organizers in the South. Kennedy talked as if he were the special friend of the working people, yet he imposed wage restraints on unions at a time workers' buying power was stagnant or declining, and he strongly opposed introduction of the 35-hour work week. He also instituted tax programs and deficit-spending policies that carried business profit rates to all-time highs without reducing unemployment.[7]

Conservative presidents, such as Richard Nixon and Gerald Ford, manifested the same tendency to *talk* for the people and *work* for the corporate elites. Both of them voiced their support for environmental

---

6. In 1973, official audits revealed that Nixon had spent $10 million of the taxpayers' money on improvements for his private estates and had made illegal tax deductions of around a half-million dollars. White House counsel John Dean testified that on occasion the president had requested the Internal Revenue Service to stop auditing the incomes of close friends. *New York Times*, June 21, 22, and 25, 1973. April 4, 1974.

7. See Ian McMahan, "The Kennedy Myth," *New Politics*, 3, Winter 1964, pp. 40–48; Richard Walton, *Cold War and Counter-Revolution: The Foreign Policy of John F. Kennedy* (Baltimore: Penguin Books, 1972); Bruce Miroff, *Pragmatic Illusions* (New York: McKay, 1976). For a treatment of the disparity between Lyndon Johnson's liberal rhetoric and his conservative policies, see Gettleman and Mermelstein, *The Failure of American Liberalism*; and Robert Sherrill, *The Accidental President* (New York: Grossman, 1967), chapters 3, 5, and 6.

protection while opening new forest lands for commercial exploitation and opposing the regulation of strip mining. Both gave lip service to the problems of the Vietnam veteran, the plight of the elderly, and the needs of the poor, yet opposed extending benefits and services to these groups and even supported cutbacks.[8]

President Carter supplied the same admixture of liberal rhetoric and conservative policy. He promised to cut the bloated military budget by some $5 billion and instead increased it $10 billion. He promised to "reduce the commerce in arms sales," but arms sales under his administration rose to new levels. While he talked of helping the needy, Carter proposed cutbacks in summer youth jobs, child nutrition programs, and other benefits. After campaigning as a friend of labor, he went on, once in office, to oppose most of the AFL-CIO legislative program. And like his predecessors, he continued to dole out multibillion-dollar credits and subsidies to big business.[9]

In his 1981 inaugural speech President Reagan said, "The solutions we seek must be equitable with no one group singled out to pay a higher price." But in his first two years in office he cut social programs by some $87 billion, in effect singling out the neediest to make the greatest sacrifices. He expressed concern about the tax burdens carried by "ordinary Americans" while he fought for a tax bill that mostly benefited the rich and powerful. After Reagan repeatedly sought to delay or cut increases in Social Security benefits, the Republican National Committee spent $1 million in television spot ads giving him credit for winning the 7.4-percent increase Congress had passed. In a press conference in April 1982, Reagan boasted of having "extended the unemployment insurance" in "some of the hardest hit states" when in fact he had imposed budget cuts and changed eligibility rules that, the Labor Department admitted, eliminated benefits for 1.5 million unemployed. In September 1982, before an audience of Black Republicans in Washington, D.C., he described himself as a champion of racial equality when in fact he had opposed an extension of the Voting Rights Act, had advocated tax breaks for segregated private schools, and had cut inner-city assistance programs. In 1982 Reagan publicly advocated a constitutional amendment that would mandate a balanced budget while he himself piled up astronomical budget deficits. During the 1980 campaign, candidate Reagan said he

---

8. See for instance, *New York Times*, September 11 and October 8, 1975.
9. Christopher Lydon, "Jimmy Carter Revealed: He's a Rockefeller Republican," *Atlantic*, July 1977, pp. 50–59; Frank Browning, "Jimmy Carter's Astounding Lies," *Inquiry*, May 5, 1980, pp. 13–17.

was opposed to Selective Service registration, but once in office he re-activated it—against much popular protest. In 1980 candidate Reagan won the endorsement of the Professional Air Traffic Control-lers union (PATCO) for supporting their claims that air-traffic condi-tions were unsafe and controllers were forced to work unreasonable hours under stressful conditions with dangerously obsolete equip-ment. But once in office, President Reagan refused to negotiate these issues with PATCO and instead broke the union by firing all 12,000 of its striking members.

In foreign affairs, Reagan repeatedly accused Cuba, the U.S.S.R., Nicaragua, and other noncapitalist countries of an unwillingness to negotiate and compromise, but he himself repeatedly rebuffed Nica-raguan and Cuban overtures for friendly relations and refused to seri-ously negotiate arms limitations with the Soviets. Through the use of blockades, embargoes, military forays, nuclear escalations, and men-acing pronouncements he launched a campaign of confrontation and destabilization aimed at socialist nations—while he assured the Amer-ican public that the U.S. government sought only friendly and peace-ful relations with other countries.[10]

The President's Systemic Bind

If presidents tend to speak one way and act another, it is less likely due to some inborn flaw shared by the varied personalities who oc-cupy the office than to something in the nature of the office itself. Like any officeholder, the president plays a dual role in that he must satisfy the major interests of corporate America and at the same time make a show of serving the people. He differs from other politicians in that the demands and expectations of his office are greater and there-fore the contradictions deeper. More than any other officeholder, he deals with the overall crises of capitalism, for he is the national execu-tive, but also the only nationally elected leader (along with the vice-president, of course), and hence the focus of mass attention and mass demand. So the president, even more than other politicians, is caught in the contradiction of attempting, or wanting to appear, to represent "all the people" but finding that he must first tend to the needs of

10. For Reagan's domestic- and foreign-policy doings see *New York Times*, March 19, 1981, and July 30 and 31, 1982; *Washington Post*, May 15, 1981, August 9, 1981, September 5, 1981, and August 29, 1982; *Daily World*, September 11, 1982, and April 8, 1982; and *supra.* chapters 6 and 7.

those who control the wealth, land, resources, technology, industry, and jobs of the nation.

Although some presidents may try, they discover they cannot belong to both the corporations and the people. Occasionally a president may be instrumental in getting Congress to allocate monies and services for the American public, but whatever his intentions, he comes no closer to solving the deep structural problems of the political economy. So, like any politician, he fills the air with promises to "fight" inflation, unemployment, and poverty and finds he has not the means of achieving these laudable ends, for he cannot both serve capitalism as capitalism needs to be served and at the same time drastically transform it. He cannot come up with a solution because he is part of the problem, or part of the system that creates the problem.

While members of Congress are the captives of the special interests, the president, elected by the entire country, tends to be less vulnerable to pressure groups and more responsive to the needs of the unorganized public—at least this is what political scientists taught after years of observing presidents like Roosevelt, Truman, and Kennedy tussling with conservatives in Congress. As we have seen, our various presidents resemble the average pressure politician to a greater extent than we were taught to believe. Nevertheless, the president is more likely to see the ramifications that issues have for the overall system than the average member of Congress, who is concerned primarily with the problems of his district or state and the desires of his campaign contributors. Since the problems of the *nation* are the president's concern, the chief executive is drawn to a broader perspective and is somewhat less likely to act as a special-interest politician. When he does represent special interests, he is less likely to be recognized as doing so, for he can define his policies on behalf of oil companies, banks, and military contractors as necessary for the security and well-being of the nation itself.

The growth of capitalism from a diverse array of small, local producers to national and multinational conglomerates has come at a cost to smaller firms and has necessitated increasingly active controls by the federal government. The government has helped secure markets for the bigger corporations by subsidizing them at the expense of smaller interests and by imposing regulations that limit the small firm's opportunity to compete successfully. Presidents have been instrumental in thus "rationalizing" the economy, a process that began at least as early as Theodore Roosevelt. In representing the more powerful, advanced financial and industrial interests, the president has played a systemic role, updating the economy and getting businessmen to accept a modern, state-regulated, state-supported capitalism.

The president must do for capitalism what individual capitalists cannot do for the system or for themselves:

1. Sometimes the president must reconcile conflicts between major producers. Thus he might go against the interests of some importing companies to protect an industry that is being hurt by foreign imports. Or he might wipe out a shellfish industry to build a shoreline plant for the nuclear industry. Generally he decides these interest-group conflicts in favor of heavy industry and big finance as against light industry and small business—again because the bigger interests play a bigger role in the entire corporate system.

2. On behalf of the capitalist system as a system the president sometimes must oppose the interests of individual companies, keeping them in line with the overall needs of the corporate economy: hence he might oppose tariff protections for particular firms in order to avoid having foreign countries retaliate by closing their markets to American trade. Or he might do battle with an industry like steel to hold prices down in order to ease the inflationary effects on other producer interests. When engaged in such conflicts the president takes on an appearance of opposing the special interests on behalf of the common interest. *In fact, he might be better described as protecting the common interests of the special interests.*

3. As the only elected officeholder accountable to a national constituency, and as the focus of popular expectation and constant attention from the media, the president does feel the pressure more than anyone else to solve the nation's problems.[11] It is his task, if anyone's, to ameliorate the hardships of the populace and discourage the tendency toward disruption, protest, and troublesome rebellion. There are limits to how inequitable and oppressive the politico-economic system can be. Those who work too single-mindedly for the privileged classes run the risk of undermining the system. So billions are spent on social programs to blunt the discontent that the underprivileged feel, wedding them to the system—by means of the dole. Here, too, the president has been the key force in the process of reform that gives a little to the many in order to keep a lot for the few. It is usually his task to convince the

---

11. During President Carter's first months in office he received more than 20,000 telephone calls a day. On Dial-a-President Day, more than nine million people called the White House. See Richard Pious, *The American Presidency* (New York: Basic Books, 1979).

business class that new concessions are needed to defend the old order. By accepting labor unions, minimum-wage laws, social programs, and the like, the president may incur the wrath of the more conservative elements of the business community who see such things as the beginning of the end. Again, the president's role is an innovative one, but it is intended to reform rather than transform the existing system.

The success any group enjoys in winning the intervention of the president has less to do with the justice of its cause than with the place it occupies in the class structure. If a large group of migrant workers and a small group of aerospace executives both sought the president's assistance, it would not be difficult to predict which of them would be more likely to win it. Witness these events of April 1971:

1. Some 80,000 to 90,000 migrant farm workers in Florida, out of work for much of the season because of crop failures and exempted from unemployment compensation, were left without means of feeding themselves and their families. Welfare agencies supplied some surplus foods that were "almost pure starch, usually unpalatable, and cause diarrhea to children." Faced with the prospect of seeing their children starve, the workers demonstrated in large numbers outside President Nixon's vacation residence in Florida. The peaceful gathering was an attempt to attract public attention to their plight and to get the White House to intercede. The workers succeeded in attracting the attention only of the police, who dispersed them with swinging clubs. The demonstration was reported in a few small-circulation radical newspapers and ignored by the establishment news media.

There was no evidence that the farm workers' message ever intruded upon the president's attention. Eventually the Florida farm counties were declared disaster areas only because of the crop losses sustained by the commercial farms. The government emergency relief money ended up in the hands of the big growers who worked with state agencies in distributing it. Since the migrant workers had no state residence, they did not qualify for relief and were "summarily left out of the decisions."[12]

2. During the very week the farm workers were being clubbed in Florida, leaders of the aerospace industry placed a few telephone calls to Washington and were invited to meet quietly with the president to discuss their companies' problems. Later that same day the White House announced a $42 million authorization to the aerospace industry to relocate, retrain, and in other ways assist its top administrators,

---

12. Tom Foltz, "Florida Farmworkers Face Disaster," *Guardian*, April 3, 1971, p. 4.

scientists, and technicians. The spending plan, an industry creation, was accepted by the government without prior study.[13]

Contrasting the treatment accorded the farm workers with that provided the aerospace industrialists (or big-farm owners, or representatives of U.S. Steel, ITT, etc.), we might ask: is the president responding to a "national interest" or a "special interest" when he helps the giant firms? Much depends upon how the labels are applied. Those who believe the national interest necessitates taking every possible measure to maintain the profits and strength of the industrial and military establishment, of which the aerospace industry is a part, might say the president is not responding to a special interest but to the needs of national security. Certainly almost every president in modern times might have acted accordingly. In contrast, a regional group of farm workers represents a marginal interest. Without making light of the suffering of the migrant families, it is enough to say that a president's first responsibility is to tend to our industrial economy. In fact, the argument goes, when workers act to disrupt and weaken the sinews of industry, as have striking coal miners, railroad operators, and steel workers, the president may see fit to deal summarily with them.[14]

Other people would argue that the national interest is not served when giant industries receive favored treatment at the expense of workers, taxpayers, and consumers and to the lasting neglect of millions like the farm workers. That the corporations have holdings that are national and often multinational in scope does not mean they represent the interests of the nation's *populace*. The "national interest" or "public interest" should encompass the ordinary public rather than a handful of big commercial farm owners, corporate elites, and their well-paid technicians and managers. Contrary to an established myth, the public monies distributed to these favored few do not "trickle down" to the mass of working people at the bottom—as the hungry farm workers can testify.

Whichever position one takes, it becomes clear that there is no *neutral* way of defining the "national interest." Whichever policy the president pursues, he is helping some class interests rather than others,

---

13. *New York Times*, April 2, 1971.

14. When Ronald Reagan complained in 1982 about the "special interests" attempting to thwart his budget-cutting efforts and his desire to serve the "national interest," he was using a motif long propagated by political scientists, who defined "special" and "national" interests by some abstract scope (local vs. nationwide) and not by the *class* interest involved (owners vs. workers, taxpayers, and consumers). Thus Reagan was able to portray the social needs of working people as limited, parochial "special" interests, while the big companies had national, indeed international, interests. It is the same argument made by presentday apologists for the framers of the Constitution: see chapter 4.

and it is a matter of historical record that presidents have usually chosen a definition of the national interest that serves the giant conglomerates. It is also clear, whether we consider it essential or deplorable, that the president, as the most powerful officeholder in the land, is most readily available to the most powerful interests in the land and rather inaccessible to us lesser mortals.

THE "NEW FEDERALISM" PLOY

In his 1981 inaugural address, President Reagan vowed "to curb the size and influence of the federal establishment." In pursuit of that goal he sought to hand over social spending programs to the states or abolish them outright. But his "New Federalism," as he called it, operated in highly selective ways, for he also advocated greater federal assistance to big business, a massive growth in the already gargantuan Defense Department, an expansion of the powers of security agencies like the FBI and CIA, and a greater role for the federal government in the regulation of public and private morals (e.g., abortion and school prayer). Reagan sought to shift power to the states but only in particular policy areas like human services, environmental and workplace protection, consumer protection, collective-bargaining rights, and unemployment benefits.

The New Federalism would be less a shift in *power* than in *responsibility*, for most states did not have the funds to pick up the multi-billion-dollar spending programs. In the absence of uniform standards and sufficient monies, the states that provided the most services would attract needy people from the states that provided less. Domestic migration, already on the upswing because of economic recession, would increase greatly. The inclination of the already overburdened states therefore would be to provide as little spending as possible. The New Federalism would greatly diminish social services and force people to rely increasingly on the private market—in a still more intensified competition for jobs that would further drive down wages and bolster profits.

The New Federalism would abolish the federal power that on occasion heeds the agitations of broad masses of people, especially around election time. Thus the president was reviving a dream, so dear to conservatives, of a marriage between Big Business and Little Government. It is easier for DuPont Corporation to control the tiny state of Delaware than deal with the federal government as a whole. Hooker Chemical Corporation would prefer to see Niagara County in New York rather than the federal government have sole jurisdiction over the land and people that Hooker poisoned in Niagara. The coal-mine companies find state safety inspectors more malleable and more easily bought off than federal inspectors. And Exxon, which is more powerful and richer than Alaska, would like to see that sparsely populated state given complete control over all federal oil and natural resources within its boundaries—which in effect would give Exxon complete control over Alaska.[15]

However, on those occasions *when corporate interests have encountered democratic regulations from the states*, Reagan discarded his states'-rights posture and acted like an early federalist, using the central government to override state powers. For instance, the Reagan administration decided (a) that the Atomic Energy Act of 1954—to the satisfaction of the nuclear and utilities industries—prohibited the states from establishing nuclear-plant emission standards more stringent than those imposed by federal authorities; (b) that the Federal Home Loan Bank Board—to the satisfaction of savings and loan associations and to the dismay of home buyers—could override state laws regulating home-sale clauses that protected low-interest mortgages; (c) that state laws protecting companies from corporate takeovers were invalid because the matter was exclusively within the province of the federal government.[16]

Like conservatives since 1787, Ronald Reagan was for stronger or weaker central government and for stronger or weaker state powers depending on which arrangement served owning-class interests on a particular issue. This is why, for all of Reagan's New Federalism talk about giving power back to the states, he has often stood firmly on the side of the "overgrown" federal power. For this, some New Right ideologues accused Reagan of abandoning true conservative principles. Not true. Like any conservative he understands that abstract notions such as states' rights are not an end unto themselves but just a means of serving the propertied class, and when they fail to do so, they are quietly put aside for more effective measures. This is not a matter of being pragmatic and compromising on conservative principles but of uncompromisingly pursuing ruling-class interests by whatever means available.

THE PRESIDENT VERSUS CONGRESS: WHO HAS THE POWER?

A glance at the Constitution seems to indicate that Congress is the more powerful branch of government. Article 2 gives the president

15. Sam Marcy, *Workers World*, January 23, 1981.
16. Alan Morrison, "New Federalism Holes," *New York Times*, September 20, 1982.

the power to appoint ambassadors, Supreme Court justices, and senior executive officers (subject to Senate confirmation) and to make treaties (subject to ratification by two-thirds of the senators present). The president can veto laws (but the veto can be overriden by a two-thirds vote in Congress), and he can call Congress into special session and do a few other incidental things. The president has two other more significant functions: he must see that the laws are faithfully executed and he is commander-in-chief of the armed forces. But Article 1 seems far more important: it gives Congress the power to declare war, make the laws of the land, raise taxes, and spend money. By all appearances, it is Congress that determines policy and lays down the law and it is the president who does Congress's bidding.

The reality, of course, is something else. In the last century or so, with the growth of industrial capitalism at home and abroad, the burdens of government have grown enormously at the municipal, state, and federal levels and in the executive, legislative, and judicial branches. But the tasks of serving capitalism's vast interests in war and peace and dealing with the politico-economic problems it has created have fallen disproportionately on the level of government that is national and international in scope—the federal—and on the branch most suited to carrying out the necessary technical, organizational, and military tasks—the executive. The responsibilities of the executive have so expanded that there is no such thing as a "weak" or inactive president nowadays, for even Eisenhower, who preferred to exercise as little initiative as possible in most affairs, found himself proposing huge budgets and participating in decisions of far greater scope than anything handled by a "strong" president a half century before. If there has been an expansion of the executive branch, it has been less due to the aggrandizing impulses of White House occupants than to the growing demands placed on the federal government.[17]

The growth of the powers of the presidency has been so great as to have occasioned a *relative* decline in the powers of Congress (even though legislative activity itself has greatly increased over the years). This is especially true in international affairs. Congressional influence over foreign policy has been exercised largely by withholding funds, passing resolutions, ratifying treaties, and other such means; but in recent times presidents increasingly have bypassed Congress or confronted it with *faits accomplis*, making covert military commitments, ignoring legislative resolutions, circumventing the Senate's power to ratify treaties by resorting to "executive agreements," and placing

---

17. On presidential powers see Pious, *The American Presidency*.

White House policymakers beyond the reach of congressional interrogation by claiming "executive privilege" for them. Although "executive privilege" is nowhere mentioned in the Constitution, it has been used to withhold information on everything from undeclared wars to illegal campaign funds and burglaries. In 1976 Ford invoked it when refusing to supply a House committee with information on the CIA.[18] The net effect of these developments has been to move important policy decisions increasingly out of public view and into the secrecy of the executive office.

By using its vast information resources, the executive branch can exercise a decisive influence over the legislators. In many instances Congress goes along with the president because it depends so heavily on what the executive departments tell it about armaments, highways, taxes, or whatever. Much of this information is provided by "congressional liaison officers" who are really lobbyists from the various departments—and, in effect, lobbyists for the defense contractors, corporations, and other groups that work closely with them on a day-to-day basis.

The legislative branch is often no better informed than the public it represents. For a number of years Congress unknowingly funded CIA operations in Laos and Thailand that were in violation of congressional prohibitions. Most of the members of the Senate who were questioned by Senator William Proxmire (D.-Wisc.) had never heard of the automated battlefield program for which they had voted secret appropriations.[19] Congress ordered a halt to further expansion of a controversial naval base on an island in the Indian Ocean, only to discover subsequently that construction was continuing and air activities had steadily increased at the base.[20] A report from two House Foreign Affairs subcommittees complained of the "unwillingness of the executive branch to acknowledge major decisions and to subject them to public scrutiny and discussion."[21]

---

18. "Executive privilege" was given a legal peg by the Supreme Court, which decided that a "presumptive privilege" for withholding information (in noncriminal cases) belonged to the president: see *U.S.* v. *Nixon*, 418 U.S. 683 (1974). Most certainly "presumptive," since it has no existence in the Constitution or in any law.

19. Paul Dickson and John Rothchild, "The Electronic Battlefield: Wiring Down the War," *Washington Monthly*, May 1971, pp. 6–14. See Richard Barnet, *Roots of War* (New York: Atheneum, 1972) for an account of the ways public opinion is manipulated by officialdom; also John C. Donovan, *The Cold Warriors: A Policy Elite* (Lexington, Mass.: Heath, 1973).

20. UPI dispatch in *Workers World*, January 2, 1976.

21. Graham Hovey, "Making Foreign Policy," *New York Times*, January 22, 1973. Yet as noted in the previous chapter, Congress seems willing enough to go along with most of the executive's secret practices and has a number of its own. (The House Foreign Affairs Committee is now the House International Relations Committee.)

In many instances, whether in foreign or domestic matters, it is not that the president acts without Congress but that he commands levers of power that leave the legislature no option but to move in a direction predetermined by him. The executive branch's control of crucial information, its system of management and budgeting, and its vast network of specialized administrators and staff workers enable it to play a greater role in shaping the legislative agenda than the under-staffed and often ill-informed legislators. Approximately 80 percent of the major laws enacted have originated in the executive branch.

The president has other resources at his command that he can use to garner support from Congress. He can endorse particular legisla-tors during election time. He can see that the lawmaker who votes the way he wants finally gets that Veteran's hospital built in his district, or White House support for an emergency farm bill, or a federal con-tract for a shipyard back home.[22] Sometimes just a personal call from the president is enough to pressure or flatter legislators into giving their support, especially if the issue is not crucial to their own inter-ests.

Congress itself has been compliant about the usurpation of its power. Since 1790, the legislature has granted each president, and a widening list of executive agencies, confidential funds for which no detailed invoices are required. The statute that created the CIA per-mitted it to expend billions without regard to the provisions of law regulating government spending and without the knowledge of Con-gress.[23] Congress has preferred to pass on to the president the task of handling crises and making troublesome and unpopular policy choices on behalf of the corporate system at home and abroad.

The peculiar danger of executive power is that it executes. Presi-dents have repeatedly engaged in acts of warfare, for instance, with-out congressional knowledge or approval because they have had at their command the military forces to do so. If the executive branch proposes, it just as often disposes, having the final word on what and how things get done, acting with the force of state, exercising daily initiatives of its own on a scale so massive and detailed, so secretive and closely linked to its military and security forces as to be held unac-countable more often than not. Indeed, the growth of the presidency has been a growth in its unaccountable and unilateral activities. The

22. Mark Green and Michael Calabrese, *Who Runs Congress?* 3rd edition (New York: Bantam, 1979), pp. 110–13.
23. Louis Fisher, *Presidential Spending Power* (Princeton, N.J.: Princeton Univer-sity Press, 1975).

crimes of Richard Nixon, then, were not an anomaly but a fulfillment of the growing capacity for abuse and evil that inheres in the office.

In the post-Watergate era, Congress felt the need to limit the expansive nature of the executive branch. To cite a few instances:

1. After seeing Nixon repeatedly impound funds appropriated by Congress for domestic programs, Congress passed the Impoundment Control Act of 1974, requiring the president to get congressional permission to defer spending appropriations—and the deferral cannot extend beyond the end of the year.

2. Congress now has budget committees with staffs that can more effectively study the president's budget, a longer budgetary review period, and better coordinating procedures within both houses—all designed to give Congress greater control over federal spending.

3. The Foreign Military Sales Act was amended to enable Congress, by concurrent resolution, to prevent any major arms sales to other nations; the president is also required to give the legislature advance notice on sales.

4. In forty years, three presidents declared states of "national emergency"—to win support for war, to break strikes, to freeze wages, and to stop bank failures. Under the National Emergencies Act of 1976, all powers held by the executive as a result of past emergencies were terminated as of 1978, and all future emergencies declared by the president must end on the date specified in a presidential proclamation or in a legislative concurrent resolution, whichever date is earlier.[24]

Many of the restrictions imposed by Congress possess more form than substance. Thus the president can still grant himself emergency powers, even if only for a specified time. And there still exist some 470 statutes that extend potentially dictatorial emergency powers to the president, allowing him to seize properties, institute martial law, control all transportation, and restrict travel.[25] Congress now requires that the president send it a copy of any secret agreement made with other governments. But if the president decides that public disclosure

---

24. For a good discussion of these points see Harvey G. Zeidenstein, "The Reassertion of Congressional Power: New Curbs on the President," *Political Science Quarterly*, 93, Fall 1978, pp. 393–409.

25. See the joint statement by Senators Church and Mathias for the Senate Committee on the Termination of the National Emergency, quoted in the *Guardian*, January 23, 1974.

might harm "national security," he can submit the text to the confidential review of only the Senate Foreign Relations Committee and the House International Relations Committee; in effect, still keeping the agreement secret.[26]

Under the guise of limiting presidential power, Congress sometimes inadvertently expands it. Thus the War Powers Resolution, placing the president under obligation to seek congressional approval within sixty days for any war he has launched, actually expands his warmaking powers, since the Constitution does not grant the president power to engage in warfare without *prior* congressional approval.[27]

Commanding the kind of media exposure that most politicians can only dream of, the president is able to direct attention to his program; and once he succeeds in defining his program as crucial to the "national interest" and himself as the key purveyor of that interest, Congress usually votes the necessary funds and enabling powers, contenting itself with making marginal modifications and inserting special amendments for special friends of its own. This is particularly the case if the president is not attempting anything of a radically deviant nature but much less true if he is hoping to initiate a program of a seemingly progressive kind.

One recalls that liberals frequently complained about the way Congress managed to thwart the desires of liberal presidents like Truman and Kennedy. They concluded from this that Congress had too much power and the president not enough. But having witnessed a conservative president like Richard Nixon regularly effect his will over a Democratic Congress, some of these same liberals concluded that the president was too powerful and Congress was too weak. Actually, there is something more to these respective complaints than partisan inconsistency. In the first situation liberals are talking about the president's insufficient ability to effect measures that might benefit the ordinary working populace. And in the second instance they are talking about the president's seemingly limitless ability to make

---

26. See Zeidenstein, "The Reassertion of Congressional Power . . . "

27. Not all the restrictions Congress imposes on the president are for the better. It is one thing when the legislature limits presidential powers in order to assert its own constitutional responsibilities and curb executive abuses, but Congress has also shown itself hostile toward the president when he tries to bring the immense federal bureaucracy, which is infiltrated by special interests and subjected to powerful centrifugal forces, under tighter White House control. Attempts by Nixon, and later by Carter, to make federal departments and agencies more accountable to White House staff members, who in turn are directly accountable to the president, have been treated by Congress as usurpation. As the elected chief executive, the president should be able to exercise control over his nonelected executive branch.

overseas military commitments and to thwart social-welfare legislation at home.

What underlies the ostensibly inconsistent liberal complaint is the fact that *the relative powers of the executive and legislative branches depend in part on the interests being served,* and that regardless of who is in what office, the political system operates more efficiently to realize conservative goals than reformist ones, both the executive and legislative branches being more responsive to the moneyed powers than to the working public. Thus the president tends to be more powerful than Congress when he assumes a conservative stance and less powerful when he wants to push in a progressive direction. This is a reflection of not only wider politico-economic forces but of the way the Constitution structures things. As the framers intended, the system of separation of powers and checks and balances is designed to give the high ground to those who would resist social change, be they presidents or legislators. Neither the executive nor the legislature can single-handedly initiate reform, which means that conservatives need to control only one or the other branch to thwart domestic actions (or in the case of Congress, key committees in one or the other house) while liberals must control both houses and both branches.

Small wonder conservative and liberal presidents have different kinds of experiences with Congress. Since a conservative president generally wants little from Congress in the way of liberal domestic legislation and, with well-placed allies in the legislature, can often squelch what Congress attempts to produce in that direction, he is less beholden to that body than a liberal president. Should Congress insist upon passing bills that incur his displeasure, the conservative president need control only one-third plus one of either the House or the Senate to sustain his vetoes. If bills are passed over his veto, he can still undermine legislative intent by delaying enforcement under various pretexts relating to timing, efficiency, and other operational contingencies. The Supreme Court has long been aware that its decisions have the force of law only if other agencies of government choose to carry them out. In recent years Congress has been coming to the same realization, developing a new appreciation of the executive's power to command in a direct and palpable way the people, materials, and programs needed for carrying out decisions.

The techniques of veto, decoy, and delay used by a conservative president to dismantle or hamstring already weak domestic programs are of little help to a liberal president who might claim an interest in social change, for the immense social problems he faces cannot be solved by executive sleight-of-hand. What efforts liberal presidents do make in the field of "social reform" legislation are frequently thwarted or greatly diluted by entrenched conservative powers in Congress. It is in these confrontations that the Congress gives every appearance of being able to frustrate presidential initiatives.

The first two years of the Reagan administration lent confirmation to the above analysis, albeit with a new twist, for here was a conservative president who was not obstructionist but activist, one who sought a major transition in taxing and spending policies. The obstructionist defenses that Congress uses so well against progressive measures were seldom in evidence against Reagan, as a coalition of Republicans and "boll weevil" conservative Democrats, backed by corporate and moneyed interests outside Congress, gave the president what he wanted, curtailing or diminishing in one session progressive programs developed over the last 50 years. So was demonstrated a new variation on an old theme: the system moves most swiftly when directed toward conservative ends.

CHANGE FROM THE TOP?

The ability of even a well-intentioned executive to generate policies for the benefit of relatively powerless constituents is, to say the least, quite limited. Not only presidents but mayors and governors have complained of the difficulties of moving in new directions. The Black mayor of Gary, Indiana, Richard Hatcher, one of the more dedicated and socially conscious persons to achieve public office, offered this observation:

> I am mayor of a city of roughly 90,000 Black people but we do not control the possibilities of jobs for them, or money for their schools, or state-funded social services. These things are in the hands of the U.S. Steel Corporation, and the County Department of Welfare, the State of Indiana. . . . For not a moment do I fool myself that Black political control of Gary or of Cleveland or of any other city in and of itself can solve the problems of the wretched of this nation. The resources are not available to the cities to do the job that needs doing.[28]

Hatcher's statement is not unique. "The speeches of mayors and governors," writes Richard Goodwin, "are filled with exculpatory claims that the problems are too big, that there is not enough power or enough money to cope with them, and our commentators sympa-

---

28. From a speech delivered by Hatcher to an NAACP meeting, reprinted in the *Old Mole* (Boston), October 5, 1968.

thize, readily agreeing that this city or that state is really ungovernable."[29]

When presidents, governors, and mayors contend that the problems they confront are of a magnitude far greater than the resources they command, we can suspect them of telling the truth. Most of the resources are preempted by vested interests. The executive leader who begins his term with the promise of getting things moving is less likely to change the political-corporate-class system than be absorbed by it. Once in office, he finds himself staggered by the vast array of entrenched powers working within and without government. He is confronted with a recalcitrant legislature and an intractable bureaucracy. He is constantly distracted by issues and operational problems that seem to take him from his intended course, and he finds it difficult to move in progressive directions without incurring the hostility of those who control the economy and its institutional auxiliaries. So he begins to talk about being "realistic" and working with what is at hand, now tacking against the wind, now taking one step back in the often unrealized hope of taking two steps forward, until his public begins to complain that his administration bears a dismaying resemblance to the less dynamic, less energetic ones that came before. In the hope of maintaining his efficacy, he begins to settle for the *appearance* of efficacy, until appearances are all he is left struggling with. It is this tugging and hauling and whirling about in a tight circle of options and ploys that is celebrated by some as "the give-and-take of democratic interest-group politics." To less enchanted observers the failure of reform-minded leaders to deliver on their promises is another demonstration of the impossibility of working for major changes within a politico-economic system structured to resist change.

The executive has grown in power and responsibility along with the increasing concentration of monopoly capital. As already noted, a centralized nationwide capitalist economy needs a centralized nationwide state power to tend to its needs. By the same token, as U.S. corporate interests grow to international scope and are confronted with challenges from various anti-imperialist forces, so the president's involvement in international affairs grows—and so grows the military establishment intended to defend "U.S. interests" abroad. The president can intervene in other countries in a variety of ways. He can also blow up the world with the nuclear arsenal at his command. Such powers do not advance the democratic interests of the American peo-

---

29. Richard Goodwin, "Reflections: Sources of the Public Unhappiness," *New Yorker*, January 4, 1969, p. 41.

ple, nor are they designed to. The immense military power the president commands, supposedly to make us all much safer, actually gives the chief executive a life-and-death power over the American people (and over other peoples). Ironically, then, as the executive power grows in foreign affairs, so the president's power over the American people becomes less accountable, less containable, and less safe for everyone.

In most domestic areas, the increase in presidential powers has not kept up with the growth in presidential responsibilities, so although the president and the government are often held responsible *for* the economy, they do not have all that much control *over* it. If anything, the growing involvement of the executive in industrial matters has increased its dependence on corporate organizations for information, cooperation, and leadership in the policy process. The purpose of executive involvement in the economy is to serve the process of capital accumulation and not to control the economy in order to bring it into line with larger, egalitarian social goals.[30] There is, then, not likely to be much progressive change from the top, no matter who is in the White House, unless there is also a mass mobilization of the people for social change.

---

30. See Frank E. Myers, "Social Class and Political Change in Western Industrial Systems," *Comparative Politics*, April 1970, p. 404.

15

The Politics of Bureaucracy

As everyone complains, bureaucracy is beset by inertia, evasion, and unaccountability, but there are reasons why bureaucrats behave as they do. Many of these reasons are profoundly political, being less a peculiarity of bureaucrats than a reflection of the wider system of power and interest in which they operate.

GOVERNMENT BY SECRECY AND DECEPTION

The first line of defense for any bureaucracy, Max Weber once wrote, is the withholding of information. Actually, it is the first line of defense of any person in authority who wishes to keep as much beyond public criticism as possible. Officials who lie or who resort to secrecy do so not only to maintain a free hand in the pursuit of their interests (or the interests they serve) but also because they distrust the public's ability to judge correctly. These two sentiments strengthen each other, as when officeholders do their best to keep the public ignorant and then use the ignorance as justification for not inviting public criticism.

Past administrations lied to the American public about the U.S. role in overthrowing popular governments in countries like Guatemala, Iran, Indonesia, the Dominican Republic, and Chile, and about U.S. covert intervention in Indochina, much of Latin America, Cuba, Angola, Portugal, Nicaragua, Jamaica, and East Timor. The government repeatedly lied to keep secret the 3,630 B-52 raids that

devastated Cambodia in 1969 and 1970. Senate investigators estimated that the United States has as many as 400 to 600 secret agreements with other countries that the White House has refused to deliver to Congress, including aid agreements with fascist governments
like Chile. After a review of its secret files, the Defense Department
declassified 710 documents and destroyed 355,300.[1]

The White House and various executive agencies frequently cooperate more closely with private business than with Congress, especially when it comes to keeping things secret. Government regulation
of prices charged by utilities and leasing of offshore drilling tracts to
oil companies are based on data supplied by the interested corporations; this information is not available to Congress or the public. The
Internal Revenue Service freely hands out tax records to agencies like
the FBI, but refused to disclose to Congress its highly questionable
ruling on a capital-gains tax for ITT.[2] The government has repressed
information concerning health and safety problems, including data
on the harmful features of certain medical drugs, pesticides, and nuclear reactors.

It was discovered—15 years after the fact—that large numbers of
the 30,000 American soldiers who had been exposed to nuclear tests
by the U.S. military in the 1950s were suffering radiation symptoms
including sterility, premature aging, and cancer. The government responded to the outcry by maintaining a wall of silence and denying
victims their basic medical benefits.[3] Although government studies
showed that herbicides like Agent Orange used as defoliants during
the Vietnam war and as weed killers in the U.S. produced birth deformities and liver cancer, the government suppressed this information. Meanwhile the U.S. military sprayed one-eighth of the acreage
of South Vietnam, causing drastic injury to its population and to the
U.S. military personnel involved in the spraying. After investigating
these and other incidents, two Stanford University scientists reported:

> We believe, as a result of our studies, that . . . the executive decision-
> making process too often sacrifices the safety and welfare of the public to
> the short-term interests of the government bureaucracy and the large in-
> dustrial interest to which it has become allied. . . . In these cases, where

1. David Wise, *The Politics of Lying* (New York: Random House, 1973); *New York Times*, October 18, 1974, and March 2 and 26, 1976.

2. *New York Times*, February 26, 1974; James Ridgeway, "How Government and Industry Keep Secrets from the People," *New Republic*, August 21 and 28, 1971, pp. 17–19.

3. Howard L. Rosenberg, *Atomic Soldiers* (Boston: Beacon Press, 1980); Harvey Wasserman and Norman Solomon, *Killing Our Own* (New York: Delacorte, 1980).

the facts and the best expert advice did not support the current administration policy, the primary interest of the Executive in the facts was to suppress them—even while stressing in public that its policies had a sound technical foundation.[4]

Public servants who defy the code of secrecy by informing a member of Congress or reporter that something is wrong risk punishment by their superiors. One such "whistleblower," Andrew Susce, an IRS agent, uncovered a multimillion-dollar tax fraud perpetrated by mobsters and politicians and was fired for his persistence in the case. When a weapons-cost analyst, Ernest Fitzgerald, testified that a Lockheed cargo plane cost $2 billion more than contracted, the Air Force abolished his job.[5] These are not isolated instances. The special board created to handle whistleblower complaints had a backlog of 1,000 cases only four months after its creation.[6] Once fired, dissidents find few employment opportunities in government or in industries dealing with government contracts.

To prevent other federal employees from "committing truth," the government has sought greater power to control and punish disclosures—even disclosures of unclassified materials. It has argued in several court cases that government information is government property; therefore when whistleblowers take and release such information they are guilty of theft. In effect, the government claims the power to make anything it does an official secret.[7] Former Attorney-General Bell denounced Justice Department personnel who leaked information to the press regarding FBI wrongdoings as having violated their oath "to uphold the law."[8] Thus, leaking information about crimes is itself treated as a crime, and "upholding the law" means collaborating in the cover-up or at least looking the other way.

In 1982, to combat public pressures for greater access to government information, the Reagan administration placed *all* government employees under orders to obtain White House clearance before talking to the press about any policy, regardless of whether it involved

---

4. The Stanford report was released in early 1971; its authors were Dr. Frank von Hippel and Dr. Joel Primack.

5. John Hayes, *Lonely Fighter* (Secaucus, N.J.: Lyle Stuart, 1979) tells Susce's story. On Fitzgerald and numerous other cases see Helen Dudar, "The Price of Blowing the Whistle," *New York Times Magazine*, October 30, 1977; also *Washington Post*, October 3, 1982, for additional cases.

6. Information provided by Lewis Clark of the Government Accountability Project (Institute for Policy Studies, Washington, D.C.), which specializes in giving support and legal guidance to whistleblowers; also *Washington Post*, October 3, 1982.

7. *New York Times*, July 12, 1978, and August 8, 1978.

8. *New York Times*, May 18, 1977.

classified information. Government officials were no longer required to establish the specific national security grounds for withholding information.[9]

It is senseless to urge people to work for a change within the system if they cannot find out what the system is doing. This is not to deny that the public is subjected to a continual barrage of "information" from federal agencies and departments (of which the Pentagon is the most prolific) in the form of hundreds of magazine articles and films, thousands of radio scripts, and tens of thousands of press releases and planted news stories—which give the establishment point of view.[10]

BUREAUCRATIC ACTION AND INACTION

The rulings of bureaucratic agencies are published daily in the *Congressional Federal Register*, a volume as imposing in size as the *Congressional Record* itself. Many of these rulings are as significant as major pieces of legislation, and in the absence of precise guidelines from Congress, they often take the place of legislation. In 1972, for instance, without a single law being passed and without a word of public debate, the Price Commission approved more than $2 billion in rate increases for 110 telephone, gas, and electric companies, thereby imposing upon the public by administrative fiat an expenditure far greater than what is contained in most of the bills passed by Congress.[11] Even when legislation does exist, it usually allows for leeway in implementation. Which laws are applied fully and which are ignored, what interpretations are made to suit what interests, what supplementary regulations are formulated—these matters, of keen concern to lobbyists, are almost unknown to the general public.

To treat public administration as a "neutral" and "nonpartisan" function is grossly misleading. The political process does not end with the passage of a bill but continues at the administrative level, albeit in more covert fashion. Succumbing to interest-group pressures, administrators will ignore statutory deadlines and delay carrying out the

---

9. *New York Times*, April 3, 1982.

10. J. William Fulbright, *The Pentagon Propaganda Machine* (New York: Vintage, 1971). More nourishing government information is being squelched. In 1981 Thorne Auchter, head of OSHA, ordered the destruction of 100,000 booklets on brown-lung disease. That same year the Reagan administration embarked on a major review to cut back on all consumer information and handbooks printed by the government. David Lindorff, "Do You Know Too Much?" *Mother Jones*, August 1981, p. 12.

11. See the report by Senator Lee Metcalf in *Ramparts*, November 1972, p. 24.

law. Thus the Federal Reclamation Act, intended to shield small farmers from the concentrated wealth and speculations of agribusiness, declares that waters from federal dams cannot be supplied to farms exceeding 160 acres per person or to absentee-owned farms. But the law has gone unenforced for decades, while corporations like Standard Oil, Purex, and Southern Pacific Railroad accumulated vast holdings and were subsidized by federal water projects.[12]

The Resource Conservation and Recovery Act, the first comprehensive law governing the disposal of garbage and toxic wastes, was supposed to clean up industrial dumping and prevent tragedies like the one at Love Canal in Niagara Falls. But at every turn industrial lobbyists stymied the Environmental Protection Agency (EPA), requiring it to spend much of its time responding to industry's com-

---

12. Kathy Keilch, "Agribusiness Skirts U.S. Water Law," *Guardian*, February 8, 1978.

plaints through Congress and the courts, so that the law remained largely unenforced.[13] Representatives of a farm-workers union complained that enforcement of existing laws, not enactment of new ones, was needed to alleviate the housing, wage, and safety problems faced by farm workers. "We've got plenty of laws, beautiful laws on housing, but they're not enforced," said one union official.[14]

Often agencies are not sufficiently staffed to handle the enormous tasks that confront them. The Bureau of Motor Carrier Safety and the Federal Railway Administration respectively have nine and sixteen full-time inspectors to monitor the truck and rail transportation of hazardous wastes over the entire country.[15] With its existing staff, EPA may take fifteen years to assess the safety of all pesticides, let alone control and restrict their use. Indeed with the budget cuts imposed by the Reagan administration, EPA may take many years more than that. Meanwhile industry pours about 1,000 new potentially toxic chemicals into the environment each year—at a faster rate than they can be monitored or controlled.[16]

While some laws go unenforced, others are so transformed during implementation as to subvert the intent of the law. Two years after Congress created a Merit Systems Protection Board to shield and encourage persons in government who report mismanagement, corruption, and discrimination, a House subcommittee charged that the board had administered the law so as to give even less protection to whistleblowers than before. For instance, the board required that employees undergo an evidentiary hearing about as rigorous as a public trial when charging their superiors with wrongdoing or when complaining of reprisals by superiors, in effect placing the burden of investigation and proof on the whistleblower instead of the agency. Such requirements were not authorized by statute.[17]

People who bemoan the "inaction" within municipal, state, and federal administrations and who insist that things don't get done because that's simply the nature of the bureaucratic beast seem to forget that only certain kinds of things don't get done—other things are ac-

---

13. Environmental Action newsletter, Washington, D.C., 1979; for other instances see *New York Times*, February 12, 1974.

14. *Guardian*, September 17, 1980. It has taken OSHA almost ten years to set a field sanitation standard for farm workers. Sanitary accommodations like portable toilets and washing facilities would greatly alleviate suffering from infectious diseases, heat exhaustion, and pesticide poisoning. But agribusiness has opposed spending money on such things, and OSHA claims it needs another five years to study whether there is a link between unsanitary field conditions and disease: *Washington Post*, November 4, 1981.

15. *In These Times*, July 16–19, 1980.

16. *New York Times*, December 12 and 25, 1977.

17. *Washington Star*, March 5, 1980; *Federal Times*, October 27, 1980.

complished all too well. A law establishing a "community development" program for a low-income neighborhood, passed by a reluctant Congress in response to the urgings of liberal spokesmen and the pressure of urban unrest, is legally the same as a law enacted to develop a multibillion-dollar, high-profit weapons system. The latter was supported by giant industrial contractors; well-placed persons within the military, scientific, and university establishments; and numerous congressmen whose patriotism is matched only by their desire to bring the defense bacon home to their districts and keep their campaign coffers filled by appreciative donors. If anything, the weapons program is of vastly greater administrative complexity than the smaller, modestly funded urban program. Yet the latter is more likely to suffer from inaction and ineffectiveness, the important difference between the two programs being not bureaucratic but political. *The effectiveness of the law depends on the power of the groups supporting it.* Laws that serve powerful interests are likely to enjoy a vigorous life, while laws that have only the powerless to nurture them are often stillborn.

Years after passage of a law making some 13 million children eligible for medical examinations and treatment, Congress discovered that almost 85 percent of the youngsters had been left unexamined, causing, in the words of a House subcommittee report, "unnecessary crippling, retardation, or even death of thousands of children." The report blamed the government for its laxity in properly enforcing the programs and for failing to penalize laggard states.[18] Such nonenforcement is less likely when the client interests are not powerless children but powerful industrialists.

Enforcement *for* the poor may be neglected but not enforcement *against* the poor. The Reagan administration increased the supervision and prohibitions imposed on welfare recipients; a family now may be cut from the rolls if it owns more than $1,000 worth of furniture and fixtures in its home. But the government did nothing to check on the royalties paid by oil companies drilling on federal lands, even though the General Accounting Office found that companies were shortchanging the government (and the American people) by hundreds of millions of dollars each year.[19]

In time, the sheer vastness of the bureaucracy lends itself to waste and duplication. The National Science Foundation made a study of automotive fuel and another of mass transportation, only to discover

18. UPI dispatch, October 8, 1976. On the failure to enforce the hospital-care program for the poor see Michael Balter, "The Best Kept Secret in Health Care," *Progressive*, April 1981, pp. 35–37.
19. Philip Stern in *New York Times*, December 26, 1981.

that the Army and the Department of Transportation had already conducted similar studies. There are thirteen different advisory committees on cancer, four on air pollution, and three on alcoholism. Seventeen agencies deal with "consumer concerns," none of them effectively.

With all the waste and duplication, important public needs remain improperly regulated or completely neglected. Millions of people staff the gargantuan federal bureaucracy, but relatively few perform the services most needed by ordinary citizens. Service goes to those who have the power to command it. The size of an agency, in any case, is a less significant determinant of its performance than the political influences bearing upon it. With a limited budget of only $3 million in 1949, the Food and Drug Administration proceeded against thousands of violators. In 1976, with a $200-million budget, FDA did not take court action against a single major drug company.[20]

With the right political support, bureaucracies are capable of carrying out policies of momentous scope. "The feat of landing men on the moon," Duane Lockard reminds us, "was not only a scientific achievement but a bureaucratic one as well."[21] The same might be said of the Vietnam war, the U.S. counterinsurgency effort in Latin America, the exploits of the Internal Revenue Service, and the farm, highway, housing, and defense programs. These endeavors represent the mobilization and coordination of stupendous amounts of energy, skill, and material resources by complex, centralized systems of command—i.e., bureaucracies. What is impressive about the federal housing program, for instance, is not how little has been done but how much, yet with so little benefit to low-income people: how many public agencies established, billions of dollars spent, and hundreds of thousands of structures built and subsidized at such profit to realty speculators, manufacturers, banks, and public officials and at such cost to the taxpayers—a stupendous bureaucratic effort. Bureaucracy's failure to serve the unorganized and needy public has led some observers to the mistaken notion that it serves no one. But as we have seen in previous chapters, for some groups the government has been anything but idle.[22]

The same can be said of Congress. As already noted, the complaint that Congress can't get things done is incorrect. While unable

20. Paul Murphy and Rene Care Murphy, "Consumer Beware," *Village Voice*, April 12, 1976, p. 12.

21. Duane Lockard, *The Perverted Priorities of American Politics* (New York: Macmillan, 1971), p. 282.

22. See Orion White, Jr., "The Dialetical Organization: An Alternative to Bureaucracy," *Public Administration Review*, 19, January–February 1969, pp. 32–41.

to accomplish certain things, especially in regard to public needs, Congress is capable of extraordinary achievements. The space, defense, highway, agricultural, and tax programs are not only bureaucratic feats, but also legislative ones. The question is not, "Why can't administrators and legislators act?" but, "Why are they able to act so forcefully and successfully in some ways and not at all in other ways?" The first question invites us to throw up our hands in befuddlement; the second requires that we investigate the realities of power and interest.

Why are reform-minded administrative bodies rarely able to operate with any effectiveness? Consider the fate of the agency set up to regulate some area of industry on behalf of consumers, workers, or the environment. In its youth, the agency may possess a zeal for reform, but before long the business-owned news media either turn their attention to more topical events or present an unsympathetic or superficial picture of the agency's doings. The president, even if originally sympathetic to the agency's mission, is now occupied with more pressing matters, as are its few articulate but not very influential friends in Congress. But the industry that is supposed to be brought under control remains keenly interested and ready to oppose government intrusions. First, it may decide to challenge the agency's jurisdiction or even the legality of its existence in court, thus preventing any serious regulatory actions until a legal determination is made.[23] If the agency survives this attack, there begins a series of encounters between its investigators and industry representatives. The industry is able to counter the agency's moves with a barrage of arguments and technical information, not all truthful but sufficiently impressive to win the respectful attention of the agency's investigators. The investigators begin to develop a new appreciation of the problems industry faces in maintaining profitable operations, and in time they begin to adopt industry's perspective.[24]

If the agency persists in making unfavorable rulings, business people appeal to their elected representatives, to a higher administrative official, or, if they have the pull, to the president himself. In its youthful days after World War I, the Federal Trade Commission moved vigorously against big business, but representatives of industry pre-

23. See the discussion in Grant McConnell, *Private Power and American Democracy* (New York: Knopf, 1966), p. 288.

24. For instance, a report by the National Academy of Sciences found that EPA "is inevitably dependent" on the industries it regulates for much of the information it uses in decision making and that such information is easily withheld or distorted to serve industry's ends: *New York Times*, March 22, 1977; also *Washington Post*, August 24, 1979.

vailed upon the president to replace "some of the commissioners by others more sympathetic with business practices: this resulted in the dismissal of many complaints which had been made against corporations."[25] Some 60 years later, in 1979, the same pattern was to repeat itself. Staffed by some consumer advocates, the FTC began vigorous action against questionable practices by insurance companies, funeral-home operators, doctors, and others, only to find itself under fire from Congress and the business community. It was not long before the commission had its jurisdictional powers abridged and its budget cut.[26]

Frequently members of Congress demand to know why an agency is bothering their constituents. Administrators who are more interested in building congressional support than in making congressional enemies are likely to apply the law in ways that satisfy influential legislators. "If the bureaucrats are to escape criticism, unfavorable publicity, or a cut in their appropriations, they must be discreet in their relations with the legislative body."[27] Some administrative bodies, like the Army Corps of Engineers, so successfully cultivate support among powerful congressmen and their big-business clientele as to become relatively free of supervisory control from department heads or the White House. "Fierce rivalries for funds and functions go on ceaselessly among the departments and between the agencies. A cunning bureau chief learns to negotiate alliances on Capitol Hill [Congress] that bypass the central authority of the White House."[28] *In the executive branch, as in Congress, the fragmentation of power is hardly indicative of its democratization.* Rather it more likely represents a distribution among entrenched special interests.

Administrators are immobilized not only by "bureaucratic infighting" but by pressures bearing upon them from the wider politico-economic system. Given a desire to survive and advance, bureaucrats tend to equivocate in the face of controversial decisions, moving away from dangerous areas and toward positions favored by the strongest of the pressures working on them. With time, the reform-minded agency loses its crusading spirit and settles down to standard operations, increasingly serving the needs of the industry it is supposed to regulate. The more public-spirited staff members either grow weary

---

25. Edwin Sutherland, *White Collar Crime* (New York: Holt, Rinehart and Winston, 1949), p. 232.

26. *Washington Post*, May 1, 1980, and October 27, 1981.

27. E. Pendleton Herring, "The Balance of Social Forces in the Administration of the Food and Drug Law," *Social Forces*, 13, March 1935, p. 364.

28. Douglass Cater, *Power in Washington* (New York: Random House, 1964), pp. 10–11.

of the struggle and make their peace with the corporations or leave, to be replaced by personnel who are "acceptable to, if not indeed the nominees of, the industry."[29]

Consider John O'Leary, who was appointed director of the Bureau of Mines in 1968. Encouraged by media attention and public concern over recent mine disasters, O'Leary ordered the bureau's inspectors to make *unannounced* spot checks of safety conditions, a step rarely tried before, although required by law. In one month, O'Leary's inspectors made 600 checks, almost four times the number for the entire previous year, and ordered workers out of more than 200 unsafe mines. O'Leary publicly charged that the coal-mining industry was "designed for production economy and not for human economy, and there's going to have to be a change of attitudes on that." The change came—but it was of a different sort. The mine companies made known to the White House their strong desire to be rid of the troublesome director. After four months, O'Leary was removed from office. His successor, a former CIA employee, reestablished close relations with the mine owners, making personal appearances at corporate gatherings and riding in company planes.[30]

More recently, without changing a word of the federal strip-mining law, the government systematically weakened the agency that enforces it by relaxing regulations and getting rid of conscientious enforcers—as in the following case:

> For four years, Bruce Boyens . . . stalked the sites of strip mines, forcing coal companies to restore the natural landscape of hills and mountains they had laid bare. When operators threatened to beat up his inspectors, he called in federal marshals to subdue them. When state officials seemed too cozy with coal companies, he leaned on them to get tough.
>
> Now his days as a fearsome enforcer in the coal fields are over. . . . He was being transferred to Washington, far from Appalachia. OSM called it a salute to his expertise. Boyens, who had no choice, took it as a "get out" [order].[31]

Many career administrators eventually leave government service to accept higher-paying jobs in companies whose interests they favored while in office. This promise of a lucrative post with a private

29. McConnell, *Private Power and American Democracy*, p. 288.

30. *New York Times*, February 17, 1969; *Christian Science Monitor*, April 8, 1970; Jack Anderson in *Washington Post*, June 17, 1973.

31. *Washington Post*, June 6, 1982.

firm can exercise a considerable influence on the judgments of the ambitious public administrator.[32]

THE ANARCHY OF REGULATION

Most administrative bodies fall under the command of department heads and the president. But the independent regulatory commissions operate outside the executive branch, making quasi-judicial rulings that can be appealed only to the courts.[33] For all the reasons just discussed, these agencies frequently become agents of the industries they are supposed to regulate, granting fixed prices and other monopoly privileges to big companies, costing the public many billions a year.[34] Industry is regulated, but not in the *public's* interest. Instead the Interstate Commerce Commission continues its long devotion to the railroad companies; the Federal Communications Commission serves the monopolistic interests of the telephone companies and the media networks; the Food and Drug Administration devotes more energy to protecting the profits of the food and drug companies than protecting the health of people; the Securities and Exchange Commission regulates the stock market mostly for the benefit of large investors; the Federal Energy Regulatory Commission maintains a permissive policy toward private utilities and natural gas producers—at a great cost to consumers.

And so with other units of government: the Department of Transportation defers to the oil-highway-automotive combine; the Agriculture Department promotes giant farming corporations; the Army Corps of Engineers and the Tennessee Valley Authority continue to mutilate the natural environment on behalf of utilities, agribusiness, and land developers; the Department of Interior serves the oil, gas,

---

32. One example: Dr. Joseph Sadusk of the FDA prevented a synthetic antibiotic from being recalled off the market despite evidence that it caused blood toxicity and even death. Soon after, he left the FDA and became vice-president of a pharmaceutical firm that produced the drug: Milton Silverman and Philip Lee, *Pills, Profits and Politics* (Berkeley, Calif.: University of California Press, 1974). For other instances see *Washington Post*, October 18, 1981.

33. The major independent regulatory commissions are the Civil Aeronautics Board, Federal Communications Commission, Federal Energy Regulatory Commission, Federal Trade Commission, Interstate Commerce Commission, National Labor Relations Board, Securities and Exchange Commission, and Consumer Product Safety Commission. While the commissions report directly to Congress, their personnel are appointed by the president, with Senate confirmation. See Louis Kohlmeier, *The Regulators: Watchdog Agencies and the Public Interest* (New York: Harper & Row, 1969). Kohlmeier finds that regulation has resulted in diminished competition, producer-controlled markets, restricted consumer choice, and higher prices.

34. See the two-year congressional investigation of regulatory agencies reported in the *New York Times*, October 3, 1976.

mining, and timber companies; and one need not speculate on the hundreds of *billions* expended each year by the Department of Defense to pay the expenses and add to the profits of favored contractors.[35]

On occasions when government agencies succeed in enforcing a regulation on behalf of the citizenry, the accomplishment requires enormous time and effort and usually has only a minimal effect, if any, on the political economy. Thus it took the Federal Trade Commission twelve years of court orders and negotiations to get the manufacturers of Geritol, a vitamin and iron preparation, to stop claiming that their product fights something called "tired blood."[36] And an antitrust action against IBM, charging it with monopolizing the computer business, dragged on for almost two decades.

Government today is an "anarchy of regulation," with hundreds of administrative units independent of the president (although most of them are not supposed to be) and independent of their departments. Congressional oversight of these agencies, a Senate report concluded, is scant and sporadic, largely because members of Congress fear reprisals from the powerful economic interests who are regulated, and congressional committees are often "stacked with members who share similar backgrounds and values with the agencies they are charged with overseeing."[37] This "iron triangle" of bureaucratic unit, congressional committee, and corporate interest—with the latter as the triangle's base—can usually withstand press exposés and attacks by public-advocacy groups.[38]

---

35. There is an ample literature documenting how administrative bodies serve the interests of the industries they are supposed to regulate. See Kohlmeier, *The Regulators;* Anthony Lewis, "To Regulate the Regulators," *New York Times Magazine,* February 22, 1959; Bernard Schwartz, *The Professor and the Commissions* (New York: Knopf, 1958); Walter S. Adams and Horace Gray, *Monopoly in America* (New York: Macmillan, 1955); The Ralph Nader Study Group Report, *The Interstate Commerce Omission: The Public Interest and the ICC* (New York: Grossman, 1970), Robert C. Fellmeth, project director; James Ridgeway, "The Antipopulists," *Ramparts,* December 1971, pp. 6–8; Richard Ney, *The Wall Street Jungle* (New York: Grove Press, 1970); Michael Parfit, "The Army Corps of Engineers: Flooding America in Order to Save It," *New Times,* November 12, 1976, pp. 25–37; John Baskin, "A Close-Up on the Corps," *Ibid.,* pp. 39–44; Robert Engler, *Politics of Oil* (Chicago: The University of Chicago Press, 1976); Henning Sjostrom and Robert Nilsson, *Thalidomide and the Power of the Drug Companies* (New York: Basic Books, 1973).

36. *New York Times,* July 5, 1969.

37. Senate Government Operations Committee report, *New York Times,* February 10, 1977.

38. Frederic V. Malek, *Washington's Hidden Tragedy: The Failure to Make Government Work* (New York: Free Press, 1978). Agencies that do not serve powerful interests but only powerless people, however, are much more vulnerable to White House control; see Ronald Randall, "Presidential Power versus Bureaucratic Intransigence: The Influence of the Nixon Administration on Welfare Policy," *American Political Science Review,* 73, 1979, pp. 795–810.

Public bureaucrats are so tightly bound to private interests that it is often difficult to tell the regulators from the regulated. *More than half the appointees to regulatory jobs are persons who previously were employed by the "regulated" industry.*[39] Eleven of the top sixteen officials appointed by President Reagan to head the Department of the Interior—including Secretary James Watt—had been employed or had served clients in the five major industries regulated by the department.[40] Administrators who have supervised such things as water-development, labor, nuclear-energy, consumer-protection, and food and drug regulations have had a history of previously serving as lobbyists, lawyers, and managers for the business firms they were to regulate.[41] A sixty-three-person National Industrial Pollution Control Council (with salaries and expenses of $475,000 a year paid by the government) was set up to advise the president on pollution reforms. All the members were businessmen from industries that, according to Senator Lee Metcalf, "contribute most to environmental pollution."

Federal meal-inspection laws have been administered by officials with a history of opposition to federal meat inspection. Federal housing programs have been supervised by conservative businessmen who were openly hostile to low-income public housing. Conservation and environmental programs have been given over to people like Secretary Watt and EPA Administrator Ann Gorsuch who have been unyieldingly antagonistic to such programs. Energy programs have been administered by former oil-company executives who are unenthusiastic about, if not openly biased against, the development of alternative energy sources. The occupational-safety program has been administered by business and government officials who were originally opposed to occupational-safety legislation. The Arms Control and Disarmament Agency has been "dominated by military men, conservatives and Wall Street types."[42]

The opportunities for corruption are plentiful. Officials in various agencies have received illegal favors and gratuities from companies or have owned stock in firms under their jurisdiction, in violation of federal rules. A GAO study found over 77,000 cases of fraud in federal agencies during a two-and-one-half-year period; nearly half were in

---

39. *New York Times*, October 3, 1976.

40. According to the Washington public-interest group Common Cause: *In These Times*, December 16–22, 1981.

41. Anthony Lewis, *New York Times*, March 26, 1981; also *New York Times*, September 1, 1982; *Washington Post*, October 6, 1981, and August 19, 1982; *Daily World*, September 25, 1981.

42. Sidney Lens, "The Doomsday Strategy," *Progressive*, February 1976, p. 28.

the Pentagon; only a small portion of the individuals involved were prosecuted.[43]

It is not enough to bemoan the fact that government agencies end up serving interests they are supposed to regulate; rather we should understand how this situation results from the politico-economic realities in which the administrators operate. Most agencies have the contradictory function of regulating a particular industry—supposedly for the public interest—and promoting the industry's profitability. But administrators find they cannot serve the people and serve the corporations, too. Before long the capital-accumulation needs of the major producer interests take precedence over the public. Thus one hears that the goal of keeping the environment free of life-damaging industrial effusions must be weighed against "industry's need to maintain production."

The special interests occupy a special position above the public interest. Indeed, in a capitalist society the special interests *are the systemic interest*, controlling the economic life of the society. Hence, regulation of the capitalist economy on anything but its own terms eventually does not work, not merely because industrialists employ shrewd lobbyists who can manipulate timid and compliant bureaucrats, but because industry *is* the economic system and sooner or later government must meet that system on its own terms or change to another. And when meeting the system on its own terms, regulation becomes a way to rig prices at artificially high levels, control markets for the benefit of large producers, secure high profits, and allow private corporations more direct and covert access to public authority.

Small wonder that reorganization schemes to eliminate the bureaucratic morass and allow for more responsible decision making seldom work. Bureaucracy is less a cause than an effect of special-interest politics. As long as private powers exist and grow, so will the bureaucratic units that serve and protect them and are in turn protected by them. The problems of the economy, affecting all dimensions of society, cannot be solved merely by redrawing bureaucratic lines, for corporate capitalism continues to recreate the conditions that defy rational regulation.

President Carter's creation of a Department of Energy (DOE) provides an apt illustration. The reorganization plan was heralded as a bold new effort to both streamline the bureaucracy and solve the en-

---

43. *Washington Post*, October 10, 1981, and June 23, 1980; for other instances of fraud see *New York Times*, March 1 and November 16, 1975, and January 20, 1976; *Christian Science Monitor*, September 1, 1978.

ergy crisis by bringing the many scattered agencies that deal with energy under one jurisdiction. It did neither, growing into a $10 billion-a-year cabinet-level department that contributes almost nothing to conservation or energy production. For behind DOE's new bureaucratic charts there stand the same old oil companies and bankers who control the resources of energy and who continue to exercise their will over DOE and the nation, while accountable to neither.[44]

What is needed to change things is not an endless proliferation of regulatory units but a change in the conditions that demand so much regulation—that is, a different method of ownership and a different purpose for production. Until fundamental systemic changes are made in the economic order, it seems regulation will continue to fail where it is most needed.

PUBLIC AUTHORITY IN PRIVATE HANDS

The ultimate submergence of public power to private interest comes when government gives, along with its funds and services, its very *authority* to business. Grant McConnell has documented how state authority is taken over by private groups in such areas as agriculture, medicine, industry, and trade. Thus Western ranches not only enjoy the use of federal land and water, they also have been granted the public authority that goes with the task of administering such resources. Control of land and water has been handed over to local "home-rule" boards dominated by the large ranchers, who thereby successfully transform their economic power "into a working approximation of publicly sanctioned authority."[45] Large agricultural producers exercise a similar authority in the administration of farm programs. "Agriculture has become neither public nor private enterprise. It is a system of self-government in which each leading farm interest controls a segment of agriculture through a delegation of national sovereignty. Agriculture has emerged as a largely self-governing federal estate," enjoying a power that has extended "through a line unbroken by personality or party in the White House."[46]

One congressional committee, investigating relations between government and industry, complained of a "virtual abdication of ad-

---

44. Janet Marinelli, "Energy Shortage at DOE," *Environmental Action*, November 4, 1978, pp. 12–14.

45. McConnell, *Private Power and American Democracy*, p. 210.

46. Lowi, *The End of Liberalism*.

ministrative responsibility" on the part of officials in the Department of Commerce, their actions in many instances being "but the automatic approval of decisions already made outside the Government in business and industry."[47] In every significant line of industry, advisory committees staffed by representatives of leading firms work closely with government agencies, making most of the important recommendations. In trying to assess their roles, it is "difficult to determine where the distinction between advice and the making of policy lies."[48] There are 3,200 committees and boards advising the executive branch and Congress, costing the government many millions a year to finance. The most influential deal with banking, chemicals, communications, commercial farming, oil, utilities, railroads, and taxation. They meet regularly with administrative leaders to formulate policies. Their reports become the basis for administrative actions and new legislation. With the coercive power of the state backing their decisions, they secure advantages over smaller competitors, workers, and consumers of a kind less easily gained in open competition.

When the government first began to gather information for legislation on water pollution, it consulted the Advisory Council on Federal Reports, a private body that describes itself as the official business consultant to the Budget Bureau; it also considers itself responsible only to the business community. The Advisory Council, in cooperation with the Budget Bureau, set up a committee on pollution, which included representatives of such big polluters as DuPont, the Manufacturing Chemists Association, and the American Paper Institute. The meetings of these business advisory committees are not open to the press or public.[49]

In many state and municipal governments, as in the federal government, business associations, dominated by the biggest firms, are accorded the power to nominate their own personnel to licensing boards, production boards, and other administrative bodies. The transfer of public authority to private hands frequently comes at the initiative of large companies. But sometimes the government will make the first overtures, organizing private associations, then handing them the powers of the state, thereby supposedly moving toward "voluntaristic" and "decentralized" forms of policymaking. In fact, these measures transfer public power to favored producers without

---

47. From a congressional report cited in McConnell, *Private Power and American Democracy*, p. 271.

48. McConnell, *Private Power and American Democracy*, p. 275.

49. Robert W. Dietsch, "The Invisible Bureaucracy," *New Republic*, February 20, 1971, p. 19.

their being held democratically accountable for the sovereign authority they exercise.

There exists, then, unbeknownst to most Americans, a large number of private decision makers who exercise public authority without having to answer to the public and who determine official policy while being primarily obligated to their private businesses. They belong to what might be called the "public-private authority." Included in this category are the various quasi-public corporations, institutions, foundations, boards, councils, "authorities," and associations, one of the most powerful being the Federal Reserve Board. The "Fed," as it is called, determines the interest rate and the money supply. Although its decisions affect the entire economy, the Fed is beholden to the banks and is run mostly by bankers. Its members are appointed to staggered fourteen-year terms by the president, who can make only two appointments during his four-year term. Once appointed, the board members answer to no one (but the banking industry). The Fed operates without even the pretense of democratic accountability, working in total secrecy, refusing to have Congress or the White House audit its books. The five regional members of its most powerful policy committee are selected not by the president but by bankers from the various regions. The bankers pick their own people to sit on a public agency and make public policy that is backed by the powers of government but is not accountable to government.[50]

Another public-private entity is the Port Authority of New York, a "public corporation" created by interstate compact for the purpose of running the bridges and tunnels between New York and New Jersey and the various metropolitan airports. Its bonds are sold to large financial institutions and rich individuals. It is answerable to none of the governing bodies in the region—not to the mayors, nor the state legislators, nor the governors of New York and New Jersey, nor the U.S. Congress—but it can condemn property and construct tax-exempt developments. The profits from its commercial ventures ($12 million annually from the JFK Airport restaurants alone) are distributed as *tax-free returns to private investors*. Millions in surpluses that could be used to salvage New York's decaying mass-transit system are kept in reserve by the Port Authority, "not for the people of New York City, but for bondholders. Thus does public authority and private

---

50. "What Is the Federal Reserve?" *Dollars and Sense*, March 1976, p. 14; Henry Bretton, *The Power of Money* (Albany, N.Y.: State University of New York Press, 1980), pp. 280–81.

power come together in a massive fusion of wealth that leaves the ordinary taxpaying New Yorkers as its victim."[51]

There are numerous "public authorities" at the federal, state, and local levels carrying out a widely varied range of activities. They all have several things in common: they are authorized by state legislatures or Congress to function outside the regular structure of government, and because of their autonomous corporate attributes, they are seldom subjected to public scrutiny and accountability. In 1972 the public authorities in New York State alone had an outstanding debt (bonds owned by banks and rich investors) of $8.9 billion, more than twice the state's debt. To meet their obligations, the public authorities float new bond issues, none of which are passed upon by the voters, and thus make demands on future tax revenues. They are creatures that have the best of both worlds, feeding off the state treasure while remaining accountable only to themselves.[52]

The public-private authority extends overseas. When the Peruvian generals nationalized the holdings of private American oil companies, the president sent a special envoy to protest the move and negotiate for reacquisition. When the Bangladesh government sought to ban the importation of hundreds of useless or harmful drugs, the U.S. State Department sent an official committee (composed of representatives of drug companies) to that country to argue against the ban. Agents of ITT, the CIA, and the White House jointly considered ways of preventing a democratically elected socialist from taking office in Chile and from remaining in office. The private interests do not merely benefit from public policy; they often *make* policy by selecting key officials, directing World Bank loans and foreign-aid investments, and offering recommendations that are treated as policy guidelines—in sum, using the United States government to pursue their interests abroad.

The corporate interests exert an influence that cuts across particular administrative departments. Within a government whose power is highly fragmented, they form cohesive, and sometimes overlapping, blocs around major producer interests like oil, steel, banking, drugs, transportation, and armaments; these blocs are composed of bureau-

---

51. Jack Newfield and Jeff Greenfield, "Them That Has Keep: Taxes," *Ramparts*, April 1972, p. 61. When the Port Authority had trouble renting space in its ugly World Trade Center, a predicament that could have meant a loss for its bondholders, then-Governor Rockefeller came to the rescue by renting 58 floors for state government offices. One of the biggest Port Authority bondholders is the Rockefeller-controlled Chase Manhattan Bank.

52. *New York Times*, December 27, 1972.

crats at all levels, regulatory commissioners, senior congressmen, lob-byists, newspaper publishers, members of trade associations, and ex-ecutives of business firms, operating with all the autonomy and unaccountability of princely states within the American polity.

MONOPOLY REGULATION VERSUS PUBLIC-SERVICE REGULATION

If government is capitalism's provider and protector at home and abroad, and if government and business are so intermingled as to be often indistinguishable, then why are businessmen so critical of "gov-ernment meddling in the economy"? There are a number of explana-tions. First, as previously noted, businessmen are not opposed to gov-ernment activity as long as it is favorable to them. "Whether we like it or not, the federal government is a partner in every business in the country," announced Lammot duPont Copeland, president of Du-Pont Chemicals. "As businessmen we need the understanding and co-operation of government in our effort to throw the economic machine into high gear."[53] The railroad owners are quite happy with regula-tion by the ICC. And the oil industry is at home with the National Pe-troleum Council. "Few industries . . . however, approve of any ag-gressive operation by the Justice Department's Antitrust Division."[54]

It is necessary to distinguish between "monopoly regulation" and "public-service regulation." *Monopoly regulation* limits entry into a market, subsidizes select industries, sets production standards that only big companies can meet, and encourages monopoly pricing. De-signed to fix rates at artificially high levels and reduce business com-petition, this kind of regulation has long been the rule in the agribusi-ness, telecommunications, energy, utility, oil, drug, rail, and (until recently) trucking and airline industries.

When business leaders denounce "government meddling," they are referring to *public-service regulations*, such as environmental protec-tions, antitrust laws, worker- and consumer-safety regulations and other safeguards that the unregulated marketplace cannot provide.

---

53. Quoted in David Bazelon, "Big Business and the Democrats," in Marvin Gettle-man and David Mermelstein (eds.), *The Failure of American Liberalism* (New York: Vintage, 1971), pp. 145–46.

54. McConnell, *Private Power and American Democracy*, p. 295. The question then is not do we need more or less regulation, but what kind? Selective preferences for reg-ulation exist also among public advocacy groups, with many calling for *more* govern-ment services for the needy; *more* health, safety, and environmental regulations; and *less* regulatory protections and services for big business.

"Uncle Sam is fine when he plays Uncle Sugar. It's just when he's Uncle Sam that he's a nuisance."[55] The business community has always been fearful that government might become unduly responsive to popular sentiments, arousing mass expectations and eventually succumbing to demands that could seriously challenge the existing distribution of wealth and power. Business attacks are directed mostly against government activities that might mobilize new constituencies, or cut into profits, or redistribute income downward instead of upward, or increase the nonprofit sector of the economy.[56] While arguing that public-service regulation interferes with "free enterprise" and "sound business practice," business is not really committed to some abstract principle of free enterprise but to its own immediate class interests.

Business attacks on government officials are a means of bringing them closer into line with industry's desires. Despite the controls exercised in the selection and advancement of government personnel, some public servants forget their commitment to the business community and entertain sympathies toward a wider constituency. Pressure must be applied to remind them of the vulnerabilities of their agencies and careers.

In addition, many of the complaints lodged against government are from firms least favored by government policies. Business is not without its interior divisions: policies frequently benefit the wealthier firms at the expense of smaller ones. The howls of pain emanating from these weaker competitors are more likely to be heard than the quiet satisfaction of the giant victors. Small businesses usually have good cause to complain of government meddling, since most regulations are written to suit the corporate giants and are often excessively burdensome for the smaller enterprise. Many government agencies more vigorously pursue their enforcement efforts against small companies because—unlike the big firms—they have less influence in Congress and cannot afford to defend themselves in drawn-out litigation.[57]

Finally, I would suggest that much of the verbal opposition to government is a manifestation of the businessman's adherence to the

---

55. Joan Claybrook, *Washington Post*, June 26, 1982; also Mark Green and Norman Waitzman, *Business War on the Law* (Washington, D.C.: Public Citizen, 1980).

56. Senator Howard Metzenbaum, "Monopoly for Everyone," *Washington Post*, September 12, 1982. A Roper poll found that people who say government is overregulating are consistently outnumbered by those who say the agencies are not doing enough in regard to consumer safety and food, drug, and environmental protection: *Washington Post*, November 10, 1981.

57. Ann Crittenden, "Big Burden for Small Business: Government Rules," *New York Times*, July 2, 1977.

business ideology, his belief in the virtues of rugged individualism, private enterprise, and private competition.[58] That he might violate this creed in his own corporate affairs does not mean his devotion to it is consciously hypocritical. One should not underestimate the human capacity to indulge in selective perceptions and rationales. These rationales are no less sincerely felt because they are self-serving; quite the contrary, it is a creed's congruity with a favorable self-image and self-interest that makes it so compelling. Many businessmen, including those who have benefited in almost every way from government contracts, subsidies, and tax laws, *believe* the advantages they enjoy are the result of their own self-reliance, efforts, and talents in a highly competitive "private" market. They believe that the assistance they get from the government benefits the national economy, while the assistance others get is a handout to parasites.

---

58. See Francis X. Sutton et al., *The American Business Creed* (New York: Schocken Books, 1962).

16

The Supremely
Political Court

All three branches of government are sworn to uphold the Constitution, but the Supreme Court alone has the power of reviewing the constitutionality of actions by the other two branches, at least in regard to cases brought before it. Nothing in the Constitution gives the Court this function, but the proceedings of the Constitutional Convention reveal that many delegates expected the judiciary to overturn laws it deemed inconsistent with the Constitution.[1] Of even greater significance is the Court's power to interpret the intent and scope of laws as they are applied in actual situations. This power of judicial *interpretation* is also limited to cases brought before the Court by contesting interests. Our main concern here is with trying to understand the *political* role the Court has played.

WHO JUDGES?

Some Americans think of the Constitution as a vital force, having an animation of its own. At the same time they expect Supreme Court justices to be above the normal prejudices of other persons. Thus they envision "a living Constitution" and an insentient Court. But a moment's reflection should remind us that it is the other way around. If

---

1. Max Farrand, *The Framing of the Constitution of the United States* (New Haven: Yale University Press, 1913), pp. 156–57. See Chief Justice John Marshall's argument for judicial review in the landmark case of *Marbury* v. *Madison* (1803).

the Constitution is, as they say, an "elastic instrument," then much of the stretching has been done by the nine persons on the Court, and the directions in which they pull are largely determined by their own ideological predilections.

Some Supreme Court justices have insisted otherwise, contending that the Court is involved in judgments that allow little room for personal prejudice. Justice Roberts provided the classic utterance of this viewpoint:

> When an act of Congress is appropriately challenged in the Courts as not conforming to the constitutional mandate the judiciary branch of the government has only one duty—to lay the Article of the Constitution which is invoked beside the statute which is challenged and to decide whether the latter squares with the former. All that the Court does, or can do, is to announce its considered judgment upon the question.[2]

This image of the Constitution as a measuring stick and the justice as measurer has been challenged by critics, including some justices. Chief Justice Hughes pointedly observed, "We are under a constitution but the constitution is what the judges say it is."[3]

By class background, professional training, and political selection, Supreme Court justices over the generations have more commonly identified with the landed interests than with the landless, the slave owners rather than the slaves, the industrialists rather than the workers, the exponents of Herbert Spencer rather than the proponents of Karl Marx, the established social elites rather than the illiterate immigrants. Over a century ago Justice Miller, a Lincoln appointee to the Court, made note of the class biases of the judiciary:

> It is vain to contend with judges who have been at the bar, the advocates for forty years of railroad companies, and all the forms of associated capital, when they are called upon to decide cases where such interests are in contest. All their training, all their feelings are from the start in favor of those who need no such influence.[4]

Nor does the situation differ much today. One study shows that persons who enjoy life tenure on federal courts, whether appointed by Democratic or Republican presidents, are drawn preponderantly

---

2. *United States* v. *Butler* (1936).
3. Dexter Perkins, *Charles Evans Hughes* (Boston: Little, Brown, 1956), p. 16.
4. Quoted in Felix Frankfurter, *Mr. Justice Holmes and the Supreme Court* (New York: Atheneum, 1965), p. 54.

from highly privileged backgrounds.[5] Another study finds that the American Bar Association's quasiofficial Federal Judiciary Committee, whose task is to pass on the qualifications of prospective judges, favors those whose orientation is conservative and supportive of corporate interests.[6] Few mavericks are appointed to the bench. As one U.S. District Court judge puts it: "Who are we after all? The average judge, if he ever was a youth, is no longer. If he was ever a firebrand, he is not discernibly an ember now. If he ever wanted to lick the Establishment, he has long since joined it."[7]

"WHAT THE JUDGES SAY IT IS"

It is said that the devil himself can quote the Bible for his own purposes. The Constitution is not unlike the Bible in this respect, and over the generations, Supreme Court justices have shown an infernal agility in finding constitutional justifications for the continuation of almost every inequity and iniquity, be it slavery or segregation, child labor or the sixteen-hour workday, state sedition laws or assaults on the First Amendment.

In its early days under Chief Justice John Marshall the Court emerged as a guardian of property, declaring in *Trustees of Dartmouth College* v. *Woodward* (1819) that a corporation was to be considered a "person" entitled to all the rights accorded persons under the Constitution. The Marshall Court also supported the supremacy of federal powers over the states. In *McCulloch* v. *Maryland* (1819) the Court forbade Maryland from taxing a federal bank and affirmed Congress's right to create a bank (a power not mentioned in the Constitution). Marshall argued that Article I, Section 8, gave Congress the right "to make all laws necessary and proper" for carrying out its delegated powers.

Throughout the 19th century and much of the 20th, when the federal government wanted to establish national banks, or give away half the country to private speculators, or subsidize industries, or set up commissions and boards that fixed prices and interest rates for manufacturers and banks, or send Marines to secure corporate invest-

---

5. Sheldon Goldman, "Johnson and Nixon Appointees to the Lower Federal Courts: Some Socio-Political Perspectives," *Journal of Politics*, 34, August 1972, pp. 934–42.

6. See Joel B. Grossman, *Lawyers and Judges: The ABA and the Politics of Judicial Selection* (New York: Wiley, 1965).

7. Marvin Frankel, *New York Times Magazine*, May 13, p. 41.

ments in Central America, or imprison people who spoke out against war and capitalism, or round up and deport immigrant radicals without a trial, or use the U.S. Army to shoot workers and break strikes, then such activities were as acceptable to the majority of the Court as to the majority of the business community. But if the federal or state governments sought to limit work-day hours, or outlaw child labor, or guarantee the rights of collective bargaining, or in other ways impose some kind of limitation on the privileges of business, then the Court ruled that ours was a limited form of government that could not tamper with the rights of property and the natural processes of the market by depriving owner and worker of "liberty of contract" and "substantive due process."[8] *Whether the Court judged the government to be improperly interfering with the economy depended less on some constitutional principle than on which social class benefited.*

The concept of "substantive due process" illustrates as well as any other judicial doctrine the way the Court manufactures new constitutional meanings under the guise of interpreting old ones. By about 1890, after years of pressure from corporate lawyers and American Bar Association spokesmen, the Court decided that due process referred not only to procedural matters, such as a right to counsel and a fair and speedy public trial, but to the *substance* of the legislation.[9] Having determined there was such a thing as "substantive due process," which ordinarily might have been considered a contradiction in terms, the Court could review legislation passed by the states brought before it by business plaintiffs. When Congress outlawed child labor, the Court found it to be a violation of "substantive due process" under the Fifth Amendment and an unconstitutional usurpation of the reserved powers of the states under the Tenth Amendment.[10] When the states passed social-welfare legislation, the Court found it in violation of "substantive due process" under the Fourteenth Amendment.[11] Thus while prohibiting Congress from supposedly encroaching on the reserved powers of the states, the Court prevented the states from using their reserved powers.

---

8. See for instance *Allgeyer* v. *Louisiana* (1897); *Lochner* v. *New York* (1905); and *Adair* v. *United States* (1908).

9. See Arthur A. North, S. J., *The Supreme Court, Judicial Process and Judicial Politics* (New York: Appleton-Century-Crofts, 1966), pp. 40–43.

10. See *Hammer* v. *Dagenhart* (1918). The Tenth Amendment reads: "The powers not delegated to the United States by this Constitution, nor prohibited by it to the States, are reserved to the States respectively or to the people." See also *Carter* v. *Carter Coal Co.* (1936).

11. *Morehead* v. *New York* (1936).

The Fourteenth Amendment, adopted in 1868 ostensibly to establish full citizenship for Blacks, says, "No State shall make or enforce any law which shall abridge the privileges or immunities of citizens of the United States; nor shall any State deprive any person of life, liberty, or property, without due process of law; nor deny to any person within its jurisdiction the equal protection of the laws." Once again the Court decided that "person" included corporations and that the Fourteenth Amendment was intended to protect business conglomerations from the "vexatious regulations" of the states.

The Court handed down a series of decisions in the latter half of the nineteenth century and the early twentieth, most notably *Plessy* v. *Ferguson* (1896), which turned the Fourteenth Amendment on its head and denied Blacks equal protection. The *Plessy* decision enunciated the "separate but equal" doctrine, which said that the forceful separation of Blacks from Whites in public facilities did not impute inferiority as long as facilities were more or less equal (which they rarely were). The doctrine gave constitutional legitimation to the racist practice of segregation.

Perhaps encouraged by the loose construction given to the word "person," or more likely convinced that they really were persons despite the treatment accorded them by a male-dominated society, women began to argue that the Fourteenth and Fifth Amendments applied to them and that the voting restrictions imposed on them by state and federal governments should be abolished. A test case reached the Supreme Court in 1894 and the justices decided that they could not give such a daring reading to the Constitution.[12] The Court seemingly had made up its mind that "privileges and immunities of citizens," "due process," and "equal protection of the laws" applied to such "persons" as business corporations but not to women and Blacks.

For more than a century, into the New Deal era, the Supreme Court was the bastion of laissez-faire capitalism, striking down reforms produced by the state legislatures and Congress and limiting government's ability to regulate the economy. The Court served capitalism almost too well—to the point of making necessary changes impossible. An increasingly centralized economy demanded a centralized regulation of business and labor. The Great Depression of the 1930s made clear to many liberal policy makers that only the federal government could revive a stagnant economy, create new investment opportunities, and subsidize business on a grand scale. At the same

---

12. *Minor* v. *Happersett* (1894).

time the government had to implement long-overdue reforms, designed to give a small share of the bounty to workers and to create some modest measure of social justice. Justice Brandeis expressed this liberal position clearly:

> There will come a revolt of the people against the capitalists, unless the aspirations of the people are given some adequate legal expression. . . . Whatever and however strong our convictions against the extension of governmental function may be, we shall inevitably be swept farther toward socialism unless we can curb the excesses of our financial magnates.[13]

Capitalism had to be reformed and updated, if only to prevent socialism. As Joan Roelofs noted, robber barons and naked exploitation had to be replaced by a more covert, technocratic form of rule that made some gesture at including working-class elements.[14] From 1937 onward, under pressure from the White House, the Supreme Court began to accept the constitutionality of New Deal legislation. Thus the Court joined the executive and legislative branches in seeking to mitigate some of the worst effects of economic depression and corporate power. At the same time the Court continued to hand down decisions that denied the Bill of Rights to persons who agitated and organized against capitalism.

NIBBLING AWAY AT THE FIRST AMENDMENT

While opposing restrictions on economic power, the Court seldom opposed restraints on free speech. The same conservatism that feared experimentation in economics also feared the radical ideas that underlay such changes. The First Amendment says, "Congress shall make no law . . . abridging the freedom of speech, or of the press." This would seem to leave little room for doubt as to the freedom of *all* speech.[15] Yet ever since the Alien and Sedition Acts of 1798, Congress and the state legislatures have found repeated occasion to penalize the

---

13. Louis D. Brandeis, *Business: A Profession* (Boston: Small, Maynard, 1933), p. 330, cited in Joan Roelofs, "The Supreme Court and Corporate Capitalism: An Iconoclastic View of the Warren Court in the Shadow of Critical Theory," paper presented at the Northeastern Political Science Association meeting, November 1978.

14. Roelofs, "The Supreme Court and Corporate Capitalism . . ."

15. Even the staunchest proponents of free speech allow that libel and slander might be restricted by law, although here too such speech when directed against public figures has been treated as protected under the First Amendment. See *New York Times Co.* v. *Sullivan* (1964), and *Time, Inc.* v. *Hill* (1967).

expression of heretical ideas. Many who expressed opposition to government policy or to the established politico-economic system were deemed guilty of "subversion" or "sedition."[16] During the First World War, Congress passed the Espionage Act, under which almost two thousand successful prosecutions were carried out, usually against socialists, who expressed opposition to the war. One individual, who in private conversation in a relative's home voiced his opposition, opining that it was a rich man's war, was fined $5,000 and sentenced to twenty years in prison.[17] The government imprisoned American socialist leader Eugene V. Debs for enunciating similar opinions from a public platform. While in prison in 1920, Debs ran for president on the Socialist party ticket and received almost a million votes.[18]

The High Court's attitude toward the First Amendment was best expressed by Justice Holmes in the famous *Schenck* case. Schenck was charged with attempting to cause insubordination among U.S. military forces and obstructing recruitment, both violations of the Espionage Act of 1917. What he had done was distribute a leaflet that condemned the war as a wrong perpetrated by Wall Street. The leaflet also urged people to oppose the draft by petitioning for repeal of the draft law and other such peaceful means. In ordinary times, Holmes reasoned, such speech is amply protected by the First Amendment, but when a nation is at war, statements like Schenck's are not protected by any constitutional right, for they create "a clear and present danger" of bringing about "the substantive evils that Congress has a right to prevent."[19] Holmes never established why obstruction of the draft was a substantive evil except to assume that prosecution of the war was a substantive good (the very idea that Schenck was trying to challenge), and therefore actions hampering the war effort were evil and Congress could stop them.

Free speech, Holmes argued, "does not protect a man in falsely shouting fire in a crowded theatre and causing a panic." Maybe so,

---

16. *Sedition* is defined in Webster's Dictionary as "excitement of discontent against the government or resistance to lawful authority."

17. Hearings before a Subcommittee of the Senate Judiciary Committee, *Amnesty and Pardon for Political Prisoners* (Washington, D.C.: Government Printing Office, 1927), p. 54. See also Charles Goodell, *Political Prisoners in America* (New York: Random House, 1973), Chapter 4.

18. In many polling places Debs failed to receive an honest count from hostile officials. Most likely his actual vote was well over a million.

19. *Schenck* v. *United States* (1919); also Holmes's decision in *Debs* v. *United States* (1919). Holmes was considered one of the more liberal justices of his day. In subsequent cases he placed himself against the Court's majority and on the side of the First Amendment, earning the title of the "Great Dissenter." See his dissents in *Abrams* v. *United States* (1919), and *Gitlow* v. *New York* (1925).

but the analogy is farfetched: Schenck was not in a theater but was seeking a forum to voice political ideas and urge opposition to policies Holmes treated as above challenge. Holmes was summoning the same argument paraded by every ruler who has sought to abrogate a people's freedom: these are not normal times; there is a grave menace within or just outside our gates; extraordinary measures are necessary and the democratic rules must be suspended for our nation's security.[20]

More than once the Court treated the allegedly pernicious quality of an idea as certain evidence of its lethal efficacy and as justification for its suppression. This was especially true if the purveyors of the idea were thought to be radicals and revolutionaries. In 1940 Congress passed the Smith Act, making it a felony to teach and advocate the violent overthrow of the government. Soon after, a group of socialists were convicted under the act and sent to prison. Ten years later the top leadership of the Communist party was convicted under the same act.

In a 6 to 2 decision in *Dennis et al.* v. *United States* (1951) the Court upheld the Smith Act and the convictions. In several concurring opinions, the majority argued that even though there did not seem to be a clear and present danger of a communist coup, the government need not wait for one. The potential "gravity" of such a danger was sufficient grounds for protective action. In any case, there was no freedom under the Constitution for those who conspired to propagate revolutionary movements. Free speech was not an absolute value but one of many competing ones. The priorities placed on these values were a legislative matter best settled by Congress—as had been done by passage of the Smith Act.

Justices Black and Douglas dissented, arguing that the defendants had not been charged with any acts nor even with saying anything about violent revolution. They were indicted for conspiring to reor-

---

20. At no time was it established that Schenck had actually obstructed anything. He was convicted of *conspiracy* to obstruct. The allegedly wrongful intent of his action, regardless of its success, constituted sufficient grounds for conviction. Under the law, "conspiracy" is an agreement by two or more people to commit an unlawful act, or a lawful act by unlawful means. In some cases, working for a common purpose, even without actual cooperative actions, has been treated as sufficient evidence of conspiracy. Thus, some antiwar demonstrators brought to trial for conspiracy to incite riot had not met each other until the time of the trial. Judge Learned Hand described the conspiracy doctrine as the "prosecutor's darling"; it can make a crime out of the thoughts in people's heads, even when these are expressed openly and promulgated by lawful means. See Jessica Mitford, *The Trial of Dr. Spock* (New York: Knopf, 1969); also Thomas I. Emerson, *The System of Freedom of Expression* (New York: Vintage, 1971).

ganize the Communist party and at some future time publish documents that would teach and advocate revolution, mostly the classic writings of Marx, Engels, and Lenin. The First Amendment was designed to protect the very views we might find offensive and dangerous. Safe and orthodox ideas rarely needed the protection of the Constitution; heretical ones did. It was one thing to argue against communist beliefs, but another to repress and imprison those who held them.

Six year after Dennis and his comrades were jailed, fourteen more Communist party leaders were convicted under the Smith Act. This time, with some of the anti-communist hysteria of the McCarthy period having subsided, a majority of the Court made a distinction between "advocacy of abstract doctrine and advocacy directed at promoting unlawful action" and decided that the Smith Act had intended to outlaw only the latter.[21] So the High Court overthrew the convictions, arguing that the law had not been applied correctly. Justice Black added the opinion that the Smith Act itself should be declared unconstitutional: "I believe that the First Amendment forbids Congress to punish people for talking about public affairs, whether or not such discussion incites to action, legal or illegal."[22]

Freedom For Revolutionaries?

Opposed to Black's view are those who argue that revolutionaries and communists should not be allowed "to take advantage of the very liberties they seek to destroy." Revolutionary advocacy constitutes an abuse of freedom, for it urges us to violate the democratic rules of the game. Hence, the argument goes, in order to preserve our political freedom, we may find it necessary to deprive some people of theirs.[23] Several rejoinders might be made to this position.

First, as a point of historical fact, the threat of revolution in the United States has never been as real or "harmful to our liberties" as the measures allegedly taken to protect us from revolutionary ideas. History repeatedly demonstrates the expansive quality of repression: first, revolutionary advocacy is suppressed, then proponents of unpopular doctrines, then "inciting" words, then "irresponsible" news

---

21. *Yates et al.* v. *United States* (1957).

22. The Federal Criminal Code Reform Act of 1977 repealed the Smith Act of 1940.

23. For samples of this thinking see the Vinson and Jackson opinions in the *Dennis* case; also Sidney Hook, *Political Power and Personal Freedom* (New York: Criterion Books, 1959); Carl A. Auerbach, "The Communist Control Act of 1954: A Proposed Legal-Political Theory of Free Speech," in Samuel Hendel (ed.), *Basic Issues of American Democracy*, 8th ed. (Englewood Cliffs, N.J.: Prentice-Hall, 1976), pp. 59–63.

reports and public utterances that allegedly might undermine our foreign policy or national security, then any kind of criticism that those in power find intolerable.

Second, the suppression is conducted by political elites who, in protecting us from what they consider "harmful" thoughts, are in effect making up our minds for us by depriving us of the opportunity of hearing, discussing, and debating revolutionary ideas with revolutionary advocates. An exchange is forbidden because the advocate has been silenced.

Third, it is debatable whether socialist, communist, and other radical revolutionaries are dedicated to the destruction of freedom. Much of the ferment in U.S. history, branded as "revolutionary," actually augmented our democratic rights. The working-class agitations of the early 19th century legitimated and widened the areas of dissent and helped extend the franchise to propertyless working people. The organized demonstrations against repressive local ordinances in the early 20th century by the revolutionary-minded Industrial Workers of the World (the Wobblies' "free-speech fights") fortified the First Amendment against attacks by the guardians of property. The crucial role Communists played in organizing the industrial unions in the 1930s and struggling for social reforms strengthened rather than undermined democratic forces. It should be remembered that Americans were never "given" their freedoms; they had to organize, agitate, and struggle fiercely for whatever rights they do have. As with our bodily health so with the health of our body politic: we best preserve our faculties and liberties against death and decay by vigorously expanding and exercising them.

Fourth, revolutionaries would argue that freedom is in grave short supply in the *present* society, where wealth and power serve mostly the interests of the few. The construction of new social alternatives and new modes of communal organization can bring an *increase* in freedom, including freedom from poverty and hunger, freedom to share in making the decisions that govern one's work and community, and freedom to experiment with new forms of production. Admittedly some freedoms enjoyed today would be lost in a revolutionary society—for instance, the freedom to exploit other people and get rich from their labor, the freedom to squander natural resources and treat the environment as a septic tank, the freedom to monopolize information and exercise unaccountable power. In many countries successful social revolutionary movements have brought a net increase in the freedom of individuals, revolutionaries argue, by advancing the conditions necessary for health and human life, by providing jobs and education for the unemployed and illiterate, by using economic resources for social development rather than for corporate profit, and by overthrowing repressive reactionary regimes and ending foreign exploitation and involving large sectors of the populace in the task of socialist reconstruction. Revolutions can extend a number of real freedoms without destroying those that never existed for the people of those countries. The argument can be debated, but not if it is suppressed. In any case, the real danger to freedom in America is from the repression exercised by those in government, the media, academia, business, and other institutions who would insulate us from "unacceptable" viewpoints. No idea is as dangerous as the force that would seek to repress it.

AS THE COURT TURNS

Far from being a bulwark against government suppression, the Court has usually gone along with it. When the Southern states imposed the tyranny of racial segregation on Black people and other non-Whites after Reconstruction, the Court, as noted, obligingly formulated the doctrine of "separate but equal" to give constitutional justification to segregation. When the U.S. government decided to uproot 112,000 law-abiding Japanese-Americans at the onset of World War II, forcing them to relinquish their homes, businesses, farms, and other possessions and herding them into concentration camps for the duration of the war on the incredible notion that they posed a threat to our West Coast defenses, the Supreme Court found that, given the exigencies of war, the government was acting within the limits of the Constitution.[24] And not one of the many laws passed by Congress throughout its history to abridge or restrict freedom of speech has the Court rendered unconstitutional.

The Supreme Court's record in the area of personal liberties is gravely wanting, yet it is not totally devoid of merit. "Let us give the Court its due; it is little enough," Robert Dahl reminds us.[25] Over the years the Court has extended portions of the Bill of Rights to cover not only the federal government but state government (via the Fourteenth

---

24. *Hirabayashi* v. *United States* (1943), *Korematsu* v. *United States* (1944) and *Ex parte Endo* (1944). For a long time the Japanese-Americans had been an object of resentment because of their successful farming and social mobility on the West Coast. The relocation left many of them destitute, and almost all their land was grabbed by agribusiness firms.

25. Robert A. Dahl, "Decision-Making in a Democracy: The Role of the Supreme Court as a National Policy-Maker," *Journal of Public Law*, 6, no. 2, 1958, p. 292.

Amendment). Attempts by the states to censor publications,[26] deny individuals the right to peaceful assembly,[27] and weaken the separation between church and state[28] were overturned. During the 1960s, the Court under Chief Justice Earl Warren took steps to safeguard individual rights in criminal-justice proceedings, including the right of a poor person to benefit of counsel in state criminal trials[29] and of an arrested person to have a lawyer at the onset of police interrogation.[30]

In some states, less than a third of the population elected more than half the legislators; the Warren Court ruled that malapportioned district lines had to be redrawn in accordance with population distribution, so that voters in the overpopulated districts were not denied equal protection under the law.[31] The Court also took the disestablishment clause in the First Amendment seriously when it ruled that prayers in the public school were a violation of the separation of church and state.[32]

The Warren Court handed down a number of decisions aimed at abolishing racial segregation. The most widely celebrated was *Brown* v. *Board of Education* (1954) which unanimously ruled that "separate educational facilities are inherently unequal" because of the inescapable imputation of inferiority cast upon the segregated minority group, an imputation that is all the greater when it has the sanction of law. This decision overruled the "separate but equal" doctrine enunciated in 1896 in the *Plessy* case.[33]

The direction the Court takes depends partly on the political composition of its majority. Refortified with Nixon and then Ford and Reagan appointees, the Court under Chief Justice Burger took a decidedly conservative turn. In the area of criminal justice, for instance, the Burger Court decided it was no longer necessary to have a unanimous jury verdict for conviction—a decision that abolished the need for having a jury agree that the prosecution has proven guilt beyond a reasonable doubt.[34] In another decision, the Burger Court ruled that

---

26. *Near* v. *Minnesota* (1931).
27. *DeJonge* v. *Oregon* (1937).
28. *McCollum* v. *Board of Education* (1948).
29. See *Gideon* v. *Wainwright* (1963).
30. *Escobedo* v. *Illinois* (1964) and *Miranda* v. *Arizona* (1966).
31. See *Baker* v. *Carr* (1962) and *Reynolds* v. *Sims* (1964). A similar decision was made in regard to congressional districts in *Wesberry* v. *Sanders* (1964).
32. See *Engles* v. *Vitale* (1962) and *School District of Abington* v. *Schempp* (1963). The First Amendment reads: "Congress shall make no law respecting an establishment of religion, or prohibiting the free exercise thereof."
33. See also the decision nullifying state prohibitions against interracial marriage: *Loving* v. *Virginia* (1967). (Loving was the plaintiff's name.)
34. *Johnson* v. *Louisiana* (1972) and *Apodaca* v. *Oregon* (1972).

police may stop and frisk people almost at their own discretion.[35] The *Miranda* decision, which forbade the use of police torture in obtaining confessions, was weakened by the Burger Court, as was the right of Black defendants to have prospective jurors questioned about their possible racial prejudices.[36]

In a 7 to 2 decision, the justices declared the death penalty to be constitutional and not in violation of the Eighth Amendment's prohibition against "cruel and unusual punishment."[37] The Court also decided that the Eighth Amendment did not apply in the case of a Texas man who got a life sentence for three minor frauds totalling $230. Legal challenges to harsh prison sentences should be exceedingly rare, for instance, when someone is given a life sentence for "overtime parking," argued the Court. Such an example leaves room for nearly any kind of unjust sentence and reduces the Eighth Amendment protection to almost nothing.[38] The Burger Court showed little sympathy for the rights of children. Ruling on two instances involving children who were seriously injured when beaten by school officials, the Court decided that the prohibition against cruel and unusual punishment did not protect school children from corporal punishment, no matter how severe.[39]

In First Amendment cases, the Court has usually favored the interests of restrictive authority over those of free speech, free press, and independent thinking. The justices handed down a decision denying reporters a right to confidential news sources.[40] By a 5 to 4 vote they refused to impose any limitation on the U.S. Army's surveillance of lawful civilian political activity. In a passionate dissent Justice Douglas called the latter decision "a cancer in our body politic. . . . The Bill of Rights was designed to keep agents of Government and official eavesdroppers away from assemblies of people."[41] The Court ruled that military posts may ban speeches and demonstrations of a "partisan" political nature and prohibit distribution of political litera-

---

35. In this instance, *Adams* v. *Williams*, the Burger Court was expanding on a policy set down by the Warren Court in *Terry* v. *Ohio* (1968); see also *United States* v. *Robinson* (1973).

36. *Michigan* v. *Mosley* (1975) and *Ristaino* v. *Ross* (1976).

37. *Gregg* v. *Georgia* (1976).

38. *Rummel* v. *Estelle* (1979). As if to prove the point, the Court subsequently upheld a 40-year prison term and $20,000 in fines meted out to a first offender in Virginia for "possession for sale" of nine ounces of marijuana. *Hutto* v. *Davis* (1982). Davis's real crime might have been that he was a Black civil-rights advocate who was married to a White woman.

39. *Ingraham* v. *Wright* (1977).

40. *United States* v. *Caldwell* (1972); see also *Zurcher* v. *Stanford Daily* (1978).

41. *Laird* v. *Tatum* (1972).

ture—thus denying American soldiers the First Amendment rights they are supposedly prepared to defend with their lives.[42] While it was all right for the Army to spy secretly on civilian political activity, it was wrong for civilians to bring political ideas openly to the Army. Both decisions were consistent with the Court's determination to keep the military and society free from anticapitalist ideas.

The Burger Court reversed decisions by two lower courts to rule 7 to 2 that the executive branch had broad legal and constitutional authority to revoke passports on national security and "foreign policy" grounds, thereby denying a passport to Philip Agee, a former CIA employee who had written books that exposed CIA covert operations in various countries (operations that themselves have no statutory mandate). The fact that neither Congress nor the Constitution granted the State Department this power to revoke passports did not bother Chief Justice Burger, who declared that in matters of "foreign policy and national security" the absence of an empowering law is not to be taken as a sign of congressional disapproval.[43] The *New York Times* described the decision as "a stupefying inversion of the law-making process."[44] The decision gave federal authorities a virtual carte blanche to deny travel to critics whom the government thought might "damage" U.S. foreign policy by word or action. All such federal actions are, Burger concluded, "largely immune from judicial inquiry or interference."

In decisions involving disputes between workers and owners, the Burger Court usually has sided with the owners. Thus it ruled that

---

42. *Greer* v. *Spock* (1976).

43. *Haig* v. *Agee* (1981).

44. *New York Times* editorial, July 2, 1981. Occasionally members of the Court's conservative majority will abandon the rightists Burger, Rehnquist, and now O'Connor (the first woman Supreme Court justice) to side with the liberal minority of Marshall and Brennan to render decisions that support rather than nibble away at the Bill of Rights. For instance, on criminal prosecution see *United States* v. *Johnson* (1982) and *Taylor* v. *Alabama* (1982); on unreasonable search and seizure, *Steagald* v. *United States* (1981). In a rare instance of unanimity the Burger Court upheld the right of groups to organize boycotts to achieve economic and social change. The decision was the first time the Court explicitly protected the boycott as a form of political protest; see *NAACP* v. *Clairborne Hardware* (1982). But for the most part the rightists have got their way in weakening the First, Fourth, Fifth, Sixth, and Eighth Amendments. In addition to cases already cited, see for the 1978–79 period *Gannet* v. *De Pasquale*, *Parham* v. *J. L.*, *Rakas* v. *Illinois*, *Smith* v. *Maryland*, and *Scott* v. *Illinois*; more recently *Tibbs* v. *Florida* (1982), *Washington* v. *Chrisman* (1982), *Rose* v. *Lundy* (1982), and *Engle* v. *Issac* (1982). For a critique of the Burger Court's attack on the Bill of Rights see the two-part series by Sidney Zion in the *New York Times Magazine*, November 11 and 18, 1979.

workers do not have the right to strike over safety issues if their contract provides for arbitration.[45] This decision, made by people who have never worked in, or even visited, a mine, denies miners the right to walk off the job in the face of immediately dangerous work conditions covered up by management. It requires that they enter the mines and risk being killed during the weeks it takes to settle the issue by arbitration. The Court reversed the findings of the NLRB and a lower federal court and ruled that employers do not have to bargain with their workers over a decision to close down operations—in effect giving owners the power to penalize workers, who had recently unionized, by breaking their union and denying them jobs.[46]

The Court held that farmers in California's Imperial Valley are entitled to federally subsidized irrigation regardless of farm size. A federal appeals court had previously directed the government to enforce a reclamation law passed by Congress, which limited water subsidies to farms of 160 acres or less and which required that farmers "were to live on or near the land." Among the "farmers" in the Valley who benefited from the ruling were Southern Pacific, Standard Oil, and Tenneco.[47]

The Burger Court manifested its dedication to class inequality with exceptional clarity when it decided that a state may vary the quality of education in accordance with the amount of taxable wealth located in its school districts. The Court seemed to say there could be any degree of inequality short of absolute deprivation: as long as the Chicano children in question had *some* kind of school to go to, this would satisfy the equal-protection clause of the Fourteenth Amendment. The decision hardly lived up to the principles enunciated in the 1954 *Brown* case, Justice Marshall pointed out in a dissent.[48]

The Court decided that the principle of "one-person, one-vote" need not be observed in elections for special-purpose governmental bodies like water districts. Instead balloting may be confined to landowners who enjoyed a voting power proportional to the amount of land they held, or "one-acre, one-vote" as dissenters in the case described it. The ruling effectively stripped thousands of Arizona citizens of the opportunity to participate in important public decisions concerning water, energy, utilities, and conservation, while concen-

---

45. *Gateway Coal Co.* v. *United Mine Workers* (1974).

46. The case involved nursing-home workers. See *First National Maintenance Corp.* v. *National Labor Relations Board* (1981).

47. Eric Nadler, "Supreme Court Backs Agribusiness," *Guardian*, July 2, 1980.

48. *San Antonio Independent School District* v. *Rodriguez* (1973).

trating voting power in the hands of a small minority of land companies and other big property holders.[49]

While unable to overrule certain Warren Court decisions, the
Burger Court sometimes did its best to erode them. Finding no way to
contravene the constitutionality of earlier reapportionment cases, it
decided that the "one-person, one-vote" rule should be applied less
rigorously to state legislative districts than to congressional ones. In
allowing for a population deviation as wide as 16.4 percent, the Court
reasoned that state districts have "indigenous" qualities that ought
sometimes to be preserved.[50]

Continuing with the fiction that corporations are "persons" and
that spending vast sums on political campaigns is a form of "free
speech," the Burger Court decided states could not prohibit corporations from spending unlimited amounts of their funds to influence the
outcome of public referenda or other elections because the Constitution guarantees freedom of speech to business firms just as it does
to human beings.[51] On the separation of church and state and on environmental, abortion, sex-discrimination, and affirmative-action
cases, the Burger Court's record has been mixed.[52]

While dominated by conservatives who supposedly seek to limit
federal powers, the Burger Court showed no reluctance to reject state
laws that restricted business interests in banking, corporate mergers,
and energy conservation, ruling that federal authority preempted
state action. So the Court further diluted the Tenth Amendment,
which reserves to the states powers not expressly given to the federal
government or to the people.[53] As with the White House, so with the
Court. When business preferred a federal policy, states' rights were

---

49. *Ball* v. *James* (1981); see also *Salyer Land Co.* v. *Tulare Lake Basin Water Storage District* (1973) and *Associated Enterprise, Inc.* v. *Toltec Watershed Improvement
District* (1973).

50. *Mahan* v. *Howell* (1973).

51. *First National Bank of Boston* v. *Bellotti* (1978) and the subsequent *Citizens
Against Rent Control et al.* v. *City of Berkeley et al.* (1981).

52. For instance, *Michael M.* v. *Superior Court of Sonoma County* (1981); *Mississippi* v. *Hogan* (1982); *Regents of California* v. *Bakke* (1978); *United Steelworkers of
America, AFL-CIO-CLC* v. *Weber et al.* (1978). For attempts by the Court to weaken
the landmark *Roe* v. *Wade* (1973), which establishes a woman's decision to terminate
pregnancy as a constitutional right (under the right of privacy), see *Harris* v. *McRae*
(1980) and *H. L.* v. *Matheson* (1981). Six months after deciding that poor women had
no constitutional right to money for abortions, the Court said that federal justices had
a constitutional right to their pay raises and that Congress lacked the authority to deny
such raises: *Washington Post*, July 3, 1981.

53. *United Transportation Union* v. *Long Island Railroad* (1982); *Fidelity Federal
Savings* v. *de la Cuesta* (1982); *Edgar* v. *MITE Corporation* (1982). For additional discussion see the section "The 'New Federalism' Ploy" in chapter 14.

forgotten; the justices discarded the "New Federalism" of Ronald Reagan (as did Reagan himself) and reverted to the old Federalism of Chief Justice Marshall as expressed in *McCulloch* v. *Maryland.*

INFLUENCE OF THE COURT

It is easier to describe the blatantly political role played by the Court than to measure its actual political influence. But a few rough generalizations can be drawn. First, as a nonelective branch occupied by persons of elitist class background, the Court has exercised a preponderantly conservative influence. For over half a century, it wielded a strategic pro-business minority veto on social welfare and reform legislation of a kind enacted in European countries one or two generations before. The Court prevented Congress from instituting progressive income taxes, a decision that took eighteen years and a constitutional amendment to circumvent. As noted earlier, the Court denied women protection under the Fifth and Fourteenth Amendments, thereby delaying universal suffrage for some 25 years and leaving women to this day without an Equal Rights Amendment (ERA).

But we should remember that the Court's ability to impose its will on the nation is far from boundless. Presidents usually get the opportunity to appoint two or more members to the Court and so exert an influence over its makeup. Furthermore, the Court cannot make rulings at will but must wait until a case is brought to it either on appeal from a lower court or, far less frequently, as a case of original jurisdiction. And the Court agrees to hear only a small portion of the cases on its docket, thus leaving the final work to the lower courts in most instances.

The Court is always operating in a climate of opinion shaped by political forces larger than itself. Its willingness to depart from the casuistry of *Plessy* v. *Ferguson* and take the Fourteenth Amendment seriously in *Brown* v. *Board of Education* depended in part on the changing climate of opinion concerning race relations and segregation between 1896 and 1954.

At the same time the Court is not purely a dependent entity. That it has had to deny women protection under the Fourteenth Amendment for almost a century and had to accept segregation for more than fifty years is not certain. The arguments used on the eve of the *Brown* decision in 1954—that the Court should not push people, that hearts and minds had to change first, that you can't legislate morality, and that there would be vehement and violent opposition—were the same arguments used during the days of the *Plessy* case. In fact there was vehement and often violent opposition to the *Brown* decision. But there also was an acceleration of opinion in support of the Court's ruling, in part activated by that very ruling. (Just as there was an increase in *segregationist* practices after the *Plessy* case, from 1896 to 1914, in part encouraged by *Plessy* and decisions like it.) Hence, some of the Court's decisions have an important feedback effect. By playing a crucial role in defining what is legitimate and constitutional, the Court gives encouraging cues to large sectors of the public. Unable to pass a civil-rights act for seventy years, the Congress enacted three in the decade after the *Brown* case. And Blacks throughout the nation pressed harder in an attempt to make desegregation a reality. Organizing efforts for civil rights increased in both the North and the South, along with "Freedom Riders," sit-ins, and mass demonstrations. The political consciousness of a generation was joined, and who is to say that the Warren Court did not play a part in that? The Supreme Court, then, probably has a real effect on political consciousness and public policy, albeit in limited ways and for limited durations.[54]

Members of the Court have been aware of the limited nature of the judicial power. They have understood that the efficacy of their decisions depends on the willingness of other agencies of government to carry them out. A Court that resists the views prevailing in the bureaucracy risks attack. Its appellate jurisdiction might be circumscribed by Congress, its decisions ignored, and itself subjected to hostile criticism. Some justices, such as Harlan and Frankfurter, were so impressed by the Court's vulnerability as to counsel a doctrine of "judicial restraint," especially when the Court tried to move in innovative ways.[55]

In similar fashion, conservatives on the Burger Court, including the Chief Justice, have argued that the Court must cease its intrusive role and defer to the policymaking branches of government. So if Congress wants to draft only men, the Court must defer to Congress.

---

54. For studies on the effects of High Court decisions see Theodore Becker (ed.), *The Impact of Supreme Court Decisions: Empirical Studies* (New York: Oxford University Press, 1969). One caveat should be given: progressive people have relied too heavily on the Supreme Court and on courts in general. For anyone engaged in the struggle for justice, the courts may occasionally be a necessary evil, but they are not the friends of progressive, democratic causes. With the exception of a brief ten-year span under Chief Justice Warren, the Supreme Court has been the most conservative branch of government. The Court, like the very laws and Constitution it interprets, is limited to a frame of reference that accepts and defends existing class and property relations.

55. For instance, see the dissents by Frankfurter and Harlan respectively in the apportionment cases: *Baker* v. *Carr*, 369 U.S. 186 (1962), and *Reynolds* v. *Sims*, 377 U.S. 533 (1964).

If the executive wants to deny freedom of travel abroad, the Court must defer to the executive. If the states have overcrowded and otherwise terrible prisons and mental institutions, the Court can do little about it and must defer to the states. In the 1980s, as conservatives in Congress, the White House, the Justice Department, and certain state and local governments launched attacks against integration, equality of women, labor rights, the right to counsel, the right to privacy, and free speech, and as they prepared legislation that would diminish federal-court jurisdiction, the Court obligingly staked out a more limited role for itself.

But this latest "judicial restraint" is applied in selective ways and may exist more in appearance than in actuality. For in numerous instances, by going along with a conservative or authoritarian action by Congress or the executive, the Court helped rewrite the law and the Constitution and in effect played a policy-making role. When the Court allows, without benefit of statute, the executive to deny passports to critics of U.S. policy, or when it weakens habeas corpus or debilitates the Eighth Amendment or gives agribusiness access to federally subsidized irrigation in violation of acreage limitations set by Congress or strikes down state regulations of nuclear industry or in other ways makes law and policy, where is the judicial restraint? Yet in such cases one hears little complaint from conservatives about judicial usurpation of policy-making powers. Judicial activism that strengthens authoritarian and corporate class interests is acceptable. Judicial activism that defends democratic working-class rights and social equality invites attack. In each case the issue is settled not by a principled adherence to some abstract judicial doctrine but by what class interests are at stake.

17

Democracy
for the Few

The United States is said to be a pluralistic society, and indeed a glance at the social map of this country reveals a vast agglomeration of groups and governing agencies, "each in competition with another, and each seeking to maximize its own interests."[1] If by pluralism we mean this multiplicity of private and public groups, then the United States is pluralistic. But then so is any society of size and complexity, including allegedly totalitarian ones like the Soviet Union with its multiplicity of regional, occupational, and ethnic groups and its party, administrative, and military factions all competing over policies.[2]

But the proponents of pluralism presume to be saying something about how *power* is distributed and how *democracy* works. Supposedly the desirable feature of a pluralistic society is that it works through *democratic means* and produces *democratic outputs*. Policies not only are shaped by competing groups but also benefit the human

---

1. Harmon Zeigler and G. Wayne Peak, *Interest Groups in American Society* (Englewood Cliffs, N.J.: Prentice Hall, 1972), p. 42.
2. See, for instance, Donald R. Kelly, "Interest Groups in the USSR: The Impact of Political Sensitivity on Group Influence," *Journal of Politics*, 34, August 1972, pp. 860–88; also H. Gordon Skilling and Franklyn Griffiths (eds.), *Interest Groups in Soviet Politics* (Princeton, N.J.: Princeton University Press, 1971). By the simple definition of pluralism offered above, even Nazi Germany might qualify as pluralistic. The Nazi state was a loose, often chaotic composite of fiercely competing groups. See Heinz Höne, *The Order of the Death's Head* (New York: Coward, McCann, and Geoghegan, 1970).

needs of the populace. Thus Ralf Dahrendorf writes: "Instead of a battlefield, the scene of group conflict has become a kind of market in which relatively autonomous forces contend according to certain rules of the game, by virtue of which nobody is a permanent winner or loser."[3] If there are elites in our society, the pluralists say, they are numerous and specialized, and they are checked in their demands by other elites. No group can press its advantages too far and any group that is interested in an issue can find a way within the political system to make its influence felt.[4] Business elites have the capacity to utilize the services of the government to further their interests, but, the pluralists argue, such interests are themselves varied and conflicting. The government is not controlled by a monolithic corporate elite that gets what it wants on every question. Government stands above any one particular influence but responds to many. So say the pluralists.

PLURALISM FOR THE FEW

The evidence offered in the preceding chapters leaves us little reason to conclude that the United States is a "pluralistic democracy" as conceived by the pluralists. To summarize and expand upon some of the points previously made:

1. Public policies, whether formulated by conservatives or liberals, Republicans or Democrats, fairly consistently favor the large corporate interests at a substantial cost to millions of workers, small farmers, small producers, consumers, taxpayers, the elderly, and the poor. Benefits distributed to lower-income groups have proven gravely inadequate and have failed to reach millions who might qualify for assistance. Government efforts in areas of social need have rarely fulfilled the expectations of reform-minded advocates. There are more people living in poverty today than ten years ago and a greater gap between rich and poor. There is more unemployment and substandard housing; more economic insecurity, immiserization, and

---

3. Ralf Dahrendorf, *Class and Class Conflict in Industrial Society* (Stanford, Calif.: Stanford University Press, 1959), p. 67.

4. One of the earliest pluralist statements is in Earl Latham, *The Group Basis of Politics* (Ithaca: Cornell University Press, 1952). See also Arnold M. Rose, *The Power Structure* (New York: Oxford University Press, 1967); Robert Dahl, *Who Governs?* (New Haven: Yale University Press, 1961); Edward Banfield, *Political Influence* (New York: Free Press, 1961); Nelson Polsby, *Community Power and Political Theory* (New Haven: Yale University Press, 1963). The criticisms of pluralism are many: the best collection of critiques can be found in Charles A. McCoy and John Playford (eds.), *Apolitical Politics* (New York: Crowell, 1967); see also Marvin Surkin and Alan Wolfe (eds.), *An End to Political Science: The Caucus Papers* (New York: Basic Books, 1970).

social pathology; more crime, suicide, and alcoholism; more environmental devastation and pollution; more deficiencies in our schools, hospitals, and transportation systems; more military dictatorships throughout the world feeding on the largesse and power of the Pentagon; more people—from South Africa to Turkey to the Philippines to Chile to Mississippi—suffering the oppression of an American-backed status quo; more profits going to the giant corporations and more corporate influence over the institutions of society; more glut in the private commodity market; and more scarcity and want in public services. Cites are on the verge of bankruptcy, and governors in almost every state are cutting back on social-service programs. And in the midst of all this, presidents and other politicians mouth platitudes, urging us to regain "faith in ourselves" and in "our institutions."

2. To think of government as nothing more than a referee amidst a vast array of competing groups (which presumably represent all the important and "countervailing" interests of the populace) is to forget that government best serves those who can serve themselves. This is not to say that political leaders are indifferent to popular sentiments. When those sentiments are aroused to a certain intensity, leaders will respond—even if only with distracting and dilatory irrelevancies, outright lies, or ameliorative programs that come nowhere near solving the problem in question. There are several reasons why so many public programs fail. Often the allocations are meager while the problem is immense, as is the case with programs relating to environmental protection and occupational safety. Other times the expenditures may be substantial but the problem is deeply ingrained in the economic system itself and is not solved by merely having public money thrown at it, e.g., job training for which there are no jobs. And sometimes, as with the housing, transportation, and medical programs, immense sums are channeled through the private sector to enrich those who supply the service. In this way public funds augment the capital-accumulation process and do not compete with the private market. But neither do they significantly answer to the needs for which they are ostensibly allocated.

Usually elites will initially oppose these kinds of policies, not realizing the gains available to them. The auto industry was against safety belts in automobiles until it realized they could be installed as high-priced accessories, which the customer was legally required to buy. And doctors opposed Medicare and Medicaid as steps toward "socialism" until they discovered gold in those programs. For with public funding available, the doctors and the hospitals were able to charge amounts they would not have dared impose had the patient been the sole payer. The result is that medical expenses zoomed upward without a commensurate improvement in medical care—although certainly some elderly people now have assistance they would not have had earlier. *To pour more money into a service without a change in the market relations enjoyed by the suppliers is merely to make more public funds available to the suppliers without guaranteeing an improvement in the service.*[5]

3. Power in America "is plural and fluid," claims Max Lerner.[6] In reality power is distributed among heavily entrenched, well-organized, well-financed politico-economic conglomerates that can reproduce the social conditions needed for continued elite hegemony. Of the various resources of power, wealth is the most crucial, and its distribution is neither "plural" nor "fluid." Not everyone with money chooses to use it to exert political influence, and not everyone with money need bother to do so. But when they so desire, those who control the wealth of society enjoy a persistent and pervasive political advantage.

4. The pluralists make much of the fact that wealthy interests do not always operate with clear and deliberate purpose.[7] To be sure, elites, like everyone else, make mistakes and suffer confusions as to what might be the most advantageous tactics in any particular situation. But if they are not omniscient and infallible, neither are they habitual laggards and imbeciles. If they do not always calculate rationally in the pursuit of their class interests, they do so often and successfully enough. It is also true that the business community is not unanimous on all issues. There are regional differences (Eastern versus Southwestern capital), ideological ones (reactionary versus liberal capitalism), and corporate ones (Ford versus General Motors)—all of which add an element of conflict and indeterminacy to economic and political policies. But these conflicts seldom include the interests of the unorganized public.[8]

5. Is then the American polity ruled by a secretive, conspiratorial, omnipotent, monolithic power elite? No, the plutocracy, or ruling class, does not fit that easily refuted caricature. First of all, it cannot

---

5. Note that the cost of Medicaid and Medicare rose from $4.8 billion in 1967 to $57 billion in 1980 to $81.7 billion in 1982. The billions have enriched the "prestigious inhabitants of Country Club America." Carl Rowan, *Washington Post*, September 15, 1982.

6. Max Lerner, *America As a Civilization* (New York: Simon and Schuster, 1957), p. 398.

7. Dahl, *Who Governs?*, p. 272. Also see Robert A. Dahl, *Modern Political Analysis* (Englewood Cliffs, N.J.: Prentice Hall, 1970).

8. Paul Sweezy, *The Present as History* (New York: Monthly Review Press, 1970), p. 138.

get its way on all things at all times. No ruling class in history, no matter how autocratic, has ever achieved omnipotence. All have had to make concessions and allow for unexpected and undesired developments. Second, the ruling elites are not always secretive. They rule from legitimized institutions. The moneyed influence they exercise over governing bodies is sometimes overt—as with reported campaign contributions and control of investments, and sometimes covert—as with unreported bribes and deals. The ruling class controls most of the institutions and jobs of this society through corporate ownership and by control of management positions, interlocking directorates, and trusteeships, the elite membership of which, while not widely advertised, is well-documented public knowledge.[9] However, these elites do often find it desirable to plan in secret, to minimize or distort the flow of information, to deny the truth, to develop policies that sometimes violate the law they profess to uphold. Instances of this are also well-documented.[10]

Third, American government is not ruled by a monolithic elite. There are serious differences in tactics, differences in how best to mute class conflict and maintain the existing system at home and abroad. "Because conflicts within the corporate ruling class must be reconciled and compromised and because of the complex and wide-ranging nature of the interests of this class, policy is dictated not by a single directorate but by a multitude of private, quasipublic and public agencies."[11] The various interest elites, be they concerned with armaments, oil, agribusiness, or whatever, are anchored in the giant corporations and banks with links extending into Congress, the executive departments, and, when pertinent, the military, the press, the professions, academia, science, and state and local governments. What holds them together when push comes to shove is the power of money and position and their common interest in preserving a system that assures their wealth and privileges.

---

9. See the discussion and citations in the section in chapter 12 entitled "The Ruling Class."

10. A common view is that conspiracy is only the imaginings of kooks. But just because some people have paranoid fantasies of conspiracies doesn't mean that all conspiracies are paranoid fantasies. There is ample evidence of real ones. The early planning of the escalation of the Vietnam war as revealed in the *Pentagon Papers*, the ITT–CIA–White House policy of destabilizing Chile, the Watergate cover-up, and the FBI COINTELPRO are some important conspiracies that have been publicly exposed. Webster's dictionary defines conspiracy as "a planning and acting together secretly, especially for an unlawful or harmful purpose." All of the above fit the definition.

11. James O'Connor, *The Fiscal Crisis of the State* (New York: St. Martin's Press, 1973), p. 68.

Although there is no one grand power elite, there is continual co-operation between various corporate and governmental elites in every area of the political economy. Many of the stronger corporate elites tend to predominate in their particular spheres of interest more or less unmolested by other elites.[12] In any case, the conflicts between pluto-cratic elites seldom work to the advantage of the mass of people. They are conflicts of haves versus haves. Often they are resolved not by compromise but by logrolling and involve more *collusion* than com-petition. These mutually satisfying arrangements among "competi-tors" usually harm public interests—as when the costs of collusion are passed on to the public in the form of higher prices, higher taxes, envi-ronmental devastation, and inflation. The demands of the have-nots may be heard occasionally as a clamor outside the gate, and now and then something is tossed to the unfortunates. But generally speaking, pluralist group politics engages the interests of extremely limited por-tions of the population, within a field of political options largely shaped by the interests of corporate capitalism.

One might better think of ours as a dual political system. First, there is the *symbolic* political system centering around electoral and representative activities including party conflicts, voter turnout, po-litical personalities, public pronouncements, official role-playing, and certain ambiguous presentations of some of the public issues that bestir presidents, governors, mayors, and their respective legislatures. Then there is the *substantive* political system, involving multibillion-dollar contracts, tax write-offs, protections, rebates, grants, loss com-pensations, subsidies, leases, giveaways, and the whole vast process of budgeting, legislating, advising, regulating, protecting, and servicing major producer interests, now bending or ignoring the law on behalf of the powerful, now applying it with full punitive vigor against here-tics and "troublemakers." The symbolic system is highly visible, taught in the schools, dissected by academicians, gossiped about by news commentators. The substantive system is seldom heard of or ac-counted for.

Interest-group politics is tiered according to the power of the con-tenders. Big interests, like the oil, banking, and defense industries, operate in the most important arena, extracting hundreds of billions of dollars from the labor of others and from the public treasure, af-fecting the well-being of whole communities and regions, and exercis-ing control over the most important units of the federal government.

12. See Peter Bachrach, *The Theory of Democratic Elitism* (Boston: Little, Brown, 1967), p. 37.

In contrast, consumer groups, labor unions, and public-interest advocates move in a more limited space, registering their complaints against some of the worst, or more visible, symptoms of the corporate system and occasionally winning a new law or regulation. Finally, the weakest interests, like welfare mothers and slum dwellers, are shunted to the margins of political life, where they remind us of their existence with an occasional demonstration in front of city hall as they attempt to make a claim on the shrinking human-services budget.

It is worth repeating that this *diversity of groups* does not represent a *democratization of power*. A wide array of politico-economic power formations does not indicate a wide sharing of power in any democratic sense, for the sharing occurs largely among moneyed interests that are becoming increasingly less competitive and more concentrated and collusive in both economic ownership and political influence. Decision-making power is "divided" in that it is parceled out to special public-private interest groups—quasiautonomous, entrenched coteries that use public authority for private purposes of low visibility. The fragmentation of power is the pocketing of power, a way of insulating portions of the political process from the tides of popular sentiment. This purpose was embodied in the constitutional structure by the framers in 1787 and has prevailed ever since in more elaborate forms.

Along with the special interests of business firms, there is the overall influence exerted by *business as a system*. More than just an abstraction, business as a system of power, a way of organizing property, capital, and labor, is a pervasive social force. Corporate business is not just another of many interests in the influence system. It occupies a strategic position within the economic system; in a sense, it *is* the economic system. On the major issues of the political economy, business gets its way with government because there exists no alternative way of organizing the economy within the existing capitalist structure. Because business controls the very economy of the nation, government perforce enters into a unique and intimate relationship with it. The health of the capitalist economy is treated by policymakers as a necessary condition for the health of the nation, and since it happens that the economy is in the hands of big companies, then presumably government's service to the public is best accomplished by service to these companies. The goals of business (rapid growth, high profits, and secure markets) become the goals of government, and the "national interest" becomes identified with the dominant capitalist interests. Since policymakers must operate in and through the private economy, it is not long before they are operating *for* it. In order to keep the peace, business may occasionally accept reforms and regulations it does not like, but government cannot ignore business's own reason for being, i.e., the accumulation of capital. In a capitalist system, public policies cannot persistently violate the central imperative of capital accumulation. Sooner or later, business as a system must be met on its own terms or be replaced by another system.

REFORM AND THE "MIXED ECONOMY"

Observing the growth of government involvement in the economy, some writers mistakenly conclude that we have become a "post-capitalist" society with a "mixed economy" that is neither capitalist nor socialist.[13] Proponents of this view avoid any consideration of what government does and whom it benefits when mixing itself with the economy. They assume that the power of government operates in a class vacuum with neutral intent and socially beneficent effect. Business elites know otherwise. They are capable of making class distinctions in public policy. So they support government services and regulations that benefit corporate interests, and they oppose government services and regulations that benefit workers, consumers, the needy, and the environment but are potentially costly to business. So they want small, weak government in the human-services areas and a big, strong national-security state to discourage and contain democratic forces at home and crush revolution abroad.[14]

Government involvement in the economy represents not a growth in socialism (as that term is normally understood by socialists) but a growth in state-supported capitalism, *not the communization of private wealth but the privatization of the commonwealth.* This development has brought a great deal of government planning, but it is not of the kind intended by socialism, which emphasizes the social ownership of productive forces and the reallocation of resources for democratic purposes. As several English socialists pointed out, in criticism of the policies of the British Labour party:

> Planning now means better forecasting, better coordination of investment and expansion decisions, a more purposeful control over demand. This enables the more technologically equipped and organized units in the private sector to pursue their goals more efficiently, more "ration-

---

13. For instance, Dahrendorf, *Class and Class Conflict in Industrial Society.*

14. One of the faithful spokesmen for the ruling elites, Samuel Huntington, advocates this position in his *American Politics: The Promise of Disharmony* (Cambridge, Mass.: Harvard University Press, 1981).

ally." It also means more control over unions and over labor's power to bargain freely about wages. This involves another important transition. For in the course of this rationalization of capitalism, the gap between private industry and the State is narrowed.[15]

In Western industrial nations, including the United States, government economic planning revolves around "the preservation and regulation of capitalism, not its demise."[16] The outcome is a more centralized blend of capitalist public-private powers. Under the notion of "rational planning" and the guise of insulating decision making from selfish interest groups and corrupt politicians, corporate-political elites will push for tighter control over the political economy while bypassing the public, the unions, and Congress. "Herein lies the fallacy of the liberal hope that planning can achieve social justice."[17] For it is state planning *for* and *by* the owning class. Its function is not social welfare or reform but the maintenance of capital profitability at home and abroad.

Given the near monopoly they enjoy over society's productive capacity, the giant corporations remain the sole conduit for most public expenditures. Whether it be for schools or school lunches, sewers or space ships, submarines or airplanes, harbors or highways, government relies almost exclusively on private contractors and suppliers. These suppliers may be heavily subsidized or entirely funded from the public treasure, but they remain "private" in that a profit—usually a most generous, risk-free one—accrues to them for whatever services they perform. The government is not a *producer* in competition with business, such rivalry not being appreciated in a capitalist economy, but a titanic *purchaser* or *consumer* of business products.

Sometimes the government will exercise direct ownership of a particular service, either to assist private industry—as with certain port facilities and research institutions—or to perform services that private capital no longer finds profitable to provide on its own—as with the nationalized companies in Great Britain and the bus and subway lines in many American cities. Public ownership in this context is often only on paper, representing nothing more than a change from private stocks to public bonds—owned by the same wealthy interests that had

---

15. Stuart Hall, Raymond Williams, and Edward Thompson, "The May Day Manifesto," excerpted in Carl Oglesby (ed.), *The New Left Reader* (New York: Grove Press, 1969), p. 115.

16. Stanley Aronowitz, "Modernizing Capitalism," *Social Policy*, May/June 1975, p. 20.

17. Ibid., p. 24. See also S. M. Miller, "Planning: Can It Make a Difference in Capitalist America?" *Social Policy*, September/October 1975, pp. 12–22.

held the stocks. In addition the government bonds offer a high interest rate and are a safe investment.[18] So private capital sells its franchise to the government for a nice price, while "ownership" in the form of a huge mortgage and the risks and losses are passed on to the public.

In sum, the "mixed economy" as found in the United States has little to do with socialism. The merging of the public and private sectors is not merely a result of the growing complexity of technological society nor is it a transition toward socialism; it is in large part a necessary development for the preservation of propertied class interests.

The Limits of Reform

Defenders of the existing system assert with pride that "democratic capitalism" provides the institutional means for peaceful change and that the history of capitalism has been one of gradual reform. To be sure, important reforms have been won by working people. To the extent that the present economic order has anything humane and civil about it, it is because of the struggles of millions of people engaged in the defense of their standard of living and their rights as citizens, a struggle that began well before the Constitutional Convention and continues to this day.

It is somewhat ironic, though, to credit capitalism with the genius of gradual reform when (a) most reforms through history have been vehemently resisted by the capitalist class and were won only after prolonged, bitter, and sometimes bloody popular struggle; (b) most of the problems needing reform have been caused or intensified by capitalism; (c) many of the actual programs end up primarily benefitting the capitalists.

The government has any number of policy options that might be pursued: it could end its costly overseas military interventions, drastically cut its military expenditures, phase out its expensive space programs, eliminate the multibillion-dollar tax loopholes for corporations and rich individuals, increase taxes on industrial profits, cut taxes for lower- and middle-income groups, prosecute industries for pollution and for widespread monopolistic practices, end multibillion-dollar giveaways, and legislate a guaranteed minimum income well above the poverty level. Government also could distribute to almost 2 million poor farmers the billions now received by rich agricultural producers, and it could engage in a concerted effort at conserva-

---

18. Note how the bond issue for "nationalized" firms in France issued by the "socialist" government in 1981 attracted big investors. *Washington Post*, September 10, 1981.

tion and enter directly into nonprofit production and ownership in
the areas of health, housing, education, and mass transportation.

Such measures have been urged, but in almost every instance government has pursued policies of an opposite kind. It is not enough to
scold those who resist change as if they did so out of obstinacy or ill
will; it is necessary to understand the dynamics of power that make
these policies persist in the face of all appeals and human needs to the
contrary. Those who bemoan our "warped priorities" should ask,
why have new and more humane priorities not been pursued? And
the answer is twofold: First, because the realities of power militate
against fundamental reform, and second, because the present politico-economic system could not sustain itself if such reforms were initiated. Let us take each of these in turn:

1. Quite simply, those who have the interest in fundamental
change have not yet the power, while those who have the power have
not the interest, being disinclined to commit class suicide. It is not
that decision makers have been unable to figure out the steps for
change; it is that they oppose the things that change entails. The first
intent of most officeholders is not to fight for social change but to survive and prosper. Given this, they are inclined to respond positively
not to group *needs* but to group *demands*, to those who have the resources to command their attention. In political life as in economic
life, needs do not become marketable demands until they are backed
by "buying power" or "exchange power," for only then is it in the
"producer's" interest to respond. The problem for many unorganized
citizens and workers is that they have few political resources of their
own to exchange. For the politician, as for most people, the compelling quality of any argument is determined less by its logic and evidence than by the strength of its advocates. And advocates are strong
if the resources they control are desired and needed by the politician.
The wants of the unorganized public seldom become marketable political demands—that is, they seldom become imperatives to which
officials find it in their own interest to respond, especially if the
changes would put the official on a collision course with those who
control the resources of the society and who see little wrong with the
world as it is.

2. Most of the demands for fundamental change in our priorities
are impossible to effect within the present system if that system is to
maintain itself. The reason our labor, skills, technology, and natural
resources are not used for social needs and egalitarian purposes is that
they are used for corporate gain. The corporations cannot build low-
rent houses and feed the poor because their interest is not in social reconstruction but in private profit. For the state to maintain whatever

"prosperity" it can, it must do so within the ongoing system of corporate investments. To maintain investment, it must guarantee high-profit yields. To make fundamental changes in our priorities, the state would have to effect major redistributions in income and taxation, cut business subsidies, end deficit spending and interest payments to the rich, redirect capital investments toward nonprofit or low-profit goals, and impose severe and sometimes crippling penalties for pollution and monopolistic practices. But if the state did all this, investment incentives would be greatly diminished, the risks for private capital would be too high, many companies could not survive, and unemployment would reach disastrous heights. State-supported capitalism cannot exist without state support, without passing its immense costs and inefficiencies on to the public. The only way the state could redirect the wealth of society toward egalitarian goals would be to exercise democratic control over capital investments and capital return, but that would mean, in effect, public ownership of the means of production—a giant step toward *socialism*.

What is being argued here is that, contrary to the view of liberal critics, the nation's immense social problems are not irrational offshoots of a basically rational system, to be solved by replacing the existing corporate and political decision makers with persons who would be better intentioned and more socially aware. Rather, the problems are rational outcomes of a basically irrational system, a system structured not for the satisfaction of human need but the multiplication of human greed, one that is grossly inequitable, exploitative, and destructive of human and natural resources at home and abroad.[19]

How then can we speak of most government policies as being products of the democratic will? What democratic will demanded that Washington be honeycombed with high-paid corporate lobbyists who would regularly raid the public treasure on behalf of rich clients? What democratic mandate directed the government to give away more monies every year to the creditor class, the top 1 percent of the population, in interest payments on public bonds than are spent on services to the bottom 20 percent? When was the public consulted on Alaskan oil leases, bloated defense contracts, agribusiness subsidies, and tax write-offs? When did the American people insist on having

---

19. It is not that state-supported capitalism is the cause of every social ill in modern society but that capitalism has no fundamental commitment to remedying social ills, despite its command over vast resources that might be directed toward such ends. And capitalism does much to create and intensify the profoundly irrational economic and social arrangements that breed ills and injustices at home and abroad.

unsafe, overpriced drugs and foods circulate unrestricted and an FDA that protects rather than punishes the companies marketing such products? When did the public urge the government to help the gas, electric, and telephone companies to overcharge them? When did the voice of the people clamor for a multibillion-dollar space program that fattened corporate contractors and satisfied the curiosity of some astronomers and other scientists while leaving the rest of us still more burdened by taxes and deprived of necessary services here on earth? What democratic will decreed that we destroy the Cambodian countryside between 1969 and 1971 in a bombing campaign conducted without the consent or even the knowledge of Congress and the public? And what large sector of public opinion demanded that the government intervene secretly in Laos with U.S. Marines in 1969, or sustain wars against popular forces in El Salvador and Guatemala, or subvert progressive governments in Chile, Indonesia, and elsewhere?

Far from giving their assent, ordinary people have had to struggle to find out what is going on. And when public opinion has been registered, it has been demonstrated in the opposite direction, against the worst abuses and most blatant privileges of plutocracy, against the spoliation of the environment and the use of government power to serve corporations, and against bigger military budgets and military intervention in other lands.

DEMOCRACY AS CLASS STRUGGLE

The ruling class has several ways of expropriating the earnings of the people. First and foremost, as *workers*, people receive only a portion of the value their labor creates. The rest goes to the owners of capital. On behalf of the owners, managers continually devise methods (including speed-ups, forced overtime, lay-offs, the threat of plant closings, and union busting) to tame labor and secure the process of capital accumulation.

Second, as *consumers*, people are victimized by monopoly practices that force them to spend more on less. They also are confronted with increasingly exploitative forms of *involuntary* consumption, as when relatively inexpensive mass-transit systems are neglected or eliminated, creating a greater dependency on automobiles; or when low-rental apartments are converted into high-priced condominiums; or when local farm products are replaced by expensive processed foods transported long distances by argibusiness.

Third, over the last 30 years or so, with each successive "tax reform" bill, working people as *taxpayers* have had to shoulder an ever larger portion of the tax burden, while business pays less and less. Indeed, the dramatic decline in business taxes has been a major cause of the growth in the federal deficit.[20] As we have seen, the deficit itself is a source of profit to the moneyed class and an additional burden to taxpayers. This regressive system of taxation and deficit spending represents a major upward redistribution of income from labor to capital.

Fourth, as *citizens*, the people get less than they pay for in government services. The lion's share of federal spending goes to large firms, defense contractors, banks, and other creditors. As citizens, the people also endure the hidden "diseconomies" shifted onto them by private business, as when a chemical company contaminates a community's ground water with its toxic wastes.[21]

These various means serve the process of capital accumulation, which is the essence of capitalism—the investment of money to extract still more money from the populace, from their labor, their consumption, their taxes, and their environment. But this process of extraction and accumulation, with all its related abuses and injustices, instigates a reactive resistance from workers, consumers, community groups, and taxpayers—who are usually one and the same people, those whom I have been calling "the democratic forces." There exists, then, not only class oppression but class struggle, not only plutocratic dominance but popular opposition to the policies and social conditions created by state-supported capitalism. *The ruling class predominates but it must continually strive to recreate the conditions of its dominance.*

Plutocratic culture would have us think that the "American heritage" consists of a series of heroic vignettes: George Washington at Valley Forge, the battle of the Alamo, the winning of the West, and U.S. Marines hoisting the flag on Iwo Jima. But there is also a tradition of *people's* struggle in the United States that has been downplayed or ignored by the dominant elites and their representatives. This democratic struggle ebbs and flows but it has never ceased. Forced to react to the exploitative conditions imposed upon them and

---

20. John McDermott, "The Secret History of the Deficit," *Nation*, August 21–28, 1982, pp. 129, 144–46.

21. As described earlier, the power of money also works its effect by controlling the communication environment, by controlling educational and other cultural institutions, by monopolizing access to, and use of, natural resources, and by predominating in the electoral party system.

moved by a combination of anger and hope, ordinary people in America have organized, agitated, demonstrated, and engaged in electoral challenges, civil disobedience, strikes, sit-ins, takeovers, boycotts, and sometimes violent clashes with the authorities—for better wages and work conditions, for a fairer allocation of taxes and public services, for political and economic equality, and for peace and nonintervention abroad. Against the heaviest odds, against courts and laws, against the clubs and guns of police and army, against the calumny and slander of well-paid propagandists—the working people, racial minorities, and women of the United States have suffered many defeats but won some important victories, forceably extracting concessions and imposing reforms upon resistant rulers.

To the extent they have sought to equalize social, legal, and economic conditions, *the democratic forces are the major limitation on capitalism's relentless exploitation of labor and on the mistreatment of the people and the environment; they are the major democratic bulwark against plutocracy*.

If we think of democracy as something more than a set of political procedures and as a system that also must produce *substantive* outcomes that sustain and advance the health, well-being, and living standards of the people (the *demos*) rather than serving the privileges of the few, then those who fight for these substantive benefits are engaged in not just "economic issues" but in advancing democracy. Through history the democratic forces have come to consider their class demands for such things as jobs and old-age security to be as much a part of their birthright as more formal political rights. Indeed many of the struggles for *political* democracy, the right to vote, assemble, petition, and dissent, have been largely propelled by the *class* struggle, by a desire to democratize the rules of the political game so as to be in a better position to fight for one's economic interests. The battle for democratic rights has not occurred in a class vacuum but has been much fortified by the fight against the moneyed interests. In a word, *the struggle for democracy has been part of the class struggle*.

Throughout the history of the United States, as noted earlier, the propertied elites have resisted the expansion of democracy. At the Philadelphia convention in 1787, the delegates showed an undisguised hostility toward the popular forces of that day and only reluctantly agreed to democratic concessions in order to assure ratification of their elitist Constitution (that among other things condones slavery). For the next 40 or 50 years in many states, the propertied classes resisted universal manhood suffrage, and for 140 years they opposed female suffrage. Through the 19th century and into the 20th, they resisted emancipation, the expansion of civil rights and civil liberties, legalized labor unions, and a whole array of social legislation. They knew that the growth of popular rights would only strengthen popular forces and put limits on the elites' ability to pursue their interests. They instinctively understood, even if they seldom publicly articulated it, that *it is not socialism that subverts democracy, but democracy that subverts capitalism.*[22]

Today as capitalism's problems deepen, as the financial powers pull everyone else (government, municipalities, consumers, other nations, and corporations themselves) deeper into debt, as the moneyed apex of the pyramid weakens its own base, so the system must work with greater haste, waste, and irrationality to maintain profit rates. As the capitalists destroy the earning power of working people in order to maintain profits, they destroy the buying power of consumers and diminish their own markets. So they need more subsidies, tax breaks, and monopolistic protections from government to maintain capital accumulation. Stagnation, inflation, underconsumption, and other economic distortions are recurrent features of this crisis.

The liberal Keynesian solution of borrowing from the future through a system of deficit spending that allows the government to maintain business profits, social programs, and huge military budgets proves increasingly difficult as the economic system contracts and fiscal resources decline.

The conservative solution is to return to the days before the New Deal. To maintain profit rates, the tax burden is shifted downward, government support of business is increased, and consumers are made to spend still more for less—all of which leads to a diminution of people's living standards. To bolster profits, government programs that cut into business earnings must be abolished regardless of their social and human value; so ruling elites attack occupational, consumer, and environmental protections under the pretense that such programs "cost jobs."

Above all, to maintain profits, wages must be held down: one way is to increase the supply of workers in relation to jobs, forcing people to compete more intensely for work on terms more favorable to employers. Historically this is done by eliminating jobs through mechanization, by bringing immigrant labor into the country, and by investing capital in countries that offer additional labor markets. More recently, the administration in Washington sought to increase the labor supply by easing child-labor laws, lowering the employable age

---

22. For a somewhat different but related discussion of this point see Peter Bachrach, "Class Struggle and Democracy," *democracy*, 2, Fall 1982, pp. 29–42.

for some jobs, and raising the retirement age, so putting millions of additional workers onto an already overcrowded job market.

Another way to hold down wages is to eliminate alternative sources of support so that people become exclusively reliant on wages and more compliant as wage earners. Wage workers are made, not born. Historically the process of creating people willing to work for subsistence wages entailed driving them off the land and into the factories, denying them access to farms and to the game, fuel, and fruits of the commons. Divorced from these means of subsistence, the peasant became the proletarian. Today, unemployment benefits and other forms of public assistance are reduced in order to deny alternative sources of sustenance.[23] Public jobs are eliminated so that still more workers will compete for employment in the private sector. Conservatives seek to lower the minimum wage for youths and resist attempts to equalize wages and job opportunities for women and minorities, so keeping women, youth, and minorities as the traditional underpaid "reserve army of labor" used throughout history to depress wages.

Still another way to hold down wages and maximize profits is to keep the work force divided and poorly organized. There is today in the U.S. a $500 million industry specializing in union busting. In addition, racism has played an important divisive role, as the economic fears and anger of Whites are channeled away from employers and toward minority fellow workers who are also competitors for jobs, education, and housing. Racism also has a deflationary effect on wages similar to sexism: when a large minority of the work force are underpaid because they are Black, this increases profit margins for the owners and holds down the price of labor in general.

Rulers have often sought to mute popular grievances by conjuring up domestic radical enemies and foreign foes. In these times of economic recession, plutocratic representatives fill the air with alarming tales of terrorists and KGB infiltration at home and of a "Soviet Menace" that is out to destroy us and enslave the world. In truth, the existing system is threatened not from without but from within, from the crisis of capitalism itself. But the cold warriors direct public attention to irrelevant foes, calling for still more sacrifices by the people in order to strengthen the repressive capacity of the state and bolster a highly expensive, dangerous—but highly profitable—military-industrial establishment. The cold warriors also use the "Soviet Menace" to justify intervention against liberation movements that threaten the re-

---

23. Frances Fox Piven and Richard Cloward, *The New Class War* (New York: Pantheon, 1982).

actionary Third World social order, which multinational capitalism finds so compliant and profitable.

Before long, the democratic forces mobilize to protect their standard of living from conservative attack and to oppose such dangerous and destructive manifestations of the cold war as the draft, the nuclear-arms race, and U.S. intervention in places like El Salvador. Once again democracy proves troublesome to capital in its war against labor at home and abroad. *So the ruling class must attack not only the people's standard of living but the very democratic rights that help them defend that standard.* Thus the right to strike is under ever more persistent attack by both the courts and legislatures. With more injunctions, fines, and jail sentences, and more restrictive "right to work" and "open shop" laws, union organizing becomes increasingly difficult—all in an era when collective bargaining was assumed to be an established right. The laws against progressive minor parties are tightened after successive third-party challenges, and public funding of the two-party monopoly is expanded.

Federal security agencies and local police violate constitutional protections in order to stifle progressive activists. The Supreme Court, packed with conservative appointees, moves to overturn or weaken many of the civil liberties and civil rights won in the past, including protections against forced confessions, arrest without warrant, invasion of privacy, and affirmative action. Even the right to distribute handbills and newspapers is under attack in some locales. In contrast, the Court decides that spending ceilings on campaign contributions place an unconstitutional limit on free speech; thus the Court gives the rich a greater capacity for speech than the rest of us and a still greater opportunity for the power of money to prevail over the power of numbers.

THE TWO FACES OF THE STATE

Some critics of capitalism believe that as the problems of the economy deepen, modern capitalism will succumb to its own internal contradictions; as the economic "substructure" gives way, the "superstructure" of the capitalist state will be carried down with it and the opportunity for a better society will be at hand. One difficulty with this position is that it underestimates the extent to which the state can act with independent effect to preserve the capitalist class. The state is more than a front for the economic interests it serves; it is the single most important force that corporate America has at its command. The power to use force, the power of eminent domain, the power to tax, spend, and legislate, to use public funds for private profit, the power of limitless credit, the power to mobilize highly emotive symbols of loyalty and legitimacy—such resources of the state give corporate America a durability it could never provide for itself. The resilience of capitalism cannot be measured in isolated economic terms. Behind the corporation there stands the organized power of the state. "The stability and future of the economy is grounded, in the last analysis, on the power of the state to act to preserve it."[24] The corporations can call on the resources of the state to rationalize and subsidize their performance, maintain their profit levels, socialize costs by taxing the many, and keep the malcontents under control through generous applications of official violence.

The state, however, is not merely a puppet of the capitalist class. As already noted, to fulfill its task of bolstering the capitalist system as a whole, the state must sometimes resist particular corporate interests. The state is also the place where liberal and conservative ruling-class factions struggle over how best to keep the system afloat. The more liberal elements see that democratic concessions sometimes can be functional to the existing politico-economic system—by keeping capitalism from devouring those who make and buy its products. If conservative goals are *too* successful, as with the upward income redistribution achieved by the Reagan administration in its first two years, then the contradictions of capitalism intensify and so do the instabilities of the system. Profits may be maintained and even increased for a time through various financial contrivances, but unemployment grows, markets shrink, discontent deepens, and small and not so small businesses perish. As the pyramid begins to tremble from conservative victories, some of the less myopic occupants of the apex develop a new appreciation for the base that sustains them and a sudden dislike for the suicidal excesses of "trickle-*up*" economics. These kinds of elite differences are fought over within the state.

The state's ability to act in the interests of the capitalist class is limited by several factors. First, government officials cannot always know what are the best policies for the corporate system, especially since particular industrial interests conflict with each other or need contradictory things—such as immediate tariff protections *and* long-range free-trade agreements, or cutbacks in wages *and* growing consumer markets. Confusions and conflicts arise within the state that reflect the irrationalities of capitalism itself.

---

24. Gabriel Kolko, *The Triumph of Conservatism* (Chicago: Quadrangle Books, 1967), p. 302.

Second, the capitalist state is limited by the historic emergence and competing appeal of socialist states and anti-imperialist forces in various parts of the world. The specter of socialism continues to haunt the bourgeois world both as a direct challenge and as an embarrassing reminder that the economic crises of capitalism are not an immutable, natural condition of all human society.

Third, just as troublesome in the immediate future are the competing interests of other *capitalist* nations. The Soviet Union may remain the *ideological* enemy, but serious market conflicts are likely to arise with *economic* competitors like Japan and Germany. As stagnation and unemployment become chronic conditions throughout the capitalist world, the competition between capitalist nations will intensify, posing problems for which the capitalist nation-state is not likely to find easy answers.

Fourth, state action on behalf of capitalism is limited by the underlying structures of capitalism itself and the ensuing realities of power and interest. So public policy will treat surface manifestations rather than systemic causes, attending to "toxic waste" rather than to the modes of production and profit of the chemical and oil industries, "unemployment" rather than the irrationalities behind capital stagnation, "the insolvency of Social Security" rather than the highly inequitable distribution of income, wealth, and taxes.

Finally, *the greatest restraint on the capitalist state comes in having to deal with the populace.* The state cannot fulfill its role of protecting the plutocratic class and legitimating exploitative social relations unless it maintains its own legitimacy in the eyes of the people. And it cannot do that without keeping an appearance of popular rule and an appearance of neutrality in regard to class interests.

More important than the constraints of appearances are the actual power restraints imposed by democratic forces. There is just so much the people will take before they begin to resist. Marx anticipated that class struggle would bring the overthrow of capitalism. Short of revolution, class struggle constrains and alters the capitalist state, so that the state itself, or portions of it, become an arena of struggle that reflects the conflict going on in the wider society. Having correctly discerned that "American democracy" as professed by establishment opinion makers is something of a sham, some people incorrectly dismiss the democratic rights and gains won by popular forces as of little account. But these democratic rights and the organized resistant strength of democratic forces are, at present, all we have to keep some ruling elites from doing what in their heart of hearts they would like to do to make this nation perfectly safe for capitalism.

The state plays a fundamentally contradictory role. The contradiction, quite simply, is the one between democracy and capitalism. More than half a century ago the great sociologist Max Weber wrote: "The question is: How are freedom and democracy in the long run at all possible under the domination of highly developed capitalism?"[25] That question is still with us. As the crisis of capitalism deepens, as surplus resources disappear and more austerity is needed, as the contradiction between the egalitarian expectations of democracy and the dominating thievery of capitalism sharpens, the state must act more repressively to hold together the existing class system. In some countries, the rulers have resorted to a dictatorial final solution, smashing all democratic organizations so better to impose a draconian economy on the people and maintain the dominance of capital over labor. But it takes more than fascists to impose fascism; many centrist and liberal interests, feeling their privileges threatened by the instabilities of the system, will also opt for an authoritarian solution—as they did in Italy, Germany, Chile, Argentina, Indonesia, and elsewhere, using fascism to protect capitalism while claiming they were saving democracy from communism.

Why doesn't the capitalist class in the United States resort to fascist rule? It would make things easier: no criticisms from the press, no organized dissent, no environmental or occupational protections, no elections or labor unions to worry about. As of now, there is no need to turn to fascism since the dominant class is getting much of what it wants behind a democratic facade. Better to break unions and hold down wages by using court injunctions, and by refusing to negotiate contracts, rather than having to put union leaders before a firing squad. Better to drown out and isolate radical opponents with a moneyed media monopoly rather than having to silence them with assassination squads. "A state based solely on the continuous resort to compulsion is revealed as an obvious instrument of class domination."[26] And a state revealed as an obvious instrument of class dominance loses popular support, generates resistance rather than compliance, and activates a revolutionary class consciousness.

Representative government is a very serviceable form of governance for capitalism, even if often a troublesome one, for it offers a modicum of liberty and self-rule while hiding the class nature of the

---

25. H. H. Gerth and C. Wright Mills (eds.), *From Max Weber: Essays in Sociology* (New York: Oxford University Press, 1958).

26. Bruce Berman, "Class Struggle and the Origins of the Relative Autonomy of the Capitalist State," paper presented at the American Political Science Association, New York, September 1981. Berman offers a good discussion of the contradictory class role of the state.

state. Rather than relying exclusively on the club and the gun, bourgeois democracy employs a cooptive, legitimating power—which is ruling-class power at its most hypocritical and most effective. By playing these contradictory roles of protector of capital and "protector of the people," the state best fulfills its fundamental class role. What is said of the state is true of the law, the bureaucracy, the political parties, the legislators, the universities, the professions, and the media. In order to best fulfill their class-control and class-dominating functions yet keep their social legitimacy, these institutions must maintain the appearance of neutrality and autonomy. To foster that appearance, they must occasionally actually exercise some critical independence and autonomy from the state and from capitalism—especially in regard to some of the more egregious transgressions against democratic appearances (for instance, the Watergate scandal).

In a country with the history and traditions of the United States, the success of a dictatorial solution to the crisis of capitalism would depend on whether the ruling class could stuff the democratic genie back into the bottle. Ruling elites are restrained in their autocratic impulses by the fear that they could not get away with it, that the people and the enlisted ranks of the armed forces would not go along. More likely, an American ruling-class-in-crisis will prefer something short of an all-out military dictatorship, a "democracy for the fewer still." This would entail keeping certain of the accoutrements of democracy such as a money-dominated two-party monopoly, an electoral system that focuses on relatively meaningless issues, a shift of policymaking power to non-elective and unaccountable public-private groups, a limited and tepid verbal dissent that leads to no serious organized opposition, politically monopolized mass media that treat existing arrangements at face value, a few tame and ineffectual labor unions, the activation and financing of organized bigotry and right-wing religionists, and an all-imposing national-security state that claims to defend the citizenry from external enemies while actually protecting capitalism from its own people. This book has tried to demonstrate that we are much closer to that democracy for the few than we might have imagined.

Another possibility is that future struggle will bring a revolutionary expansion of class democracy and the eventual replacement of capitalism with socialism.[27] Whether the existing modern capitalist state can be used to bring about socialism or must be overthrown by

---

27. For suggestions on what is to be done in the immediate future see Martin Carnoy and Derek Shearer, *Economic Democracy: The Challenge of the 1980s* (New York: Random House, 1980); Andre Gorz, *Strategy For Labor* (Boston: Beacon, 1964).

popular revolution so that a new order can be formed is a question unresolved by history. So far there have been no examples of either road to socialism in modern industrial society. But because something has never occurred in the past does not mean it cannot happen in the future. In the late 19th century, knowing persons, relying on the fact that a successful workers' revolution had never taken place, concluded that one never would. Yet early in the next century the Bolshevik revolution exploded upon the world. And bourgeois pundits scoffed at the idea that "native" peoples could overthrow modern colonial powers and achieve self-rule, yet such things have happened.

The question of what kind of socialism we should struggle for deserves more extensive treatment than can be given here. American socialism cannot be modeled on the Soviet Union, China, Cuba, or other countries with different historical, economic, and cultural developments. But these countries ought to be examined so that we might learn from their accomplishments and problems. Whatever else one wants to say about existing socialist societies, they have achieved what capitalism cannot and has no intention of accomplishing: providing adequate food, housing, and clothing for all; economic security in old age; free medical care; free education at all levels; and the right to a job—in countries that are not as rich as ours but which use productive resources in more rational ways than can be done under capitalism.[28]

The wasteful, destructive, and unfair effects of capitalism upon our nation, the pressures of competition between capitalist nations, the growing discontent and oppression of the populace, the continual productive growth within socialist nations, the new revolutionary victories against Western imperialism in the Third World, all these things make objective conditions increasingly unfavorable for capitalism. Yet people will not discard the system that oppresses them until they see the feasibility of an alternative one. It is not that they think society *should* be this way, but that it *must* be. It is not that they don't want things to change, but they don't believe things *can* change—or they fear that whatever changes might occur would more likely be for the worse.

What is needed is widespread organizing not only around particular issues but for a socialist movement that can project both the desirability of an alternative system and the *possibility* and indeed the

---

28. See, for instance, Albert Szymanski, *Is the Red Flag Flying? The Political Economy of the Soviet Union Today* (London: Zed, 1979); Mike Davidow, *Cities Without Crisis* (New York: International Publishers, 1976); P. Bonovsky, *Are Our Moscow Reporters Giving Us the Facts About the USSR?* (Toronto: Progress Books, 1982).

ALIVE AND WELL

great *necessity* for democratic change. Throughout the world and at home, forces for change are being unleashed. There is much evidence—some of it presented in this book—indicating that Americans are well ahead of the existing political elites in their willingness to embrace new alternatives, including public ownership of the major corporations and worker control of production. With time and struggle, as the possibility and necessity for progressive change become more evident and the longing for a better social life grows stronger, people will become increasingly intolerant of the monumental injustices of the existing capitalist system and will move toward a profoundly democratic solution. We can be hopeful the day will come, as it came in social orders of the past, when those who seem invincible will be shaken from their pinnacles and a new, humane, and truly democratic society will begin to emerge.

There is nothing sacred about the existing system. All economic and political institutions are contrivances that should serve the interests of the people. When they fail to do so, they should be replaced by something more responsive, more just, and more democratic. Marx said this, and so did Jefferson. It is a revolutionary doctrine, and very much an American one.

Information and Resource Guide

The following books are useful in expanding the discussion of issues encountered in *Democracy for the Few*.

Howard Zinn, *A People's History of the United States* (New York: Harper, 1980)

Richard Boyer and Herbert Morais, *Labor's Untold Story* (New York: United Electrical, Radio and Machine Workers, 1972)

These two excellent titles are enjoyable reading and give much historical information on the struggles of labor, women, and minorities.

Dick Cluster and Nancy Rutter, *Shrinking Dollars, Vanishing Jobs* (Boston: Beacon Press, 1980)

Mark Green and Robert Massie, Jr. (eds.) *The Big Business Reader* (New York: Pilgrim Press, 1980)

These two books provide a good deal of information on the instabilities and crises of the big-business system in the United States.

Frances Fox Piven and Richard Cloward, *The New Class War* (New York: Pantheon, 1982)

A good discussion of the struggle between capitalism and democracy, giving special attention to Reaganism's attack on the human-services system.

James Aronson, *The Press and the Cold War* (Boston: Beacon Press, 1970)

A good analysis of the cold-war distortions of the capitalist press.

John Downing, *The Media Machine* (London: Pluto Press, 1980)

A sophisticated and clear analysis of the system-supporting role of the mass media, giving special attention to the media's anti-labor, racist, and sexist aspects.

Michael Parenti, *Power and the Powerless* (New York: St. Martin's Press, 1978)
Something of a sequel to this book, but with a more theoretical approach, it focuses on the conservative socialization and class-control functions of the capitalist social order and institutions.

Mark Green and Michael Calabrese, *Who Runs Congress?* Third edition (New York: Bantam, 1979)
The best critical treatment of Congress, from a liberal perspective. Readable and anecdotal.

Grant McConnell, *Private Power and American Democracy* (New York: Knopf, 1966)
A sophisticated study of the pressure-group system, corporate power, and the politics of bureaucracy.

Noam Chomsky and Edward Herman, *The Washington Connection and Third World Fascism* (Boston: South End Press, 1979)
Naom Chomsky and Edward Herman, *After the Cataclysm* (Boston: South End Press, 1979)
These two books compose volumes one and two of *The Political Economy of Human Rights*, a monumental work that discusses how U.S. foreign policy maintains fascism throughout the Third World and how the press distorts and covers up this activity. Written clearly and forcefully.

Daniel Guerin, *Fascism and Big Business* (New York: Pathfinder, 1973)
A superb study of the class basis of fascism and the link to big business. Very revealing and with a good theoretical analysis. A good antidote to the work of present-day academics who labor hard to deny the link between capitalism and fascism.

Karl Marx, Frederick Engels, V. I. Lenin, *The Dynamics of Social Change* (New York: International Publishers, 1970)
Selections from Marx, Engels, and Lenin on economics, sociology, politics, and history. Edited by Howard Selsam, David Goldway, and Harry Martel. Probably the best reader of its kind.

Albert Szymanski, *Is the Red Flag Flying?* (London: Zed, 1979)
Mike Davidow, *Cities Without Crisis* (New York: International Publishers, 1976)

George Morris, *Where Human Rights Are Real* (Moscow: Progress Publishers, 1980)

These three books offer an eye-opening view of the Soviet Union that is not found in most of the academic literature or in the U.S. media.

Interested students should consult the book lists of such publishers as Beacon Press, International Publishers, Monthly Review Press, South End Press, Workers World Press, and Zed Press as well as the publication list of the Institute for Policy Studies in Washington, D.C. For newspapers and other periodicals offering a viewpoint that differs from the prevailing orthodoxy see *The Progressive, Monthly Review, Political Affairs, Nation, Daily World, Guardian, Radical America, Workers World, In These Times, Dollars and Sense, Economic Notes, Multinational Monitor, The Witness,* and *National Catholic Reporter.* Following is a very incomplete list of progressive organizations that students may wish to contact in continuing their political development.

General Political

Democratic Socialists of America, 853 Broadway, Suite 801, New York, N.Y. 10011

Communist Party U.S.A., 235 West 23 St., New York, N.Y. 10011

Citizen's Party, 1605 Connecticut Ave., Washington, D.C. 20009

Workers World Party, 46 West 21 St., New York, N.Y. 10010

Peace

Women Strike for Peace, 145 South 13 St., Philadelphia, Pa. 19107

Women's International League for Peace and Freedom, 1213 Race St., Philadelphia, Pa. 19107

People's Anti-War Mobilization (PAM), 19 West 21 St., New York, N.Y. 10010

Coalition Against Registration and the Draft (CARD), 201 Massachusetts Ave., Washington, D.C. 20002

U.S. Peace Council, 7 East 15 St., New York, N.Y. 10003

Nuclear Weapons Freeze Campaign, 4144 Lindell Blvd., Suite 404, St. Louis, Mo., 63108

Labor and Human Services

Trade Unionists for Action and Democracy (TUAD), 343 S. Dearborn, Rm. 600, Chicago, Ill. 60604

Association for Union Democracy, 215 Park Ave. South, New York, N.Y. 10003

Gray Panthers (for old and young people), 3700 Chestnut St., Philadelphia, Pa. 19104

Shelterforce (housing), 380 Main St., East Orange, N.J. 07018
Health PAC, 17 Murray St., New York, N.Y. 10007

Anti-Repression and Anti-Racist
National Emergency Civil Liberties Committee, 175 Fifth Ave., New
York, N.Y. 10010
National Lawyers Guild, 853 Broadway, Rm. 1705, New York, N.Y.
10003
National Alliance Against Racist and Political Repression, 27 Union
Square West, New York, N.Y. 10003
National Black United Front, 415 Atlantic Avenue, Brooklyn, N.Y.
11217
Mexican-American Legal Defense and Education Fund, 28 Geary
Street, San Francisco, Calif. 94108
New Jewish Agenda, 150 Fifth Ave., Rm. 1002, New York, N.Y.
10011

Women, Gays, and Anti-Sexist
Coalition of Labor Union Women, 15 Union Square West, New
York, N.Y. 10003
Radical Women, 2661 21 St., San Francisco, Calif. 94110
Working Women, 1258 Euclid Ave., Cleveland, Ohio 44115
National Alliance of Black Feminists, 202 South State St., Chicago,
Ill. 60604
National Abortion Rights Action League, 825 15 St., Washington,
D.C. 20005
Catholics for a Free Choice, 2008 17 St., Washington, D.C. 20009
Gay Activists Alliance, P.O. Box 2554, Washington, D.C. 20013

Religious
Methodist Federation for Social Action, 76 Clinton Ave., Staten Is-
land, N.Y. 10301
American Friends Service Committee, 1501 Cherry St., Philadelphia,
Pa. 19102
Christians for Socialism, 3540 14 St., Detroit, Mich. 48208
Clergy and Laity Concerned, 198 Broadway, New York, N.Y. 10038

Other
Institute for Policy Studies, 1901 Q St. NW, Washington, D.C. 20009
Environmental Defense Fund, 1525 18 St. NW, Washington, D.C.
20036
Science for the People, 897 Main St., Cambridge, Mass. 02139
Union of Radical Political Economics, 41 Union Square West, New
York, N.Y. 10003

About the Author

Michael Parenti received his Ph.D. from Yale University and has taught political and social science at various colleges and universities. In addition he has been a guest lecturer on campuses throughout the country. His writing has appeared in the *Progressive*, the *Nation*, *Monthly Review*, *In These Times*, *Political Affairs*, the *National Catholic Reporter*, the *New York Times*, *New Political Science*, the *Journal of Politics*, the *American Political Science Review*, and numerous other publications. His books include *The Anti-Communist Impulse*, *Ethnic and Political Attitudes*, *Trends and Tragedies in American Foreign Policy* (a book of edited readings), and *Power and the Powerless*; the latter is published by St. Martin's Press. He is currently a Visiting Fellow at the Institute for Policy Studies in Washington, D.C., where he is completing a book on the mass media entitled *Inventing Reality*.

Index